PAGANINI

The 'Demonic' Virtuoso

PAGANINI
The 'Demonic' Virtuoso

Mai Kawabata

THE BOYDELL PRESS

First published 2013
The Boydell Press, Woodbridge

ISBN 978 1 84383 756 5

The Boydell Press is an imprint of Boydell & Brewer Ltd
PO Box 9, Woodbridge, Suffolk IP12 3DF, UK
and of Boydell & Brewer Inc.
668 Mount Hope Ave, Rochester, NY 14620-2731, USA
website: www.boydellandbrewer.com

A catalogue record for this book is available
from the British Library

The publisher has no responsibility for the continued existence or accuracy of URLs for
external or third-party internet websites referred to in this book, and does not guarantee that
any content on such websites is, or will remain, accurate or appropriate

Papers used by Boydell & Brewer Ltd are natural, recyclable products
made from wood grown in sustainable forests

Printed and bound in Great Britain by
CPI Group (UK) Ltd, Croydon, CR0 4YY

For my father, mother and sister

Contents

Illustrations, Musical Examples, and Tables

The author and publishers are grateful to all the institutions and individuals listed for permission to reproduce the materials in which they hold copyright. Every effort has been made to trace the copyright holders; apologies are offered for any omission, and the publishers will be pleased to add any necessary acknowledgement in subsequent editions.

Acknowledgements

I AM grateful to all the wonderful people who have contributed to this book in so many ways. It simply could not have taken shape without them. Any errors that remain in it are entirely my own.

Susan McClary expertly advised the doctoral dissertation of which this book is a spin-off. At UCLA, I also learned much from Professors Robert Fink, Raymond Knapp, Elisabeth Le Guin, Anne Mellor, Mitchell Morris, and Robert Walser, as well as David Ake, Daniel Goldmark, Jonathan Phillips, and especially Nadya Zimmerman. Thanks to my congenial colleagues at the University of East Anglia and Stony Brook University and to countless students who have taught me so much over the years.

In writing this book, I have benefitted greatly from lively exchanges with Keith Chapin, Daniel Chiarilli, James Deaville, Katherine Ellis, Bonnie Gordon, Sasha Gurevich, James Masland, Simon McVeigh, Jonathan Neufeld, Edwin Outwater, Jonathan Pearl, and Aidan Thomson. Professor Lydia Goehr has inspired me by her brilliant example. Violinists Gilles Apap, Ilya Gringolts, Soovin Kim, Kurt Nikkanen, Philippe Quint, Giulio Rovighi, and Tracy Silverman kindly shared their virtuoso expertise with me. Dana Gooley has thought, and continues to think, more deeply about virtuosity than anyone else I know.

Kevin Lavine of the Library of Congress Music Division in Washington, DC, has been an invaluable help; permission to reproduce materials from their Gertrude Clarke Whittall Foundation Collection is gratefully acknowledged. Anna Alberati at the Biblioteca Casanatense in Rome and all the music staff at the Bibliothèque Nationale and the Bibliothèque-Musée de l'Opéra National de Paris, the Staatsbibliothek zu Berlin, and the British Library in London have been very helpful. I would like to thank the editorial staff at *19th-Century Music*, *Current Musicology*, and *Ad Parnassum*—especially Ruth Solie, Karen Hiles, Tyler Bickford, and Roberto Illiano; permission to reprint material that originally appeared in those journals is gratefully acknowledged. I owe a debt of gratitude to everyone at the 'Diabolus in Musica' Conference in La Spezia (2009) for stimulating discussions, and to Anna Rita Certo of the Uficio Paganini (City of Genoa) and Marvi Rachero of the Amici di Paganini for access to Paganiniana in the Palazzo Tursi. Thanks also to Jason Dixon for setting the examples, and to Beate Dölling, Keith and Emmanuelle Chapin, Lina Glede, Beatrice Poubeau, Meike Reintjes, and Giulio Ventura for generous assistance with translations.

At Boydell, I could not have wished for a more patient and hard-working editor than Michael Middeke.

Last but not least, thanks from the bottom of my heart to Michael Beckerman for his unfailing brilliance, humour, and friendship, and to the late Leonard Stein, whose wisdom and ebullience are greatly missed.

CHAPTER 1

Introduction

THE aura of Paganini in the popular imagination as a 'demonic' violin virtuoso, a mysterious figure hovering in a grey area between reality and myth, has not changed greatly in nearly two hundred years. It has endured in a range of visual and print media such as the caricature 'Le Spectre de Paganini' (1889, Figure 1.1), Giuseppe Fiorini's famous forged daguerreotype (1900), Anatoli Vinogradov's novel *The Condemnation of Paganini* (n.d.), and Klaus Kinski's biopic *Paganini* (1989).[1] A consistently romanticised image has had the effect of keeping the figure of Paganini fixed in a single dimension and of obscuring his importance as a musician and as a historical personage. What he achieved as a virtuoso extended well beyond the 'demonic' cultivation of technique.

This book explains the cultural phenomenon of Paganini's virtuosity by examining the unprecedented ways in which his performances 'signified' in the musical culture of his time. The rumour that he had made a pact with the devil was only the most famous aspect of this. Yet beyond the familiar image of a player over-endowed with technical skills there lies a little-understood figure whose powers were even more mysterious, dangerous, and immediate than the stereotypical 'demonic' label suggests,simmering with sexual tension, a Gothic aura, and a personal magnetism. The power Paganini's audiences sensed in his playing blended together taboos and myths, attraction and repulsion.

Paganini himself was only a participant in the creation of this phenomenon. Take the reasons behind his 'demonic' image, for instance. On the one hand he resembled a corpse and drew seemingly impossible sounds from his violin; on the other, he was living in a culture overrun by Faust-mania, Byronism, and Gothic novels. The 'demonic' virtuoso thus emerged through the cultural

---

[1] 'Le Spectre de Paganini', *Le Plaisir à Paris* (1 May1889), Bibliothèque de l'Opéra, Paris: 'Dossier d'artiste: Nicolo Paganini'. The daguerreotype by Giuseppe Fiorini (1861–1934), an Italian violinmaker who lived in Bologna, Munich, and Rome, is often reproduced in studies of Paganini and virtuosity. See for instance, Edgar Istel, 'The Secret of Paganini's Technique', *The Musical Quarterly* Vol. 16 No. 1 (1930), 101–16, Leslie Sheppard and Herbert R. Axelrod, *Paganini* (Neptune City, NJ: Paganiniana Publications, 1979), and the front cover of Heinz von Loesch, Ulrich Mahlert, and Peter Rummenhöller, eds., *Musikalische Virtuosität. Perspektiven musikalischer Theorie und Praxis (Gebundene Ausgabe)* (Mainz: Schott, 2004). See also Anatoli Vinogradov, *The Condemnation of Paganini: A Novel*, trans. Stephen Garry (London: Hutchinson, n.d.) and Klaus Kinski, *Kinski Paganini* (SPV Recordings DVD, 2003).

Figure 1.1 'Le Spectre de Paganini', *Le Plaisir à Paris* (1 May, 1889) Archive of the Bibliothèque de l'Opéra, Paris.

contextualisation of the violinist. A wide range of contemporary concerns were reflected in this web-like context: secularism and the power of mankind over nature, expressions of eros and sexuality, questions of egocentrism and self-definition, musical entrepreneurialism, hero-worship and cult-formation, all in the ever-changing landscape of Europe in the years following the French Revolution. Paganini's performances touched on or reflected all of these issues, and so does this book.

Each chapter takes a theme or set of themes to explore. Chapters do not need to be read consecutively as they are not ordered chronologically. Chapter 2 delves beneath the surface of Paganini's 'demonic' image to examine the multitude of meanings that this label encompassed. Chapter 3 brings to light gender and sexuality issues that were hidden or disguised in Paganini's time. Chapter 4 draws parallels between three ideas: 'musical sovereignty' (i.e. a form of music-making that models soloist dominion), the entrepreneurialism of virtuoso concert tours, and Napoleonic conquest. Chapter 5 turns to the history of violin virtuosity following Paganini's death and takes a fresh look at his role in shaping it. It then addresses directly a theme running throughout the previous chapters, the interrelation of the performer's on-stage persona and his private self, and suggests that their close correlation in Paganini's case is his most enduring legacy. The Epilogue considers the enduring mythology of Paganini as a 'demonic' virtuoso after his death by examining the investments made in it by his successors and followers. Finally, the Appendix presents examples of Paganiniana from the British press in the period 1840–1900 to give readers a chance to experience how strongly the myth persisted in a given body of literature. This chapter is designed as a general introduction to Paganini's place in music history and to what his virtuosity comprised, giving a new perspective on his techniques and performing style, his background, his public, and his 'cult'. It also explains the method and approaches I have taken and briefly considers the problems and challenges that arise in theorising virtuosity specifically and in performance studies more broadly.

Paganini's Historical Context as a Violinist

Paganini's standing in the history of virtuoso violinists is unique. His supreme technical ability and idiosyncratic performance style were undoubtedly indebted to the Italian violin tradition.[2] Certainly, he followed in the footsteps of seventeenth- and eighteenth-century precursors such as Arcangelo Corelli, Francesco Geminiani, Antonio Lolli, Pietro Nardini, Gaetano Pugnani, Giovanni Battista Somis, Giuseppe Tartini, Giuseppe Torelli, Francesco Veracini, and Antonio Vivaldi.[3] As the violin historian David Boyden stated, 'the eighteenth century was truly the century of the violin'.[4] In the realm of violin playing, the Italians led over the English, Germans, and the French during this era. This was partly because, as Boyden wrote, 'the musical prestige of Italy was never higher

---

[2] See Luigi Alberto Bianchi, 'Il virtuosismo violistico nell'opera di Rolla e Paganini', *Nuova Rivista Musicale Italiana* 1 (1975), 10–34.

[3] See, among others, James Deaville, 'La figura del virtuoso da Tartini e Bach a Paganini e Liszt', in *Enciclopedia della musica*, Jean-Jacques Nattiez, ed., with the collaboration of Margaret Bent, Rossana Dalmonte, and Mario Baroni, Vol. IV (Torino: Giulio Einaudi, 2004), 807–09, for a discussion of Corelli, Locatelli, Tartini, and Lolli as precursors to Paganini's violin virtuosity.

[4] David Boyden, *The History of Violin Playing from its Origins to 1761* (New York: Oxford University Press, 1965), 312.

than in the early eighteenth century'.[5] Another reason was that, as Boris Schwarz has observed, 'the art of violin building peaked in Italy at about the same time as the art of violin playing. Amati and Stradivari were contemporaries of Corelli and Vivaldi, while Tartini used a Guarneri instrument'.[6]

Boyden rightly refutes the widespread opinion that the progress of violin playing was slow until the emergence of Paganini; as he argues,

> Alberto Bachmann is a case in point when he says: 'When we consider the time which has elapsed from the creation of the violin, properly speaking, to the appearance of Paganini, it must be admitted that the evolution of progress was slow up to the moment when the tremendous genius of the great Italian illumined the firmament of art by the deploy of his magic powers'. Such a statement cannot be taken seriously today. The achievements of Vivaldi and Locatelli—to select two—show that the 'evolution of progress' in the technique and idiom of the violin was remarkably rapid, and Paganini's 'deploy of magic powers' would have been impossible without theirs a century earlier.[7]

But Bachmann's view is widely held even today among leading violinists, adding to the Paganini mystique. For example, the violinist Ivry Gitlis (b. 1922) once said, 'For me, Paganini was not a 'development' in the sense that there was Viotti, Corelli, 'Tatee', 'Tataa' . . . and then on . . . . There was all this, and then there was . . . Paganini'.[8]

An important historical precursor for Paganini was Pietro Locatelli (1695–1764), who supposedly had unusually flexible fingers like him. According to Schwarz, Locatelli 'could be called the father of violin virtuosity. He achieved in the eighteenth century what Paganini was to accomplish in the nineteenth—an unprecedented expansion of the violin technique of the time'.[9] Locatelli's *Capricci* (1733) probably served as a model for Paganini's own *Caprices*, some of which bear a striking resemblance to Locatelli's.[10] As Paganini himself later told the music

---

[5] *Ibid.*, 314.

[6] Boris Schwarz, *Great Masters of the Violin* (New York: Simon & Schuster, 1983), 77.

[7] Boyden, *The History of Violin Playing*, 312–13. The quotation comes from Bachmann's *Encyclopedia of the Violin* (New York, 1925), 188.

[8] From an interview he gave for the documentary *The Art of Violin* by Bruno Monsaingeon (Idéale Audience, 2000).

[9] Schwarz, *Great Masters of the Violin*, 92.

[10] See Alberto Cantù, *Invito all'ascolto di Nicolò Paganini* (Milan: Mursia, 1988), 56–7. See also Geraldine I. C. De Courcy, *Paganini, the Genoese* (Norman: University of Oklahoma Press, 1957) Vol. I, 34 and 46–7.

critic Fétis, Locatelli's example 'opened up a world of new ideas and devices that never had the merited success because of excessive difficulties'.[11]

The span and dexterity of Paganini's left fingers can be deduced, for example, from the double and triple harmonics in *Le Streghe,* variation III (Example 1.1a-d): (a) requires the simultaneous use of all four fingers of the left hand (first and third fingers on the D string and the second and fourth fingers on the A string); (b) demands that the third finger hover in a double stop over the D and A strings with the first and fourth fingers on the E string; (c) is a conglomerate of double-stopped artificial harmonics on the E and A strings with a natural harmonic on the D string; and (d) combines three stopped harmonics on the D, A, and E strings, involving a considerable stretch of the hand.

Example 1.1a–d Paganini, *Le Streghe*, variation III, multiple harmonics

But Paganini's performing style cannot be fully explained by reference to the classical Italian violin tradition alone: he also drew on an alternative genealogy of violin performance as a form of popular entertainment. This ranged from playing dance music to performing tricks and competitive 'duels', as exemplified by certain violinists excluded from the canonical tradition just identified. The Polish violinist Auguste Frédéric Duranowski, also known as Durand (1770–1834), left an indelible impression on Paganini as a boy with his 'marvelous [*sic*] magic'.[12] The eighteenth-century Bohemian violinist Jakob Scheller (1759–1803), to whom

[11] De Courcy, *Paganini, the Genoese* I, 46.

[12] Quoted in Andreas Moser, *Geschichte des Violinspiels*, ed. Hans-Joachim Nössel, 2nd ed. (Tutzing: Hans Schneider, 1967), 145. Very little is known about Duranowski. He studied with Viotti, according to Warwick Lister, *Amico: The Life of Giovanni Battista Viotti* (Oxford: Oxford University Press, 2009), 115. Paul G. Gelrud noted that Durand toured Italy and Germany from 1794 to 1814, served in the French army, and led the Strasbourg theatre orchestra in 'Foundations and Development of the Modern French Violin School' (MA thesis, Cornell, 1940), 45. Gelrud quoted a review from the *Allgemeine musikalische Zeitung* (7 November 1810), Vol. 12, no. 58, col. 933 marvelling at Durand's 'defeat of the greatest difficulties': 'his precision and skill must always excite the liveliest admiration; and every listener can get carried away with his fiery, bright, piquant humour' (quoted 46, my translation). See also De Courcy, *Paganini, the Genoese* I, 34 and the story of Duranowski's foiled attempts at petty thievery and subsequent imprisonment, from which the legend of Paganini's incarceration may have arisen, as he claimed himself in the *Revue musicale*.

Figure 1.2 Tightrope-walking fiddler, reproduced from John Durant and Alice Durant, *Pictorial History of the American Circus* (New York: A. S. Barnes, 1957).

Ludwig Spohr compared Paganini, was known for his dazzling parlour tricks, such as making the windows shake by imitating the sound of thunder on his violin. Peter Knappes of Stuttgart supposedly played entire pieces with the violin behind his back in the eighteenth century. The theatrical use of the violin echoed the circus featuring a tightrope walker playing the violin on top of his head in England in around 1700 (Figure 1.2 shows the unidentified circus performer).

Paganini's virtuosity also drew on the vocal control, dramatic power, and expressivity of the castrati he admired, such as Velluti, Crescentini, Pacchierotti, and Marchesi, alongside whom he made his debut at the opera house of Genoa (1795).[13] His high regard for their singing is evidenced by a comment he once made about soprano Angelica Catalani, (in)famous for treating her voice like an instrument: 'she would have *more soul* if she had been trained by such celebrated masters as Crescentini, Pacchierotti, Babini, and our celebrated Serra'.[14] Paganini particularly admired those castrati renowned for their pathos and depth of feeling (as did Rossini) and would have been very pleased to know that Wilhelm Speyer, a German music connoisseur (and a friend of Spohr's), once said of him, 'the *cantabile* passages and the *Adagio* he sings in a melancholy, deeply moving and albeit eloquent way such as I have never heard from any instrumentalist—about as I heard Crescentini sing in Paris'.[15] Paganini's ascent coincided with the decline of that vocal tradition, and because the leading castrati were revered as larger-than-life virtuoso celebrities at the peak of their popularity in the 1700s, they could be considered forerunners to his standing as a violin virtuoso. By providing a substitute spectacle he filled the space they left as they fell out of favour with audiences and disappeared from the opera stages.[16]

Carmela Bongiovanni's observations on Genoa in the time of Paganini give us a sense of the city buzzing with music in a variety of settings.[17] Drawing on a wealth of documentary evidence including journals, diaries, and church and theatre records, she has identified four broad themes within music in Genoa in the eighteenth and nineteenth centuries: 1) the music of numerous confraternities, based in churches and organised by societies particularly around religious festivals; 2) military bands, which played an important role in civil ceremonies during the period of the Ligurian Republic by performing military symphonies

---

[13] Marchesi was said to 'control his voice as one would a violin' according to Pietro Verri in Sven Hansell, 'Marchesi, Luigi', *Grove Music Online*, accessed 15 April 2009. <www.oxfordmusiconline.com/subscriber/article/grove/music/17732>.

[14] Quoted in De Courcy, *Paganini the Genoese* I, 222, my emphasis. NB Crescentini and Pacchierotti were legendary castrati, Babini was one of Italy's leading tenors, and Serra a respected composer and conductor.

[15] When Crescentini attended a concert of his in Bologna in 1818, Paganini was genuinely humbled and honoured that an artist of his stature would take any interest in his performance.

[16] By the 1830s, there were none left on the opera stage (although they continued to sing in church choirs until around 1900). John Rosselli, 'Castrato', *Grove Music Online* accessed 1 February 2010 <www.oxfordmusiconline.com/subscriber/article/grove/music/05146>.

[17] Carmela Bongiovanni, 'Osservazioni sulla musica a Genova nell'età di Paganini', in Maria Rosa Moretti, Anna Sorrento, Stefano Termanini, and Enrico Volpato, eds, *Paganini divo e comunicatore, atti del convengo internazionale* (Genoa, 3–5 December 2004) (Genoa: Serel International, 2007), 101–60.

and other kinds of music to help promote patriotism and to glorify Napoleon; 3) church and theatre orchestras (e.g. Chiesa di S. Lorenzo, Teatro Carlo Felice) assembled to perform on religious holidays, for public dances, and 'academies', the rosters of which list Paganini's teachers Costa and Cervetto as *primo violino* and section viola respectively; 4) the musical patronage of the Marchese Gian Carlo Di Negro (1769–1857), who was involved in the affairs of the Carlo Felice and became acquainted over the course of his long life with virtuosi such as Antonio Bazzini, Max Bohrer, and Sigismund Thalberg.

At the risk of over-generalising, the musical environment in which Paganini grew up in the 1780s and 1790s was one that gravitated more to the theatrical than the literary; to opera than to instrumental music; to the public visual spectacle of carnival, church rituals, and military splendour than to the private act of listening. Paganini was also firmly rooted in the popular music traditions of the time— with an informal approach to performance, taking requests, and improvising on traditional songs and dances transmitted by oral tradition. The instruments he played (violin, guitar, and mandolin) all carried folk associations to some degree; the traces of his early immersion in popular music genres such as the *trallalero* (a traditional Genoese singing style) and dances from the Apennines such as the *Alessandrine, Perigordino,* and *Monferrine* brought to Genoa by travelling troupes can be seen in many of his compositions, as Mario Balma has shown.[18] As he puts it, Paganini 'transformed traditional language giving it a bourgeois destination without greatly altering the coordinates'.[19]

Paganini was almost certainly taught to improvise on certain stock musical patterns or 'schemata', as Robert Gjerdingen has called them; as he has noted, eighteenth-century musicians used a template for improvisation similar to the *zibaldone*, 'a manuscript of assemblage of stock speeches, slapstick, jokes, and plots passed down from actor to actor, usually within the same family or troupe'.[20] Originating in the *commedia dell'arte* tradition, *zibaldone* was 'also the word used to describe a music student's notebook of exercises and rules'.[21] For example, Francesco Galeazzi (1758–1819) used the term in this way, and indeed the 'Pulcinella cadence' was named for the character. Melodic patterns, harmonic sequences, and cadential formulas could be strung together to create entire pieces.

[18] Mario Balma, 'La tradizione popolare fonte di ispirazione per Paganini', in Moretti *et al*, eds. *Paganini Divo e Comunicatore*, 227–54.

[19] Balma, 'La tradizione popolare', 234. Having this background undoubtedly helped Paganini to compose new works based on the well-known melodies at his tour destinations once he set out for the capitals of Europe ('God Save the King', 'St Patrick's Day', etc.).

[20] Robert O. Gjerdingen, *Music in the Galant Style* (Oxford: Oxford University Press, 2007), 8.

[21] *Ibid.,* 10.

The 'Ponte' was a bridge-shaped melody (i.e. ascending and descending), the 'Romanesca' a harmonic pattern exemplified by Pachelbel's canon (the first six chords), and the diatonic 'Monte' a bassline motion constructed entirely out of root-position chords—just to name a few. Gjerdingen has provided a kind of morphological lexicon of these, from research conducted at the conservatory libraries of Naples, Milan, and Bologna, and shown their usage in the music of numerous composers including Pugnani, Locatelli, and Viotti—the forefathers of the Italian violin tradition—as well as Cimarosa and Paisiello, typifying the Italian opera tradition in which Paganini was immersed.

Paganini was a paradox as an 'un-Romantic Romantic'. In the words of musicologist Joël-Marie Fauquet, he was 'a supreme incarnation of Romanticism for his generation while his syntax, form, and techniques were classical'.[22] The uncomfortable fit between Paganini's own outlook and the typical traits of Romanticism have also been noted by Hugh Macdonald, who characterises him as 'an eighteenth-century violinist-craftsman' and thus an un-Romantic figure, and by Dana Gooley, who places him in the Italian *commedia dell'arte* tradition.[23] Indeed, by the early nineteenth century, Paganini's compositional language and musical aesthetics seemed as antiquated as his Italian ancestry seemed next to the new stars of the French School.

It was significant that Paganini was an *Italian* violinist at a time when the French School was becoming the leading violin school in Europe, marking the end of the era of Italian ascendancy. This was due in part to the fact that Viotti, the last proponent of the great Italian violin tradition and dubbed 'the greatest violinist in Europe' in the 1790s, settled in Paris. By the 1820s and 1830s his pupils Rode, Baillot, and Kreutzer had established the Conservatoire as the pre-eminent training-ground for violinists and established the dominance of the 'French School'.[24] Through direct multi-generational teacher–pupil relationships, the subsequent development and proliferation of various national 'schools' of violinists (Franco-Belgian, Viennese, German, Czech, Russian, American, etc.) in retrospect underlines Paganini as an isolated figure lacking a genealogical tree of descendants. The fact that he left no true disciples or 'school' stemming from his style of playing has been interpreted as a sign of the robustness of alternative

---

[22] Joël-Marie Fauquet, 'Quand le diable s'en mêle', *Romantisme: Revue de la Société des Études Romantique* 128 (2005), 35.

[23] Hugh Macdonald, 'Paganini in Scotland', in Raffaello Monterosso, ed., *Nicolò Paganini e il suo tempo [Nicolò Paganini and his times]* (Genoa: Comune di Genova, 1984), 217; Dana Gooley, 'La Commedia del Violino: Paganini's Comic Strains', *Musical Quarterly* Vol. 88 No. 3 (2005), 370–427.

[24] Boyden, *The History of Violin Playing*.

schools (for instance, in Schwarz's view, '[Viotti's] legacy survived the tidal wave of virtuosity brought about by the rise of Paganini').[25] However, historiographically speaking, Paganini remains an anomaly, contributing to his aura of ultimate individualism. The widely accepted belief that 'with Paganini's contribution the art of violin playing may be considered as having completed its evolution' (attributed for instance to Marc Pincherle in a review of his book *Les Violinistes compositeurs et virtuoses*) locates him in a singular position, an apex of finality.[26]

Demystifying Virtuosity

Paganini's virtuosity comprised an array of musical and extra-musical elements that have so far received little or no attention. The trademark virtuoso techniques themselves (left-hand pizzicato, double harmonics, *due corde, jeté,* left-hand pizzicato, perpetual motion, prestidigitation, *ricochet, scordatura,* staccato, *sul ponticello, una corda,* etc.), have been analysed and classified across his extant oeuvre by violinists and scholars from Guhr (1829) to Cantú (1988).[27] Yet how Paganini deployed these techniques performatively has been little explored. The following three examples illustrate some of the ways he used techniques to create drama.

1. Caprice No. 1 is famous for featuring the technique of flying staccato, ascending and descending in continuous semiquavers across all four strings through a series of arpeggiated chord changes (Example 1.2). The motoric propulsion of the right arm coupled with the increasingly convoluted and higher positions of the left hand create a striking effect. While this is well known, the fact that the perpetual motion stops suddenly at bar 56 is not. There is a crotchet rest, then the mechanism begins again. The unexpected silence shows the hand of the dramaturge: he draws attention to the continuity of the technique by disrupting it.[28] Thus, the dramatic effect of this Caprice derives not only from the use of the flying staccato technique, as widely recognised, but also from its momentary suspense—a rhetorical decision that highlights the technique.

[25]   Schwarz, *Great Masters of the Violin*, 145, 148.
[26]   M.-D. C., 'Les Violinistes compositeurs et virtuoses', *Musical Times* Vol. 64 No. 965 (July 1923), 471.
[27]   Techniques are discussed in Carl Guhr, *Ueber Paganini's Kunst die Violin zu spielen* (Mainz: Schott, 1829), Cantú, *Invito all'ascolto*, and other texts.
[28]   The moment is further heightened by the harmonic structure. As a basic musical analysis reveals, the previous twelve bars do not so much modulate as they ratchet up the tonality a semitone at a time, the root G becoming the third of the V^7 chord leading to Ab, and so on, as follows: $G–(E\flat^7)–A\flat–(E^7)–A–(F^7)–B\flat–(F\sharp^7)–B–(G^7)–C–(A\flat^7)$ (as shown in the example). At the point where the music breaks off, the Ab^7 is left hanging unresolved—until the Db chord arrives, in bar 56, with the 'false reprise'.

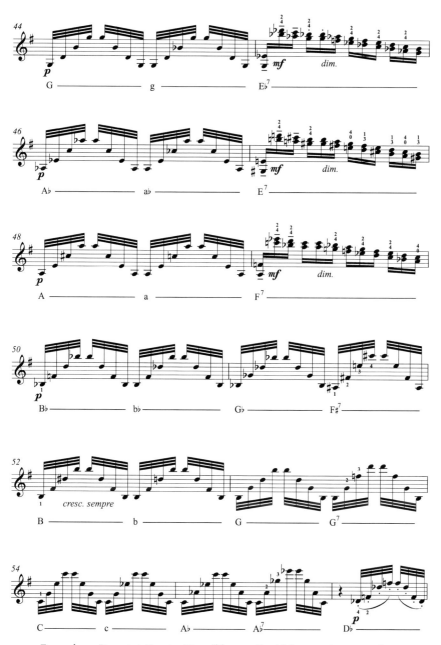

Example 1.2 Paganini, Caprice No. 1 (bb. 44–56) with harmonic progression

2. Paganini's technique of performing entire pieces on only one string was one of the hallmarks of his virtuosity, yet in the Introduction and Variations on 'Dal tuo stellato soglio' from Rossini's *Mosè in Egitto* (ca. 1819), the effect of this technique was heightened further by its extra-musical meaning. In the original operatic

scene from which the theme was taken, Moses implores God to part the sea so that the Israelites may pass—by saying a prayer, repeated by his followers Elisero and Elcia. Paganini's version imitated their voices in three different registers, moving higher up the G string and into harmonics. He thus represented Rossini's characters and carried the dramatic import of the scene over into his playing, giving the one-string technique an extra expressive dimension.

3. Paganini used *glissandi, sul ponticello, ricochet*, and very high pitches not only as stand-alone performance techniques but also as devices of mimesis, imitating the cries of animals, human voices, and musical instruments other than the violin. Following in the tradition of Farina's *Capriccio Stravagante*, he imitated donkey brays, birdsong, cats meowing, and dogs barking, thereby introducing elements of improvisation and humour into his performances.[29] Paganini is also said to have made the violin say 'buona sera' so realistically that the audience said 'good evening' back to him,[30] and he imitated the nasal whining of an old witch in *Le Streghe*.[31] In forging an informal connection with the audience, in an era before the stiff behaviour of concertgoers became a social convention (in the later nineteenth and twentieth centuries), Paganini used his techniques as a communicative device. They were not just put on display, to be marvelled at passively, but rather they served an extra-musical function, to provoke and involve his audiences— as when performers actually talk from the stage in jazz clubs and increasingly in cutting-edge classical concert venues today. Virtuosity then was not only a musical aesthetic but also a concert aesthetic, in the sense that spontaneous, humorous interjections using dazzling technical effects created a certain mood that went beyond display for its own sake.

   Although there are no surviving notations of such improvisations, the *24 Caprices* contain hints as to how Paganini went about imitating flutes and hunting horns (No. 9), trumpets (No. 14), birdsong (No. 19) and even donkey brays (Nos. 7 and 17) (see Examples 1.3–1.7).[32] As these examples show, Paganini dramatised his

---

[29] His 'imitations of a donkey, a dog, a rooster, etc., [were] enough to make you lose your mind!' according to Boucher de Perthes in a letter to his father from Livorno (9 February 1810), quoted in De Courcy, *Paganini, the Genoese* I, 113.

[30] Lilian Day, *Paganini of Genoa* (London: Victor Gollancz, 1966 [1929]), 106.

[31] Two accounts can be found in *Harmonicon* Vol. 6 No. 9 (September 1828), 211 and De Courcy, *Paganini, the Genoese* I, 123–4.

[32] The proximity to flute timbre in Caprice No. 9 may have been increased through the use of double harmonics—given as an 'ossia' in Niccolo Paganini, *Op. 1: Twenty-Four Caprices For the Violin*. Study-version and Preface by Harold Berkley (New York: Schirmer, 1944). Albi Rosenthal has also noted the proximity of Caprice No. 19 to birdsong in 'An intriguing copy of Paganini's "Capricci" and its implications', in Monterosso, ed. *Paganini e il suo tempo*, 243. The way Caprice No. 17 leaps down from

display of techniques through performative decisions. This differed from the drama inherent in the display of technical skill itself deriving from the element of risk in live performance. That kind of drama was nothing new. Diderot parodied it in the story of Rameau's nephew, who performs a pantomime of a violinist struggling with the acrobatic passagework of a Locatelli *Allegro*.[33] To heroically overcome technical difficulty was a basic principle of virtuoso performance long before Paganini, and was still very much operative in his time. His performance of his Concerto No. 1 impressed the virtuoso violinist Karol Lipinski, who stated that 'with remarkable ease he overcame such terrible difficulties as previously no one had dreamt it possible to surmount, and which I myself had considered insurmountable'.[34]

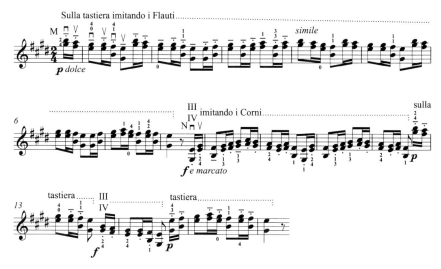

Example 1.3 Paganini, Caprice No. 9, excerpt

From Paganini's point of view, technical difficulties posed little or no challenge; he hardly ever practised on tour. He also helped himself by spacing out technically demanding passages in the structure of his compositions, and pacing himself by gradually introducing faster and faster note values, with the fastest (semiquavers or demisemiquavers) saved for the finale. The structure of the potpourri concert,

the upper two strings to the lower two bears some resemblance to Mendelssohn's depiction of Bottom's brays in his *A Midsummer Night's Dream Overture* (1842), an effect easily made grotesque by playing a crescendo and simulating a guttural stop by stopping the bow in the midst of crossing strings.

[33] Denis Diderot, *Rameau's Nephew and D'Alembert's Dream*, trans. Leonard Tencock (Harmondsworth: Penguin, 1966), 53.

[34] Quoted in Czeslaw Raymond Halski, 'Paganini and Lipinski', *Music and Letters* Vol. 40 No. 3 (1959), 275.

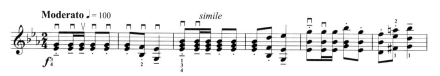

Example 1.4 Paganini, Caprice No. 14, excerpt

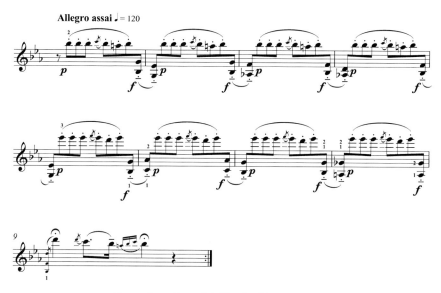

Example 1.5 Paganini, Caprice No. 19, excerpt

whereby he took the stage in alternation with other performers (usually singers, who also 'warmed up' the crowd) allowed him to rest in between pieces. Paganini did not wish to look like he was working hard.

So far, we have drawn the emphasis away from *what* he played onto *how* he played. Now we turn away from Paganini to the role of the audience, as no exploration of how meaning arose in virtuoso performance can be complete without considering it as a form of mediation, as a ritualised social contract.[35]

[35] Vernon Howard has reached a similar conclusion in 'Virtuosity as a Performance Concept: A Philosophical Analysis', *Philosophy of Music Education Review* Vol. 5 No. 1 (Spring 1997), 42–54. Concerning the ritual aspect, I have found Victor Turner's idea of 'communitas' illuminating; for an application of it to denote Paganini's performance uniting his audience in a shared experience, see David L. Palmer, 'Virtuosity as Rhetoric: Agency and Transformation in Paganini's Mastery of the Violin', *Quarterly Journal of*

Example 1.6 Paganini, Caprice No. 7, excerpt

Example 1.7 Paganini, Caprice No. 17, excerpt

Speech Vol. 84 No. 3 (August 1998), 341–57. Similarly, Éric Bordas's 'Ut musica poesis? Littérature et virtuosité, *Romantisme: Revue de la Societé des Études Romantique* 128 (2005), 109–28' presents the idea that virtuosity's meaning is constructed and not posed, a 'cultural proposition' arising (in music as in literature) in the relations between the internal structure of works and the reactions of the listeners or readers of a certain epoch in a given culture.

From the audience's point of view, Paganini's difficult techniques could be divided into those that were within the realm of the comprehensible and those that were not. His performance of a *moto perpetuo* led a Parisian orchestral violinist to calculate that he had executed a staggering 2,272 notes in the space of three minutes and twenty seconds.[36] For the performer, it was possible to see how it could be done in theory, since the fast-moving fingers corresponded to the fast-moving sounds. Similarly, his *una corda* playing was realistically understandable. Other techniques like left-hand pizzicato runs, harmonics, and the flying staccato defied emulation, either because they were too difficult or simply inexplicable.

While trained violinists had it in their power to discern the difference between a technique that looked difficult because it was hard to play and one that merely seemed difficult, they constituted only a small minority among Paganini's audiences. For the vast majority, Paganini simply seemed to exceed the limits of human capability. His playing was incomprehensible, unbelievable, bringing on a type of cognitive failure in the viewer. As Meyerbeer put it, 'Paganini begins where our reason stops';[37] and as one critic wrote after a Milan concert of 1813, 'his playing is truly *inexplicable*'.[38] This inexplicability was key to the power of virtuosity to fascinate.

Two of Paganini's favourite techniques were singled out as defying explanation. One was the production of harmonics, which sounded high-pitched despite the left hand not being positioned high on the fingerboard—an illusion without the knowledge that artificial harmonics can be produced by lightly pressing on the string in a low hand position. As a reviewer for the *Athenaeum* wrote, 'the phenomenon of producing higher sounds by receding from the bridge is matter of wonder to such only as are not musicians'.[39] Double harmonics sounded improbable even to trained violinists, such as Carl Guhr, who was mystified as to how they were played until he had observed Paganini many times. The other technique was up- and down-bow staccato, which created the illusion that the bow moved by itself. As a reviewer for *The Observer* noted: 'Paganini does the staccato in a manner quite different from all other performers. He strikes his bow once on the string, and it seems to run by a tremulous motion over as many notes as he chooses to include in the staccato passages. This, too, he does with the quickness almost of

[36]   As quoted in Anne Penesco, 'Portrait de l'artiste violiniste en virtuose', *Romantisme: Revue de la Société des Études Romantiques* 128 (2005), 22.

[37]   Quoted in Schwarz, *Great Masters of the Violin*, 175.

[38]   Peter Lichtenthal, *Leipziger allgemeine musikalische Zeitung*, quoted in De Courcy, *Paganini the Genoese* I, 125–6.

[39]   Quoted in Vanda Delfino, 'Niccolo Paganini e la critica musicale inglese', *Nuova Rivista Musicale Italiana* Vol. 14 No. 4 (October–December 1980), 557–8.

thought itself.'[40] By moving from the difficult to the inexplicable, Paganini crossed a certain threshold, leaving comprehensibility behind and stepping into another realm. This act of transgression from the known to the unknown provided fertile grounds for transforming a mortal violinist into an immortal demon in the public imagination.[41]

Exactly how Paganini acquired the virtuosity that stunned so many people has been kept shrouded in mystery by the legend of his 'secret'.[42] Numerous attempts to divine the nature of the 'secret' have served to fuel its legendary status, from the obsessive repeated observations of Guhr to mid-twentieth-century academics re-examining his conclusions and Paganini's manuscripts for further clues.[43] The belief that there must exist some key to unlock the 'secret' served and continues to serve a mythological or symbolic function like the Holy Grail. This was partly responsible for creating the 'Paganini cult'.

The 'Paganini Cult'

The 'Paganini cult' is a familiar phrase today.[44] Yet to my knowledge it was not used in any of the literature about Paganini during his lifetime.[45] That is not to suggest that the phenomenon it describes, the quasi-religious worship of Paganini's virtuosity, was not recognised then. To adopt the language of a contemporary critic, what Paganini inspired was a pseudo-spiritual 'craze': as Ludwig Boerne wrote of his Paris debut (1831), 'it was a divine, a diabolic enthusiasm. The people have all gone crazy and will make everybody else crazy'.[46] The following

---

[40] *The Observer* (4 June 1831) quoted in Arturo Codignola, *Paganini intimo* (Genoa: Edito a cura del municipio, 1935), 343.

[41] As Dana Gooley has posited, 'virtuosity is about shifting borders' (*The Virtuoso Liszt*. New Perspectives in Music History and Criticism (Cambridge and New York: Cambridge University Press, 2004), 1).

[42] According to Federico Mompellio, the legend of Paganini's secret arose 'first of all, because anyone who heard him—even expert violinists—could not understand how he could perform such hitherto unimaginable difficulties. Then because he himself helped voluntarily or involuntarily (very likely the first) to surround with mystery his own performance'. Quoted in De Courcy, *Paganini, the Genoese* I, 373.

[43] Carl Guhr, *Ueber Paganini's Kunst die Violin zu spielen*, Istel, 'The Secret of Paganini's Technique'; see also Warren Kirkendale 'Segreto comunicato da Paganini', *Journal of the American Musicological Society* Vol. 18 No. 3 (Autumn, 1965), 394–407.

[44] Sheila M. Nelson states, for example, that 'there is ample evidence that a Paganini cult swept through Europe' (comparable to Beatle-mania in the 1960s) in *The Violin and Viola: History, Structure, Techniques* (Mineola, NY: Dover, reprinted 2003), 141.

[45] I have not found any references to a 'cult', 'culte', 'kult', or 'culto' in nineteenth-century writings on Paganini.

[46] Quoted in De Courcy, *Paganini, the Genoese* II, 15.

the violinist gained was like a cult: people travelled great distances to see him as if making a holy pilgrimage; women became infatuated with him; he became a god for violinists obsessed with perfecting their technique (and in this sense Paganini still has a cult following today).

The 'Paganini cult' was primarily a bourgeois phenomenon. The majority of the virtuoso's public was middle class, and it was their characteristics, their psychological needs, that the 'cult' reflected in the 1820s–1830s, just as 'Lisztomania' would in the 1840s.[47] Indeed, Paganini and Liszt epitomised the Romantic 'cult of the virtuoso' with its emphasis on soloistic, heroic performance as part of the bourgeois era's obsession with the cult of personality, individualism, and the self.

The historian Peter Gay has defined 'the cult of virtuosos like Paganini and Liszt' as 'a collective mania that responsible music critics derided as the vulgar overvaluation of mere entertainers'.[48] In his view, 'the cult of virtuosos' was a cultural phenomenon that, along with the 'virtual deification of Beethoven', exemplified 'the worship of music'—in other words, making music a secular religion. The distinction between a cult and deification lay in the legitimacy of the object of worship. The virtuosi were spurious deities, akin to pseudo-gurus who inspired undeserved devotion in their followers. As Gay points out, the philistinism of the bourgeois public made them susceptible to worshipping false gods, as did 'the uncomfortable feeling that one's pacific, safe, unadventurous class was hopelessly unheroic'.[49] The 'cult of virtuosos' sprang up to fill a psychological void just as, for instance, the 'cult of nature' provided an object of worship in 'the pit of modern godlessness'.[50] Similar needs were served in the nineteenth century by Bach, Wagner, Goethe, Joan of Arc, conductors, and violins, all of which became the objects of cults.

'Lisztomania' was symptomatic of the need for an object of public enthusiasm, as Dana Gooley has shown.[51] Berlin audiences in the early 1800s who went mad for Liszt also idolised the singer Henriette Sontag and the dancer Fanny Elssler. The 'Paganini cult' similarly instantiated the need of his followers for idols, which

---

[47] Roberto Grisley's reference to 'Paganinimania' is a retroactive adaptation of 'Lisztomania' in *Niccolò Paganini, epistolario 1810–1831* (Rome: Accademia Nazionale di Santa Cecilia and Milano: Skira editore, 2006), 11. Liszt's followers were described as a 'cult' at least as early as 1844, when Henri Blanchard referred to a 'new musical cult . . . of which Liszt is at least the high priest if not the Mohammed' in the *Revue et gazette musicale* Vol. 11 No. 17 (28 April 1844), 151, quoted in Dana Gooley, *The Virtuoso Liszt*, 210.

[48] Peter Gay, *The Naked Heart*. The Bourgeois Experience, Victoria to Freud, No. 4 (New York and London: Norton, 1995), 23.

[49] *Ibid.*, 61, 159.

[50] Ibid., 80–1.

[51] Gooley, *The Virtuoso Liszt*, Chapter 5.

could be fulfilled by other virtuosi. Even in his home town of Genoa, for example, the arrival of the singer Catalani in 1825 was heralded as follows: 'A person who has earned more than an English conqueror general, more than Lord Byron with his poems, more than Walter Scott with his novels'.[52]

Like Liszt, Paganini caught the imagination of the bourgeois audiences who dominated concert life, but also appealed to the nobility and the lower classes. At the Redoutensaal in Vienna, for example, in his first appearances outside his native land (1828), his audience included the empress and her children as well as burghers, musicians (including Schubert), music critics, and friends and colleagues from Italy. Permission to use the venue came from the court; Paganini also played for the emperor's private birthday party. His Paris début (1831) was a celebrated affair with a litany of luminaries in attendance as well as the court and the diplomatic corps.[53] In London, Paganini's appeal across class lines, West End and East End, was evidenced by the fact that he could 'never leave [his] house without being mobbed by people . . . and not only the common people, but even the upper classes'.[54] Paganini therefore illustrates William Weber's observation that in early nineteenth-century London, Paris, Leipzig, and Vienna, 'the fashionable virtuoso concert . . . brought together people from diverse social levels under the aegis of a unifying musical outlook'.[55]

This was noteworthy considering that social segregation by class was a very recent memory in German towns like Stuttgart, Dessau, Hanover, and Darmstadt and still in practice in Weimar, where 'nobility and townspeople sat on different sides of the theater'.[56] In many of the places Paganini visited, the presence of women in the public audience was a novelty; as Weber has also noted, 'women were barred from membership in the great majority of amateur music societies in the eighteenth century'.[57] The hysterical responses of women at Paganini's concerts thus need to be gauged against the fact that they were among the first women in European history to experience public concerts at all.

---

[52] *Gazzetta di Genova* 91 (12 November 1825), quoted in Grisley, *Niccolò Paganini, epistolario*, 282 n.3.

[53] As listed by De Courcy, *Paganini, the Genoese* II, 14–15: 'Théophile Gautier, Jules Janin, Charles Nodier, Alphonse Kerr, Alfred de Musset, Eugène Délacroix, George Sand . . . Jules Sandeau, Heine, Boerne, Baillot, Beriot and Malibran, Rossini and his friend Baron Aguado, Liszt, Castil-Blaze, Alfred de Vigny, Émile de Girardin, Donizetti, Auber, Halévy, the Rothschilds, Prince Demidoff.'

[54] Paganini's letter to Germi (June–July 1831) quoted in De Courcy, *Paganini, the Genoese* II, 53.

[55] William Weber, *The Great Transformation of Musical Taste: Concert Programming from Haydn to Brahms* (Cambridge: Cambridge University Press, 2008), 91.

[56] De Courcy, *Paganini, the Genoese* I, 308.

[57] Weber, *The Great Transformation*, 23.

On Theorising Virtuosity and 'Performance Studies'

This book departs from most previous studies of Paganini, which have tended to focus either on historical/biographical aspects or purely analytical ones (concentrating on explaining his compositional or violinistic techniques), by combining both avenues of inquiry.[58] It draws on the evidence of two kinds of primary sources: 1) scores of Paganini's compositions, and 2) historical and biographical documents including reviews, caricatures, treatises, letters, and so on from Paganini's time to our own.

There are several reasons why a book-length study of this kind has not been undertaken until now. Obviously, the difficulty of establishing the 'text' in the study of any musician before the age of recording has deterred musicologists from focussing on nineteenth-century performance styles. Paganini died approximately half a century before violinists were first recorded.[59] While an 'objective' assessment of his sound production and performance style will never be possible, they can nonetheless be 'reconstructed' to a certain extent on the evidence of his compositions, which bear the traces of the player they were designed to showcase, and verbal accounts describing his gestures and movements by audiences, critics, and the player himself. Paying close attention to the musical clues offered by his most representative solo repertory (the *24 Caprices*, the concertos, and variation sets, rather than his chamber music, duos with guitar, or other incidental works—for the simple reason that they are the best known today) enables an approximation of Paganini's performance to come into view.[60] So does examining the kind of language contemporaries used. It is

---

[58]   In the first category, see De Courcy, *Paganini, the Genoese* (on which I have relied extensively), Edward Neill, *Nicolò Paganini: la vita attraverso le opere, i documenti e le immagini* (Genoa: Cassa di risparmio di Genova e Imperia, 1978), Paul Metzner, *Crescendo of the Virtuoso: Spectacle, Skill and Self-Promotion in Paris during the Age of Revolution* (Berkeley and Los Angeles: University of California Press, 1998); in the second, Cantú, *Invito all'ascolto*, and Istel, 'The Secret of Paganini's Technique'. The exceptions are articles by Anne Penesco, 'Paganini et l'école de violon Franco-Belge', *Revue Internationale de Musique Française* 9 (1982), 17–60, Dana Gooley, 'La Commedia del Violino: Paganini's Comic Strains', Joël-Marie Fauquet, 'Quand le diable s'en mêle', and Camilla Bork, 'Theatricality in the Concert Hall: Paganini's Virtuosity', Paper read at the 3rd German-American Frontiers of Humanities Symposium, Humboldt University, Berlin (2006).

[59]   Some of the earliest recordings of Joachim, Sarasate, and Ysaÿe date from 1903–04, as reissued by Pearl (2003) under the title *Joseph Joachim: The Complete Recordings (1903). Pablo de Sarasate: The Complete Recordings (1904). Eugène Ysaÿe: A Selection of his Recordings (1912).*

[60]   There are limitations to establishing the 'text', especially in the case of his improvisations, in which even intimate familiarity with Paganini's stock-in-trade devices only goes so far.

perhaps worth mentioning that this book is not intended as a study in historical performance practice, since the goal is not to recover and replicate the original performance conditions in the name of 'authenticity', but to shed light on the nature of performance itself.

Taking the performance rather than the score as the authoritative 'text' not only poses a practical challenge, it also shifts the locus of musical meaning. For various reasons, musicology as a discipline has traditionally been biased towards locating musical meanings in works, with performers playing only an ancillary role. For instance, Carl Dahlhaus considered Paganini's development of violin virtuosity interesting as a fact of 'cultural history' but insignificant in terms of music history; in his view, virtuosity only became a 'legitimate' consideration of music history when Liszt combined it with conceptions of organic form—by blending together improvisatory and sonata elements in his compositions.[61] The historiographic decision to cast composers as the protagonists of music history needs to be revised, not by simply replacing composers with performers—that would be to replace one problematic hierarchical paradigm with another—but by viewing the activities of composing and performing as continuous, overlapping, and non-hierarchical.

Recent studies eschewing a radical separation between composed and performed musical meanings have illuminated aspects of virtuosity in, for example, Boccherini and Liszt.[62] These have gone beyond the limitations of 'performance studies', a subfield that tends to invert or leave unaddressed the hierarchy just described. In addition, new ways to critique the act of performance itself have been advanced in popular music studies as an alternative to the traditional

---

[61] Carl Dahlhaus discusses The *Dante Sonata* and the Piano Concerto No. 1 in Eb major in this regard in *Nineteenth-Century Music*, trans. J. Bradford Robinson (Berkeley, Los Angeles and London: University of California Press, 1989), 134–42.

[62] Elisabeth Le Guin has theorised the figure of Boccherini as a sphinx-like enigma whose relationship with his cello, far from being straightforward, was fraught with uncertainties over the philosophical category of self that was typical of the Enlightenment era. In his reception study of Liszt, Dana Gooley has emphasised the remarkable chameleon-like transformations of the pianist's identity in meeting the demands and needs of his audiences, while James Deaville has shed light on the pianist's star status. Elisabeth Le Guin, *Boccherini's Body: An Essay in Carnal Musicology* (Berkeley and Los Angeles: University of California Press, 2006); Dana Gooley, *The Virtuoso Liszt;* James Deaville, 'The Making of a Myth: Liszt, the Press, and Virtuosity', in James Deaville and Michael Saffle, eds, *Analecta Lisztiana II: New Light on Liszt and His Music* (Stuyvesant, NY: Pendragon Press, 1997), 181–95. I have also benefited from the 'cultural history' approach epitomised by Peter Gay's *The Naked Heart* and Arthur Loesser's *Men, Women and Pianos: A Social History* (New York: Simon and Schuster, 1954).

musicological separation of cultural and musical issues.[63] Such approaches have informed and guided the present study, as have two excellent general studies of musical virtuosity, one in French, the other in German, that have appeared in recent years.

An admirable collection of essays on Romantic virtuosity edited by Cécile Reynaud appeared as a special issue of the journal *Romantisme* (2005).[64] It contains two essays focusing on Paganini's legacy of instrumental singing and pictorial effects as well as 'transcendental mechanisms', and on the role of the Tartini legend in his reception in Paris, which have proved particularly invaluable in broadening my own perspective.[65] The other essays in the volume, which shed light on virtuoso aspects of Liszt and Chopin, French music (e.g. Berlioz as composer and as conductor), French literature (e.g. Balzac, Hugo, Zola), and French ballet, demonstrate the breadth of virtuosity as a Romantic phenomenon in French culture well into the nineteenth century.[66]

Musikalische Virtuosität (2004), edited by Heinz von Loesch and others, fills a long-standing gap in musicological scholarship by bringing together twenty essays on a broad range of topics concerning musical virtuosity—broad in historical scope (from Frescobaldi and C.P.E. Bach to rock guitarists and DJs), coverage of musical genres (not just common practice classical repertoire but popular music as well as North Indian tabla-drumming) and approaches (philosophical and music-theoretical as well as historical, performer-centric as well as composer-centric). In particular, the contributions of Beatrix Borchard (on Joseph Joachim),

[63] Robert Walser's study of heavy metal guitarists gives insight into the power ideology of performance. *Running with the Devil: Power, Gender and Madness in Heavy Metal Music* (Hanover, NH: Wesleyan University Press, 1993).
[64] *Romantisme: Revue de la Société des Études Romantiques* 128 (2005): 'La Virtuosité'.
[65] Penesco, 'Portrait de l'artiste violiniste en virtuose'; Fauquet, 'Quand le diable s'en mêle'.
[66] Bruno Moysan's 'Virtuosité pianistique: les écritures de la subjectivité' (51–70) asserts that the project of romantic virtuoso piano writing is to present a subjectivity, a heroic 'I', in a 'discourse of me'. Peter Bloom's 'Virtuosités de Berlioz' (71–94) explores Berlioz's 'virtuosities'—as an orchestral conductor and as a composer (for example in *Harold in Italy*). Sylvie Jacq-Mioche's 'La virtuosité dans le ballet français romantique: des faits à une morale sociale du corps' (95–108) discusses virtuosity in French Romantic ballet, with a focus on the emergence of Antoine Paul and Antoine Coulon in 1820s Paris, as well as the introduction of the art of 'la pointe', which enabled ballerinas Geneviève Gosselin and Marie Taglioni to execute pirouettes with greater speed and elegance than ever before. Éric Bordas's 'Ut musica poesis? Littérature et Virtuosité' (109–28) examines literary and poetic virtuosity, particularly in the use of the rhythms of the French language, in the works of Balzac, Hugo and Zola. On this last topic, see also Susan Bernstein, *Virtuosity of the Nineteenth Century: Performing Music and Language in Heine, Liszt, and Baudelaire* (Stanford, CA: Stanford University Press, 1998).

Cornelia Bartsch (on women virtuosi), and Peter Wicke (on guitar heroes) shed light on performer mythology, gender issues, and the sociological significance of virtuosi, thus demonstrating that the study of virtuosity is growing into the latest developments in musicology as a field.[67] As Heinz von Loesch writes in his introduction to the volume, 'virtuosity' is 'a musicological object'.[68]

Demythologising Paganini

Paganini's performing career spanned over four decades, yet the tours that took him to the musical capitals of Europe lasted only six years (1828–34). This period of activity saw the peak of the Paganini craze, as evidenced by the appearance of biographies (beginning in 1829), eyewitness accounts by notable historical personages, and masses of reviews in the numerous music journals of the time.[69] Liszt's claim that hearing Paganini revolutionised his approach to the piano and launched his virtuoso career dates to 1832. Ecstatic or else vitriolic, the accounts are remarkably consistent in their high emotional temperature—especially given the diverse backgrounds and musical expectations of his audiences.

It was during this concentrated six-year span that the 'Paganini mythology' surged, as we will see in subsequent chapters. Paganini contributed to his own mythologisation by overdramatising his recollection of childhood duress in the hands of his demanding father, the better to earn comparison with Beethoven as a boy.[70] The distortion and embellishment of the facts of his life by writers after his death further added to his myth. A good example of this is Fétis's false claim in his biographical sketch (1851) that Paganini played for Princess Pauline Borghese, Napoleon's sister, in Livorno; this episode was given a romantic twist in Elise Polko's quasi-fictionalised biography (1876); Kapp (1914) then described the pair's 'bliss' and Codignola (1936) assumed without any factual basis whatsoever that she retired with him to Piedmont.[71]

---

[67] Beatrix Borchard, 'Der Virtuose—ein 'weiblicher' Künstlertypus?', 63–76; Cornelia Bartsch, 'Virtuosität und Travestie: Frauen als Virtuosinnen', 77–90; and Peter Wicke, 'Virtuosität als Ritual: Vom Guitar Hero zum DJ-Schamanen', 232–43.

[68] Heinz von Loesch, 'Virtuosität als Gegenstand der Musikwissenschaft', 11–16. No comparable studies have been published in English to date; publication of translations of both volumes would be welcome, as would original contributions from anglophone scholars.

[69] Literature on Paganini's life and work began to be published in 1829–30 with the appearance of Julius Max Schottky, *Paganini's Leben und Treiben als Künstler und als Mensch* (Prague: Calve, 1830), G. Imbert de Laphelèque, *Nicolo Paganini. Notice sur ce célèbre violiniste* (Paris: Guyot, 1830), and Guhr, *Ueber Paganinis Kunst die Violin zu spielen.*

[70] De Courcy, *Paganini, the Genoese* I, 13.

[71] François-Joseph Fétis, *Notice biographique sur Nicolo Paganini: Suivie de l'analyse de*

The process of mythologising Paganini further escalated in the early twentieth century. Pulver's 1936 biography fabricated Paganini's reception in northern France, Holland and Belgium, saying 'the Catholic papers dwelt upon the sinister aspects of his life and warned their readers to ignore him. The risk of coming under the influence of Satanic spells was even considered'.[72] A 1914 article by a Dr Julius Siber asserted that Paganini was homosexual.[73] The 'Psychological Study' purported that the 'hysteria, the tendency to break into tears easily, and hypersensitivity' that a contemporary doctor supposedly observed in Paganini along with his 'vanity, effeminate facial expressions, and long, flowing hair' were typical homosexual traits.[74] Siber even attributed to Heine, without identifying the source, the insinuation that Paganini's relationship with Sivori resembled that of Socrates with Alcibiades.[75] To fully understand Paganini entails stripping away layers of myth and identifying reliable sources.

In addition to archival materials, I have relied heavily on De Courcy's comprehensive biography in two volumes (1957). This aims, in her own words, to 'present a full-scale narrative of his life', not 'to appraise Paganini's influence on the world of music'.[76] However, such an appraisal does form part of this book, and will be supported by commentary on specific works. The five biographical accounts of Paganini De Courcy deems to be of lasting value are the subject's own biographical sketch and works by Schottky, Harrys, Codignola, and Pulver.[77] Codignola's *Paganini intimo* was a particularly valuable resource for De Courcy, and in turn her work has been a valuable resource for me. Her book accumulates voluminous evidence to sketch Paganini's portrait so that he 'emerges from this process of demythicization infinitely more inspiring than the gravely distorted figure associated with his legend'.[78]

ses ouvrages (Paris: Flute de Pan, 1981 [originally published 1851]), Elise Polko, *Nicolo Paganini und die Geigenbauer* (Leipzig: Bernhard Schlicke, 1876), Julius Kapp, *Paganini: Eine Biographie mit 60 Bildern* (Berlin: Schuster & Loeffler, 1922 [1914]), Codignola, *Paganini intimo*. For more details, see De Courcy, *Paganini, the Genoese* I, 104.

[72] De Courcy, *Paganini, the Genoese* II, 148–9. Jeffrey Pulver, *Paganini: The Romantic Virtuoso* (London: Herbert Joseph Limited, 1936).

[73] Dr. Julius Siber, 'Niccolò Paganini. Eine psychologische Studie von Dr. Jules [sic] Siber', *Jahrbuch für Sexuelle Zwischenstufen* (1914), 39–44.

[74] *Ibid.*, 44.

[75] *Ibid.*, 43.

[76] De Courcy, *Paganini, the Genoese* I, viii.

[77] *Ibid.* II, 345–61. Schottky, *Paganinis Leben und Treiben*, George Harrys, *Paganini in seinem Reisewagen und Zimmer, in seinem redseligen Stunden, in gesellscaftlichen Zirkeln und seinen Konzerten* (Tutzing: Schneider, 1982 [originally published 1830]), Codignola, *Paganini intimo*, and Pulver, *Paganini: The Romantic Virtuoso*.

[78] *Ibid.* I, x.

Yet, with all due respect to De Courcy's tremendous achievement, this 'inspiring' figure also has certain troubling aspects that have come to light with the advent of feminism in musicology and new evidence that has surfaced since 1957. For example, Roberto Grisley has revealed previously censored material in Codignola's collection of Paganini's letters containing 'rather colorful expressions' which Codignola probably had no choice but to censor at the time of publication.[79] This important work together with the publication of proceedings of conferences devoted to Paganini studies, and the ongoing production of a new critical edition of Paganini's music, have made a new perspective possible as well as timely.[80]

Today the mythology of Paganini as a 'demonic' virtuoso remains as seductive, appealing, and historically entrenched as the image of Beethoven as a singular compositional genius, or the idea that Liszt was born to be great, transcending historical contexts. Musicologists such as Tia DeNora and Dana Gooley have shown us how culturally constructed and mediated such ideas of transcendent genius are, and have introduced new critical perspectives.[81] In doing so, they follow in the footsteps of Pierre Bourdieu, who showed that the glorification of 'great individuals' obscures the social agents and power structures that constitute what he called the field of cultural production.[82] This book shares their spirit of historical revisionism, exposing the beliefs and value judgements underlying constructs of Romanticism for what they were—hence the 'scare quotes' around the word 'demonic' in my title. To demythologise the 'demonic' virtuoso is to reveal 1) the realities of the violinist's life in the conditions of the era; and 2) the investments (psychological, monetary, emotional) that his contemporaries and followers made in him. As it turns out, we do not know very much about either yet, a fact that our enchantment with the myth has served to obscure.

---

[79] Grisley, *Niccolò Paganini*, 25. This includes the use of words such as 'Coglione' [Asshole] and 'fica', a derogatory sexual reference to women (188, 610).

[80] Monterosso, ed. *Paganini e il suo tempo*; Moretti, *et al.*, eds. *Paganini divo e comunicatore*; Andrea Barizza, and Fulvia Morabito, eds, *Nicolò Paganini Diabolus in Musica*. Studies on Italian Music History, Vol. 6 (Lucca: Brepols, 2010); Raffaello Monterosso, *et al.*, eds, *Nazionale delle opere di Niccolò Paganini*, Vols I–IX (Rome: Istituto Italiano per la Storia della Musica, 1976-ongoing).

[81] Tia DeNora, *Beethoven and the Construction of Genius: Musical Politics in Vienna, 1792–1803* (Berkeley: University of California Press, 1997); Gooley, *The Virtuoso Liszt*.

[82] Pierre Bourdieu, *The Field of Cultural Production* (New York: Columbia University Press, 1993), 29.

CHAPTER 2

'Demonic' Violinist, Magical Virtuosity

AT first glance, it is not difficult to explain why Paganini was described as 'demonic'—his virtuosity seemed inhuman. More precisely, he embodied the acquisition of virtuoso ability by forfeiture of a human heart, a human soul—an idea most clearly articulated by the poet Heinrich Heine in an essay of 1843:

> When it comes to violinists, virtuosity is not entirely the result of mechanical finger velocity and sheer technique, as it is with pianists. The violin is an instrument which has almost human whims—it is attuned to the mood of the player in a sympathetic rapport: a minute discomfort, the tiniest inner imbalance, a whiff of sentiment elicits an immediate resonance . . . probably because the violin, pressed against the chest, can perceive our heart's beat. But this happens only with artists who truly have a heart that beats, who have a soul. The more sober, the more heartless a violinist is, the more uniform will be his performance, and he can count on the obedience of his fiddle, any time, any place. But this much-vaunted assurance is only the result of a spiritual limitation, and some of the greatest masters were often dependent on influences from within and without. I have never heard anyone play better—or, for that matter, play worse—than Paganini . . .[1]

Heine distinguished violin virtuosity from piano virtuosity on the grounds that the violin closely reflected the inner state of the player in a way that the piano did not. The fact that Paganini's mastery of technique approached pianistic mechanicalness was a reflection of his heartlessness, his soullessness—which made him at once the best and worst violinist Heine had ever heard.

Paganini's ghostly presence on stage and his eradication of seemingly insurmountable technical difficulties suggested that he had exchanged his humanity for virtuoso powers. Yet beyond the famous story of his Faustian pact with the devil, there lay a variety of less penetrable meanings of the word, each with their own social and symbolic currency. This chapter begins by showing how Paganini was constructed as a 'demonic' violin virtuoso in his reception. This cannot fully

---

[1] Heinrich Heine, 'Musikalische Saison in Paris', *Zeitungsberichte über Musik und Malerei*, ed. Michael Mann (Frankfurt am Main: Insel-Verlag, 1964), 145–6, as quoted in and translated by Boris Schwarz, *Great Masters of the Violin*, 23.

be understood without examining contemporary reactions to his performances in their cultural contexts. By surveying reviews, caricatures, and portraits, the nuances and motivations behind the 'demonic' label come into view. The diverse monikers by which Paganini was known ('Zamiel', 'Mephistopheles', etc.) carried specific subtexts, associations, and value judgements—often by reference to literature, theatre, opera, or instrumental music—that reflect the preoccupations of Romanticism. Various cultural currents in early nineteenth-century European society provided multiple settings for Paganini's identity as a 'demonic' figure to proliferate: the popularity of Goethe's *Faust* and the cult of Byron highlighting post-Enlightenment secularism, the resurgence of interest in the middle ages, the breaking of sexual taboos, the rise and fall of Napoleon, and the birth of capitalist enterprise. In contrast to Liszt, whose demonic side was dialectically offset by his humanitarianism (e.g. giving charity concerts to raise money for the poor), Paganini seemed 'demonic' through and through.[2]

A second aim of this chapter is to establish the extent to which Paganini himself earned, or contributed to earning, these labels. The violin and bow each had their own 'magical' connotations independently of Paganini, for example. He himself even spoke of the 'magic' of his violin that sent charges through his body like electricity. His transgressive virtuosity and 'undead' appearance were therefore not the sole factors in projecting the illusion of dark magic. The widely held belief that Paganini consciously cultivated and exaggerated his ghoulish physical traits and unholy reputation does not hold up to close inspection. He was Catholic, and although his famous denials of criminality and sacrilege did serve to amplify his fame and fortune, it is far from conclusive that he deliberately planned his actions to produce that outcome.

Constructions of Paganini as 'Demonic'

The eyewitnesses who remarked upon Paganini's 'demonic' quality as a person and as a performer were legion, yet what they meant by this description and the seriousness of tone they carried varied greatly depending on the context. The combination of poor education and devout Catholicism then prevalent in some parts of the rural Italian states may have caused a small minority to truly believe he was possessed.[3] But the majority of commentary identifying Paganini

---

[2] Gooley rightly observes that having this 'glow of goodness' was where Liszt differed most from Paganini, in *The Virtuoso Liszt*, 237.

[3] Even as late as 1871, literacy rates were under 50% in the north, 16% in the south, and 25% in the central regions, according to Derek Beales, *The Risorgimento and the Unification of Italy* (London: George Allen & Unwin, 1971), 46.

as 'demonic' came from the educated classes of the major European capitals; they were mostly music critics, amateurs, and connoisseurs, in the 1820s and 1830s. In this public discourse, eyewitnesses freely interchanged terms like *magia, dämonisch*, and *sorcière* in response to virtuoso performance, more often intended sardonically than sincerely. When, where, and how did this discourse first arise?

Early in his career, a series of pamphlets circulating in Lucca (ca. 1800–05) identified him as a 'sorcerer' and a 'charlatan'.[4] The latter perhaps carried the connotation of trickery and the use of artificial or dishonest methods to acquire special powers, akin to cheating at, say, gambling (one of Paganini's favourite pastimes, as it happens). In 1809, Boucher de Perthes (a customs officer and music lover who knew him fairly well) described him as 'the grand clown of violinists'.[5] The overriding impression Paganini seems to have made during these early years on Italians outside of his hometown was that he was an offbeat personality—a clown, a gambler, a trickster—but the 'demonic' image was simply not present yet.

That reputation originated in the period 1810–13, when details of his life are so sparse that a gap has resulted in his biography. These 'wastrel years', as De Courcy calls them, were, according to her,

> the years of vagabondage when many of the silly tales were started, which then clung to him like burrs; for these were the years when he was gradually taking on the external qualities, was developing the mannerisms, poses, affectations, that contributed so greatly to his epic: his emaciation, something Mephistophelian in his cast of features, his amazing dexterity, his readiness to exploit but not reveal his personality, the innate showman's instinct, with its *besoin d'étonner*, and last of all the tremendous magnetism that emanated from his person and his music and threw his audiences into beatific ecstasies.[6]

By around 1814–15, the clownish youth had transformed into a *diabolus*. Three factors come into consideration when establishing this date as the origin for this change. First, his new composition *Le Streghe* (1814) associated Paganini with witchcraft on the strength of its title alone. It was called that because it was based on the theme that signals the witches' entrance onto the stage in Salvatore Vignano and Franz Xaver Süssmayr's ballet *Il noce di Benevento* (*The Walnut-tree*

---

[4] Renée de Saussine, *Paganini*, trans. Marjorie Laurie (London: Hutchinson, 1970 [1953, 1954]), 42.

[5] De Courcy, *Paganini, the Genoese* I, 108.

[6] De Courcy, *Paganini, the Genoese* I, 116–17.

of Benevento) (1802), which Paganini had seen in 1813.[7] Reviewing one of the earliest known performances of *Le Streghe*, the *Gazzetta di Genova* remarked: 'this man is so extraordinary throughout, and has learned the harmony of the angels in heaven, that of birds in the air, from the terrain of men to the Witches from the Noce of Benevento, and will not rest until he leads us to hell to tell us about devils better than Tasso, Dante, Virgil, Orpheus, all of [whom] he has already exceeded with his miraculous violin'.[8] Leigh Hunt wrote that with *Le Streghe* Paganini dropped 'the clownish and tastelessly grotesque ... raised the imitative effect to a higher level and incorporated it in a diabolically difficult and time-resisting work that remained one of the most admired and sensational numbers of his repertory'.[9]

Second, his supposed 'abduction' of the twenty-year-old prostitute Angelina Cavanna to Parma (1815–16) earned him the reputation of a rake. That the child he fathered with her was stillborn was perceived as the inevitable result, according to contemporary theological dogma, of the 'cooled off seed' of an incubus.[10] The Cavannas filed a lawsuit and Paganini ended up paying damages as well as serving a brief term in the Parma jail. (Consider that Paganini was by then thirty-three years old; in comparison, both his father Antonio and older brother Carlo were already married at age twenty-three, and Antonio was twenty-eight when Niccolo was born.)

Third, the legend (probably originating in his brief imprisonment) of a long period of incarceration for murder during which he supposedly whiled away the hours by teaching himself difficult violin techniques, dates to this time. We know from the diary of a Colonel Montgomery, a British military commander stationed in Genoa at the time, that rumours were circulating in the city by 1814.[11] Paganini's abominable, rakish conduct, exaggerated reputation as a violent convicted felon, and use of the 'witches' theme combined into one potent 'demonic' image.

---

[7] The ballet, known as *Die Zauberschwestern* in German, was 'given in German and Italian theatres up to about 1835'. Linda Tyler, and Caryl L. Clark, 'Süssmayr, Franz Xaver', in Stanley Sadie, ed., *New Grove Dictionary of Music and Musicians*, 2nd ed. (London: Macmillan, 2001) Vol. 24, 734.

[8] *Gazzetta di Genova* (21 September 1814) quoted by Grisley, *Niccolò Paganini, epistolario*, 75 n.76.

[9] Quoted in De Courcy, *Paganini, the Genoese* I, 124.

[10] Pascal Fournier, *Der Teufelsvirtuose: eine kulturhistorische Spurensuche* (Freiburg im Breisgau: Rombach, ca. 2001), 161–2. According to Fournier, this interpretation is reinforced by observing the devastation of Europe and the widespread 'devil propaganda' of the Inquisition at the time.

[11] Montgomery, an aide-de-camp for Sir William Bentinck, commander of H.M. 36th Regiment in Genoa, was 'intimately acquainted with Di Negro, Mme de Stael, the Durazzos, and their circle' according to De Courcy, *Paganini, the Genoese* I, 131–2.

The 1820s cemented the image that had gained momentum in the previous decade. Another period of a few months during which his whereabouts are unaccounted for (mid-November 1821 to February 1822) probably added to his growing mystique. Around 1823, he began to take the extreme mercury treatments for his long-term syphilis, the disease also known as 'morbo gallico' (or 'mal francese', because it was spread by French soldiers), the debilitating effects of which were plain to see in his physical appearance.[12] In 1824 the Bishop of Venice banned him from the cemetery on the Lido, where he had dared to play his violin, on the grounds that the holy place was profaned by any person who had sold his soul to the devil.[13] This incident is the first known documentation of the myth.

It is worth noting here that during the 1820s Paganini's reputation within and beyond the Italian states differed. In Great Britain, for example, where he was not seen performing until 1831, the story of the demonic pact mattered less than his alleged criminal past, as a search of the British Periodicals database reveals.[14]. Indeed, the word 'devil' was not used in connection with him until he was reviewed on English soil for the first time following his début there on 3 June 1831.[15] This word did not appear at all in any of the British reports of the previous ten years. Rather, his Gothic image was constructed in the press principally through three interlinked themes: 1) the rumour that he had murdered his wife and served time in prison where he had practised for long hours, which first appeared in print in 1826 and was repeated several times between 1828 and 1830, the prison sentence growing from seven to twelve years in each retelling;[16] 2) his decrepit physical appearance—his cadaverous face, his pale cheeks, skeletal frame—of which there are numerous examples;[17] and 3) his strange personality and stage demeanour, described as 'eccentric'. 'His style is wild, strange, and severe', wrote one reviewer,

[12] He contracted the disease some time 'between puberty and his thirty-seventh year' according to Pietro Berri, *Il Calvario di Paganini* (Savona: Liguria, 1941), 85.

[13] According to Ghetaldi, cited in De Courcy, *Paganini, the Genoese* I, 325.

[14] See britishperiodicals.chadwyck.co.uk, a database of numerous nineteenth-century British publications on a wide variety of topics (not just music), of which selected examples can be found in the Appendix.

[15] 'A very Zamiel in appearance, and certainly a very devil in performance!' in Anon., 'Paganini!!!' *Athenaeum* 188 (4 June 1831), 364.

[16] Anon., 'Monthly Theatrical Review', *Review* Vol. 2 No. 8 (August 1826), 211; Anon., 'Music', *Literary Gazette* 609 (20 September 1828), 605; Anon., 'Paganini, and the History of the Violin', *Monthly Magazine* Vol. 8 No. 48 (December 1829), 631; Anon., 'Varieties', *Literary Gazette* 682 (13 February 1830), 108; Anon., 'Haymarket Theatre' *Theatrical Observer* 2662 (25 June 1830), 1; Anon., 'Paganini', *Athenaeum* 120 (13 February 1830), 92. The last of these, quoting from Laphelèque, debunked the story that Paganini had poisoned his wife.

[17] See for instance Anon., 'Haymarket Theatre', *Theatrical Observer* 2662 (25 June 1830), 1 and Anon., 'Paganini', *Literary Gazette* 748 (21 May 1831), 332.

while his 'peculiar smile . . . I believe made more than [the reviewer] shudder', according to another.[18] The reception seems to suggest that previous to his arrival, Paganini's image was that of a man tinted with criminality, strange in appearance—as a person and as a performer. It was not however until the London public actually saw him play that the word 'demonic' started to circulate in the press.

By the late 1820s and early 1830s, as Paganini reached ever-wider audiences, the myth was in full swing—a demonic package enmeshing the mysterious person with virtuoso powers. Unsurprisingly perhaps, the 'demonic' label became popular and important as more and more people of diverse backgrounds went to see him during his European tour in the years 1828–34, and documented their reactions in print. Table 2.1 shows a selection of the diverse appellations by which he was known, in chronological order, from the four countries where he garnered the most press. While these nicknames all connote devilry in some way, they are obviously not synonymous.

The most popular labels by far were those identifying Paganini as a 'magician' or a 'wizard'. 'Let us rejoice that this enchanter is our contemporary', wrote the music critic Castil-Blaze in the *Journal des débats* (15 March 1831), 'let him be glad of it himself; if he had played his violin like that two hundred years ago, he would have been burned as a magician'.[19] The 'Magician of the South' was a play on the nickname for Sir Walter Scott, 'The Wizard of the North', so called because of the enormously popular Gothic novels that Scott published anonymously.

Some commentators identified the violin bow as an instrument of sorcery: 'Paganini has been recently waving his magic wand', wrote one reviewer for the *Harmonicon* after a Leipzig performance in 1829, and Heine remarked that he 'swept the air with his bow [and] he seemed like some sorcerer who commands the elements with his magic wand'.[20] The French caricaturist Jean Ignace Isidore Grandville even depicted Paganini's bow as a witch's broomstick in one of his humorous illustrations of the violinist.[21] A reviewer from the *Birmingham Journal*

---

[18] Anon., 'Monthly Theatrical Review', *Review* Vol. 2 No. 8 (August 1826), 211; Anon., 'Paganini at Prague', *Quarterly Music Magazine and Review* Vol. 10 No. 38 (April 1828), 203–5, quote from 204.

[19] Quoted in Metzner, *Crescendo of the Virtuoso*, 131 from François-Henri-Joseph Castil-Blaze [Anon.]. 'La Chronique Musicale', *Journal des débats* (15 March 1831), reprinted in Castil-Blaze, *L'Académie impériale de musique de 1645 à 1855*, 2 vols (Paris, Castil-Blaze, 1855), II, 222–3.

[20] Anon., 'Foreign Musical Report [Leipzig]', *Harmonicon* Vol. 7 No. 12 (1829), 311; Havelock Ellis, ed., *The Prose Writings of Heinrich Heine* (London: Walter Scott, 1887), 205.

[21] In the Gertrude Clarke Whittall Foundation Collection, Library of Congress, Music Division (n.d.), no call number given.

Table 2.1. Paganini's 'demonic' epithets

Appellation	From whom (where known), where, when, and citation
Genoese wizard	Lipinski, Warsaw ca. 1829 in Halski, 'Paganini and Lipinski', 275
Magician	Castil-Blaze, *Journal des débats* (15 March 1831) in Metzner, *Crescendo of the Virtuoso*, 131
Magician	Heine, Hamburg, 1830, *Florentine Nights,* trans. Frederick Carter (London: Gerald Howe, 1933), 48
Magician of the South	Zelter, Berlin 1829 in Saussine *Paganini,* 113
Hexensohn	Zelter, Berlin 1829 in Saussine *Paganini,* 113
Goethe's Mephisto	Rellstab, Berlin 1829 in De Courcy, *Paganini, the Genoese* I, 318
Hexenmeister	Rellstab, Berlin 1829 in Saussine *Paganini,* 114
Dr Faustus	A. B. Marx, *Allgemeine Musikalische Zeitung* 16 (Berlin 1829) in Saussine, *Paganini,* 114
Mephistopheles	D'Ortigue, Paris 1833 in *Le Balcon d'opera* (Paris: Renduel, 1833), 247
Demonic	Goethe, Weimar 1831 in De Courcy, *Paganini, the Genoese* I, 361–2
Zamiel	*Athaeneum* (London 1831)
Devil	*Athaeneum* (London 1831)
Satan	*L'Entracte* Paris 1831, quoted in James Johnson, *Listening in Paris: A Cultural History* (Berkeley, Los Angeles, and London: University of California Press, 1995), 267
Devil's spawn	Vienna 1828 in De Courcy, *Paganini, the Genoese* I, 259
Wandering Jew	*Vienna 1828 in De Courcy, Paganini, the Genoese I, 259* incarnate

attributed the 'magic' of making difficult things appear easy to 'the wonders of Signor Paganini's bow':

> both staccato and legato, his harmonics and double notes, were admira-
> bly exhibited in ... passages of the most extraordinary difficulty. Such,
> however, is his mastery over the violin, that he appears more to play with
> the instrument than labour upon it. A mere jerk or touch with this magic
> wand is obeyed by a responding flow of notes.[22]

Attributing Paganini's remarkable abilities to magic reflected the helplessness of viewers irrespective of their background when faced with explaining how Paganini made difficulties of violinistic technique and execution vanish. It was not only critics and laypersons but also other violin virtuosi who made such comments: in 1829, Karol Lipinski admiringly called him 'the 'Genoese Wizard', for example.[23] Ludwig Spohr, who had encountered Paganini as early as 1816, stated, 'he

---

[22] In the Gertrude Clarke Whittall Foundation Collection, Library of Congress, Music Division (n.d.), no call number given.

[23] Lipinski quoted in Halski, 'Paganini and Lipinski', 275.

is a complete wizard, and brings tones from his violin which were never heard before from that instrument'.[24] The reputation of Paganini's 'magical' virtuosity throughout Europe thus expanded on his Italian reception in the 1810s–1820s, which tended to emphasise his ability to 'magically' make the violin sound like anything but one.[25]

Each of the labels—magician, wizard, sorcerer, witch's son, and witch-master—was a variation on the popular theme of Paganini as a *maleficus*—commonly defined as a person who makes a pact with Satan. Viennese artist Johann Peter Lyser's illustration captures this perfectly (see the cover to this book). Another famous version of this caricature, 'Karikatur auf die Wiener Konzerte', ca. 1828 depicts the violinist balanced at mid-skip inside a 'magic circle', hair on end as if charged with electricity, having supposedly gained access into the secrets of witchcraft.[26] Talismans associated with black magic surround him, such as a black cat, a magic sword, a human skull, a pyramid, the bones of a human hand, and a snake wrapped around a staff, along with various alchemical, astrological, occult, and invented symbols including the Star of David, Mars, Gemini, and approximations of signs for Sun, Fire, and the Black Mass. Floating in the background like apparitions are images from folklore and legend: a possessed nun with hands outstretched in the act of devil-worship, a languishing maiden cradling a skeleton (a reference to 'Death and the Maiden', perhaps), a number of monstrous creatures at various stages of materialisation, and a round of skeletons dancing the *Totentanz* (or 'Dance of Death') where the central figure parallels Paganini's posture with his violin. In its detailed references to occultism, this caricature provides a visual expression for the famous legend that Paganini had sold his soul to acquire superhuman powers on the violin.

While that explanation was by far the most popular, some people concluded that the violinist was actually possessed by the devil. The distinction between the two lay in the fact that a *maleficus* entered into the pact voluntarily, whereas, alternatively, the devil could possess bodies without permission. Stories of extraordinary musical virtuosity arising from demonic possession can be traced to the middle ages; for example, a monk named Caesarius at the monastery of Heisterbach (in present-day Germany), wrote in the thirteenth century that:

---

[24]   Louis Spohr, *Louis Spohr's Autobiography*, trans. anon. (New York: Da Capo Press 1969 [1865]), I, 280.

[25]   For instance, according to the *Gazzetta Piemontese* (14 February 1818): 'Often times it is no longer his violin; it is a flute, or the very clear voice of a well-trained canary', quoted in Grisley, *Niccolò Paganini, epistolario*, 112 n.2 (my translation).

[26]   See, for example, Julius Kapp, *Paganini: Eine Biographie mit 60 Bildern* (Berlin: Schuster & Loeffler, 1922 [1914]), plate 9.

There was once a priest whose singing was a joy to all . . . until one day another priest heard it, and realized that such perfection must come not from a human being but from a demon. So he exorcized the demon, which promptly departed . . . whereupon the singer's body fell lifeless to the ground, showing that for some time it had been animated by the demon alone.[27]

Because it was commonly believed that demons took possession of the dead, Paganini's 'Undead' appearance was taken as evidence of his possession. To Heine, he resembled 'a corpse risen from the grave, a vampire with a violin' with his 'cadaverous face' and his bow arm guided by the devil himself.[28]

In numerous cases across Europe, Paganini was viewed as a manifestation of the devil himself, blurring the line between demonic collusion and demonic personification. The critic François-Joseph Fétis wrote acerbically, 'in reality, everyone had noticed and had guessed for a long time that Paganini and Satan were in the most intimate relationship; that is, provided they are not one and the same thing'.[29] The French journal *L'Entracte* carried a review in the language of Gothic poetry: 'He's Satan onstage, Satan knock-kneed, bandy-legged, double-jointed, twisted . . . fall to the knees of Satan and worship him'.[30] Similarly, London's *Athenaeum* described him as 'truly a Zamiel in appearance'—a reference to Weber's *Der Freischütz*, in which the devil is known as Samiel.[31]

As we have seen, the identification of Paganini's 'magical' powers—whether acquired through demonic possession or collusion—was widespread across the European continent and the United Kingdom. While many of the epithets given in Table 2.1 derived from this shared understanding, some arose from specific, localised contexts. The German nicknames 'Hexensohn' (son of a witch) and

[27] Caesarius of Heisterbach, Book XII, Chapter 4 quoted in Norman Cohn, *Europe's Inner Demons: The Demonization of Christians in Medieval Chistendom*, rev. ed. (Chicago: University of Chicago Press, 2000), 27.

[28] Ellis, ed., *The Prose Writings of Heinrich Heine*, 199 and 201. A recent study of the aesthetics of horror has also noted that Paganini and vampires—largely products of romantic imagination—were described in very similar ways and with similar attributes. See Hans Richard Brittnacher, *Ästhetik des Horrors. Gespenster, Vampire, Monster, Teufel und künstliche Menschen in der phantastischen Literatur* (Frankfurt am Main: Suhrkamp, 1994), I, 117–80, quoted in Pascal Fournier, *Der Teufelsvirtuose*, 157 n.79.

[29] François-Joseph Fétis, *Notice Biographique sur Nicolo Paganini*, 40.

[30] *L'Entracte* quoted in James Johnson, *Listening in Paris: A Cultural History* (Berkeley, Los Angeles, and London: University of California Press, 1995), 267.

[31] See n.15. Weber's opera had been staged numerous times in London by the time of Paganini's first appearance there in 1831. Understandably, he is compared with Samiel rather than with Max, the character who barters with Samiel for a magic bullet that will enable him to win the competition and marry his beloved.

'Hexenmeister' (witch-master) specifically referred to *Le Streghe*, which was known to German audiences as *Hexentanz* (Witches' Dance).[32] (In French the work was known as *Danse des Sorcières*.) Paganini frequently programmed it on his European tour, in his 1829 Berlin concerts, for example.

Paganini's demonic aura also tapped into the story of the devil appearing in a dream to Baroque violinist Giuseppe Tartini, which was popularised especially in Paris in the early nineteenth century, approximately forty years after it was supposed to have happened.[33] Upon making his Paris debut in 1831, Paganini came to be identified as the anti-muse in the story, which had been in vogue for the previous two years.[34] A French critic wrote, 'Tartini saw in a dream a demon, who played a diabolical Sonata. That demon could have been none other than Paganini.' But the critic appears to have changed his mind already in the next sentence: 'And yet Tartini's sprite, with his double trills, his weird modulations, his rapid arpeggios, was the merest tyro compared to the virtuoso we now possess'.[35]

Similarly, in England, Tartini's dream and Paganini's legend were conflated in James Minasi's lithograph 'Il violino magico' (n.d., Figure 2.1), which paralleled James Marshall's painting 'Tartini's Dream, or the Devil's Trill Sonata' (1868). (Both echoed Henry Fuseli's *The Nightmare* (1781), depicting an incubus hovering over a fainted woman.) Strikingly, Minasi chose to depict Paganini not as a substitute for the devil, but as his companion, implying, as the artist himself explained, that the violinist was the more 'demonic' of the two:

> In this Vision the Devil being conquered is represented in the Act of giving up the Violin to Paganini (thinking it enchanted by some superior power) as the only person in the world capable of executing his own peculiar, and wondrous Composition! The Streghe (witches) are seen flying under *La Noce di Benevento* ... it being the title of one of his most extraordinary [compositions].[36]

---

[32] *Allgemeine Musikalische Zeitung* 14 (6 April 1814) and 32 (5 August 1824). N.B. 'Hexentanz' was the alternative title for Clara Schumann's 'Impromptu' op. 5 no. 1, the first of *Quatre pièces caractéristiques* of 1836, when it was republished in Vienna, 1838.

[33] Jean-Baptiste Cartier, *L'Art du violon* (Decombe: A l'Accord Parfait, ca. 1796).

[34] As Joel-Marie Fauquet has shown, a ballade by Auguste Panseron entitled *Le Songe de Tartini* and a novella by Samuel-Henri Berthoud in the style of Hoffmann, entitled *La Sonate du diable*, prepared the musical public for Paganini's candidacy as the personification of the demon Tartini saw in his dream. See Fauquet, 'Quand le diable s'en mêle'.

[35] Castil-Blaze, *L'Académie impériale de musique* II, 222–3.

[36] From the Gertrude Clarke Whittall Foundation Collection, Library of Congress, Music Division.

Figure 2.1 James Minasi, 'Il violino magico', from the Gertrude Clarke Whittall
Foundation Collection, Library of Congress, Music Division.

In this iconography, replicated in numerous other vehicles, the figure of Paganini
was placed directly against the backdrop of Italian folklore, Benevento's tree being
a favourite meeting place for witches in stories passed down through oral trans-
mission (even though Paganini's relation to the folklore was mediated through
his borrowing Süssmayr's theme). It is possible that the use of trees 'charged' with
electromagnetism in Mesmerist treatments of the time further contributed to the
muddled-up association of Paganini with enchanted trees and forests.

The focal point for the swirl of speculation and aura of mystery was Paganini's
decrepit body. It was a source of endless fascination to his public: contorted,
cadaverous, and disease-ravaged, it spoke of abnormality, alterity, excess. A
recent German literary study has even suggested that Paganini's 'tall, thin frame
. . . conformed to a devilish prototype carrying the stigma of expressing "the
sensual"'.[37] His extremes of physiognomy allowed and indeed encouraged the
view that he had sacrificed his physical well-being in his barter with the devil.

---

[37] Brittnacher, *Ästhetik des Horrors* Kapitel I, n.184, quoted in Fournier, *Der Teufelsvirtuose*,
      162.

Paganini's extremely pale complexion, accentuated by his dark hair and attire, led his contemporaries to divergent conclusions concerning what caused it. Placed in the context of ethnic stereotyping in certain socially conservative parts of Europe, Paganini's features elicited derogatory assertions that he was Jewish (despite the fact that he was a Catholic).[38] The writer Friedrich von Mathieson (1761–1831), who saw Paganini at the Hotel Riesen in Weimar in 1829, noted in his journal that Paganini had a 'Jewish cast of features'.[39] This echoed the private diary of Colonel Montgomery, which similarly noted his 'large black eyes, hooked nose, and jet black hair, which is long and more than half hides his expressive Jewish face'.[40] Such remarks recycled alarming stereotypes and reinforced negative associations with Jewishness. This was true especially in Vienna, where one journalist went so far as to call Paganini 'the devil's spawn, the Wandering Jew incarnate'.[41]

That Paganini 'looked like a dying man' (in Heine's words) was elsewhere interpreted as a symptom of cholera. After an epidemic struck Paris during his stay there in 1832, his contorted posture was said to mimic the death throes of a patient afflicted with stomach cramps. As art historian Nina Athanassoglou-Kallmyer has shown, the horrors and degenerative effects of the Paris cholera epidemic provided a metaphor for contemporary aesthetics of the grotesque. Personified in contemporary culture as a Death-like skeleton, the disease exposed the 'medieval' state of medicine (cholera was still incurable despite scientific advances) and provoked fears of death on a massive scale. As Athanassoglou-Kallmyer further notes, Paganini's Death-like image, iconised by Delacroix's portrait (1832), determined that, 'in the popular imagination, the violinist merged with the diabolical disease, became its live embodiment'.[42] The fact that Paganini liked to visit hospitals and

---

[38] Note that he once met 'a beautiful English girl' in Rome who 'instantly lit him up', but he renounced any possible union with her upon learning that she was Jewish. Anna Maria Salone, 'The Paganini–Cavanna event', 'La vicenda Paganini–Cavanna', in Moretti *et al.*, *Paganini divo e comunicatore*, 374.

[39] Friedrich von Mathieson, quoted in De Courcy, *Paganini, the Genoese* I, 131.

[40] Colonel Maxwell Montgomery's memoirs, *My Adventures*, quoted in De Courcy *Paganini, the Genoese* I, 356.

[41] Anonymous Viennese journalist quoted in De Courcy, *Paganini, the Genoese* I, 259. Meanwhile, Jewish authors in Eastern Europe (writing mostly in Yiddish) had their own set of iconographic meanings associated with Paganini. The fact that Paganini's composition *La sinagoga* was based on a traditional Hebrew song also may have contributed to perceptions of his Jewishness. The nickname of Salomone Rossi, violinist at the court of Mantua, Il Ebreo (The Hebrew) was probably irrelevant; in any case, he 'was so highly regarded that he was exempt from wearing the yellow badge of the Jew', according to Schwarz, *Great Masters of the Violin*, 35.

[42] Nina Athanassoglou-Kallmyer, 'Blemished Physiologies: Delacroix, Paganini, and the Cholera Epidemic of 1832', *The Art Bulletin* Vol. 83 No. 4 (2001), 691–9.

cemeteries to watch cholera patients dying and corpses being buried could only have linked him more closely to the disease, at least in the minds of those who knew about it.[43] By 1834—the year Paganini concluded his tour of the European continent—he had held the 'demonic' reputation for roughly twenty years.

Paganini on Paganini

As we have now seen, the 'demonic' was a portmanteau term with specific resonances encompassing a vast array of cultural trends in Italy, France, Germany, Austria, and England. We now turn to the question of the degree to which he participated in creating his 'demonic' image. Born and raised a Catholic, Paganini in no way saw himself as 'demonic'. Contrary to popular opinion, of which he was aware, he was not a devil-worshipper. As he confided in a letter to his friend and lawyer Luigi Germi (1832):

> Now no one ever asks if one has heard Paganini, but if one has seen him. To tell you the truth, I regret that there is a general opinion among all classes that I'm in collusion with the Devil. The papers talk too much about my outward appearance, which arouses incredible curiosity. [44]

The only instance of his using the word 'diabolical' with reference to his performances was to describe not himself but rather the overwhelming enthusiasm shown by his audiences while on tour in England: in Liverpool and Manchester, his performance on his instrument produced 'diabolic fanaticism'.[45] As he saw it, it was not he who was possessed, but his fans.

The previous year, Paganini had denied rumours of demonism and criminal conduct in a letter published in the *Revue musicale* (23 April 1831):

> As the tales persist despite their utter improbability, once more I must give in; yet I still have one hope and that is that after my death calumny will

---

[43] 'I amuse myself by watching them bury the victims at the cemetery', Paganini wrote to Germi from Paris (18 April 1832), quoted in De Courcy, *Paganini, the Genoese* II, 102. She attributes his morbid curiosity to the fad for necrophilia. See also 79–81, 103, 191.

[44] In a letter from Manchester (15 January 1832) translated by De Courcy in *Paganini, the Genoese* II, 89. The original Italian can be found in Codignola, *Paganini intimo*, 357: 'Ora non si domanda più se hanno inteso Paganini, ma si domanda se lo hanno veduto. A dirti il vero mi ricresce che si popaghi l'opinione in tutte le classi ch'io abbia il Diavolo addosso. I giornali s'intrattengono troppo sulla mia figura, la qual cosa semina una curiosità incredibile.'

[45] *Ibid.* His use of the word 'diabolical' in reference to a painful inflammation of the oesophagus is documented in Berri, *Il Calvario di Paganini*, 106.

consent to abandon its prey and those who have so cruelly avenged my triumphs will let my ashes rest in peace.[46]

Some have suggested that, in denying the rumours, Paganini was not without a certain cynicism, and willingly permitted the fiction to be believed.[47] The publication of a letter from his mother declaring that an angel had prophesied his glittering future as a virtuoso has also been interpreted as a public-relations manoeuvre reinforcing the 'demonic' legends.[48] However, Paganini's abovementioned letter (1832) expressing sorrow over the rumours casts doubt on the insincerity of his rebuttal.

That he 'actively cultivated repulsion as an aspect of his charm' is another myth.[49] While it is true that Paganini appeared 'ghostly', this was the result of aging and disease rather than a conscious tactic for the stage (he hardly set out to ruin his health and parade the results). He also avoided 'demonic' themes and characteristics in his compositions, even when such devices were in vogue and accessible to him. At a time when composers were drawing extensively on the rich musical vocabulary of musical *diablerie*—tritones (the so-called *diabolus in musica*), diminished seventh chords, and quotations of the medieval plainchant *Dies irae*—Paganini conspicuously left it unmined. Berlioz's *Symphonie fantastique* (1830) and Liszt's *Totentanz* (1839–65) exemplified 'infernal' music, as did numerous operas associating diminished sevenths with sinister characters and forces: Bertram in Meyerbeer's *Robert le diable* (1831), Samiel in Weber's *Der Freischütz* (1821), and the supernatural realm in Spohr's *Zemire und Azor* (1819). Weber's *Euryanthe* (1823) even had a section that the critic D'Ortigue described as the 'violins shrieking in triplets expressing their diabolical joy'.[50] Such devices had no place in Paganini's music, however; indeed, it appears that the *Dies irae* was not used in a solo violin work until Eugene Ysaÿe's solo Sonata No. 2 'Obsession' of 1924.

Not only were Paganini's compositions devoid of the conventions of demonism, their character contrasted sharply with his contemporaries' offerings of

---

[46] *Revue musicale* (23 April 1831), quoted in De Courcy, *Paganini, the Genoese* II, 29. Paganini sought to correct his misidentification (instead of Duranowski) as the culprit in the account of an assassination attempt on a wealthy priest.

[47] Fauquet, 'Quand le diable', 38–9.

[48] See, among others, Corina Caduff, 'Heinrich Heine: Die Musikperson als Medium der Musikkritik' [Heinrich Heine: The musician as a medium of music criticism], *Musik & Ästhetik* Vol. 6 No. 22 (April 2002), 103, n.42.

[49] Richard Taruskin, *The Oxford History of Western Music* (Oxford: Oxford University Press, 2005), III, 253.

[50] D'Ortigue was probably referring to the duet 'Komm denn, unser Leid zu rächen' for Eglantine and Lysiart in Act II of that opera. D'Ortigue, *Le balcon de l'Opéra*, 247.

diablerie, even when his titles carried Gothic overtones. The theme of *Le Streghe*, for example, is an *Allegretto* tune in D major, lilting along in compound meter towards an open cadence with a banal arpeggio: music more at odds with the 'diabolical' cemetery scene from *Don Giovanni* or Weber's 'Wolf's Glen' scene is hardly imaginable. When he imitated the nasal voices and laughter of witches in this piece, his apparent intention was to produce a comic effect.[51] Paganini did not intend to portray himself or his music as 'demonic', even when the opportunity to do so—with its promise of fame and fortune—was present. He did not invite the Gothic associations of *Le Streghe* any more than he invited spectators to check and see if he had hooves like the devil because of his habit of stamping his foot on the stage to keep the beat.[52]

Paganini himself identified a certain intangible quality arising from his performances that emanated not from within himself but rather from the violin. He mentioned 'magic' (*magia*) several times in his private correspondence with Germi:

> Monday I will give an academy [concert], then I leave for Rome, and in mid-April I will return here to give half a dozen concerts and throughout my violin there is magic [Naples, 26 March 1819].[53]

> I'm not going to tell you of the magic generated by my instrument here on the 5th [Karlsruhe, 8 February 1831].[54]

The idea of magic was a recurrent theme in Paganini's reception throughout his career, as we have seen, because he made difficulties vanish, or because he made the violin sound like anything but a violin. What Paganini called 'magic' was more closely aligned to superstitious beliefs in the mysterious power of violins or, more

---

[51] Indeed, the work's sinister aura was supplied by its superficial reception latching onto the 'witches' in the title—i.e. an extra-musical element. (Likewise, the nickname 'Rire du diable' for Caprice No. 13 supplied a diabolical meaning externally.) The title of *The Witches* alone was reminiscent of the Walpurgis orgy in *Faust* or the weird sisters plotting around a steaming cauldron in *Macbeth*, judging from the elaborate frontispiece illustrations of numerous popular editions of the time. These were published in simplified form for amateurs under titles such as 'The Celebrated Witches' Dance'. Typically covered in Gothic lettering, they often depicted a nocturnal scene with Paganini lying on a craggy rock surrounded by dancing witches, flying goblins, snakes, bats, and sleepwalking maidens.

[52] In the *Leipziger Kometen* 41 (October 1829), a reporter described the 'great stamping of his right foot', for example; quoted in Codignola, *Paganini Intimo*, 294.

[53] Quoted in Grisley, *Niccolò Paganini, epistolario*, 17.

[54] *Ibid.*

precisely, in a kind of charge that was sparked in his virtuoso manner of handling them. 'The electricity that I feel in dealing with the magical harmony harms me horribly', Paganini wrote to Germi from Manchester (15 January 1832).[55] His use of the word *elettricismo* is notable, as distinct from 'elettrismo' and 'elettricità', which had been in the Italian vocabulary since 1753 and 1775 respectively. The neologism arose from Faraday's startling discovery of induced electric currents between magnets and the earth, news of which swept across England during Paganini's visit.[56]

More specifically, Doctor Bennati (author of a famous 'medical report' on the violinist following a physical examination) observed that 'the first bowstroke is like an electric spark that comes to give new life . . . All his nerves vibrated with the strings of his violin and his brain had no other faculty than to express the transports in his musical soul'.[57] Expanding on this observation, Pietro Berri has more recently explained that 'electricity' was 'a state of excitation, indeed of nervous excitement, that seized the artist when he was before the public . . . an exceptional nervous tension, which arose in the act of drawing sound from the instrument, which exalted him in a kind of Dionysian intoxication and which transmitted itself to listeners, leaving him exhausted'.[58] While Berri has speculated that Paganini's susceptibility to nervousness was due to his highly emotional temperament and a slightly neurotic tendency, others have taken it as 'evidence' of epilepsy.

Originating in eyewitness accounts, the notion that Paganini was an epileptic persisted long after his death. In London in 1830 the *Theatrical Observer* reported:

> The French critics describe his efforts as 'almost superhuman chef d'oeuvres of genius,' that after having finished some admirable *morceau*, he manifests the symptoms of a man under the influence of epilepsy. He experiences an abundant perspiration, and only answers in monosyllables to the questions put to him.[59]

A year later, a review from *Le globe* appeared in English translation observing that at a Paris concert 'a sort of shuddering and rage appears to seize him'.[60] As late as

[55] 'L'elettricismo che provo nel trattare la magica armonia mi nuoce orribilmente', quoted in Berri, *Il Calvario di Paganini*, 89.
[56] Della Corte, cited in *ibid.*, 90.
[57] Quoted in *ibid.*, 75.
[58] *Ibid.*, 18, 20, 32, 90.
[59] Anon., 'Drury Lane Theatre', *Theatrical Observer* 2586 (27 March 1830), 1
[60] Anon., 'Paganini', *Literary Gazette* 748 (21 May 1831), 332.

1893, it was simply stated that 'Paganini, an inveterate gambler, was epileptic and consumptive'.[61]

Epilepsy and demonism were linked due to the obvious fact that the violent paroxysms of a person having an epileptic fit superficially resembled the external manifestations of a person thought to be demonically possessed. This was clearly articulated by the author of a medical treatise on the symptoms, diagnosis, and treatment of epilepsy published in London in 1823, a decade before Paganini's arrival:

> The powerful contractions of muscles, especially of the face, are often such as to terrify the beholder. The body is sometimes bent forwards, till the chin touches the breast; sometimes it is drawn backwards with prodigious force. The eyes roll furiously, or are so distorted that the white part of them can only be seen; the lips are dreadfully convulsed, and covered with a frothy saliva; the tongue is thrust violently from the mouth, and is sometimes shockingly lacerated by the spasmodic contraction of the muscles of the jaws, which bring the teeth together suddenly, and with great violence. The face is very pale, or else livid, or almost black. The muscles, expressive of various and as it were contending passions of the mind, are sometimes together thrown into a state of powerful involuntary action; which, with the rolling of the eyes, the foaming at the mouth, and the gnashing of the teeth, give to the countenance a horribly wild, and, as some fancy, supernatural expression, as if the wretched patient were possessed, or, in the language of Scripture, *torn* by some malignant demon.[62]

It seems plausible that, for non-violinists, Paganini's jerky, unpredictable movements on the violin and with the bow could resemble epileptic or demonically induced convulsions. Moreover, the notorious association of mental illness (e.g. hysteria) with demonic possession, which allowed the work of Mesmerists to be compared with that of exorcists, placed Paganini in the position of an afflicted patient or victim.[63] At the same time, the analogy that Paganini 'touched' his

---

[61] John Ferguson Nisbet, *The Insanity of Genius and the General Inequality of Human Faculty Physiologically Considered*, 3rd ed. (London: Ward & Downey, 1893), 172.

[62] John Cooke, *History and Method of Cure of the Various Species of Epilepsy* (London: Longman, 1823), 11–12. The author noted this as a historical curiosity; he did not entertain a supernatural explanation for the disease and, in fact, did not mention possession or demons again throughout the rest of the treatise.

[63] Allen Putnam, *Mesmerism, Spiritualism, Witchcraft, and Miracle: A Brief Treatise, showing that mesmerism is a key which will unlock many chambers of mystery* (Boston: Bela Marsh, 1858) and R.B. Ince, *Franz Anton Mesmer, His Life and Teaching* (London: William Rider and Sons, Ltd, 1920), esp. 55.

listeners with a kind of nervous energy arising from an electromagnetic force and passed through sound vibrations resonated with Mesmerism in another way. The mysterious power of the male magnetiser to induce in helpless women a state of hypnosis, or somnambulism as it was then called, was erotically charged—'a sort of sexual magic' (as in Hoffmann's story 'Der Magnetiseur').[64] Paganini implied the existence of an invisible force of this kind with his observation on the effect on Princess Elisa when he played harmonics (the violin timbre most closely resembling that of the glass harmonica): 'the flageolet tones of my violin were too much for her nerves'.[65] Paganini's powers over the violin and over women, in parallel with the magnetiser's role, also carried sexual connotations (which we will explore in the next chapter).

Conditions for 'Demonisation'

As we have now seen, the 'demonisation' of Paganini was due not to one reason alone but rather to an array of motivations, such as the willingness to explain the inexplicable by recourse to occultism, and interpretations of his physical attributes through the lenses of fantasy, fear, or prejudice. Joël-Marie Fauquet has rightly suggested that we should look to elucidate the myth of the 'demonic virtuoso' less in the singular characteristics of the individual than in the fundamental traits of a society in which the conditions arose to permit the virtuoso to be produced.[66] Contributing factors to the historical moment in which Paganini emerged included the symbolism of the violin as a magical instrument and the popularity of images of the devil and Gothic themes in nineteenth-century Europe.

The mythological-symbolic properties of the violin and its prototypes pre-dated Paganini's lifetime. The instrument had always radiated an aura of mystique, seeming to contain hidden powers waiting to be unleashed; its mysterious origins in the Middle East promoted its status as a 'magic box' whose deepest secrets could only be unlocked by the most gifted virtuosos.[67] In medieval folklore

---

[64] Wolfgang Müller-Funk, 'E.T.A. Hoffmanns Erzählung *Der Magnetiseur*, ein poetisches Lehrstück zwischen Dämonisierung und neuzeitlicher Wissenschaft', in *Franz Anton Mesmer und die Geschichte des Mesmerismus*, ed. Heinz Schott (Stuttgart: Franz Steiner, 1985), 200–15 and Robert Darnton, *Mesmerism and the End of the Enlightenment in France* (Cambridge, MA: Harvard University Press, 1968), esp. 52–3.

[65] 'Origin of Paganini's Magical Command over a single violin string. As related by himself. [From a Memoir lately written by M. Schottky]', *Athenaeum* 153 (2 October, 1830), 620.

[66] Fauquet, 'Quand le diable', 36.

[67] The violin's origins can be traced to the medieval *rebec*, a small two- or three-stringed instrument primarily used for dance music and first brought to Europe around AD 1000; the *rebec* was a descendant of the even older *rabab*, a bowed stringed instrument

the violin was associated with the Grim Reaper, who led the *Totentanz* playing a pair of human bones like a violin, a mythology that became popularised as part of the Romantic interest in the middle ages. In southern Italy the violin was traditionally used in rituals associated with tarantism, the frenzied condition believed to be caused by poisonous spider bites.[68] In northern Italy at the turn of the eighteenth century, Cremona violins coated with special varnishes concocted from secret recipes recalled alchemists' attempts to transform ordinary materials into rare metals. Thus when Paganini's friend Germi wrote an acrostic on the name 'Niccolò Paganini' with references to 'il magico stromento', he was tapping into existing perceptions of the instrument's occult powers, which were in turn enhanced by Paganini's reputation. Similarly, Martin Piaggio recycled a familiar theme as the pre-eminent contemporary poet of the Genoese dialect with the lines: 'Of what magic is your violin made? That by playing it you moralise the heart? What is there inside? A nest of nightingales, or an orchestra of flutes and guitars?'[69]

The popularity of Goethe's *Faust,* Part One (1805), greatly influenced Paganini's reception. Framed in terms of *Faust,* alternate views of Paganini as a *maleficus* or the devil himself translated into both a Faustian and Mephistophelean figure. Unsurprisingly, many of the references to *Faust* came from German writers who saw parallels between Paganini's quest for virtuosity and Faust's thirst for power and knowledge. The Berlin music critic A. B. Marx called him 'Dr. Faustus' (undoubtedly referring to Goethe's version rather than Christopher Marlowe's play of 1620).[70] Heine's description of Satan accompanying Paganini 'disguised as a black poodle' recalled the first appearance of the devil in the guise of a dog in Faust's study.[71] Another prominent critic, Ludwig Rellstab, remarked, 'Never in my whole life have I heard an instrument weep like this . . . I never knew that music contained such sounds! He spoke, he wept, he sang! . . . There is something demonic about him. Goethe's Mephisto would have played the violin like this.'[72]

'Faust-mania' provided a setting that would prove receptive to Paganini, nowhere more so than in Paris, where the play was extremely popular. The

of Arab origin. For more on this topic, see David D. Boyden *et al* . . ., *New Grove Violin Family* (New York: Norton, 1989), 129–36.

[68] According to superstition, the poison would not kill victims as long as they kept up a manic dance that came to be known as 'the tarantella'. See Grisley, *Niccolò Paganini, epistolario*, 15 n.16.

[69] Quoted in Roberto Iovino, *Niccolò Paganini: un genovese nel mondo* (Genoa: Fratelli Frilli Editori, 2004), 49–50.

[70] A.B. Marx, *Allgemeine Musikalische Zeitung* 16 (1829), quoted in Saussine, *Paganini*, 114.

[71] Ellis, ed. *The Prose Writings of Heinrich Heine*, 200.

[72] Rellstab quoted in De Courcy *Paganini, the Genoese* I, 318.

first French edition of *Faust*, Part One, had appeared in 1814, and by 1831 it had resurfaced in numerous translations and stage productions.[73] Spohr composed an opera version of *Faust* (1830), and Berlioz's *Symphonie fantastique* of the same year was partly inspired by the play.[74] When Paganini played his debut at the Paris Opéra in March 1831, the city's music-lovers had already been swept up in the craze for nearly two decades, and Joseph D'Ortigue could write: 'Yes, it's him, it's Mephistopheles . . . I saw him and heard him play the violin'.[75]

Paganini's Parisian audiences were primed for a 'Mephistophelean' performer before he even set foot in the city, and no one knew this better than Louis Véron, the ambitious new director of the Opéra (as of early 1831). Véron had his own agenda—to popularise the institution as a symbol of bourgeois power—and saw a way to entice the public by offering entertaining spectacles of marauding devils and witches' Sabbaths.[76] Meyerbeer's opera *Robert le diable*, due to premiere that November, featured (according to James Johnson) a scene of 'debauched nuns who slid out of their habits to swivel and gyrate and guzzle down wine'.[77] As far as Véron was concerned, Paganini's arrival could not have come at a better time—Paganini biographer Renée de Saussine has suggested, 'here was the Mephistopheles of Véron's dreams, the very person for his scenes of hell'.[78]

Paganini fit the bill perfectly because of the French tendency to sensationalise and simplify the character of Mephistopheles, moving away from the philosophical elements of Goethe's original.[79] The visual orientation of French interpretations of *Faust,* with dazzling special effects and elaborate stagings of dancing demons, predisposed audiences to the spectacle and display of Paganini's abnormal appearance and magnetic performance style. French audiences gravitated towards viewing Paganini as a sort of quasi-caricatured Mephistophelean, playing into Véron's hands as he seized the cultural moment and turned it to his advantage.

The Mephistophelian Paganini also matched the idea of grotesque Sensualism conceived by Heine, German by birth but resident in Paris from 1831 until his

[73]   Sarah Hibberd, '"Cette diablerie philosophique": *Faust* Criticism in Paris c. 1830', in Roger Parker and Mary-Ann Smart, eds., *Reading Critics Reading* (New York: Oxford University Press, 2001), 111–36.

[74]   Spohr wrote to his friend Speyer (5 June 1830) after a performance of his *Faust*, 'he [Paganini] heard it for the first time and it seemed to interest him greatly'. Quoted in De Courcy, *Paganini, the Genoese* I, 392.

[75]   D'Ortigue, *Le balcon de l'Opéra*, 247.

[76]   For more on Véron's mission to associate the Opéra with an increasingly powerful economic and political class on the heels of the July Revolution, see Sandy Petrey, 'Robert le diable and Louis-Philippe the King', in *Reading Critics Reading*, 137–54.

[77]   Johnson, *Listening in Paris*, 240.

[78]   Saussine, *Paganini*, 153–5.

[79]   Sarah Hibberd, 'Cette diablerie philosophique', 111–36.

death. Under the influence of the Saint-Simonians, Heine had sought a new dialectical synthesis of Sensualism and Spiritualism, for instance the 'wild physicality' of the can-can, which emerged in the 1840s, contrasted with 'the tedium of a respectable Paris ball'.[80] He advocated the sensual—linked to the lasciviousness of dancing, worldly pleasures associated with the devil—but also recognized that 'Sensualism could survive only in gross and brutish forms'.[81] In Heine's own *Faust* ballet (1847), for example, the witches' festival is 'a crude parody of ecclesiastical ceremonies'.[82] (It is also worth noting here that in Heine's *Atta Troll* (1841), the character Laskaro is a witch's son—recalling one of Paganini's nicknames.)[83]

In German aesthetics around 1800, the word 'demonic' (*dämonisch*) signified a quality that, together with 'divine' (*himmlisch*), described the dual nature of music itself, as musicologist Mario Puppo has shown. For example, E. T. A. Hoffmann spoke of music's 'divine miracles and diabolical magic', on the one hand exalting 'the capacity of music to transport man's spirit to a "luminous, ultra-terranean" life filled with a divine force' and on the other evoking the terror, thrill and pain of Beethoven's music, which can be linked to the diabolical and the sinful, to madness and death.[84] This opposition also echoed the dual aesthetic of the demonic and divine identified by W.H. Wackenroder in his treatise *Phantasien über die Kunst für Freunde der Kunst* (1799).[85]

For Goethe himself, the concept of the demonic or, more accurately, the daemonic, had a particular resonance, as Angus Nicholls has shown.[86] The word daemon (or *Dämon*) originated in the ancient Greek word *daio*, which meant to distribute or divide, as between realms of secular and divine. For Plato and Aristotle, this was tied up with ideas of genius, fate, and godlike human gifts. It

[80]   Ritchie Robertson, *Heine* (London: Halban, 2005), 42–3.
[81]   *Ibid.*, 48.
[82]   *Ibid.*, 43.
[83]   Heine himself was 'always fascinated by folk-tales and superstitions' (*ibid.*, 26). He believed that they were 'remnants of the ancient Germanic religion' (*ibid.*, 27). As a boy in Düsseldorf he had heard stories of witchcraft and ghosts, including the one that eventually became the basis for Wagner's Flying Dutchman.
[84]   Mario Puppo, 'Divinità e demonismo della musical nella cultura romantica', in Monterrosso, ed., *Paganini e il suo tempo*, 83–4.
[85]   Wackenroder's 'divine/demonic duality', according to Puppo, 'describes music as being divine—but with an ambiguous turn, reflecting together joy and pain, joking and a shudder of fear, innocence and crime, light and darkness'. See Puppo, 'Divinità e demonismo', 83 (my translation).
[86]   Angus Nicholls, *Goethe's Concept of the Daemonic: After the Ancients* (Rochester, NY: Camden House, 2006). This concept runs through all of his writings and 'addresses key philosophical debates concerning the relationships between human subjectivity, reason, and nature' (3).

was the Judeo-Christian tradition that split the daemonic into demonic (devilish) and divine (angelic). The German *Dämonische* in Goethe's time and its usage combined the meanings of daemonic and demonic.[87]

In *Faust*, this duality mapped onto the union of Faust and Gretchen: the 'devilish' man who removes all obstacles to satisfying his desires, and the 'angelic' woman who radiates pure innocence. The title character of *Robert le diable* also personified this duality, endowed with both his mother's angelic and his father's Satanic natures. But if the 'demonic' constituted only half of a double aesthetic, and it was a quality identified in Paganini, then who or what served as his 'divine' or 'angelic' counter-pole?

Ironically, Paganini himself was praised by some of his listeners for precisely those celestial qualities, but these comments were often overlooked or ignored because they contradicted his prevailing image. For instance, after hearing Paganini, Schubert claimed, 'I have heard an angel sing in the Adagio'.[88] The unnamed Paris correspondent of the *Frankfurt Journal* gushed over Paganini's little-known composition *Adagio religioso* (which he performed as a prelude to his concertos):

> He played an introduction which he modestly described as 'religious' but which his audience unanimously acclaimed as divine. To compose melodies so sweet he must have been carried away in an ecstasy to hear the singing of the cherubim. It vibrates with the awe, adoration and love that nature feels in the presence of the Creator.[89]

It was generally agreed, however, that characteristics related to the 'divine' were external to Paganini. Based on the number of 'diabolical' violinists throughout history who had been paired with 'angelic' ones (because of contrasting playing styles), one might expect that the demonic Paganini would have been set into relief by his own opposite figure. In 1728, for example, Pietro Antonio Locatelli performed at the court of Kassel followed by Jean-Marie Leclair. The court-jester commented, 'one plays like an angel, and the former plays like a

---

[87] *Ibid.*, 13.

[88] Quoted in Raymond Erickson, ed., *Schubert's Vienna* (New Haven, CT, and London: Yale University Press, 1997), 110.

[89] *Frankfurt Journal* (2 April 1831), quoted in Saussine, *Paganini*, 97–8. Paganini had originally composed this work for a concert in Berlin on 13 May 1829, the so-called Day of Penitence. According to the critic Ludwig Rellstab, 'Paganini composed an introduction stemming from the monastic forms and customs of his fatherland in the naïve belief that only such a prelude was appropriate for the Day of Penitence' (quoted in De Courcy, *Paganini, the Genoese* I, 326 from the journal *Vossiche Zeitung*).

devil'; Locatelli was devilish because 'he runs over the violin like a rabbit'.[90] Earlier in the eighteenth century Arcangelo Corelli was apparently so impressed by the nimble playing of German violinist Nicolaus Adam Strunck that he is supposed to have said, 'If my first name is Arch-Angel, then yours should be Arch-Devil'.[91] Earlier still, Thomas Baltzar's virtuosity led his listeners to suspect that he had a cloven foot.[92]

Despite such historical precedents, however, and despite the fact that such comparisons persisted well into the nineteenth century, no violinist was put forward as Paganini's 'heavenly' counterpart, undoubtedly because it was clear that no other violinist played on his level, as even his French contemporary Pierre Baillot conceded.[93] But that was not the only reason the critics positioned him as a singular figure. In fact, Paganini already had a Marguerite to his Faust: his own violin. Just as Marguerite ends up deranged and committing infanticide under Faust's maleficent influence, the violin was understood by the Romantics to symbolise an 'angelic' woman victimised by destructive forces (as we shall see in Chapter 3).[94]

The word 'demonic' was polysemous, used by contemporaries to reflect a great number of concerns and not just to refer to occult power. The magic of the

---

[90] Quoted by Boris Schwarz, *Great Masters of the Violin*, 94, from Albert Dunning, *Pietro Antonio Locatelli, der Virtuose und seine Welt*, 2 vols (Buren: F. Knuf, 1981), I, 118–19.

[91] Quoted in Schwarz, *Great Masters of the Violin*, 53, from a Dutch translation of Charles Burney's *Music in the Netherlands*. Such pairings can be found even earlier in music history to describe Marin Marais and Antoine Forqueray, France's most accomplished viol players; for example, 'L'un jouait comme un diable et l'autre comme un ange' (Hubert Le Blanc, quoted in Arthur Pougin, *Le violon, les violonistes et la musique de violon du XVIe au XVIIIe siecle* (Paris: Fischbacher, 1924), 37).

[92] Anon., 'Review of the History of Music before Mozart', *Musical World* Vol. 33 No. 42 (20 October 1855), 670–1. Apparently Viotti said of Dragonetti, 'he has the Devil in his body or in his double bass!' after they 'engaged in a friendly contest, each trying to outdo the other with ever more difficult variations improvised on a tarantella melody' in London in around 1804 (Lister, *Amico*, 213).

[93] According to the *Gazetta musicale di Milano* (13 March 1859), for example, 'Sivori plays like a goblin, Bazzini sings like an angel'. Quoted in Claudio Sartori, *L'avventura del violino: l'Italia musicale dell'Ottocento nella biografica e nei carteggi di Antonio Bazzini* (Turin: Edizioni Rai radiotelevisione italiana, 1978), 80, my translation. Baillot wrote, 'We saw from the very first that his manner of playing the violin was generally his own, and had but very little resemblance to that of any other virtuoso . . . The violin in his hands becomes a different instrument, just as the artist himself has gained a place which is out of the ordinary'. Pierre Marie François de Sales Baillot, *The Art of the Violin* (Paris, 1835), trans. Louise Goldberg (Evanston, IL: Northwestern University Press, 1991), 9.

[94] The demonic player and his angelic violin formed a complementary pairing, bound together as one by oppositional qualities—a model later echoed by Freud's theory of god and the devil sharing an origin in a single entity. See Fauquet, 'Quand le diable', 39.

violin had nothing to do with *Faust*, yet the two overlapped in the reception of Paganini's virtuosity. Both romanticised notions of power. The next two chapters are devoted to examining other forms of power that Paganini was thought to wield—namely, sexual domination, sovereign rule, and economic prowess. These ultimately reveal how contemporaries thought about power and not just about Paganini.

CHAPTER 3

Hypereroticism and Violence

THE *Variations on 'La ci darem la mano'* was a favourite virtuosic vehicle of Paganini, based on Mozart's opera *Don Giovanni*; he programmed it at least five times between 1828 and 1832 at various locations on his European tour.[1] Though it is no longer extant, it is likely, judging by what is known of his approach to composing variation sets, that he differentiated the voices of Don Giovanni and Zerlina in a comparable fashion to the dialogues and techniques of multivocality he developed in the *Scena amorosa* and *Moïse* variations, incorporating virtuoso techniques such as multiple stops, trills, pizzicato, and harmonics. Along with Beethoven, Chopin, Liszt, and others, Paganini was drawn to the theme of Mozart's duet. This number was famous for dramatising Zerlina's resistance, ambivalence, and ultimate acquiescence—Don Giovanni's diabolical seduction of a peasant girl on her wedding day.

Where Paganini departed from these other composers, however, was his candidacy as a stand-in for the absent figure of Don Giovanni himself. On a superficial level, the violinist's reputation as a serial seducer of women, a persona sensationalised by the publication of salacious biographical details, formed a striking homology with his erotically charged performances. Paganini was not regarded as handsome by anyone, but he exuded a certain magnetism towards women as a demonic seducer enhanced by the allure of genius. As distinct from that of pianists or poets, his virtuosity connoted demonic eros for contemporaries by infusing the violin (as we shall see, a symbolically and mythologically chaste, feminine entity, like Zerlina), with diabolical energy.

This chapter examines how the demonic and the erotic overlapped in figurations of virtuoso violin performance as a violent sexual attack. With the violin serving as his 'erotically alluring muse'[2] and his bow as a phallic weapon, playing amorous melodies and explosive bowstrokes, the symbolism of Paganini's virtuoso performance suggested that it stemmed from deep sexual urges. There is some

---

[1] He played the *Variations* in Vienna (1828), Berlin and Leipzig (1829), Frankfurt (1830), and Birmingham (1832), sometimes using it as an introduction to the *Sonatina e Polacchetta*.

[2] Stephen Downes has traced the figure of the 'erotically alluring muse' as a source of inspiration for composers such as Schumann, Mahler, and Sibelius. Stephen Downes, *Muse as Eros: Music, Erotic Fantasy and Male Creativity in the Romantic and Modern Imagination* (Aldershot: Ashgate, 2006).

evidence to suggest that Paganini did intend to seduce women as he performed, thereby reflecting in public his libidinous behaviour in private. But ultimately what is more important to note from a historical point of view is that his audiences attributed such urges to Paganini himself, by forming a link between his performing style and his legendary sexual exploits, which were widely publicised to satisfy the public's appetite for details of his private life. This link instantiated a classic case of investment in the Romantic ideal of music's purpose as self-expression: that is, the desire to take musical expression for the personal expression of the artist. The reciprocally feeding fascination with his personal biography and his stage persona made him a 'rock star' prototype. The visual impact of his right arm wielding the bow high in the air and attacking the strings, which were sometimes pictured snapped and broken, may even have anticipated the modern spectacle of male rock guitarists smashing their instruments in 'macho' displays of masculinity.

Hypereroticism

Paganini's biographers agree on the fact that their subject had an unusually developed libido, which he articulated in terms of pleasure, recreation, and conquest more often than romance and courtship. Geraldine De Courcy gives a vivid picture of what she calls Paganini's 'highly erotic temperament', referring to him as a 'Don Juan', a 'Dionysiac' and a libertine with a 'sexual drive' that led him to 'taste pleasure to the full'.[3] Roberto Iovino has stated that Paganini 'collected more conquests than Don Giovanni touring Italy and Europe, doing justice to the maxim of the celebrated Mozartian personage: 'he who is true to one is cruel to the rest . . . etc.'.[4] Pietro Berri describes Paganini's life as one full of 'donne, altre donne, sempre donne'—in a word, a life of hypereroticism.[5]

The biographies document enough affairs and pursuits of girls and women to fill a catalogue. Musicologist Anna Maria Salone has compiled a chronological list of the women who held a place in Paganini's heart in some way: Elisa and Paolina (Napoleon's sisters), Angelina Cavanna, Taddea Pratolongo, an unnamed Protestant girl from Torino*, Elena, Marietta (or Marina) Banti*, Lauretta of Venice, an unnamed English girl in Rome, Angelica Catalani of Naples, Carolina Banchieri*, Antonia Bianchi, Hélène von Dobeneck, an unnamed businessman's

---

[3] De Courcy, *Paganini, the Genoese* I, 5, 19, 22, 64, 133, 365 and *passim*.

[4] 'Collezionò in giro per l'Italia e per l'Europa più conquiste di Don Giovanni, facendo proprio il motto del celebre personaggio mozartiano' (Iovino, *Niccolò Paganini*, 67).

[5] Berri, *Il Calvario di Paganini*, 26–7.

daughter in Frankfurt*, and Charlotte Watson*. He considered marrying some of them, going so far as to propose to several (those marked with an asterisk).[6] Salone goes on to note that the opportunities to meet women undoubtedly multiplied, considering that Paganini left Genoa as a lad to dedicate himself to his musical studies, and that his fame as a concertiser and the wealth he had accumulated played important roles in gaining the attention of women.[7]

Paganini's hypereroticism is very well known yet, amazingly, it has attracted very little attention from musicologists seeking to understand his music and historical significance.[8] This has had the effect of leaving his sexuality uncritiqued from a historical point of view, and the relation between his sexuality and his musicality unexamined. By re-examining his sexual exploits, partly with the help of new documents, and drawing on recent studies on the relation between eros and music, this situation can be changed.[9]

Paganini's libido informed his performing style, his compositions, and his attitude towards music in a number of ways. First and most obviously, at the court of Lucca between 1801 and 1805, he mimicked the sighs and moans of erotic arousal on the violin when he improvised a 'dialogue' between Adonis and Venus. Giving this work the title *Scena amorosa*, he used only the highest and lowest strings to simulate the voices and possibly employed 'sigh' figures and *glissandi*, as seen in the *Caprices* and in interpretations of Concerto No. 1.[10] He used the term 'amore' and its cognates 'amoroso' and 'amorosamente' in numerous movement and section titles, the most famous being in Caprice No. 21. The majority appeared

---

[6] Salone, 'The Paganini–Cavanna event', 'La vicenda Paganini–Cavanna', 372. NB Her list accords with and supplements the names given in the section 'Paganini e le donne' in Iovino, *Niccolò Paganini*, 67–72 and De Courcy, *Paganini the Genoese, passim*.

[7] *Ibid.*, 372.

[8] M.O.C. Döpfner and Thomas Garms have speculated that Paganini's prestidigitation and rapid, rhythmic bowing accompanied by foot-tapping carried sexual innuendo, in *Erotik in der Musik* (Frankfurt: Populäre Kultur, 1986), 78.

[9] Recent studies exploring issues of eros and sexuality in nineteenth-century music have arrived at divergent conclusions. Döpfner and Garms have identified eros as a transhistorical property of music irrespective of type or genre, in *Erotik in der Musik*. Jeffrey Kallberg has argued in his work on Chopin against an essentialist reduction of sexuality as a musical property of works that can be uncovered by formalist analysis (see 'Small Fairy Voices' in *Chopin at the Boundaries: Sex, History, and Musical Genre* (Convergences: Inventories of the Present) (Cambridge, MA: Harvard University Press, 1996), 62–86). Susan McClary has used sexual drive as a metaphor for the narrative drive of tonal structures such as sonata form, the most famous example being her reading of Beethoven's Ninth Symphony in *Feminine Endings: Music, Gender, and Sexuality* (Minneapolis: University of Minnesota Press, 1991), 128–30.

[10] Maiko Kawabata, 'Violinists "Singing": Paganini, Operatic Voices, and Virtuosity', *Ad Parnassum* Vol. 5 No. 9 (April 2007), 7–39.

Table 3.1. Movement headings containing 'amore' and its cognates

Movement heading	Work
'Romance— più tosto Largo, Amorosamente'	*Grand sonata* for violin and guitar
'Andante Amoroso'	*Sonata movimento perpetuo*
'Adagio amoroso'	Sonata for violin and guitar Op. 3 No. 5
'Adagio con Amore'	Sonata for violin and guitar Op. 5 No. 2
'Adagio Amorosamente'	Sonata violin and guitar. Op. 6 No. 4
'Adagio Amorosamente'	Sonata No. 1 for violin and guitar
'Andantino Amorosamente'	*Serenata* for violin, cello and guitar
'Amoroso'	Sonata No. 1 for violin and guitar
'Quasi adagio amorosamente'	6 Sonate, No. 4.
'Andantino amoroso'	37 Sonatas for guitar, No. 28
'Amoroso espressivo'	Six Duets for violin and guitar, No. 1
'Amoroso'	*In cuor più non mi sento for two violins and cello*

in the Sonatas for violin and guitar composed in Lucca between 1803 and 1808 (see Table 3.1).

He probably used them as vehicles for seduction, judging from the expressive markings 'Adagio con passione' (in the Sonata for violin and guitar, Op. 5 No. 1), 'appassionatamente' (Quartet No. 9), 'appassionatissimamente' (Sonata for violin and guitar No. 6), and, in one case, 'seducentemente' (Sonata for violin and guitar, Op. 6 No. 1, Adagio). He dedicated numerous works to women who interested him romantically or sexually. For example, the abovementioned Sonata No. 1 for violin and guitar containing the 'Amoroso' movement was dedicated to Madama Frassinet, a lady-in-waiting at the court of Lucca; in Bologna in 1818 Paganini dedicated minuets for guitar to Marietta Banti, whom he was pursuing at the time.[11]

In one anomalous case, Paganini viewed one of his works not as a vehicle for seduction but as a substitute for it. In advance of the premiere of his Concerto No. 4 in France, he supposedly referred to the work in terms of sexual conquest, saying, 'I want to deflower it in Paris'.[12] This cryptic comment could be dismissed as apocryphal but for the fact that when he listed the concerto's slow movement (*Adagio flebile*) in an itemised catalogue of his compositions some time later, he drew the symbol of a heart in the margin (Figure 3.1). The symbol, which may have

---

[11] Grisley, *Niccolò Paganini, epistolario*, 144 n.5.
[12] Quoted in Schwarz, *Great Masters of the Violin*, 186 and Hans-Günter Klein's liner notes to *Accardo Plays Paganini*, trans. Clive Brown (Deutsche Grammophon, 1988), 10. Paganini made this comment notwithstanding the fact that he had already performed the concerto in Frankfurt nearly a year earlier.

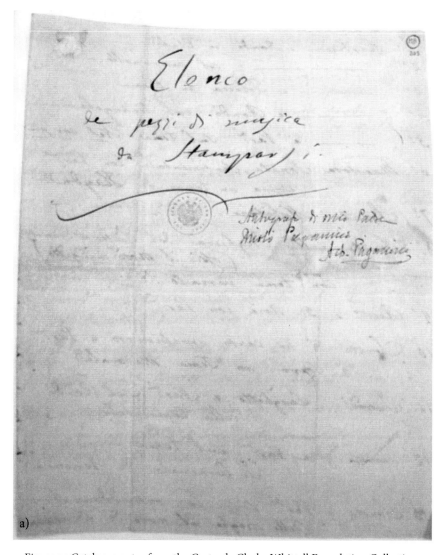

Figure 3.1 Catalogue entry from the Gertrude Clarke Whittall Foundation Collection, Library of Congress, Music Division. (a) Front page: 'Elenco'; (b) heart sign (c) heart sign detail.

referred to the love affair with Hélène von Dobeneck that preoccupied Paganini during the concerto's genesis, has never been mentioned let alone explained in the existing literature.[13]

---

[13] Cantù, *Invito all'ascolto* mentions the affair. Without new documentary evidence coming to light, the meaning of the heart symbol will remain unexplained.

b)

Figure 3.1 (continued)

By his own admission, Paganini led a hedonistic lifestyle as a libertine. As he told his biographer Schottky in 1830:

> As a man who has spent a very lively and often stormy life, I must confess that my youth was not immune from the errors of all young people who, after having spent a long time almost enslaved, find themselves suddenly free again and abandoned as before, and so after a long deprivation want to accumulate pleasure upon pleasure.[14]

De Courcy has noted that the 'scorpionic urge towards sensuality' was in his nature, and that since 'the age imposed no moral curbs ... [he] should not be harshly judged for early sensual excesses when temptation lay everywhere around him'.[15] Even taking into account the patriarchal society in which Paganini lived, it is difficult to share her assessment from 1957 (i.e. before the development of feminist musicology).

Paganini's casual attitude towards women as objects of sexual conquest is evident from his language in letters to Germi. In January 1820, for example, he wrote: 'in Turin I suffered the cold as well as boredom. There are many females to make a pass at'.[16] In February 1830, he used a phrase previously censored by Codignola that Roberto Grisley's new edition of Paganini's correspondence has revealed for the first time: 'These beauties have a feeling for romance; but my friend Mr Azzeretto, Rebizzo's cousin, put it well: *fica in*

---

[14] Quoted in Iovino, *Niccolò Paganini*, 67 from C. M. Rietmann: 'Come uomo, il quale ha trascorso una vita molto movimentata e spesso tempestosa, debbo confessare che la mia giovinezza non fu immune dagli errori di tutti i giovani i quali, dopo aver trascorso lungo tempo pressocché schiavi, si ritrovano improvvisamente liberi e abbandonati a se stessi, e allora dopo una lunga privazione vogliono accumulare piacere e piacere.'

[15] De Courcy, *Paganini, the Genoese* I, 4, 19, 65. She also points out that he did not cultivate libertinism deliberately in order to outrage the public.

[16] 'In Torino [ho] sofferto il freddo non che della noja. Vi sono molte femmine da maneggio', quoted in Salone, 'The Paganini–Cavanna event', 374.

tavola.'[17] The censored phrase Grisley reveals is a *double entendre* in Genoese dialect meaning 'stay at the table' and a crude sexual reference to the presence of women. In other letters to Germi, close (male) friends, and lovers, Paganini also made references to the Gardens of Cythera, and the letters of Eloise and Abelard.[18] At the time of his death, Paganini had 'obscene pictures' hanging in his house.[19] What Romantics were prone to viewing as the behaviour of a 'Byronic anti-hero' rebelling against his Italian Catholic heritage is apt to strike us today as sexual addiction. This is especially the case when considering Paganini's preference throughout his life for young girls, some as young as fourteen—echoing Don Giovanni's paedophiliac taste for 'la piccina'.[20] Moreover, the way he dealt with Angelina Cavanna's accidental pregnancy—forcing her to take a miscarriage-inducing potion—was against Catholic doctrine and coded as 'demonic' (as we saw in Chapter 2).

Gendered Power Dynamics in Performance

One of the many meanings of the word 'demonic' as applied to Paganini pointed to the moral corruption of the archetypal Gothic villain; in such cases it denoted an intent to harm women physically and sexually for selfish pleasure. The violinist's apparently altered state while performing was seen to resemble a deviant's extreme excitement while in the midst of a criminal act, as reviewers in Berlin, Paris, and London wrote:

> He seemed to be striking his instrument, like the unhappy youth, who after conjuring up the image of his murdered mistress, destroys it again

---

[17] 'Queste bellezze hanno un sentimento romanzesco; ma dice benissimo un mio amico cugino di Rebizzo ed è il Sig. Azzeretto: *f . . . in tavola'* (Codignola, *Paganini intimo*, 308, and Grisley, *Niccolò Paganini, epistolario*, 610). Azzeretto or Asseretto was a Genoese businessman who had dealings with one of Paganini's bankers.

[18] Paganini played down his libertinism in a letter to an unnamed friend (1834–35), writing, 'more than once the things they said about me might have very well been true if I had not regarded Europe as a field of honour rather than as the Gardens of Cythera'. Quoted in De Courcy, *Paganini, the Genoese* II, 184–5. He described the letters of Hélène von Dobeneck (1830) as 'worthy of publication, and carrying a sentiment far beyond those of Eloise to Abelard', a reference to the steamy letters exchanged illicitly between a monk and a nun in twelfth-century France.

[19] According to the priest who offered Paganini holy sacraments on his deathbed, 'there were no visual expressions of religious belief in the house' and 'four obscene pictures hanging in the vestibule, one a Venus in a most shameful and disgraceful posture'. Quoted in De Courcy, *Paganini, the Genoese* I, 326.

[20] Salone, 'The Paganini–Cavanna event', 376, 379, 384, 385.

in a fit of amorous rage; then once more seeks to revive it with tears and caresses.[21]

His bow shimmers like a steel blade; his face is as pale as a crime; his smile is beautiful, like Dante's Inferno; his violin cries like a woman.[22]

He literally imparts an *animal sensibility* to his instrument, and at moments makes it wail and moan with all the truth and expression of conscious physical suffering.[23]

Here the unusually charged quality of Paganini's performance was explained in terms of a dramatic spectacle of eros and murderous destruction. This spectacle comprised a rich nexus of metaphors and symbols for gender, sexuality, and the body: the violin was a woman subjected to the licentious assaults of a violent rapist using the bow as a phallus/weapon. Arising in response to Paganini's virtuosity, this imagery drew on ancient folkloric associations of the violin, and it was the combination of these elements that created an explosively violent and pornographic allegory out of his performances.

Long before Man Ray's famous photograph 'Ingres's Violin' (1924) made the visual pun explicit, the violin stood in for the female nude—it was a favourite subject of Ingres himself and other early nineteenth-century painters, of course. The objectification of the female form evident in his *La Grande Odalisque* (1814), for example, mirrors Paganini's treatment of the violin; the passivity implied by the violin's resemblance to a woman's torso reflected the subjugated status of the odalisque (a virgin slave-girl employed in Turkish harems).[24] The dynamic of patriarchal power / feminine submission in this act of objectification is too obvious to require a full feminist critique.[25] It is perhaps worth noting, however, that Paganini's image was built with the violin positioned as 'other' in more than one respect: like odalisques, violins originated in the 'Orient'.

The gender symbolism of the violin as feminine stemmed partly from the obvious fact that its body resembled a woman—with its curved shape and

---

[21] A. B. Marx in *Allgemeine Musikalische Zeitung* (1829), quoted in De Courcy, *Paganini, the Genoese* I, 108–10.

[22] Anon., *L'Entracte* (1831), quoted in Johnson, *Listening in Paris*, 267.

[23] *Athaeneum* (London 1831) quoted in Codignola, *Paganini intimo*, 340 n.1, my italics.

[24] François Girard's *The Red Violin* (1998), in which a violin-maker uses his dead wife's blood to varnish an instrument and thereby gives it her soul, shows that the issues under discussion still have resonance today.

[25] Such a critique could be launched by observing that the 'femininity' of the violin and 'masculinity' of the player were not essential qualities but rather constituted through repeated acts of being performed—borrowing ideas from Judith Butler, 'Performative Acts and Gender Constitution: An Essay in Phenomenology and Feminist Theory' in Sue-Ellen Case, ed., *Performing Feminisms: Feminist Critical Theory and Theatre* (Baltimore, MD, and London: The Johns Hopkins University Press, 1990), 279.

anatomically named parts: 'belly', 'back', 'shoulders', 'ribs', and 'neck'. Another
was the attribution of personhood to the violin upon being played: 'if the instrument could be said to speak and to feel, it does so in his hands', as a reviewer
wrote for *The Observer* (4 June 1831).[26] Coupled with male players, the anthro-
pomorphism of violins noted by an unnamed author in the *Allgemeine Wiener
Musikzeitung* (1843) encompassed a variety of gendered personalities:

> We have heard several violins: Paganini's was bizarre in sorrow and bur-
> lesque in joy; Lipinski's a heroine or indeed *une brave*; Lafont's a Parisian
> salon-lady, elegant, insinuating; Spohr's German, powerful, more thoughts
> than words; Beriot's a lovely girl, touching, naïve, enticing, without strong
> tendencies; Ole Bull's a Cachucha-dancer, striking castanets, pirouet-
> ting thoughtlessly; Ernst's a charming, languishing, melancholy beauty,
> somewhat wistful, a dove still in flight.[27]

The personas of the violins in the hands of these virtuosi were all described as
girls or women, notable not only for the fact of sharing a gender but also for their
human-like characteristics. The voices of violins were often compared to those of
the leading prima donnas: Paganini's with Giuditta Pasta's and Maria Malibran's,
Bériot's with Malibran's, Sivori's with Malibran's and Giulia Grisi's, and so on.[28]
What was highlighted in particular by Paganini's playing, however, was the sexual
significance of the violin's gender symbolism; no other player tapped nearly as
much into the association of 'chastity' with untouched violins. For example,
Stradivari's 'Le Messie' (1716) was legendary for its chastity, like a virgin, as it
remained unplayed for nearly 150 years.[29] Unlike other violinists, whose playing
resembled only operatic singing, Paganini's performances also voiced primal
expressions of eros and pain—as the language of the abovementioned reviews
indicates.

---

[26] Quoted in Codignola, *Paganini intimo*, 342, n.1.

[27] Freia Hoffmann, *Instrument und Körper* (Frankfurt and Leipzig: Insel, 1991), 188–9.

[28] See Kawabata, 'Violinists "Singing" '.

[29] The Italian luthier Carlo Bergonzi told Luigi Tarisio (the violin dealer who discovered and disseminated many priceless Cremona instruments, including 'Le Messie'),
'Remember, "Le Messie" has never been played, therefore one can only guess at the
voice. You have looked upon women who were pure and women who were just beautiful. No? . . . So, when you look up on the face of purity, somehow you know it. Your
eyes say something to your heart. It is the sort of feeling one has when one gazes upon
the features of a sleeping infant. That will be your impression when you finally feast
your eyes on Le Messie.' Allegedly, the violin was not played until as late as 1855, when
Delphin Alard, the son-in-law of French violin-maker Jean Baptiste Vuillaume, finally
touched a bow to its strings. See William A. Silverman, *The Violin Hunter* (Neptune
City, NJ: Paganiniana Publications, 1981), 115 and 245.

In early German Romanticism, women singers were linked to violins by occult forces.[30] Heine wrote after Maria Malibran's tragically early death (from complications following a horse-riding accident), 'sometimes I cannot rid myself of the idea . . . that the soul of his defunct spouse is confined in the violin of Bériot and that she sings'.[31] This echoed the story of Antonia in E. T. A. Hoffmann's 'Councillor Krespel (or The Cremona Violin)' (1816) [32]: afflicted with a mysterious terminal illness triggered by singing and thus forbidden to sing by her father, an eccentric violin-maker, she discovers that she can 'channel' her voice through his prized Italian violin. But when she falls in love with a young composer and gives into the temptation to sing for him in the throes of passion, she dies in a dramatic *Liebestod*. At the same moment the violin shatters into pieces. 'It could only live in and through her', her father sobs. Antonia's father crafts instruments only to play them once, and longs to dispossess his daughter of her virginity; his desire to penetrate both bodies is tinged with dark psychological undertones of 'incestuous desire sublimated through music', as Heather Hadlock has argued.[33] The violin and woman were interchangeable objects of a demonic erotic desire subjected to the discipline/punishment of a patriarch. Such stories that blurred the lines between human and supernatural agency overlapped notions of envoicement and ensoulment, and attributed subjectivity to the instrument, supplying a set of meanings through which the inexplicable power of Paganini's playing could be filtered and explained. The violin was 'sexualised' to a degree commensurate with Paganini's reputedly monstrously overdeveloped libido.

Rumours of Paganini's violent and criminal past helped create his reputation as a remorseless sadist who piled abuse onto women and violins for his own edification. This earned him notoriety as an immoral rake in the mould of Lovelace, the licentious hero/villain of Richardson's novel *Clarissa*.[34] Stories of evisceration led people to draw parallels between the violinist and the Marquis de Sade by speculating that Paganini had practised the violin to while away his time in prison just as the Marquis had written *Les Infortunes de la vertu* inside the walls of the

[30] 'The Ensouled Violin', a story attributed to the Theosophist Madame Blavatsky, recycled this theme.

[31] Quoted in Michael Goldstein, 'Charles de Bériot', trans. Simone Luciani, *Cahiers Ivan Tourgéniev, Pauline Viardot et Marie Malibran* Vol. 10 (1986), 69.

[32] E. T. A. Hoffmann, *Tales of Hoffmann*, trans. R. J. Hollingdale (London: Penguin Books, 1982), 159–83.

[33] Heather Hadlock, *Mad Loves: Women and Music in Offenbach's* Les Contes d'Hoffmann. Princeton Studies in Opera (Princeton, NJ: Princeton University Press, 2000), 40.

[34] See De Courcy, *Paganini, the Genoese* I, 133–42. The much-publicised story of Paganini supposedly abducting singer Charlotte Watson could not have shaped his reception on tour in Europe because it allegedly took place in June 1834 (at the end of his tour).

Bastille. Such stories, popularised in writing as well as through lithographs depicting imaginary scenes of Paganini in captivity, conflated his identity with that of another violinist-libertine, Giacomo Casanova.[35]

Paganini's persona as a Gothic libertine touched on various literary and historical figures (Lovelace, Sade, Casanova). Paganini seemed to exemplify the figure of the brooding villain who attacked innocent women, consorted with depraved monks and nuns, and personified the Catholic 'South' as a diabolical 'other'.[36] Not coincidentally, the disturbing power dynamic of total male domination and female submission he enacted was a convention of such Gothic novels.[37]

The stereotype of violinists as morally loose, low-class scoundrels predated Paganini's emergence, as it stemmed from associations with dancing, beer-halls, and drunken debauchery. In 1711, for instance, author Jonathan Swift wrote in a private letter concerning the case of a man accused of rape whose guilt he assumed on the grounds that the man 'was a fiddler, and consequently a rogue'.[38] Moral aspersions were cast on fiddlers because their music encouraged dancing, an activity abhorred by pious individuals for resembling or leading to debauched behaviour.[39] Paganini was hardly original in being an Italian violinist with a bent

---

[35] Such stories were printed in, for instance, Laphelèque, *Nicolo Paganini*, 48–9. One of the best-known lithographs imagining Paganini in prison is by Louis Boulanger (1831). Casanova was in reality a professional violinist briefly incarcerated in 1755 by the authorities on suspicion of witchcraft, an imprisonment which temporarily interrupted the amorous adventures for which he is best known today.

[36] See for example discussions of Matthew Gregory Lewis's *The Monk* (1796) as typifying the anti-Catholic, pornographic, and transgressive bent of Gothic literature in Clara Tuite, 'Cloistered Closets: Enlightenment Pornography, the Confessional State, Homosexual Persecution, and *The Monk*', *Romanticism on the Net* Vol. 8: www.erudit. org/revue/ron/1997/v/n8/005766ar.html (online article, accessed 1 March 2007), Marie-José Tienhooven, 'All Roads Lead to England: *The Monk* Constructs the Nation', *Romanticism on the Net* Vol. 8: www.erudit.org/revue/ron/1997/v/n8/005777ar.html (online article, accessed 1 March 2007), and James Whitlark, 'Heresey Hunting: *The Monk* and the French Revolution', *Romanticism on the Net* Vol. 8: www.erudit.org/ revue/ron/1997/v/n8/005773ar.html (online article, accessed 1 March 2007).

[37] Recall the grisly murder of Elisabeth, Victor Frankenstein's fiancée, near the end of Mary Shelley's novel. For more on this literary convention, see Anne Williams, *Art of Darkness: A Poetics of Gothic* (Chicago and London: University of Chicago Press, 1995), 104 and Anne K. Mellor, *Romanticism and Feminism* (Bloomington and Indianapolis: Indiana University Press, 1988), 220–32.

[38] Jonathan Swift, *Journal to Stella*, ed. J. K. Moorehead (London: J. M. Dent and Sons, 1948 [1924]), 203.

[39] Heinrich Heine even wrote a poem in which 'a ghostly fiddler entic[es] a young maiden to dance herself to an early death' in the 'Heimkehr' series of 1823–24. See Rita Steblin, 'Death as Fiddler: A Study of a Convention in European Art, Literature and Music', *Basler Jahrbuch für historische Musikpraxis* XIV (1990), 286–7.

towards seduction; in the eighteenth century, Pugnani's 'weakness for women was known', according to Schwarz.[40] But to construe a violinist as a wicked brute whose performance staged a vicious attack was new with Paganini. Fellow violinist Charles Lafont described him as 'a woman-hunter, with a face like a vulture'[41] while the London periodical *Athenaeum* reported that 'the poor violin was a transformed victim in the demon's hand, uttering the anguished complaints of his inflicted torture'.[42]

His libertinism and erotic transgressions put him in the league of Lord Byron himself, the poet whose sexual excesses were so legendary that, in the words of one historian, 'his promiscuity seemed almost superhuman'.[43] Moreover, he appeared to emulate the behaviour of Laclos's Valmont like Byron did, thereby prolonging an eighteenth-century brand of libertinism that was unfashionable by the early nineteenth century.[44] With his 'Byronic' traits—pale countenance, dark passions simmering beneath a calm veneer, and a 'Satanic smile'—Paganini resembled the character types of the corsair or the giaour. The title character of the dramatic poem *Manfred* (inspired by Goethe's *Faust*) says of Astarte (his mistress, his victim, and possibly his sister), 'I loved her, and destroy'd her'—these are the kind of words audiences might have imagined Paganini to have uttered about his violin after an impassioned performance.[45]

The graphic symbolism of violin performance combined with Paganini's reputation as a dangerous rake served to exemplify a Gothic archetype: the close links between sex and death, pleasure and pain. In music probably the best-known example is 'Death and the Maiden', Schubert's *Lied* for baritone and piano (1817), later reworked for his String Quartet in D minor, D. 810 (1824). Lyser's depiction of a young girl overcome by the skeleton in her lap (in the aforementioned illustration) echoed the medieval theme of Death and the Maiden, which resurfaced in

---

[40] Pugnani also 'was vain and easily offended if not treated with deference . . . . Because of his vanity, Pugnani was often the butt of jokes. His appearance was unattractive; at times he looked grotesque, with a high wig, modish frock coat, and a bouquet of flowers on his chest.' Schwarz, *Great Masters of the Violin*, 105.

[41] Quoted in Saussine, *Paganini*, 157.

[42] Quoted in Codignola, *Paganini intimo*, 340.

[43] Gay, *The Naked Heart*, 93. According to Gay, Byron was said 'to have committed incest with his half sister, sodomized his wife, conducted a string of love affairs with women of all ranks, and varied them with homosexual flings'.

[44] As Jonathan Gross has pointed out in his study of Byron, eighteenth-century libertinism involved a revolt against Christianity and was later not only unfashionable but even politically dangerous for Byron to emulate. See his *Byron: The Erotic Liberal* (Lanham, MD: Rowman & Littlefield, 2000), 10.

[45] See Mario Praz, *The Romantic Agony*, trans. Angus Davidson, 2nd ed. (London: Oxford University Press, 1951), 53–94, for more on Byron's hero-villains.

the Romantic revival of Gothic art, such as 'Death as Lover' by the Swiss painter Niklaus Manuel Deutsch (1484–1530), which depicts a young girl being ravaged by a skeleton. Delacroix's *The Death of Sardanapalus* (1827), supposedly inspired by Byron's play *Sardanapalus* (1821), eroticises the slaughter of a voluptuous odalisque as the notoriously perverted King of Assyria watches. According to art historians, this 'sado-masochistic fantasy' 'with its provocative intermingling of sexuality and death, voyeurism and erotic pleasure',[46] highlights 'carnality under the knife, orgiastic passion flaring up briefly before extinction overwhelms it'.[47] The proximity of extreme sexual excitement and death represented here was precisely how reviewers described Paganini's performances.

Paganini exemplified *par excellence* Freia Hoffmann's observation that men who handled the violin's body and brought it to sound experienced an increase in masculinity.[48] The most obvious sign of this was the phallic symbolism of the bow reflected in certain metaphors favoured by Paganini's contemporaries. The poet and aesthetician Friedrich August Kanne merged images of weaponry and sexual potency by imagining Paganini grasping his bow and a magic tone shooting up like an arrow to penetrate the soft clouds in the heavens.[49] Paganini's bow was said to be loaded with 'magic pellets'—reminiscent of Max's 'magic bullets' in *Der Freischütz* (1821) with their overlapping sexual symbolism and supernatural powers.[50] With a precedent in Renaissance writer Pietro Aretino's description of a debauched Abbess 'rubbing the boy's little bow on her lyre' as a metaphor for sexual relations, the bow as a phallic symbol was firmly established by Paganini's lifetime.[51]

---

[46] Timothy Wilson-Smith, *Delacroix: A Life* (London: Constable, 1992), 82; Elisabeth A. Fraser, *Delacroix, Art, and Patrimony in Post-Revolutionary France* (Cambridge and New York: Cambridge University Press, 2004), 134. See also Jack Spector, *Delacroix: The Death of Sardanapalus*. Art in Context (New York: Viking Press, 1974), 89–105.

[47] F. W. J. Hemmings, *Culture and Society in France, 1789–1848* (Leicester: Leicester University Press, 1987), 185–7. For a colour reproduction of the painting, see René Huyghe, *Delacroix*, trans. Jonathan Griffin (London: Thames & Hudson, 1963), 123.

[48] Women violinists meanwhile carried the taboo connotation of homosexuality in handling the violin's 'feminine body'. See Freia Hoffmann, *Instrument und Körper*, 187–94.

[49] Schottky, *Paganinis Leben und Treiben*, 21. The sexual imagery of Kanne's poetry can be seen as part of the rise of German erotic writing around the turn of the nineteenth century, lagging behind France and England.

[50] Silverman relates the story that 'the reason Paganini can play staccato so marvelously is that his bow is hollow and filled with little leaden pellets which run up and down the bow when required to, and stop at once when so desired', in *The Violin Hunter*, 77.

[51] 'di fregare l'archetto del fanciullo su per la sua lira'. See the *First Giornata* of Antonia and Nanna in Pietro Aretino, *Ragionamento*, ed. Giorgio Barberi Squarotti and Carla Forno (Milan: Biblioteca Universale Rizzoli, 1988), 97, 140 n.420. Exceptionally, the

It is worth noting here that in spite of appearing aggressive and literally break-ing strings and bow hairs (which were easily replaceable), Paganini did not actu-ally destroy his instruments—in fact, he took care of his violins with great pride and protectiveness, and was especially attached to certain ones. According to a famous story from the early 1830s (possibly apocryphal) he took his favourite Guarneri, 'The Canon', to the luthier Vuillaume for repairs following an accident in which it fell off the front bench of a horse-drawn carriage; when Vuillaume began to work with his tools, Paganini reportedly began 'moaning and grimacing, uttering loud exclamations which plainly revealed the affection he had for his violin' (as if it were his own body under the chisel).[52]

Paganini's innovations of bowing technique, the violent physical dimension of which has until now received little attention from scholars, tapped into and enhanced the symbolism of the bow as a weapon. He used a Cramer bow, which is now considered a transitional model between the earlier Corelli–Tartini bows and the later Tourte bow, and which had a springier action than its predeces-sor.[53] His trademark bowings such as *jeté* and *ricochet* involved 'throwing' the bow at the string, thus emphasising the visual image of the player 'lashing' at the instrument with a weapon. Paganini used such bowstrokes in numerous compositions, notably in the finale to his Concerto No. 1, where he employed a *ricochet* stroke of four notes to a single bow (as shown in Example 3.1). Paganini left no written records as to how he executed these bowstrokes—despite plans he never wrote a treatise—but others did. Leading French soloist and pedagogue Pierre Baillot, for one, explained 'How to Play the Ricochet' as follows (with startling exactitude):

> The player *throws* the bow at the [lower] end of the middle [third], and from about 2.13 inches above the string; the bow rebounds and 'bites' several notes by itself . . . . In order to articulate a greater number of notes in a single up-bow or down-bow in the ricochet, the player has only to let the

use of the violin as a dildo ('violon anal') was advised in the French sex manual by a certain 'Doctor Jacobus X', *L'Amour au colonies* (Paris, 1893). For more on the gendered language used to describe strong bowstrokes (as 'masculine') and the sexist bias in the reception of women violinists, see Maiko Kawabata, 'Virtuoso Codes of Violin Performance: Power, Military Heroism, and Gender (1789–1830)', *Nineteenth Century Music*, Vol. 28, No. 2 (November 2004), 89–107.

[52] Silverman, *The Violin Hunter*, 73.

[53] David D. Boyden, 'Der Geigenbogen von Corelli bis Tourte', in Vera Schwarz, ed., *Violinspiel und Violinmusik in Geschichte und Gegenwart: Bericht über den Internationalen Kongress am Institut für Aufführungspraxis der Hochschule für Musik und Darstellende Kunst in Graz, vom 25. Juni bis 2. Juli 1972* (Vienna: Universal Edition, 1975), 305–6.

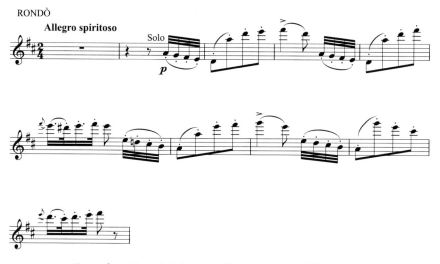

Example 3.1 Paganini, Concerto No. 1, movement III, opening

bow fall from higher above the string. This will increase the number of rebounds made by the bow.[54]

Baillot went on to note that Paganini was the first violinist he had witnessed executing the multiple-rebound *ricochet*. He then directed the interested reader to Carl Guhr's treatise on Paganini's playing style, the relevant section of which employs telling language:

Paganini allows the bow ... to make a *jumping, whipping* [*springende, peitschende*] movement and uses for that purpose almost the middle of it and only as much of its length as is necessary to put the string into vibration.[55]

Another technique that might have resembled assault was Paganini's use of the bow in the midst of passages employing left-hand pizzicato. In the second variation of *Le Streghe*, for example, where bowed semiquavers are interspersed with plucked ones (indicated by a cross (+) in Example 3.2), Paganini would have touched the bow to the string momentarily, with more of a vertical motion (dropping the bow) than a horizontal one (drawing the bow). Because the bow would have hit the string so rapidly and in such an irregular pattern (on the 2nd, 3rd, and

[54] Baillot, *The Art of the Violin*, 184–85, my italics.
[55] Quoted in Clive Brown, 'Bowing Styles, Vibrato and Portamento in Nineteenth-Century Violin Playing', *Journal of the Royal Musical Association* 113 (1988), 105, my italics.

Example 3.2 Paganini, *Le Streghe*, variation II

5th quaver beats of bar 2; on beats 1, 2 1/2, 4, and 5 1/2 of bar 4; on beats 1, 2, 4, and 6 of bar 6, and so on), the viewer would have seen a blur of repeated and erratic 'lashings'. This effect, which becomes more pronounced the greater the height from which the bow is dropped, has been exploited by some modern performers of Paganini's music who exaggerate the bow's height for show.[56]

In addition to 'thrown' bowings and left-hand pizzicato, which were the most famous of the percussive effects Paganini employed, there were several other less well-known techniques among his arsenal. The jerking movements of the right arm in executing passages involving rapid string crossing would have resembled assaults of various kinds. His technique of fixing the left hand in high positions and crossing the bow rapidly between the G string and the E string to create a compound melody would have created the visual effect of 'lashing' with the bow, as seen in Caprice No. 21 (Example 3.3). In such passages, Paganini may have appeared to approach the basic mechanics of the violin like a percussion instrument, hitting or whipping the strings with the bow as if striking a drum with a stick.[57]

Example 3.3 Paganini, Caprice No. 21, 'lashing'

[56] The extraordinary Alexander Markov, for example, whips his bow theatrically through the air in rendering the left-hand pizzicato variation to the Caprice No. 24 in Bruno Monsaingeon's film, *The Art of Violin* (Idéale Audience, 2000).

[57] This aspect of Paganini's virtuosity was untranslatable to the keyboard. When Liszt transferred Paganini's devices to the piano, rendering the ricochet arpeggios of Caprice No. 1 as staccato arpeggios, for instance, the visually spectacular, percussive dimension was lost. Although Liszt's performing style called up its own set of violent metaphors—the masculine 'aggression' of pounding the keys with his hands in fortissimo octave-scales, for example—this substituted direct manual contact for assault with a weapon.

Figure 3.2 Anon., illustration, from the Gertrude Clarke Whittall Foundation Collection, Library of Congress, Music Division.

The inherent theatricality of violent bowstrokes was laden with connotations of heroic, sexual conquest. Numerous contemporary illustrations and carica-tures depict Paganini holding his bow high up in the air ready to deliver a good lashing (see Figure 3.2, for example).[58] The broken strings gave the impression that they had snapped under excessive force brought on by excessive passion (echoed later in accounts of piano strings giving out under Liszt's overpowering hands). Augustin Edouard's caricature (1832) figured Paganini's performance as 'bodice-ripping'—snapped strings dangling like corset-laces—and depicted his

[58] The desk with the open score that stands behind Paganini in Figure 3.2 was a figment of the artist's imagination—there is no evidence to suggest that Paganini ever performed from scores.

Figure 3.3 Augustin Edouard's caricature of Paganini (October 1832), from the Gertrude Clarke Whittall Foundation Collection, Library of Congress, Music Division.

Figure 3.4 Melchior von Hugo, 'Der Geiger', from Eduard Fuchs, *Geschichte der erotischen Kunst* (Munich: A. Langen, 1922-26), vol. I, 'Das zeitgeschichtlichte Problem', 405.

fingers creeping over the violin's body all the while keeping his bow-arm raised, poised to 'undo' the remaining string (Figure 3.3).[59]

The implications of murder and rape in the colourful language of Paganini's reviewers were not represented pictorially until the early twentieth century. Melchior von Hugo's 'Der Geiger' (n.d.) depicted Death dragging a grotesque phallus-bow across a naked female torso, thus bringing together cruelty, sexual arousal, violence, the gender symbolism of the violin and bow, and the 'Death and the Maiden' theme (Figure 3.4). Although it does not date from Paganini's time, this drawing is iconic in that it summarises all the cultural references underlying his Gothic attributes.[60] Similarly, what Paganini's contemporaries could only imply through verbal choices was captured in a surrealist caricature by Alberto

[59] Also consider again the caricatures first mentioned in Chapter 2.
[60] I am grateful to Lisa Parkes for bringing this illustration to my attention.

Figure 3.5 Alberto Martini, 'Paganini', from the Gertrude Clarke Whittall Foundation Collection, Library of Congress, Music Division.

Martini (1876–1954). In his 'Paganini' (n.d.), a naked succubus with trailing locks and a long tail arches her back in ecstasy as she emerges from the violin's scroll like an organic outgrowth, a perversion of Eve being moulded out of Adam's rib (Figure 3.5). Its allusion to the story of original sin leaves no doubt as to the corrupting influence of Paganini's hands.

Paganini as Rock Star

There are obviously close parallels of symbolism and gendered power relations between Paganini's violin-playing and guitarists in 'cock rock' and heavy
metal bands—with the guitar as a phallus/girl-substitute and performance as
a display of masculine potency.[61] Eddie van Halen, Yngwie Malmsteen and
others have not only 'appropriated' Paganini's Caprice No. 5 and virtuoso violin
music from the Baroque onwards, as Robert Walser has shown, but have also
inherited from Paganini a hypersexualised aura as a performer fuelled by the
public's fascination with off-stage sexual exploits.[62] This aspect of Paganini's
legacy tends to get obscured every time we collapse his 'demonic' aura into
the single dimension of a Faustian pact, ignoring its undertones of sexuality,
deviancy, and so on. Paganini's performance style prefigured the innuendo of
virtuoso dexterity as a measure of sexual prowess. Jimi Hendrix's fast finger
movements, hand gestures imitating masturbation, and 'fellating' the strings
(later copied by Steve Vai and others) demonstrated 'the erotic relationship
with the instrument as a symbol of femininity and fetish';[63] *Newsweek* reported
that the artist 'loved his guitar with the passion and imagination of Casanova'.[64]
These comments echo the above-mentioned descriptions of Paganini's intimacy
with the violin. The origins of instrumental virtuosity as filtered through tropes
of gender and sexuality (given such ample attention in popular music studies)
lie in the nineteenth century.[65]

Paganini also anticipated modern rock stars in the role that his reception, especially among women, played in his construction as a public performer. His quasi-
pornographic performances were inextricably linked to his rumoured sexual
insatiability, just as rock stars channel a hypersexualised stage persona consistent
with their backstage sexual promiscuity. The idolisation of Paganini produced a

---

[61] In 'cock rock', stereotypically, 'performance is an explicit, crude, and often aggressive
   expression of male sexuality' in which 'mikes and guitars are phallic symbols' and
   'male physicality (hardness, control, virtuosity)' are brought to the fore (Simon Frith
   and Andrew Goodwin, eds, *On Record: Rock, Pop, and the Written Word* (New York:
   Pantheon Books, 1990), 374).

[62] Walser, *Running with the Devil*, chapter 3.

[63] Döpfner and Garms, *Erotik in der Musik*, 171–201.

[64] Döpfner and Garms, *Erotik in der Musik*, 191. 'Cock rockers' musical skills become
   synonymous with their sexual skills (hence Jimi Hendrix's simultaneous status as stud
   and guitar hero)', according to Simon Frith and Angela McRobbie, 'Rock and Sexuality
   (1978)' in Frith and Goodwin, eds, *On Record*, 374.

[65] Paganini could further be said to have embodied the kind of Gothic image of alterity
   popularised by Marilyn Manson and others today.

mass ecstasy akin to 'Beatle-Mania' (as numerous critics have noted).[66] This set a precedent for 'Lisztomania' (Heine's coinage in the 1840s), which, as Dana Gooley has shown, carried a medical connotation because of the nervous excitement brought on by witnessing the pianist's virtuoso playing, to which women were thought to be particularly susceptible.[67]

The Paganini craze swept up men and women, as we can see from scenes of euphoria at his concerts. An 1829 lithograph from Berlin depicted its citizens in a state of pandemonium, clutching at each other and collapsing in the attempt to enter the hall where Paganini was playing.[68] A London reviewer wrote in 1831: 'at the end of every performance, and especially after the last, the applause, cheers and waving of handkerchiefs and hats, altogether presented a most extraordinary scene'.[69] Wilhelm Smets (1796–1848), a priest and writer who later became canon at Cologne Cathedral, spontaneously burst into tears upon meeting Paganini, in a small town near Bonn in 1829.[70]

This kind of extreme emotional response was more commonly found among women. They pressed him for autographs, dedicated poetry to him, and mobbed his hotels.[71] Hélène von Dobeneck left her husband for the violinist and, when the affair came to an end, considered becoming a nun:

> She entered the Benedictine convent Mariastein, near Basel, to serve her novitiate. Failing, however, to find in a religious life the peace of mind she sought, she abandoned the idea before taking her final vows, and from then on led a restless, unhappy existence, making religious pilgrimages to Rome and wandering from place to place like a lost spirit.[72]

Mary Shelley drew on personal experience when she wrote in a private letter to her friend Maria Gisborne in 1831:

---

[66] See, for instance, Döpfner and Garms, *Erotik in der Musik*, 76, McClary, *Feminine Endings*, 200, and Deaville, 'The Making of a Myth: Liszt, the Press, and Virtuosity', 182.

[67] Gooley, *The Virtuoso Liszt*, 210.

[68] The caption beneath Ad. Schrödter's lithograph 'Karikatur auf die Berliner Konzerte' (Berlin, no publisher given, 1829) reads 'How the Berliners lost two thalers by force' ['Wie die Berliner zwei Taler mit Gewalt loswerden'] in Karl Storck, *Musik und Musiker in Karikatur und Satire* (Oldenburg: Stalling, 1910), 327.

[69] *The Observer*'s review (4 June 1831) of his London appearances is quoted in Codignola, *Paganini intimo*, 343.

[70] The encounter occurred six months after Smets saw Paganini play according to De Courcy, *Paganini the Genoese* I, 389.

[71] Among them were Louisa Anne Twambley of Birmingham, England (a poetess), Mrs Benjamin Curtis (wife of a wealthy American silk merchant in Paris) and Madame d'Obrée. De Courcy, *Paganini, the Genoese* I, 217 n.11.

[72] De Courcy, *Paganini the Genoese* I, 418.

What effect Paganini would have had on you I cannot tell—he threw me
into hysterics—I delight in him more than I can express—his wild etherial
[*sic*] figure rapt look [*sic*]—& the sounds he draws from his violin are all
superhuman—of human expression … It is interesting to see the astonishment & admiration of Lindley Spagnoletti & Mori as they watch his
evolutions.[73]

Paganini himself noted the overpowering effect of his playing on women: 'True,
when they hear the language of my music, the lilting cadence of my notes makes
them [women] weep'.[74] Goethe observed, 'it is curious to hear people, especially
women, talk about it [Paganini's performance]. Without any hesitation they give
utterance to what are in fact confessions'.[75] Vinogradov's novel parodied this by
describing how Paganini's concerts caused 'devout women to lose the simplicity
of faith natural to them and become filled with sinful agitation'.[76]

It did not matter that he was not 'physically attractive and vigorous' like Liszt
(or Byron).[77] As Anna Maria Salone has noted, young women were fascinated
with Paganini's mysterious artistic temperament and the promise of escape from
a mundane life, which made them forget his appearance as well as his character.[78] As for the question of why women went crazy for a performer who symbolically enacted sexual violence, we can turn to Pascal Fournier's argument that
Paganini's reputation as a 'girl hunter' actually made him sexually attractive to
women.[79] This paralleled the appeal the 'Byronic (anti-)hero' supposedly held for
female readers—by representing the dangerous seducer they secretly longed for.[80]
As literary critics and cultural historians have claimed, the element of transgression was key to the thrill readers derived from Byron's writings, which included
behaviour that overstepped accepted social codes.[81]

---

[73] Betty T. Bennett, ed., *The Letters of Mary Wollstonecraft Shelley* (Baltimore, MD and
     London: The Johns Hopkins University Press, 1983) II, 210. Robert Lindley (1776–1855)
     was an English cellist and composer, Paolo Spagnoletti (1768–1834), an Italian violinist,
     and Nicholas Mori (1796–1839), a violinist and music publisher.
[74] Letter to Germi (30 July 1830), quoted in De Courcy, *Paganini, the Genoese* I, 415.
[75] Letter to Zelter (9 November 1829), quoted in *ibid.* I, 361.
[76] Vinogradov, *The Condemnation of Paganini*, 204.
[77] Deaville, 'La Figura', 816.
[78] Salone, 'The Paganini–Cavanna event', 376, 379, 385. In Salone's opinion, the women
     who chased after Paganini were interested above all in his capital.
[79] Fournier, *Der Teufelsvirtuose*, 162.
[80] As Jacques Barzun has suggested (among others), in *From Dawn to Decadence: 500
     Years of Western Cultural Life* (New York: Perennial, 2001), 485–6.
[81] For men, an identification with the violent symbolism of a Paganini performance
     might also have served to provide a necessary outlet for aggressive impulses that might

More broadly, it was the Romantic cult of the virtuoso highlighting the protagonism of the individual amidst massive social changes that anticipated the veneration of rock stars, as James Deaville has shown.[82] Specifically, he notes that Liszt captured Europe by involving the press, by being a model of heroic individual success during a time of identity crises, and by using his subject position to give form to a bourgeois aesthetic identifying the messenger (the soloist) as the message (the art of music).

Recently, popular music scholars have advocated the need to consider the active role played by female fans in constructing Elvis as an 'object'. The argument against a monolithic portrayal of Elvis as an all-powerful 'subject' displaces attention onto the way women explored and shaped their sexual subjectivities through active rather than passive engagement with Elvis as a figure.[83] Nineteenth-century women differed from Elvis fans in many ways, notably in their limited opportunities for self-determined expressions of sexuality. Their manifestations of enthusiasm and excitement as 'hysteria' and/or throwing themselves at him reflected not so much on themselves as on the patriarchal society they lived in. The 'flying squadron of infatuated women' (De Courcy's expression) that encircled Paganini wherever he went reflected not only on the powers he had over women but also on their newfound freedom, however limited, to respond to him publicly.[84]

The model of active-male-performer/passive-female-listener inscribed patriarchal power in precisely the kind of way feminists have been eager to expose (the same power structure sustained libertinism, i.e. total subjugation of the female

---

otherwise have manifested in more troubling ways. Mario Praz has described what he calls Byron's 'criminal erotism' as hinging on the act of transgression in *The Romantic Agony*, 53–94; Anne Williams has posited the eroticisation of 'obsession with transgression, with violating taboos' as one of a set of literary conventions underpinning Gothic poetics in *Art of Darkness*, 172; and Peter Gay has written about the ambivalence of bourgeois men and women in their attitudes towards the libertinism of exhibitionistic romantics like Byron—outraged and enthralled at the same time—in *The Naked Heart*, 93–4. Lastly, David Punter's *The Literature of Terror: A History of Gothic Fictions from 1765 to the Present Day* (New York: Longman, 1980) points out that one characteristic feature of Gothic novels is 'precisely that they are not realistic' (20), thereby underscoring the element of fantasy.

[82] Deaville, 'La Figura', 821.

[83] Walser has noted that 'instead of a subject who caused his helpless fans to go into frenzies, Elvis was for many women an object by means of which they explored their own desires and formed friendships' in *Running with the Devil*, 132. Similarly, the feminist critic Sue Wise has pointed out the need to revise the male-centered, ego-enhancing view of Elvis by considering him as an 'object' constructed by his female fans in 'Sexing Elvis', *On Record*, Frith and Goodwin, eds, 396–8).

[84] De Courcy, *Paganini, the Genoese* I, 271.

body to male control). At the risk of reductionism, we could conclude that the dynamics of performer/listener and player/instrument brought into play a host of binaries: active/passive, male/female, sexualised/chaste.

The main reason why the erotic, violent, and gendered subtexts to Paganini's performances have been overlooked for so long is that the 'demonic' stereotype has remained unexamined. As we saw in Chapter 2, beneath that label resided a wide range of meanings with multiple connotations depending on diverse points of view. The figuration of Paganini as a kind of 'Don Giovanni with a violin'—a twisted libertine clutching his latest deflowered victim by the throat—formed one strand of his 'demonic' image. In the next chapter, we turn to an altogether different kind of 'demonic' conquest of Paganini's that has similarly received scant attention—his campaign to dominate Europe and pocket the spoils.

CHAPTER 4

Sovereignty, Domination, and Conquest

A CCORDING to Kierkegaard, the 'demonic' power of music was channelled by certain performers to 'grip and capture a multitude, especially women, in the seductive snare of fear'.[1] Kierkegaard did not make an example of Paganini—indeed he could not have witnessed any performances first hand. But this description of 'demonic' power fits the quasi-hypnotic control the violinist seemed to exert over his massed concert audiences, holding them captive and provoking extreme emotional responses ranging from stunned to tearful.[2] We saw in Chapter 3 that the creation of this power dynamic was in reality more complex (due to the emerging social dynamics of public concerts) than the wholesale attribution of power to Paganini and powerlessness to his audience suggests. The sheen of omnipotence and how this potency was balanced warrant further investigation: while the direction of the orchestra by a conductor has been examined and compared to dictatorship, the figure of the virtuoso has largely escaped such critique.[3]

Michel Foucault defined power as something arising in strategic interactions among social groups or institutions rather than possessed and wielded by a sovereign individual.[4] Taking this definition as a jumping-off point, this chapter examines the way Paganini dominated his audiences, dominated the music market, and dominated the orchestra. He swept across Europe emptying the pockets of audiences wherever he went in what was the most lucrative concert tour yet undertaken in history. His virtuosity constituted a form of 'symbolic capital', to use Bourdieu's term for subverted or substituted economic capital that can be used to make economic profits.[5]

---

[1] See Søren Kierkegaard, *Either/Or*, trans. D. and L. Swenson (Princeton, NJ: Princeton University Press, 1944 [1843]), 72.

[2] Franz Farga has described Paganini's effect on his audiences as 'Massenhypnose' in *Paganini: Der Roman seines Lebens* (Zürich: Albert Müller, 1950), 26.

[3] Theodor W. Adorno remarked that 'the virtuoso—a pianist of Liszt's type, for instance—shows similar traits' to the orchestral conductor, a figure who 'is an imago, the imago of power, visibly embodied in his prominent figure and striking gestures', in 'Conductor and Orchestra: Aspects of Social Psychology', in *Introduction to the Sociology of Music*, trans. E. B. Ashton (New York: Continuum, 1989), 104. See also Elias Canetti, *Crowds and Power*, trans. Carol Stewart (London: Phoenix Press, [1962] 2000), 394–6.

[4] See, for instance, Michel Foucault, *Power/Knowledge*, ed. Colin Gordon (New York: Pantheon, 1980).

[5] Bourdieu, *The Field of Cultural Production*, esp. 75.

The word 'virtuosity' does not come from 'virtue' as it is commonly understood. The common root is *virtù* (Italian) or *virtus* (Latin), which means power or strength—this original meaning is preserved in the English usage 'by virtue of the power vested in me'. The first definition of the term 'virtuoso' to denote a musician of exceptional ability appeared in Sebastien de Brossard's entry 'Virtù' for the *Dictionnaire de musique* (1703): 'that superiority of genius, skill or ability that makes us excel in the fine arts, whether in theory or in practice'.[6] *Virtù*, in the sense of potency or agency, has little to do with observing a moral code, still less to do with notions of Victorian virtue. In fact, it is more apropos to see virtuosi as virtueless: as Ernest Newman suggested in his essay 'The Virtuous and the Virtuoso', the two were mutually exclusive.[7]

Paganini's reception played a major part in this. His virtuosity harnessed, enabled, channelled, and symbolised various kinds of power—military, political, economic, social, and sexual—which he wielded to his advantage. Because his virtuosity was coded as 'demonic', as he was himself, and these forms of power were self-serving, egoistically driven, and self-gratifying, they became enmeshed as a big jumble of anti-virtues—the seven deadly sins with violin virtuosity thrown in. His *Geldsucht*, his lust for social standing, his personal autonomy, his heroic image, his celebrity—all of this was driven and supported by his virtuosity, and inseparable from its demonicism.

As we shall see, his single-minded quest for personal glory, for social and material advantages of every kind, paralleled Napoleonic campaigns of conquest, pillage, and destruction. His self-promoting entrepreneurialism and self-centred worldview were closely related to the self-glorification of virtuoso solo performance, in which he subjugated the orchestra to the imperative of individualistic display. Taking the First Concerto as an example, I will show that Paganini designed his music not only to showcase his virtuosity but also as unabashed self-aggrandisement, modelling the egocentric assertions of sovereignty that he manifested economically and as a social being. Not only did he enact domination through social and musical means, he gave the impression that his virtuosity generated power from within—from some inner 'demonic' impulse.

---

[6] 'Quella superiorità di genio, destrezza o abilità che ci fa eccellere sia nella teoria che nella pratica delle belle arti.' Sebastien de Brossard, 'Virtù', *Dictionnaire de musique* (Paris: Ballard, 1703), [no page number], my translation.

[7] Ernest Newman, 'The Virtuous and the Virtuoso', *More Essays from the World of Music* (London: John Calder, 1958), 160–2. This essay, focusing on late nineteenth-century music history, contrasted virtue and virtuosity against the backdrop of both the Brahms–Wagner debate and Victorian codes of morality.

Self-Advancing Entrepreneurialism

Paganini's career outlines the classic rags to riches story. Born the son of a dock-worker in the port city of Genoa, he won his first professional appointment as a violinist at the court of Lucca at age eighteen. He quickly progressed to soloist status, leaving behind his older brother Carlo, who had also joined the court orchestra, and gave numerous lucrative concerts while officially engaged to the court. The next two decades saw Paganini travelling throughout the Italian states as a freelance concert violinist using business skills that he may have inherited from his business-minded father (as De Courcy suggests).[8] By the time of his European tours (1828–34), his average annual income soared to more than 300 kg of gold.

The kind of lucrative career Paganini had as a touring virtuoso simply would not have been possible until after the French Revolution, which, to put it briefly, changed the role of the musician in society.[9] (By comparison, in the 1760s, the virtuoso violinist Antonio Lolli had been unable to give up his court position in order to tour full-time.) In the standard narrative of Western music history, Beethoven is the figurehead for the emergence of the financially and artistically autonomous musician emancipated from the constraints of the patronage system. What he achieved as a composer Paganini could be said to have achieved as a performer. A dozen years his junior, Paganini followed a similar trajectory—he abandoned the limitations of being a court musician and took advantage of the new socio-economic conditions that enabled capitalist entrepreneurialism.

As Paganini told George Harrys, 'in my early years I had much dissension with the court at Lucca, and for a piffling little salary had to suffer many a vexation. Then one day I suddenly decamped, living first in once place, then another, and falling into the company of gamblers where I often risked more than I possessed . . . . When I became my own master, I enjoyed life in rich, full draughts.'[10] Becoming his 'own master' meant controlling every detail of his concerts personally, including finding suitable venues, placing advertisements in the papers, printing and posting flyers, hiring the orchestra and rehearsing with

---

[8] 'To his Ligurian birth he undoubtedly owed his commercial instincts . . . Antonio had the astute business head of all Genoese' (De Courcy, *Paganini, the Genoese* I, 23–4). Within a few years Ole Bull, recognising himself as a 'brand', would begin to mass-produce his own busts and soaps embossed with his signature—which it never occurred to Paganini to do.

[9] For more on this topic, see William Weber, *Music and the Middle Class: The Social Structure of Concert Life in London, Paris and Vienna Between 1830 and 1848* (London: Ashgate, 2003).

[10] De Courcy, *Paganini, the Genoese* I, 119–20.

them (usually on the day of the concert, if at all), providing the supporting artists and the orchestral parts, setting ticket prices (by finding out how much audiences were accustomed to paying, then doubling and tripling the amount), and staffing the box office. Sometimes he even sold tickets himself in disguise right up to the time of the performance, at which point he would lock the doors and walk out onto stage with his violin, and go back to the box office at intermission to sell yet more tickets (at a discount). Of the gross receipts, Paganini typically took about two-thirds. He hired managers to administer his affairs. As William Weber has noted, Paganini and Liszt were the first virtuosi to employ managers, unlike their predecessors even up to the 1800s–1820s, including Spohr and Hummel, who managed themselves.[11]

Paganini benefitted from living at a time when concert culture was burgeoning; as William Weber has shown, there was a 'rapid explosion in [the] number and significance' of concerts in London, Paris, and Vienna in the period 1813–48, especially in the 1830s and 1840s.[12] The overall pattern was the emergence of an upper-middle class, who joined aristocrats as the new 'high-status' public.[13] He exploited the novel patterns of bourgeois consumption enabled by the virtuoso public concert, and became a 'brand', helping to sell everything from violin lessons to cakes and sheet music by hack musicians: in Parisian patisseries, cakes 'à la Paganini' were in vogue; in Vienna, the 5-florin note (the cost of admission) became known as the 'Paganini-note'; and a giraffe sent as a gift by the Pasha of Egypt that had been all the rage until Paganini's arrival was promptly forgotten.[14]

Paganini kept meticulous accounts of his finances, recording various calculations, profit margins, and detailed travel and accommodation expenses in his letters to Germi and in the so-called 'Secret Red Book'.[15] The latter document

[11] William Weber, 'The Musician as Entrepreneur and Opportunist, 1700–1914' in Weber, ed., *The Musician as Entrepreneur, 1700–1914: Managers, Charlatans, and Idealists* (Bloomington: Indiana University Press, 2004), 18, and 'From the Self-Managing Musician to the Independent Concert Agent' in the same volume, 108. As Weber further notes, Paganini's managers (Laporte, Pettet, Freeman, Watson and Pacini) 'tended to push the musician too hard, setting up more concert engagements than his health could tolerate'. Disagreements broke out over dividing profits and non-payment as the roles were not yet defined or codified (111–12).

[12] Weber, *Music and the Middle Class*, 3, 16.

[13] Ibid., 29, see also 36–40.

[14] See De Courcy, *Paganini, the Genoese* I, 271, Alice Hanson, *Musical Life in Biedermeier Vienna* (London: Cambridge, 1985), 183, and Pulver, *Paganini: The Romantic Virtuoso*, 142–4.

[15] The 'Secret Red Book', now kept in the Gertrude Clarke Whittall Foundation Collection, Library of Congress, Music Division (no call number), has never been published.

contained page upon page of calculations; the fact that Paganini kept this notebook hidden—there is no 'secret' to his technique, it is rather a document of obsessive record-keeping—attests to the intensity and private ambition Paganini brought to maximising his generation of income. He tried to keep secret his avarice, the selfish motivation to move 'from city to city collecting fees'—like prima donnas Pasta and Malibran, 'without contributing to society around them'.[16] But unlike them (and Liszt), he was rarely moved to perform altruistic acts of charity (which created a mythology of divas as angelic humanitarians, as Poriss has shown) and alongside these women he appeared all the more demonic.

From the subsequent publication of such details in various secondary sources we know, for instance, that in Vienna receipts from his first eight concerts totalled nearly 22,000 florins, roughly equal to Schubert's lifetime earnings.[17] In Berlin, he made nearly 11,000 thalers over three months; compare this with the 4 or 5 thalers a typical orchestral musician earned per concert in that city.[18] (As a point of reference, the most lavish two-room suite at the best hotel in Breslau cost 1 thaler per night.[19]) In Paris, between 9 March and 24 April 1831, he made a total of more than 120,000 francs, whereas Paganini's first job at Lucca paid a mere 1,146 francs per annum in the period 1801–03.[20] The concert of 20 March 1831 alone brought in nearly 22,000 francs; by comparison, the highest-earning concert of Baillot's quartet series on 7 May of the same year netted just over a tenth of that amount (2,300 francs).[21] In London between May and July of the same year, Paganini received over £10,200 from his concerts, while the diva Giuditta Pasta received £3,500 for the entire season.[22] According to a report by Paganini's London manager (held in the Library of Congress), his gross nightly income peaked at £1,463/9 on 22 June.[23] In provincial English towns such as Brighton, his fee was usually £200 per concert; general admission at such venues typically cost ten shillings.[24] In Scotland in 1831, he played eight concerts in one week and

[16] Hilary Poriss, 'Prima Donnas and the Performance of Altruism', Rachel Cowgill and Hilary Poriss, eds, *The Arts of the Prima Donna in the Long Nineteenth Century* (Oxford: Oxford University Press, 2012), 42–60.

[17] De Courcy, *Paganini, the Genoese* I, 276 and Newman Flower, *Franz Schubert: The Man and His Circle* (London: Cassell, 1928), 155.

[18] De Courcy, *Paganini, the Genoese* I, 314 and 328–9.

[19] *Ibid.*, I, 345.

[20] *Ibid.*, I, 96 and II, 21.

[21] *Ibid.*, II, 21 and Joël-Marie Fauquet, *Les Sociétés de musique de chambre à Paris de la Restauration à 1870* (Paris: Aux Amateurs de Livres, 1986), 75.

[22] *Ibid.*, II, 44 and 66 n.37.

[23] Harold Spivacke, 'Paganiniana', *The Library of Congress Quarterly Journal of Current Acquisitions* Vol. 2, No. 2 (February 1945), 58.

[24] *Ibid.*, II, 83 and 90.

made £450; by comparison £400 was considered 'a comfortable annual salary for a gentleman'.[25]

Paganini's earning power was immense, setting a precedent for Liszt and Herz, also instrumentalists who 'built substantial fortunes'.[26] While on tour, he made large deposits at Heath Furse Co. in London and Arnstein & Eskeles in Vienna. He acquired precious instruments: seven Stradivaris, two Guarneri del Gesùs (including the famous Il Cannone), and two Amatis, as well as violas, cellos, and mandolins. He provided for his immediate and extended family, bought expensive jewellery for his paramours, and showered his son with expensive presents. He also squandered away a considerable sum gambling and in the disastrous business venture that was the Casino Paganini in Turin.

His strategy of maximising profits by inflating ticket prices to an unprecedented degree came under attack numerous times during his tours. In London, for instance, he caused an uproar by raising the cost of admittance to the pit at the King's Theatre from 8s 6 to a whole guinea (21 shillings), leading the music journals of 1831 to print page upon page of vitriol. Mary Shelley, who sought to buy tickets but found them prohibitively expensive, wrote in May to her friend John Howard Payne, who knew the manager of the King's Theatre (Pierre François Laporte), to obtain a discount for her:

> My dear Payne
>
> Is it in your power to do me a pleasure? If it is I am sure you will—and it will be a very great one to me if you can—I am an enthusiastic admirer of Paganini—& wish excessively to go to hear him but the tariffe they put on the boxes renders this impossible—This tariffe is arbitrary, because not half the boxes are filled—& still fewer at the stated price. Could you through your acquaintance with Laporte arrange that I should have a box at a moderate price—such as I have given at the beginning of the opera season—a good box on the pit tier or the ground tier or the one above it—not higher—on taking three tickets at half a guinea each—if you can manage this I can't tell you how obliged I should be to you—let me know speedily yes or no—. . .[27]

From this letter it is clear that Shelley considered half a guinea to be a reasonable price for a box ticket, an expectation founded on personal experience of attending the opera earlier that season. As William Weber's research has uncovered, 21s was

[25] Macdonald, 'Paganini in Scotland', 214.
[26] Weber, 'The Musician as Entrepreneur and Opportunist', 14.
[27] Quoted in Bennett, ed., *The Letters of Mary Wollstonecraft Shelley* II, 136.

the highest price charged for a concert ticket in London, the top end of the 'upper expense bracket' of all concert prices there in the 1830s and 1840s.[28]

As Simon McVeigh has observed, Paganini 'simply rewrote the rules as far as individual promotion was concerned. Paganini milked the market for all it was worth, with endless repeat performances, extensions in to the City [sic] and provincial tours'.[29] The fact that London reporters thought that what Paganini did amounted to robbery is well known and evidenced by the following commentary of 1839, which is also unsympathetic to reports that Paganini had by then lost his voice:

> Englishmen always make a great fuss [over] two sorts of people, those who rob them and those who humbug them, and as Paganini the fiddler continued to do both, the English will always make a fuss about him, and paragraphs respecting him in the English papers will always be acceptable ... The last intimation we have of him is, that he has lost his voice, though we had never yet received any official account of his having ever had any. So as he does not lose the use of his fingers to play upon his own fiddle and our pockets, it is very likely that his loss will not greatly signify.[30]

His seemingly insatiable hunger for wealth and personal glory was seen as a kind of vampiric blood thirst. Perhaps the harshest critique of Paganini capitalising on his virtuosity came from Heine: 'is that a man brought into the arena at the moment of death, like a dying gladiator, to delight the public with his convulsions? Or is it one risen from the dead, a vampire with a violin, who, if not the blood out of our hearts, at any rate sucks the gold out of our pockets?'[31] This critique anticipated Marxist discourse, which figured capital as vampiric.[32]

---

[28] See Table 5 in Weber, *Music and the Middle Class*, 160.

[29] Simon McVeigh, '"An Audience for High-Class Music": Concert Promoters and Entrepreneurs in Late–19th Century London' in Weber, *The Musician as Entrepreneur*, 173.

[30] Anon., 'Paganini's Voice', *Figaro in London* 392 (10 June 1839), 170.

[31] Quoted in Steblin, 'Death as Fiddler', 282. With Gothic imagery, Heine called into question the aesthetic value of a virtuoso who 'fiddle(s) millions of money' (Ellis, ed., *The Prose Writings of Heinrich Heine*, 201). Heine located the beginning of the cult of the public star in the propagation of urban virtuosity—a phenomenon of the industrialisation of music, as Corinna Caduff has shown in 'Heinrich Heine', 101.

[32] As Marx later wrote in *Das Kapital*, 'Capital is dead labour which, vampire-like, lives only by sucking living labour, and lives the more, the more labour it sucks.' Karl Marx, *Das Kapital* (Volume I, published 1867) quoted in, among other sources, Terrell Carver, *The Postmodern Marx* (University Park: Penn State Press, 1999), 14. See also Mark Neocleous, 'The Political Economy of the Dead Marx's Vampires', *History of Political Thought* Vol. 24 No. 4 (2003), 668–84.

Heine's perspective on Paganini was typical of his outlook as a music critic and social commentator trained in the Hegelian tradition. Briefly put, in his view, art history tended to move away from material objects (such as buildings, sculptures, and paintings) towards the intangible, the spiritual—i.e. music, the most extreme example being late Beethoven.[33] For Heine, Paganini's music fell short of the art form's spiritual potential by a wide margin. Moreover, his opinion that the violinist's business-mindedness compromised his musical aims paralleled his condemnation of fellow critic Ludwig Börne for 'sacrific[ing] his artistic conscience to his political loyalties'.[34] In *The Town of Lucca* (1831), Heine wrote 'the Catholic priest behaves rather like a salesman employed in a large business'.[35] Any instance of commercial or economic interests trumping or displacing higher interests met with Heine's staunch disapproval. This can be seen as part of Heine's overall 'disillusionment with the middle-class society that flourished under the July Monarchy' after his initial 'excitement over the revolution of July 1830 in France', as Ritchie Robertson has observed.[36]

Heine was certainly not alone in accusing Paganini of robbing the citizens of the cities and towns where he toured, some of whom reportedly skipped meals in order to buy tickets. The satirical writer Serafino Siepi (1776–1829) wrote, after Paganini visited his hometown of Perugia and gave a concert at the Teatro del Verzaro (on 1 July 1827): 'It is said that some poor workmen did not have dinner that evening to hear Paganini, imitating the great Napoleon, who starved the monks, and meanwhile assigned a pension of 36,000 francs to the famous singer Crescentini'.[37] Zelter wrote to Goethe on Good Friday, 1829, that Paganini 'with his cursed violin concertos, maddens men and women, and he will take 10,000 thalers from Berlin, as if [they were] losing them all over again to the Pharaoh'.[38] Also recall in this context the caption underneath the Berlin lithograph mentioned in Chapter 3: 'How the Berliners lost two thalers by force' (p. 72). Like the 'mesmerist charlatan, his pocket bulging with money' or the numerous 'mountebanks with their universal remedies and weird concoction, magicians who professed to

[33] Robertson, *Heine*, 4–5.
[34] *Ibid.*, 23.
[35] *Ibid.*, 88.
[36] *Ibid.*, 50.
[37] 'Diario comico', from *Efemeridi Comiche*, quoted in Biancamaria Brumana, *Teatro musicale e accademie a Perugia. Tra dominazione francese e Restaurazione* (Firenze, Olschki, 1996), 118–119. Yet Siepi also noted that Paganini charged nobles triple and cittadini double the price of admission for the others (119).
[38] Johann Wolfgang Goethe, *Sulla musica*, a cura di Giovanni Insom (Pordenone: Studio Tesi, 1992), 157.

call up spirits, and fortune tellers',[39] a virtuoso becoming rich by means of a spurious talent caused suspicion.

Attacks on Paganini were also implicit social critiques of the capitalist underpinnings of musical enterprise. As Eric Hobsbawm has written, the rise of capitalism saw the degeneration of the arts (with the exception of the novel, which concerned itself with the changing fortunes of the bourgeoisie), an argument framed within his Marxist view that the consumption of art is necessarily shaped by socio-economic trends.[40] Since there is no question that Paganini turned the newly emerging market structures to his advantage, the critiques are understandably focused on his motivations. Moreover, behind the critiques there lay deepseated suspicions of the dangerous extremes to which capitalism could lead the arts and, by extension, society. As Heine implied, commodification under false pretences amounted to robbery, and promoted self-interest rather than subsuming the artist to art for the betterment of society; one need hardly invoke Adorno to point out the logical end-result, a collapse of aesthetic worth under the weight of commercialism.

Heine's critique of Paganini's commercial success at the expense of artistic priorities provides a focal point for a latent factor in perceptions of his demonism. For centuries, performers in the Western European art music tradition had served their patrons, whether the aristocracy or the Church. In the aftermath of the French Revolution, with a turn to a man-centred worldview (the classic exposition of which M. H. Abrams gave in *The Mirror and the Lamp*), the artist himself could become his own self-serving institution.[41] Acquiring economic independence and with it a personal autonomy exalted the power of the individual artist, which, if left unchecked, could quickly escalate into a kind of God-complex, demonic greed, self-cultification.

As Weber has pointed out,

> The careers virtuosi launched during the period transformed not only the commercial aspect of concert life but also its class structure. In making concert life a commercial field of the modern kind, they eroded the traditional power of the aristocracy in musical life and forced it to accept the upper-middle class on a more equal basis. . . . Musicians no longer acted as employees or small-scale enterprises but rather as powerful independent

---

[39] Donald Walmsley, *Anton Mesmer* (London: Hale, 1967), 92 and Darnton, *Mesmerism and the End of the Enlightenment in France*, 52–3.

[40] Eric Hobsbawm, *The Age of Capital: 1848–1875* (London: Vintage, 1996).

[41] M.H. Abrams, *The Mirror and the Lamp: Romantic Theory and the Critical Tradition* (London: Oxford University Press, 1953).

entrepreneurs. Just like commerce and industry, their profession found new opportunities for actively controlling the market in which they worked.[42]

He gives the example of Paganini's refusal to play at private salons upon visiting Vienna in 1828, thereby forcing Viennese aristocrats to attend his public concerts along with everybody else (in contrast, Liszt and Thalberg did play at salons).[43] As Weber has also pointed out, Paganini and Liszt 'used concert tours to build personal capital . . . . The competitiveness essential to the virtuoso was "performative" in nature, intensifying the theatricality of virtuoso showmanship.'[44] Liszt's success as a virtuoso strategist was the result of reading and controlling his audiences—for example, by taking advantage of the popularity of Beethoven's music among affluent Parisians, as Dana Gooley has shown.[45] Paganini similarly capitalised on local tastes by composing variations on familiar melodies designed to ingratiate himself to the public (the Austrian national anthem, 'St Patrick's Day', 'God Save the King', etc.).

Paganini's entrepreneurialism differed from Liszt's in significant ways, however. Unlike the pianist, who exhibited a humanitarian streak, Paganini did not customarily give concerts for charity. With only a few exceptions, he hoarded all his earnings for his own personal benefit or that of those closest to him.[46] Paganini not only lacked Liszt's *caritas*, he also lacked his sensitivity to adjust his strategy according to time and place, sticking instead to the principle of maximising profits no matter what: he was undiscerning as to the social composition of his audiences, as long as they could line his pockets. Unlike Liszt, who adjusted his identity like a chameleon to appeal to various factions (as a Hungarian patriot,

---

[42] Weber, *Music and the Middle Class*, 36–7.

[43] *Ibid.*, 40.

[44] Weber, *The Great Transformation*, 141–2. Similarly, Weber has suggested elsewhere that since 'the most basic act of the opportunist was self-display—indeed, self-promotion . . . the virtuoso performer was intrinsically an opportunist' (Weber, 'The Musician as Entrepreneur and Opportunist', 5–6).

[45] In his for-profit chamber music concerts with Urhan and Batta in 1837 Paris, Liszt programmed Beethoven trios, 'capitalizing upon the recently developed cult of Beethoven to draw in a high-paying audience' (Dana Gooley 'Franz Liszt: The Virtuoso as Strategist', in Weber, *The Musician as Entrepreneur*, 145–6).

[46] In Paris, he raised 6,115 francs for orphanages, needy families, and the Department of Public Charities; he also played concerts for charity in Vienna, Dresden, Berlin, Warsaw, and Frankfurt. Although he did not always refuse to play in concerts to benefit the poor, contrary to newspaper reports, these were not high-profile concerts, and certainly Paganini does not appear to have been motivated by humanitarianism. Uncharacteristically, he gave Berlioz 20,000 francs believing him to be the one true successor to Beethoven, after attending a concert of his music in Paris and learning of Berlioz's financial struggles.

as a Napoleonic hero, etc.), Paganini seemed to hold himself apart from society, maybe even above it, even as it was changing everywhere around him.[47]

His wealth and lack of geographical rootedness brought him the freedom to be without ideology or rather to be a blank slate on which any political creed could be written. Consider in this regard the grab-bag of titles he amassed, titles he took pride in for the prestige they lent him without regard for the beliefs and social structures they represented: Knight (Cavaliere, Ritter) a title awarded by Pope Leo XII as part of the 'Order of the Golden Spur'; Chamber Virtuoso (to the Austrian Emperor); Baron and Commander of Westphalia.[48] He collected honours a Genoese boy growing up in the aftermath of the French Revolution could hardly have imagined, conferred by (respectively) the Vatican, the very Austrian Empire that was holding back Italian nationalism, and a Prussian province. This was cosmopolitanism of an undiscriminating kind, motivated by personal advancement at whatever cost, no matter how contradictory the 'glories' he attained were.

'Napoleonic' Conquests

Emptying coffers across Europe without a care for the havoc wreaked along the way, seemingly driven by nothing but individualistic impulse, Paganini's musical 'campaign' was seen to resemble Napoleon's military conquests. Both men exhibited the ruthless, uncompromising ambition to conquer unchartered terrains and wield sovereign power over them. By the time of the Congress of Vienna (1815), intended 'to prevent France from attempting to dominate Europe', a Napoleonic violinist had emerged who would go on to do just that.[49]

I have written elsewhere about the image of violinists as 'heroic' military generals commanding their troops using their bows like swords.[50] Here, I am interested in drawing attention to the demonic thirst for power that Paganini and Napoleon supposedly had in common. This was identified as a shared personality trait that found its expression in virtuoso conquest and military conquest respectively. Like the brilliant young general who went on to become a despotic emperor, the violinist exuded a power that propelled him across Europe and went to his head. Paganini 'had the gift of electrifying men ... like Napoléon' according to critic

---

[47] For more on the many faces of Liszt, see Gooley, *The Virtuoso Liszt.*

[48] The episode in 1832–33 when he supposedly bought himself the last of these titles is detailed in De Courcy, *Paganini, the Genoese* II, 116–33. Westphalia (Westfalen) was a province of the kingdom of Prussia at the time.

[49] Beales, *The Risorgimento and the Unification of Italy*, 41.

[50] Kawabata, 'Virtuoso Codes'.

Peter Lichtenthal, who saw the violinist perform in 1813.[51] Goethe had a similar response in 1831:

> The demonic is that which cannot be explained in a cerebral and a rational manner. It is not peculiar to my nature but I am subject to its spell. Napoléon possessed the quality to the highest degree. Amongst artists one encounters it more often with musicians than with painters. Paganini is imbued with it to a remarkable degree and it is through this that he produces such a great effect.[52]

Around the same time in Paris, two lines of scribbled verse appeared on one of the orchestral parts for Paganini's Concerto No. 2:

> Nature wanted in our century to display her infinite power;
> To astonish the world she created two men: Bonaparte and Paganini![53]

By the time of Fétis's monograph (1851), which was instrumental in promoting the violinist's legend for posterity, Paganini's name had been linked with Napoleon's (as well as Rossini's) as one the three most famous geniuses of the early nineteenth century (Beethoven is conspicuously absent).[54]

Here, too, a comparison with Liszt is apt. As Gooley has shown, Liszt tapped into the cult of Napoleon because his virtuosity formed 'a displaced image of heroic military valor'.[55] Gooley also states that, for Liszt, the 'Napoleonic' and 'diabolical' described different modes of performing, because they pulled audiences in opposite directions (towards worldliness and fantasy respectively).[56] Yet in Paganini's case the 'Napoleonic' and the 'demonic' stemmed from a common root, the thirst for power and the will to conquer.[57]

---

[51] In a review of Paganini's concert at Milan's La Scala (29 October 1813) for the *Leipziger Allgemeine Musikalische Zeitung*, quoted in De Courcy, *Paganini, the Genoese* I, 125–6.

[52] Goethe's comments of 2 March 1831 as reprinted in Johan Peter Eckermann, *Gespräche mit Goethe* (Leipzig: Brockhaus, 1925), 373–4, quoted in De Courcy, *Paganini, the Genoese* I, 361–2.

[53] Lecarpentier, a cellist at the Académie Royale de Musique, wrote this verse on one of the orchestral parts to Paganini's Second Concerto ca. 1831 (quoted in Penesco, 'Portrait', 202).

[54] See Fétis, *Notice Biographique sur Nicolo Paganini*.

[55] Gooley, *The Virtuoso Liszt*, 78.

[56] *Ibid.*, 116.

[57] Note also Joel-Marie Fauquet's description of Paganini as being 'satanic' like the French Revolution, adapting historian Joseph de Maistre's observation that 'the French revolution has a satanic character' because of the bloodshed and destruction it caused. Fauquet, 'Quand le diable', 49.

Soloistic Domination

The musical power Paganini wielded in performance took a number of different forms. First, he directed the orchestra assuming the function of the modern
orchestral conductor, giving cues and establishing tempos through physical gestures. As Fétis observed in 1834, Paganini took it upon himself 'to give the beat,
to stamp with his foot, to turn round to indicate the entry of the instruments'.[58]
That Paganini stamped his feet as he played, an aspect of his performance style
that is not well known, gives us an idea of his domineering physical presence on
the stage. At a concert in Trieste in 1824, Matteo Niccoló de Ghetaldi found it
distracting that 'while [Paganini] played he continuously struck time with his left
foot' (Ghetaldi).[59] For a German reviewer who saw Paganini in 1829, his stamping
and gestures contributed to an overall 'demonic' appearance:

> So with his frail appearance, strange bowing and great stamping of his right
> foot, with the cadaverous nature of his pale countenance, the southern glow
> of his eyes and the Italian liveliness of his gesticulations, so with the quietest
> Pianissimo of the orchestral accompaniment which, upon his signal, sud-
> denly becomes Fortissimo with drum and cymbals, so with the comical in
> the manner of overcoming of difficult passages the profound earnestness in
> the always calm facial features.[60]

Second, Paganini's playing could dominate the orchestra with sheer volume
of sound. When he played the variations on the Austrian national anthem in
Berlin in 1829, for example, the reviewer for the *Revue musicale* wrote: 'a remarkable occurrence, testifying to the prodigious power of Paganini's sound, is that,
while he played the theme, the orchestra deployed all its forces in a tutti, and

---

[58] Fétis is quoted in De Courcy, *Paganini, the Genoese* II, 154. Döpfner and Garms point
to foot stamping as evidence of a body-based, 'jazz'-like approach to performance, in
Erotik in der Musik, 78. Also it is possible that Lyser's drawing of Paganini hopping on
one foot was not just some fantastic portrayal of a spritely figure but also an exaggerated
one of his posture, standing on one leg while keeping time with the other.

[59] Quoted in Bruno Tonazzi, *Paganini a Trieste* (Trieste: Edizioni LINT, 1977), 44.

[60] 'So mit dem Hinfälligen in seiner Haltung die merkwürdige Bogenführung und
das gewaltige Stampfen seines rechten Fusses, so mit dem Leichenhaften des blas-
sen Antlitzes die südliche Glut des Auges und die italienische Lebhaftigkeit in den
Gestikulationen; so mit dem leisesten Pianissimo der Orchesterbegleitung auf seinem
Wink das plötzliche Eintreten des Fortissimo mit Trommel und Becken, so mit dem
Komischen in der Art der Überwindung schwieriger Passagen der tiefe Ernst in des
stets ruhigen Gesichtszügen.' *Leipziger Kometen* 41 (October 1829) quoted in Codignola,
Paganini intimo, 294 (my translation).

even then they were dominated by the single string of the solo violinist'.[61] He thus exemplified his contemporary Baillot's dictum that 'the violin must develop all its power; born to dominate, it reigns supreme in the concerto and speaks as the master'.[62]

Third, Paganini had the power to silence his audiences in an era when intent listening was not yet customary. As *The Examiner* reported of his English listeners from the early 1830s, 'the real magic is not the novelty of the feat, but the surprising beauty of the effect, an effect that hushed his audiences into an attention more profound than we ever witnessed in this usually gossiping theatre'.[63] Paganini's domination of the amassed orchestra thus seemed to extend beyond the stage into the auditorium.

Fourth, Paganini composed soloistic domination into the structure of his concertos. By this, I do not simply mean he designed them as virtuoso vehicles—that much is already well known—but, rather, that the soloist's role actively subjugates the orchestra and controls the musical narrative. The following analysis of excerpts from Paganini's Violin Concerto No. 1 in D major (1818) relies on methods developed by musicologists for interpreting concertos in terms of personas, plots, and relationships.[64]

From its very first notes the solo violin exhibits virtuosity as a given (Example 4.1). The melody of the opening *tutti* receives an elaborate, 'hyperactive' treatment—at the furthest imaginable remove from the bland original statement (Example 4.2). Then follows an array of dazzling techniques: runs of parallel

---

[61] *Revue musicale* (17 April 1829), 281.

[62] Baillot, *The Art of Violin*, 480.

[63] Quoted in Delfino, 'Niccolo Paganini e la critica musicale inglese', 555, n.d. (between 1831 and 1834). It is interesting to compare this to James Johnson's account of audiences being silenced in *Listening in Paris*.

[64] Narrative thinking also lies at the heart of concerto critiques. Edward Cone has observed that 'among sonata-related forms, the solo concerto especially cries out for dramatic interpretation, for it displays attitudes on the part of the protagonist and the orchestra that vary from mutual support to downright opposition' in *The Composer's Voice* (Berkeley and Los Angeles: University of California Press, 1974), 113–14. Joseph Kerman has interpreted numerous concertos as conversations, anthropomorphising the roles played by the orchestra/solo (e.g. 'master/servant' or 'mentor/acolyte'), and traced the way these roles change over time in what he calls 'relationship stories in *Concerto Conversations* (Cambridge, MA: Harvard University Press, 1999). Susan McClary has suggested that concertos contain 'plots' dramatising tensions between individual freedom and social harmony, in 'The Blasphemy of Talking Politics during Bach Year,' in Richard Leppert and Susan McClary, eds, *Music and Society: The Politics of Composition, Performance and Reception* (Cambridge: Cambridge University Press, 1987), 13–62, and 'A Musical Dialectic from the Enlightenment: Mozart's *Piano Concerto in G Major, K.453*, Movement 2', *Cultural Critique* (1986), 129–69.

Example 4.1 Paganini, Concerto No. 1, I, solo entry

thirds, diminished-seventh chords in rising inversions, left-hand pizzicato, and virtuoso bowings such as up-bow staccato and *jeté* (the 'flying' bow-stroke). This first entry already presents a full-fledged persona, confident and brash, unleashing a barrage of attention-grabbing effects.

The solo then proceeds to flout the rules of convention when it launches

Example 4.2 Paganini, Concerto No. 1, I, opening tutti

Example 4.3 Paganini, Concerto No. 1, I, 'cadenza' (bb. 231–234)

without warning into an impromptu cadenza, at a place in the musical form where none usually occurs (Example 4.3). With this cadenza, the solo abandons the metre established by the orchestra. It is utterly brazen, following its impulses with total disregard for any consequences or impact it may have on others. As the solo indulges in the melodramatic gestures of the cadenza, the orchestra is relegated to the role of providing a basic accompaniment. The violin controls the development of the musical 'plot', and holds the power to chart its own fate in its hands.

Further evidence of this 'narrative control' can be seen later on in the first movement, in the lead-up to an important structural juncture, the arrival of the tutti in the dominant (A major). Instead of resolving as the phrase structure suggests (at b. 197), the solo extends the phrase by a bar, thereby delaying not only the resolution, but also the orchestra's big entrance. By making them wait, the solo displays its power, which it then flaunts by turning the extra bar into an ostentatious display of virtuosity (Example 4.4). Breaking the cadential momentum with a brilliant left-hand pizzicato, then taking the trill up an octave via a daring leap of blind faith up the E string, the solo is clearly in charge—and knows it.

These examples illustrate the solo's musical sovereignty, seemingly oblivious to everything but itself, everything but the pursuit of its own virtuoso agenda. This precludes any possibility of dialogic engagement with the orchestra. Dialogue would open up the possibility of change, of negotiation, but it is doubtful that the solo even *hears* the orchestra—which seems to be there merely for support or amplification. In fact, Paganini told Schottky (responding to criticism that he had overused *musica turca* in the tuttis), 'I only use it to fill in the gaps between my solo passages so that I can get my breath'.[65]

The only interaction between solo and tutti to speak of is one-way—with the violinist commandeering the proceedings, bending the orchestra to his will. The solo violin persona remains unchanged throughout the concerto; its character does not develop at all. This is an immutable 'self' defined by a predominant trait—virtuosity—that is always already there. It is a finished product, merely confirmed in subsequent episodes ('here we have leaps . . . then we have left-hand pizzicato . . . then we have runs in thirds . . . then we have harmonics', and so on) in an additive narrative structure.

In contrast to the plot-driven narrative of a concerto such as Beethoven's Violin Concerto,[66] solo–tutti relations in Paganini's concerto lack interaction, argument, and collaboration. The solo bends to no one, refusing to be subordinated to the development of the motivic and tonal argument advanced by the orchestra. It is a *violinistic* drama with the orchestra merely providing a framework for the soloist rather than a *musical* drama in which the grappling between violin and orchestra generates the story. Virtuosity in Paganini's concertos is

---

[65]   De Courcy, *Paganini, the Genoese* I, 408–9.
[66]   The second chapter of my 'Drama and Heroism in the Romantic Violin Concerto' (PhD dissertation, UCLA, 2001) explains this in detail.

Example 4.4 Paganini, Concerto No. 1, I (bb. 195–203)

its *raison d'être* as opposed to being a dramatic device to heighten tension and advance a plot.[67]

The musical sovereignty outlined in the above analysis serves as a metaphor for the sovereignty of self. The philosopher Charles Taylor has posited a definition of modern identity extending from a Romantic notion of self: 'One is a self only among other selves. A self can never be described without reference to those who surround it'.[68] This refers to the familiar idea that individual selfhood is subject to negotiation with other 'selves', whether through mutual recognition and affirmation, or through working through challenging encounters that trigger deep transformative experiences, or through any of a range of interactions lying between those two extremes. A sovereign self arrogantly assumes distance from the forces of influence, believing his uniqueness to be entirely of his own making.

Bruno Moysan has noted that 'a characteristic of the relationship between modern subjectivity and romantic virtuosity is that of "solisme": a self-affirming position of the individual vis-à-vis the society around him.'[69] By the dramatization of technical prowess, the virtuoso places himself at the center, astonishes, and causes all eyes to converge upon him. Although he focuses on works of Liszt (e.g. *Réminiscences de Robert le Diable*) and Chopin (e.g. the *Ballade*, op. 23) and does not mention Paganini at all, we can see that the above example illustrates a similar notion of soloism.

Egoistic 'apartness' is key, I believe, to understanding Paganini as a virtuoso. He demanded admiration and worship as *object*, standing apart from ordinary people, framed like a picture. He seemed to have powers that came from 'somewhere else', a place inaccessible and invisible to other people, which suggested that taking the arduous steps to Parnassus could be circumvented. As he told Boucher de Perthes, he wanted to make the world believe that he was self-taught, self-made, and self-directed, that 'great ideas sprang spontaneously from the inner flame that animated him'.[70]

---

[67] The history of nineteenth-century concertos can be divided into 'virtuoso' (e.g. Wieniawski) and 'symphonic' (e.g. Brahms)—see, for instance, Robert Layton, ed., *A Guide to the Concerto* (Oxford and New York: Oxford University Press, 1996), which divides 'The Concerto after Beethoven' into precisely these two categories (131–76). This dividing line is not always strict, however; for example, as we saw earlier, Carl Dahlhaus observed that Liszt's Piano Concerto No. 1 achieved a synthesis of virtuosity and organicism (p. 21).

[68] He goes on to explain further: 'The full definition of someone's identity [. . .] usually involves [. . .] some reference to a defining community'. See Charles Taylor, *Sources of the Self: The Making of the Modern Identity* (Cambridge, MA: Harvard University Press, 1996), esp. 35–6.

[69] Bruno Moysan, 'Virtuosité pianistique', 52ff.

[70] Francesco Bennati, 'Notice psychologique sur Niccolò Paganini', *Revue de Paris* (May, 1831), quoted in De Courcy, *Paganini, the Genoese* I, 27 (her translation).

This unabashed self-centredness exemplified an extreme form of Romantic individualism and the typical iconoclasm of the artist on the fringes of society. Paganini certainly lived his life on his own terms: his indifference to social changes, his lack of interest in them, is particularly conspicuous considering that he lived in an era of tumult. Despite his youthful enthusiasm for Jacobin ideals and reputation as a Genoese radical, from around the age of thirty onwards he 'carefully abstained from politics and concentrated his attention on his music, with little or no interest in the calamities of his native land'.[71] The opportunity to involve himself in advancing the cause of Italian nationalism was wide open but not taken, even as others hailed him as a national hero.[72] He could have held concerts to raise money for cholera victims but instead chose to watch their suffering for entertainment. He refused to marry the mother of his child and paid her a flat settlement to relinquish maternal rights and future financial claims. He kept his compositions and techniques to himself, avoided teaching as much as he could, and lacked regular musical collaborators. In De Courcy's overwhelmingly positive biographical sketch, Paganini is noted for his 'fatal susceptibility to flattery, his egoism, coupled with natural avarice'.[73] Recall too that, ten years after being swept up by Paganini fever, even Liszt came to see self-serving virtuosity as ego-driven, writing of the violinist, 'his god was never any other than his own gloomy, sad "I"'.[74] Can the greed, lust, pride, and vainglory that manifested in multiple aspects of the virtuoso's life be viewed any longer as separate from the aesthetic of virtuoso performance?

---

[71] De Courcy, *Paganini, the Genoese* I, 128. British forces briefly occupied Lucca in 1813–14; Carbonari patriots led revolutionary outbreaks in Naples, Sicily, and Piedmont in 1820–21 and again in 1831–32 following the July revolution in France. Paganini seemed to take no notice.

[72] For example, Mazzini praised the City of Genoa's commission of a bust honouring Paganini in 1835. A critic for *Il caffè di Petronio* (no. 4, January 1825) wrote: 'One of the men who currently honors Italy is the renowned professor of violin Niccolò Paganini', quoted in Grisley, *Niccolò Paganini, epistolario*, 267 n.1. In contrast to Paganini, the tenor Mario Candia (Giulia Grisi's husband) and later Giuseppe Verdi helped to sustain the nationalist cause via their dealings with Mazzini.

[73] De Courcy, *Paganini, the Genoese* II, 251.

[74] *Gazette musicale* (23 August 1840), quoted in Alan Walker, *Franz Liszt*, Vol. 1: *The Virtuoso Years 1811–1847* (Ithaca, NY: Cornell University Press, 1987), 177.

CHAPTER 5

Paganini's Legacies

THIS chapter considers Paganini's legacies in the realms of violin performance and cultural history. It does not examine compositions drawing upon the theme from Caprice No. 24 (Brahms, Rachmaninov, Lutosławski, Milstein, Ichiyanagi, and so on). Rather, my aim is to assess the manifold ways in which his technical prowess on the one hand, and his Romantic notion of self on the other, have been subjected to interpretation, reinterpretation, and misinterpretation.

The association of Paganini's name with the 'soulless' pursuit of technique divorced from musical expression came about through the development of instrumental virtuosity in the generations after his death, but it was based on only a partial and skewed understanding of Paganini's achievements as a virtuoso. His name was invoked as synonymous with 'demonic' technical prowess across Europe from about 1830 on, and with growing momentum in the decades after his death in 1840 as legion imitators emerged on the violin and other instruments, of whom Liszt was only the most famous. The proliferation of violin virtuosi in the nineteenth century—a roster of such familiar names as Antonio Bazzini, Heinrich Ernst, Pablo de Sarasate, Camillo Sivori, Henri Vieuxtemps, Henryk Wieniawski, and Eugene Ysaÿe—also included lesser-known ones.

Isaac Collins (1797–1871), the self-styled 'English Paganini', specialised in performing with the bow held between his knees and rubbing the violin against it using both hands (Figure 5.1). He promoted his son Viotti Collins (1822–99) as 'the Infant Paganini'.[1] The prodigy Apollinaire de Kontski (1825–79) was known as 'le Petit Paganini' (a nickname that Mazzini, for instance, considered well-deserved).[2] Ole Bull (1810–80) was known as 'the Norwegian Paganini' or 'the Nordic Paganini'. Sophie Humler (1842–?) was praised as a 'female Paganini'.[3] Sarasate (1844–1908) was named the 'Spanish Paganini' by the Queen of Spain.[4]

---

[1] *The Morning Chronicle* (9 July 1832).

[2] Penesco, 'Violon', 204 and Marco Battaglia, 'Mosaico Ottocentesco. Mazzini e Paganini tra musica, filosofia, lettere, memorie e due storiche chitarre', in Moretti *et al.*, eds, *Paganini divo e comunicatore*, 211.

[3] Anon., 'A Female Violinist—(From Punch)', *Musical World* Vol. 36 No. 32 (7 August 1858), 509.

[4] Anon., 'Musical Gossip', *Literary Gazette* Vol. 5 No. 126 (24 November 1860), 447.

Aug.¹ 1831, London, Published for the Proprietors, by G.S.Tregear. N.º 123, Cheapside.

Figure 5.1 'Mr. Collins, the English Paganini', anonymous illustration, from the Gertrude Clarke Whittall Foundation Collection, Library of Congress, Music Division.

The appellation 'the Eighteenth-century Paganini' was invented with historical hindsight to refer to Arcangelo Corelli and Johann Walther.[5] Joseph Joachim (1822–82) was 'the Modern Paganini', as was August Wilhelmj (1845–1908), who was also proclaimed 'the German Paganini' by Henriette Sontag in 1854 and

[5]   See Anne Penesco, 'Le Violon en France au Temps de Baillot et de Paganini', *La Musique en France à l'époque romantique: 1830–1870* No. 25 (1991), 204.

'the future Paganini!' by Liszt in 1861.[6] More recently, Vassil (Vasko) Abadgiev (1928–78) came to be known as the 'Bulgarian Paganini' for his virtuosity and the caprices he composed in the style of Paganini, one of which has been called the '25th'.[7]

The title 'the Second Paganini' was conferred on several candidates: Josef Slavík (1806–33) earned it after composing a supposedly unplayable Concerto in F♯ minor and, according to legend, teaching himself to play Paganini's *La Campanella* after a single hearing.[8] Izydor Lotto (1840–1927) of Warsaw, who won the Paris Conservatoire's *Premier Prix* (1855) and wrote his own cadenza to one or more of Paganini's concertos, was hailed as 'a Second Paganini' by the *Athenaeum*'s Leipzig correspondent.[9] Charles Vondra (?1868–?) was expected at the age of eleven in Bucharest on the basis of 'the greatest ease in overcoming difficulties . . . [to] become, in five or six years, a second Paganini'.[10]

The association of Paganini's name with technical skill for its own sake was further reinforced by the characterisation of certain violinists as being 'of the Paganini school', a designation that falsely implied the existence of a codified system. The playing style of Camillo Sivori (1815–94), Paganini's sole violin pupil, resembled his teacher's in that, among other things, he slid around the fingerboard.[11] Sivori described Paganini as 'probably the worst teacher of the violin who ever lived', since all he would do was watch his pupil struggle with difficulties then show off his own superior technique.[12] Sivori went on to have a brilliant virtuoso career performing Paganini's *Carnival of Venice* and other works, including a *Fantasia* he composed on themes from *Norma* in the manner of Paganini. According to *La France musicale*, Antonio Bazzini (1818–97) owed to 'l'école fantastique de Paganini' his 'admirable clarity in harmonics and purity of attacks'.[13]

[6]   H. Morgan-Browne, 'An Approximation to the Truth about August Wilhelmj', *Music & Letters* Vol. 3 (1922), 220. Liszt's letter to Ferdinand David is quoted in E. Heron-Allen and Lynda Macgregor, 'Wilhelmj, August', in Stanley Sadie, ed., *The New Grove Dictionary of Music and Musicians*, 2nd ed. (London: Macmillan, 2001), vol. 27, 386. Caricatures by Charles Lyall of Joachim and Wilhelmj appeared alongside each other in the *Musical World* (6 January 1877), Vol. 55 No. 1, 14–15.

[7]   Bozhanka Mocinova, 'Compositori bulgari ispirati a Paganini', in Moretti *et al.*, eds, *Paganini divo e comunicatore*, 517–26.

[8]   Unpublished pamphlet from the Dvořák Museum, Prague, by Ljuba Medkova-Strakova.

[9]   Anon., 'A Second Paganini', *Musical World* Vol. 40 No. 21 (25 May 1861), 334.

[10] Anon., 'A New Prodigy', *Musical Standard* Vol. 16 No. 765 (29 March 1879), 195.

[11] Ernst was also noted for sliding back and forth on the fingerboard, while Vieuxtemps avoided it. Michael Mann, ed., 'Kommentar', in *Zeitungsberichte über Musik und Malerei*, 336.

[12] Quoted in De Courcy, *Paganini, the Genoese* I, 219.

[13] Escudier in *La France musicale* (28 March 1852), quoted in Claudio Sartori, *L'avventura del violino*, 61.

Kontski was known as 'the celebrated protegé of Paganini'[14] on the basis of having received a few lessons from him in 1837.[15] And because other violin virtuosi such as Arthur Saint-Léon (1821–70) and Agostino Robbio (1840–?) claimed to have studied with Paganini despite there being no evidence that they ever did, the illusion that a 'Paganini School' existed was maintained.[16]

Nineteenth-century virtuosi on instruments other than the violin came to be known as 'the Paganini' of their instruments. Adrien-François Servais (1807–66) was 'the Paganini of the Cello'; Ernesto Cavallini (1807–73) was 'the Paganini of the Clarinet'; Franz Liszt (1811–86) was 'the Paganini of the Piano'; Giovanni Bottesini (1821–89) was 'the Paganini of the Double Bass'; Jules Demersseman (1833–66) was 'the Paganini of the Flute'; Antonino Pasculli (1842–1924) was 'the Paganini of the Oboe'; Ermenegildo Danovaro (1889–1950) was 'the Paganini of the Mandolin', and so on.[17] The common denominator among these instrumental performers linked with Paganini's name was an emphasis on extreme technical facility. Not all of them assumed a 'demonic' persona, of course, but some did actively adopt one or else had it thrust upon them.

The best-known example is Liszt, whose Mephistophelean piano works (Piano Concerto No. 1, *Mephisto Waltz*, etc.) and fast, aggressive keyboard technique most closely resembled Paganini's demonicism. From the viewpoint of Clara Schumann, Liszt's virtuosity comprised a 'demoniac force' (as she wrote in her diary in 1872), causing an unhealthy devotion similar to Wagner-mania and thereby positioning him firmly on one side of the Brahms–Wagner debate (and herself on the other).[18] In the words of Liszt biographer Alan Walker,

> Demonic, Mephistophelian, satanic: such words have often been used to describe Liszt's new style of keyboard diablerie. The emotional impact of his

[14]   Anon., 'M. de Kontski's concert', *Mirror Monthly Magazine* Vol. 6 No. 1348 (August 1849), 130–1, quote from 130.

[15]   According to Anon., 'Chronological Biography of Ernesto Camillo Sivori', *Violin Times* Vol. 1 No. 5 (March 1894), 67–70, 69.

[16]   Agostino Robbio 'called himself a pupil of Paganini' when he visited Japan in 1863, becoming the first European violin virtuoso to travel there according to Margaret Mehl, 'Japan's Early Twentieth-Century Violin Boom', *Nineteenth-Century Music Review* Vol. 7 No. 1 (2010), 26.

[17]   Penesco, 'Violon', 204, H. G. Farmer, 'Military Music and its Story', *Musical Standard* Vol. 36 No. 934 (25 November 1911), 342, and Giorgio De Martino, *Giuseppe Gaccetta e il segreto di Paganini: la biografia del violinista anche scelse di non essere il più grande* (Genoa: De Ferrari, 2001), 20. Roberto Grisley also notes that the 'Paganini of . . .' eponym indicated excellence on another instrument or on the violin by players from other countries in *Niccolò Paganini, epistolario*, 461, n.2.

[18]   Quoted in Ernest Newman, 'The Virtuous and the Virtuoso', 162.

playing on the Parisians has been well documented. Storm and stress had entered the concert hall. The scene was sometimes like a séance in which some unknown spirit stirred and swept the audience with fear and ecstasy. Only Paganini had conjured up such a dark atmosphere before, and his influence on the history of virtuosity can never be eradicated.[19]

Moreover, Liszt's immersion in Romantic poetry and musical language, and his instrument being the epitome of individual musical 'heroism' for the nineteenth century (as the violin had been for the eighteenth), made him more convincingly the demonic virtuoso than Paganini had ever been. Indeed, without Liszt's fame and stature, and his outspoken indebtedness to Paganini's example, the violinist's own demonic image may never have become quite as legendary beyond his lifetime or the realm of violinists. Liszt certainly developed and extended the 'demonic' mode further than any post-Paganinian violinist, even those who cultivated a Gothic aura in one way or another.

Bazzini was dubbed 'le violiniste demon' by the *Revue et gazette musicale de Paris*;[20] his 'Paganinian' showpiece *La Ronde des lutins* (with its 'Gothic' title, an anachronistic choice by 1852), foregrounded flashy techniques such as left-hand pizzicato and the gimmick of playing $f_\sharp 2$ on each string in quick succession.[21] His ability to span three octaves on the fingerboard without shifting, placing his thumb on the G-string and his little finger on the E-string, recalled Paganini's left-hand flexibility.

A little-known work, *Valse diabolique*, op. 10, for violin and piano by Swiss violin virtuoso Louis Eller (1820–62), similarly took advantage of the diabolical association of Paganini's virtuosity. This salon piece, published several times but bearing no date (by Gustav Heinze in Leipzig, Guillaume Paul in Dresden and Richault in Paris—one in an edition by Wilhelmj) comprises a triple-metre theme in E minor marked *Presto* followed by a series of variations incorporating bariolage, left-hand pizzicato, *moto perpetuo*, double and triple stops, octaves, trills, double trills, harmonics, and so on. The most idiomatically Paganinian touch comes at the end with a diminished seventh chord ($A_\sharp$–$C_\sharp$–E–G) in rising inversions spread across all four strings as per Paganini's Caprice No. 1.[22] (Quadruple-

---

[19]   Alan Walker, *Franz Liszt*, Vol. 1: *The Virtuoso Years 1811–1847*, 175.

[20]   Henri Blanchard, 'Antonio Bazzini', *Revue et gazette musicale de Paris* Vol. 20 No. 17 (24 April 1853), 152.

[21]   Clara Schumann also composed a piece with that title.

[22]   Eller composed several other works in a Paganinian mould, including not only show pieces containing the expected virtuoso techniques but also an Adagio and Rondo, op. 17, very similar to *La campanella* in key, metre, and character. For more on Eller, see Anon., *Zur Erinnerung an Louis Eller* (Dresden: Rudolf Kuntze, 1864);

stopped diminished chords in rising inversions were exactly what Liszt wrote out as characteristic of Paganini's playing in a letter he sent to a pupil after hearing the violinist play in 1832.[23])

The Frenchman Arthur Saint-Léon (1821–70) was a dual virtuoso in that he performed as a violinist and as a ballet dancer. In the 1849 ballet *Le Violon du Diable*, he played the role of a man who uses 'a magic instrument given him by a sinister doctor [to win] the affections of a beautiful girl of noble birth', then loses the violin because he 'refuses to barter his soul for it' (Figure 5.2).[24] Saint-Léon's performance, in which 'he use[d] his fingers with as much agility, aplomb, and brio, as his legs', according to a reviewer, drew exaggerated attention to the technical, dexterous, and athletic aspects of virtuosity.[25] Later in the nineteenth century, Frenchman Alexandre Ropicquer impersonated Paganini's typical postures and gestures; another (anonymous) violinist specialised in performing the *Caprices* in a darkened hall under an 'oxyhydrique' spotlight.[26]

Bazzini, Eller, Saint-Léon, Ropicquer, and the unnamed violinist adopted a 'demonic' image to be linked with Paganini, piggy-backing on his legend; they were its beneficiaries, while at the same time helping to sustain it and escalate it further. By comparison, Sivori, the only violinist to have a direct link to Paganini, did not cultivate a 'demonic' aura. None of his compositions contained references to diabolism in their titles, and his reviewers generally avoided devilish themes— an exception being the following undated commentary from the London periodical *The Globe*: 'it is said of Sivori and his master, that they never feel the full inspiration of play till they see devils' tails come out at the S holes [*sic*] of the fiddle. He is either in the infernal regions or in paradise.'[27]

In addition, the phenomenon of the 'Paganini Redivivus'—Paganini come

Baker's Biographical Dictionary of Musicians, rev. Nicolas Slonimsky, 7th ed. (New York: Schirmer Books, 1984), 657; and Andrea Harrandt, 'Eller, Louis', in Rudolf Flotzinger, ed., *Oesterreichisches Musiklexicon* (Vienna: Österreichischen Akademie der Wissenschaften, 2002) I, 380.

[23] Walker, *Franz Liszt* I, 174.

[24] He is ultimately saved by a saintly monk who magically appears with another violin that transports him to an Edenic paradise where he is united with his beloved angel . . . and together they dance *Les Fleurs animées*. Ivor Guest, *Fanny Cerrito: the Life of a Romantic Ballerina*, 2nd ed. (London: Chameleon, 1974), 129.

[25] 'P.S.', 'Théâtre de la Nation (Opéra), *Le Violon du Diable*', *Revue et gazette musicale de Paris* Vol. 16 No. 3 (21 January 1849), 18–19. Saint-Léon's inclination to gimmickry is also evident in his own compositions such as 'Dodo', a *berceuse burlesque* (1854), and 'L'Express Train' (1853–54), in which he mimicked the sounds of an express-train.

[26] For more about the French violinists, see Penesco, 'Portrait', 19–32.

[27] Quoted in Luigi Inzaghi, *Camillo Sivori: carteggi del grande violinista e compositore allievo di Paganini* (Varese: Zecchini, 2004), 206.

Figure 5.2 Arthur Saint-Léon in *Le Violon du Diable* (1849), lithograph from a drawing by Janet Lange, Bibliothèque de l'Opéra, Paris, reproduced in Ivor Guest, *Fanny Cerrito: the Life of a Romantic Ballerina*, 2nd ed. (London: Chameleon, 1974), Illustration xxa, opposite p. 145.

back to life—may also be said to have contributed to the legend of the 'demonic' virtuoso living on beyond the span of his natural life. No other violinist in history has had 'Redivivus' suffixed to his name, nor had so many aspirants to the title. Sivori, Wilhelmj, Jan Kubelík (1880–1940), Willy Burmester (1869–1933), and Juan Manén (1883–1971) all earned the title during their careers as violin virtuosi.[28] Apart from Sivori, these were violinists active only late in the nineteenth century at the earliest and the label came from critics who could not have seen or heard Paganini himself. That did not stop them from making direct comparisons, however. Following Burmester's 'Paganini-Abend' in October 1894 in Berlin at which he performed the First Concerto, a variation-set, *Le Streghe*, and a few *Caprices* (three or five, depending on the source), the *Lokal-Anzeiger* declared, 'Paganini himself might have played something like that'.[29] (One of the *Caprices* he played was No. 11 in C major, which he had supposedly practised a record 4,276 times.[30]) In the case of Manén, outdoing Sarasate was enough to merit the title a 'Second Paganini': 'he has inherited from Sarasate his sweetness of tone, the elegance of his bowing, his noble style of interpretation, but he surpasses him as regards technique: in this respect all the critics have unanimously proclaimed him a "Paganini Redivivus"'.[31] Interestingly, with the exception of Sivori, none of these 'revived Paganinis' was Italian. (The fate of virtuosity among Italian violinists after Paganini is dealt with in the next chapter.)

One more 'Paganini Redivivus' needs to be mentioned, although, since his identity was shrouded in mystery and deliberately withheld, we do not know who he was. This violinist, who performed mostly in the United Kingdom during the 1860s and 1870s and also toured to France, Germany, Belgium, and Italy around that time, billed himself as the 'Paganini Redivivus'. According to reviews of concerts he gave in Belfast, Carlisle, London, and elsewhere, his repertory extended beyond Paganini's *Carnival of Venice* to a random assortment of works, including one by Mendelssohn (the title is not given), a Bach fugue, Beethoven's *Kreutzer Sonata*, a version of *William Tell* played on one string, and a *Fantasia on Scotch Airs*. However, he was best known to London audiences for his performances

---

[28] P. R., 'Current Notes', *Lute* No. 150 (June 1895), 417; W. Meredith Morris (Rev.), 'My Impression of Kubelík', *Violin Times* Vol. 11 No. 122 (January 1904), 13; Anon., Untitled item, *Musical World* Vol. 18 No. 12 (23 March 1843), 107; Anon., 'Joan [*sic*] Manen, Violinist', *Musical Standard* Vol. 37 No. 957 (4 May 1912), 20.

[29] 'Paganini selbst mag sie so ähnlich gespielt haben.' *Lokal-Anzeiger* (2 November 1894), quoted in Joachim W. Hartnack, *Grosse Geiger unserer Zeit* (Zurich: Atlantis, 1993), 45. Burmester played three Caprices according to Harnack, five according to Farga, *Paganini*, 189.

[30] Farga, *Paganini*, 189.

[31] Anon., 'Joan [*sic*] Manen, Violinist', 20.

at the Royal Polytechnic Institution, where 'he drew crowds daily and nightly by a weird and clever impersonation, entitled 'Paganini's Ghost', which he gave upwards of two hundred times in that establishment'.[32] He succeeded in maintaining his anonymity, even signing his name 'Paganini Redivivus' when he wrote letters to the *Musical World* in 1872. All that is known about him is that he was supposedly first heard at the Paris Conservatoire *Concours* in 1850.[33] The link with Paris suggests that he may have been the same violinist who impersonated Paganini along with Ropicquer there in the late nineteenth century.

Paganini's Misconstrued Legacy of Technique Fetishisation

Over the course of the nineteenth century and into the twentieth, instrumental virtuosity came to acquire a litany of pejorative connotations. Critiqued as superficial, vainglorious, and aesthetically bankrupt, many of Paganini's imitators fetishised technical display at the expense of artistic expression. As the *Musical Standard* put it in 1901, 'a new era of violin technique was born: an era of struggle and ambition in which every violinist sought to scale the heights unveiled by Paganini'.[34] They were seen as promoting sensationalism, gimmickry, and the 'stuntsman' mentality of performance art over the artistic imperatives of emotional expression and musical soulfulness.

While his imitators made technical display their *raison d'être*, it constituted only one aspect of Paganini's virtuosity, in conjunction with improvising, *cantabile* playing and composing his own music. Paganini could not have anticipated the one-dimensional imitations of him by aspiring violinists of his and subsequent generations, as in complaints regarding 'legions of violinists thrown into a state of spasmodic palsy for life by Paganini',[35] or Zelter holding Paganini responsible for 'ruining all our young orchestral violinists' (as he wrote to Goethe in 1829).[36] But Joseph Joachim noted that 'Paganini exercised a disastrous influence *through no fault of his own*'.[37] In Joachim's view, the tendency of 'ambitious young violinists to focus on technique while ignoring all other musical concerns ('purity and beauty of tone, intonation . . . material and essential matters [of music-making]'),

---

[32] Anon., 'Paganini Redivivus', *Musical Standard* Vol. 24 No. 973 (24 March 1883), 185.

[33] *Ibid.*

[34] Anon., 'Hints to violinists', *Musical Standard* Vol. 15 No. 3476 (16 March 1901), 163–4, quote from 163.

[35] Anon., 'Art. VII.–1. The Life of Mozart', *The Foreign Quarterly Review* Vol. 36 No. 72 (January 1846), 389.

[36] Zelter's letter of 5 May 1829 is quoted in De Courcy, *Paganini, the Genoese* I, 322.

[37] *Ibid.* I, 322; my italics.

meant that, 'what with Paganini was only the means to an end was for them an end in itself, and so became a monstrosity, a caricature'.[38] Joachim recognised that the skewed, slavish worship of technique in the name of being 'Paganinian' was a misnomer.

Nor could Paganini have anticipated the changes in the very meaning and value of virtuosity resulting from a historical shift around 1850 in the primary role of the soloist from composer–improviser to interpreter of a musical work (as we will see below). For Paganini, the purpose of composition had always been to serve the needs of performance; since the degree of success of a composition depended on its effectiveness as a virtuoso vehicle, he preferred to play his own music, tailor-made for bravura. An examination of his performance repertory reveals that in his early career (and in rare circumstances) he relied on concertos of Pleyel, Viotti, Kreutzer, and Rode, but that once he had composed enough concertos and virtuoso showpieces of his own to fill up his programmes, he quickly phased out nearly all trace of other composers. As he told his biographer Schottky around 1830:

> I've often sworn off playing compositions by others, and I've already destroyed all such music. But in Vienna they made me break my vow. For it is foreign to my nature to play the works of others, to perform borrowed material. Not that I can't play these works. Everybody knows quite well that I can play the most difficult music at sight, but I want to maintain my own individuality and none can blame me for this since it seems to satisfy the public.[39]

Performing his own music almost exclusively (as did most other virtuosi of the time) entailed another kind of musical sovereignty, allowing him to avoid having to subordinate himself to the wishes of another composer. When Paganini did play the works of others, he still strove to maintain his own individuality by embellishing them (concertos by Viotti, Kreutzer, and Rode), adding his own improvisations (imitations of barnyard animals, etc.), and sometimes even substituting entire movements (e.g. replacing the slow movement of a Rode concerto with his own *Adagio religioso*).[40] At a private soirée in 1829, Paganini supposedly

[38] Quoted in Istel, 'The Secret of Paganini's Technique', 115–16, from the introduction to Albert Bachmann, *Les Grands Violinistes du passé*, trans. Theodore Baker.
[39] Schottky, *Paganinis Leben und Treiben*, 278 quoted and translated by De Courcy, *Paganini, the Genoese* I, 266. What Paganini described as 'maintaining individuality' was sarcastically rephrased by Goethe as: 'there is no violinist who would not prefer to play his own melodies' (quoted on the same page of the same volume).
[40] See De Courcy, *Paganini, the Genoese* I, 266–7. Many years later, during a performance

played Beethoven's *Spring Sonata*, adding embellishments in demisemiquavers and hemidemisemiquavers in the slow movement and playing the theme of the finale 'in harmonics' and 'double-stopped octaves'.[41] Paganini commissioned music from composers only under exceptional circumstances, once because he reasoned that working with a Viennese composer would win him favour there, and on another occasion because he was simply too exhausted from travelling to compose himself a new viola concerto.[42]

For Paganini, a score served merely as a point of departure, subject to 'improvements' in the act of performance. While some critics objected to the 'complete disregard of the composer's intentions', others praised him, for example, for 'add[ing] a Scherzo to the Kreutzer Rondo which the work stands very well, even if the original composer never thought of it'.[43] A Viennese critic observed: 'to date we have only heard him play a work of Kreutzer's and one of Rode's but on both occasions the composer's individual style disappeared in the ingenious treatment of the executant, and the composition might easily have been taken for his own'.[44] Since the performance of works, whether his own or not, could include improvisations—in effect, recomposing the music in the moment—it is questionable to what degree there is meaning to drawing a sharp distinction between the acts of performing and composing when speaking of Paganini. As for his own concertos, Paganini was extremely protective of them (they were all published posthumously), preventing other violinists from treating them as he did their works.

As far as I know, no one else performed Paganini's concertos in public during his lifetime. Sivori stated that he only played the *Carnival of Venice* variations 'in public after Paganini's death'—presumably out of a sense of deference to its composer while he was still alive, a sensibility Ernst ostensibly did not share (he supposedly performed this work in London in 1837).[45] A 'Paganini canon' of works, those selected frequently for concert programmes, emerged through the publication in Paris in 1851 by Schott of opp. 6 to 14 (i.e. the Concertos Nos. 1 and

of Paganini's *La Campanella*, Sivori introduced a theme from a Spohr string quartet, claiming to have been taught this type of gambit by Paganini himself (quoted in De Courcy, *Paganini, the Genoese* I, 267 n. 24.)

[41] Wilhelm Speyer, a violinist, wrote about Paganini's 'whimsical' interpretation in a letter to his teacher Pierre Baillot. Quoted in *ibid.* I, 350–1.

[42] The resulting works were *La tempesta*, co-authored with Joseph Panny (1794–1838), and Berlioz's *Harold in Italy*.

[43] *Zeitung für die Elegante Welt* (1828), quoted in De Courcy, *Paganini, the Genoese* I, 267.

[44] *Theaterzeitung* (1828), quoted in *ibid.* I, 267.

[45] Quoted in Anon., 'Ernst v. Sivori', *Musical World* Vol. 18 No. 30 (27 July 1843), 251. The assertion that Ernst played *Carnival of Venice* is that of the anonymous author of the article (252).

2, *Le Streghe , God Save the King, Carnival of Venice, Moto perpetuo, Nel cor più non mi sento, I palpiti,* and the *Baracuba Variations*). Sivori recycled the same few Paganini works in his performances over and over again, often playing several in the course of the same programme. He maintained Paganini's practice of *scordatura* tuning for the First Concerto (a practice that had died out by the 1890s) and often performed *La campanella* as an excerpt.[46]

Notably absent from the list of 1851 publications were the Concerto No. 4 and the *Sonata militare*, as the reviewer from the *Musical World* noted and deplored.[47] An even more glaring omission from the performing repertory of Sivori and that of other virtuosi were the *Caprices*. Indeed, the *Caprices* appeared infrequently on public programmes, most likely because of the difficulty presenting them as stand-alone pieces, even as they were studied in private. Nos. 1, 14, 17, 18, 19, and 21 were listed under 'Junior Examinations—Fellows' in London's 'College of Violinists' in 1892.[48]

When Joseph Joachim gave a series of concerts in Vienna in 1880 with orchestra and sharing the bill with pianists and singers, he played a mixture of concertos (Bruch, Beethoven, Spohr) and smaller-scale works (Brahms, Joachim, Tartini). At one of these concerts, he performed a Paganini Caprice (we do not know which one); on the same evening, he also performed Spohr's *Gesangs-Szene*, Brahms's Concerto, Tartini's Sonata in G major, two Hungarian Dances by Brahms, and the *Romanze* from his own Hungarian Concerto. (The rest of this programme included an aria from Gluck's *Orpheus* and *Lieder* by Brahms, Reinecke, and Franz.) The inclusion of the Caprice on that lengthy list of works carries the whiff of a spice thrown in to an already abundant dish.[49] Jan Kubelík gave six concerts in Vienna between February and November of 1900, in the course of which he performed works by Mendelssohn, Brahms, Beethoven, Vieuxtemps, Wieniawski, and Saint-Saëns, along with Sarasate's Bach Prelude. In all but one concert he included at least one work of Paganini's (Violin Concerto No. 1, Variations on

[46] 'In modern times the Paganini concerto is mostly played in D ... Sivori ... always played it in E flat ... Lotto did the same, but he had two fiddles' according to Alert Payne, 'Paganini's Violin Concerto', *Violin Times* Vol. 4 No. 37 (November 1896), 12.

[47] W. G., 'Oeuvres posthumes de N. Paganini, pour violin, avec acct. de piano. L'Orchestre séparement et en partition', *Musical World* Vol. 16 No. 329 No. 52 (27 December 1851), 821–22.

[48] Anon., 'The College of Violinists', *Musical Standard* Vol. 43 No. 1466 (3 September 1892), 186.

[49] Vera Schwarz, 'Zur Programmgestaltung des Violinabends in Wien 1880–1920', in Vera Schwarz, ed., *Violinspiel und Violinmusik in Geschichte und Gegenwart: Bericht über den Internationalen Kongress am Institut für Aufführungspraxis der Hochschule für Musik und Darstellende Kunst in Graz, vom 25. Juni bis 2. Juli 1972* (Vienna: Universal Edition, 1975), 52–3.

God Save the Queen [*sic*], *Hexentanz, I palpiti*), but no Caprices. The last concert, on 26 November 1900, was billed as a 'Paganini-Abend' with singers and pianists, and it is possible he included a Caprice or two if not on the programme itself then as an encore.[50]

Wilhelmj circumvented the problem of how to programme the *Caprices* by stringing several of them together in his own arrangements. For instance, *Einleitung. Thema und Variationen nach Nicolo Paganini für Violin mit Orchester oder Clavier-Begleitung* by 'Paganini–Wilhelmj'[51] proceeds in three sections, with an orchestral interlude between parts I and II:

I.   *Andante pastorale* (an accompanied version of Caprice No. 21, 'Amoroso')
II. A brief cadenza elaborating on an E major arpeggio (alluding to Caprice No. 1)
III. *Moderato* (Caprice No. 24)

Even more elaborate is his *Italienische Suite nach Nicolo Paganini für Violin mit Orchester oder Clavier-Begleitung*,[52] a 'greatest hits' medley with the violin soloist playing Paganini originals (enhanced in places) accompanied by orchestra or piano. Three Caprices, a concerto slow movement, and the *Moto perpetuo* follow each other consecutively, packaged as a 'suite' in five parts:

I.   *Air. Andante.* Eight-bar orchestral introduction. Caprice No. 11
II. *Marsch. Allegretto marziale.* Two-bar orchestral introduction. Caprice No. 14
III. *Barcarole. Grazioso.* Caprice No. 13
IV. *Romanze. Largo.* Ten-bar orchestral introduction. Violin Concerto No. 1, second movement (with new orchestration and the solo part amended in the last three bars, replacing the two-octave leap down from b^2 to B with a B-major rising arpeggio)
V.   *Moto perpetuo. Allegro vivace* [in C major]

Scored for 2 flutes, 2 oboes, 2 clarinets, 2 bassoon, 2 horns, timpani and strings, Wilhelmj's orchestration brings added character to Paganini's music as well as imaginative contrapuntal lines in the manner of Schumann's piano accompaniments to the *Caprices*. Part II for example makes liberal use of trumpets and drums and pits violas and cellos in a triplet-quaver cross-rhythm against the

---

[50] *Ibid.*, 53.
[51] Paganini–Wilhelmj, *Einleitung. Thema und Variationen nach Nicolo Paganini für Violin mit Orchester oder Clavier-Begleitung* (Mainz: Schott, n.d.).
[52] August Wilhelmj, *Italienische Suite nach Nicolo Paganini für Violin mit Orchester oder Clavier-Begleitung* (Berlin: Schlesinger, n.d.).

martial rhythms of the solo violin. Above all, this arrangement is clearly designed for ease of programming, making it practical and recital friendly.

In the same spirit of facilitating performance, Wilhelmj made his own edition of Paganini's Violin Concerto No. 1, pared down to just the first movement, with recomposed and significantly curtailed tutti. 'Known as the Paganini–Wilhelmj concerto, it effectively displaced the original three-movement version, which was revived in the 1930s', according to Boris Schwarz.[53]

Similarly, a number of new publications around the turn of the twentieth century in London purported to ease the plight of the would-be Paganinian virtuoso. In 1900 a revised edition of *Moto perpetuo* by Ernst Heim was published in London by Augener & Co. with the innovation of eliminated page turns: 'by the use of smaller type and by printing the staves very near to each other, [it] contrived to give the student a part from which the whole movement can be played without stopping to turn over'.[54] The 1904 publication *Five Violin Solos, for Concert Use, composed or arranged by Ferdinand Israel* featured as 'No. 3a . . . the *Andante* from Paganini's little known composition "In my heart no longer do I feel", and No. 3b, Paganini's *Surprise Solo*'.[55] A new edition of Guhr's treatise, revised by C. Egerton Lowe, was published by Novello in 1915. Reporting this, the *School Music Review* advised that 'those who are ambitious to conquer all the puzzling complications would do well to have a violin specially strung with extra thin strings, as these produce the harmonics more easily'.[56]

Werktreue *and Virtuosity*

As we have now seen, Paganini's performances relied on an unapologetic foregrounding of his individuality. As arrogant as this stance was, it came to be regarded as even more so over the course of the nineteenth century for reasons that had little to do with Paganini. After mid-century, virtuosi became unfashionable as part of a fundamental change in European musical culture. Discourses surrounding this change were wide-ranging and complex, the single most important factor in this being the growing influence of the German concept of the musical 'work' in the early 1800s.[57] The related notion of *Werktreue*—being true or faithful

---

[53]   Schwarz, *Great Masters of the Violin*, 317.

[54]   Anon., 'Moto perpetuo', *Musical News* Vol. 18 No. 485 (16 June 1900), 574.

[55]   Anon., 'Five Violin Solos, for Concert Use, composed or arranged by Ferdinand Israel', *Monthly Music Record* Vol. 34 No. 408 (December 1904), 231. 3a refers to *Nel cor più non mi sento*; 3b is unknown.

[56]   Anon., 'Paganini's "Art of Playing the Violin"', *School Music Review* Vol. 24 No. 279 (August 1915), 72.

[57]   As philosopher Lydia Goehr has observed in *The Imaginary Museum of Musical Works:*

to a work—whereby the performer functioned as a transparent medium for the music, minimised the interference of the performer's own personality. The valuation of the work and the valuation of performer personality were fundamentally incompatible; as the former grew in importance and prestige, self-promoting virtuosity became devalued. Moreover, because performers who abided by *Werktreue* came to be seen as 'priests of the public' (as Joachim put it), preaching the 'gospel' of the composer, those who failed to do so risked appearing irreligious, demonic, or self-aggrandising.[58] For example, Joachim was enraged by Adolphe Jullien for 'introduc[ing] his charlatanism into the works of Mozart and Beethoven'.[59] Virtuosi in the later nineteenth century were denigrated for opposing *Werktreue* in a musical culture where it gradually became the normative practice.

To be sure, Paganini's virtuosity was self-serving. But it was grounded in improvisation-based Italian musical practice in which the notion of *Werktreue* held no sway; it also was not a 'style of performance' separate from the impulses of composing and improvising. The performer-centric approach to interpreting works by others was a post-Paganinian historical development.

The single-minded pursuit of technique did not acquire its extreme fetishistic character until later in the nineteenth century with the full-fledged emergence of 'empty' virtuosity as a denigrated performance aesthetic. It was exemplified in the later nineteenth century by violinists such as Sarasate, whose complaint about the Brahms Violin Concerto ('why should I stand there while the oboe has the only proper melody in the whole piece?') betrayed his expectation that the soloist be paramount.[60] Similarly, Ysaÿe was criticised because he 'seemed bent rather on impressing his own individuality on the music than on the reverent interpretation of Beethoven's ideas'.[61] It was precisely in the act of bringing attention to oneself *and away from the music* that virtuosity became 'empty'.

An Essay in the Philosophy of Music (Oxford: Clarendon Press, 1992), the 'work' concept arose along with the rise of conductors and concert halls and the decline of improvisation, as copyright laws and the notion of plagiarism came increasingly to regulate music publishing. See also Lydia Goehr, *The Quest for Voice: Music, Politics, and the Limits of Philosophy* (Berkeley and Los Angeles: University of California Press, 1998).

[58] Joachim's phrase is quoted in Michael Musgrave, *A Brahms Reader* (New Haven, CT, and London: Yale University Press, 2000), 61. For accounts of the public's treatment of music as a 'secular religion' by listening intently and communing silently with the composer, thereby penetrating an inner world, see Johnson, *Listening in Paris*, Chapter 15, and Gay, *The Naked Heart*, 3–35, esp. 24–33.

[59] Quoted in Weber, *The Musician as Entrepreneur*, 15.

[60] Quoted by Eric Wen, 'The Twentieth Century', in Robin Stowell, *The Cambridge Companion to the Violin* (Cambridge: Cambridge University Press, 1992), 79.

[61] Anon., 'Mr. Ysaÿe's concerts', *The Musical Times* Vol. 16 No. 580 No. 32 (1 June 1891), 340.

This was reflected in criticisms such as 'the egotism of self-display is irrelevant and unartist-like', and 'virtuosi do not generally like being made subservient to the general effect—thinking the display of the solo everything, and the design of the composer nothing'.[62] 'Empty' virtuosity (as it came to be called) was thus not synonymous with Paganini's own virtuosity and should therefore be distanced from Paganini himself.[63]

In contrast to 'empty' virtuosity, 'true' virtuosity resulted from the performer channelling his virtuosity in the service of interpreting the work, and even then only when it was compatible with the nature of that music.[64] When Pierre Baillot played Beethoven's Violin Concerto, Fétis praised him as 'a virtuoso of the first order' because he met this condition.[65] A London critic praised Sainton's 1850 performance of the same work because he avoided 'look[ing] to mechanical facility for the means of producing effect'.[66] Similarly, in Vieuxtemps's 1852 performance, 'there was nothing which did not spring naturally from the composition'.[67]

The performance and reception history of Beethoven's Violin Concerto in the nineteenth century encapsulates in microcosm the shift in purpose from the work serving the performer to the performer serving the work. Early proponents such as Franz Clement (1806) and Adolf Wiele (1829) seemed to highlight its unsuitability as a virtuoso vehicle; the remark that 'many listeners wished that [Wiele] had chosen a different composition' implies that the primary purpose of the concerto, was to showcase the soloist.[68] (Baillot was an exception to the trend.) By the mid-nineteenth century, 'a virtuoso of a very uncommon class' had appeared,

---

[62] In a review of Joachim by Anon., 'Philharmonic concerts', *The Musical World* 36/18 (1 May 1858), 284. In the 1930s, the French writer André Suarès described the figure of the virtuoso as obscene, foolish, vain, and immodest in his *Pensées sur la musique*, quoted in Marc Pincherle, 'Virtuosity' (trans. Willis Wager), *Musical Quarterly* Vol. 16 Vol. 335 No. 2 (April 1949), 236.

[63] Pincherle's term in 'Virtuosity' 226–43.

[64] Pincherle's terms in 'Virtuosity'. Similarly, in *Music and the Ineffable*, trans. Carolyn Abbate (Princeton: Princeton University Press, 2003), Vladimir Jankélévitch distinguished true virtuosity from mere exhibitionism on the basis of its power to 'charm' (an 'Apollonian' power akin to the virtues of love, eros, caritas, soulfulness) and not merely to intoxicate (a Dionysian ploy lacking taste, decency, and longevity).

[65] *Revue musicale* 3 (1828), 205. Translation quoted from Louise Goldberg's preface to Baillot's *The Art of Violin*, xvii.

[66] From a review of Sainton, whose playing was judged to go beyond mechanical display. Anon, 'Philharmonic Concerts', *The Musical World* Vol. 25 No. 17 (27 April 1850), 254–5.

[67] Anon., 'Philharmonic Society', *The Musical World* Vol. 30 No. 27 (3 July 1853), 419.

[68] See Robin Stowell, *Beethoven: Violin Concerto* (Cambridge: Cambridge University Press, 1998).

in the form of Joseph Joachim.[69] He embodied the ideal as an interpreter of Beethoven's music as attested by two typical reviews of the era:

> Never, for one instant, is the player made conspicuous at the expense of the composer. Beethoven speaks throughout.[70]

> What Beethoven has written must be performed as it is written, and that in faith and humbleness. Joseph Joachim is one of those who best understand and most willingly accept this condition. He knows and feels that in giving a tongue to Beethoven's thoughts he is glorifying his art, and he has too much modesty to regard himself at such a moment.[71]

Baillot, an important precursor to Joachim, stated that his aim was 'to extend the limits of execution, not to bring astonishment by means of an increased number of difficulties conquered, but to offer increased means of eloquence or increased effects that influence the soul'.[72] Baillot also professed great admiration for Paganini: 'His is an admirable talent, truly prodigious, a phenomenon in music, doing marvelous things and doing them with a facility and perfection of which nothing can give a true idea'.[73] So did Joachim, as we saw earlier. Neither of these 'true' virtuosi confused Paganini's virtuosity with the 'empty' virtuosity of his imitators.

The wholesale attribution of technique-fetish to Paganini is not entirely justified because it ignores the development of virtuosity and its discourse in the nineteenth century. While he revolutionised violin technique and the fundamental tenets of soloistic performance, the importance of technique to Paganini has been exaggerated by a reductionist historical view of his music and misinterpreted through being taken out of context.

Paganini's Legacy of Self-Expression

We turn now to consider an aspect of Paganini's legacy that has remained unexamined until now; it lies not in the realm of composition or performance—not in

---

[69]   Anon., 'Philharmonic Concerts', *The Musical World* Vol. 36 No. 18 (1 May 1858), 284.

[70]   Anon., 'Musical Society of London', *The Musical World* Vol. 40 No. 24 (14 June 1862), 372.

[71]   Anon., 'Philharmonic concerts', *The Musical World* Vol. 22 No. 20 (15 May 1847), 312–13.

[72]   Baillot, *The Art of the Violin*, 12.

[73]   Letter to his friend Montbeillard of 20 March 1831, quoted in *The Art of Violin*, xvii-xviii from Brigitte François-Sappey, 'Pierre Marie François de Sales Baillot (1771–1842) par lui-même', *Recherches sur la Musique Française Classique* 18 (1978), 194 n.1.

music at all—but rather in the realm of cultural history. Digging deep beneath the association of virtuosity with demonism and its negative aesthetic valuation, we can see that Paganini's importance as a historical figure is rooted in his establishing the idea of performance as an expression of the self; in other words, as the externalisation of 'authentic' traits of identity.

By this I do not mean that Paganini himself created a fixed, stable identity and engineered its projection on the stage; rather, the close connection between Paganini's persona and virtuosity promoted the idea that exceptional musical skills emanated from an exceptional person. The powerful image of the 'demonic' violinist whose inborn traits compelled him to play virtuosically was a spin on the Romantic 'cult of personality'.[74] According to a related Romantic idea, Paganini suffered for his art, living an unhappy, tormented life due to illness, gruelling practice, and the nervous tension that resulted from constantly performing.[75] This promoted the image of Paganini as a genius engaged in 'titanic combats' with physical pain and yet 'heroically' overcoming them for the sake of producing great art—just as Beethoven struggled against his deafness.[76]

Of course, to view a virtuoso's on-stage characteristics as extensions of his off-stage personality was nothing new in itself; for example, in the eighteenth century, the violinist Antonio Lolli's immodest, impulsive behaviour in private was seen to carry over into his egoistic performance style.[77] But by Paganini's era the strong tendency of audiences to take the persona for the person was enfolded in the Romantic discourse on genius.[78] Paganini's audiences had no reason not

---

[74] As Peter Gay has shown, the 'cult of personality' originated in the Renaissance and blossomed in the nineteenth century as the 'modern doctrine [of] individualism' (*The Naked Heart*, 346).

[75] For example, Berri, *Il Calvario di Paganini* venerates the violinist as a hero and romanticises his pain.

[76] *Ibid.*, 21.

[77] The German critic Wilhelm Triest criticised Lolli for his 'immoral characteristics: lack of modesty, strange moodiness, and an addiction to sensual indulgences such as gambling, women, and drink', which could only be detrimental to the music, for him 'an art whose ethical purpose can only be served by virtuous performers', quoted in Dana Gooley, 'The Battle Against Instrumental Virtuosity in the Early Nineteenth Century', in *Franz Liszt & His World*, ed. Christopher H. Gibbs and Dana Gooley (Princeton: Princeton University Press, 2006), 89. Contemporaneously, the critic Carl Gollmick was 'disgusted with the virtuoso bigwigs who sweep into town, seduce the public, and leave with huge quantities of money', and Gollmick attacked the personal character of the virtuoso: 'Despite external fine manners, impressive medals, despite the salon style, etc., he looks very weak on the inside' quoted in Gooley, 'The Battle', 89.

[78] As Gooley has argued, building on an observation of sociologist Richard Sennett, the disconnect between behaviours in a person's private life and public role in early nineteenth-century society made the virtuoso into an exemplar for bridging the divide.

to believe that the demonic, licentious, power-hungry, avaricious, egomaniacal 'Gothic' persona they saw on the stage was not the man himself.

Paganini's decrepit body provided a focal point because many of his contemporaries believed that only someone with such extreme physiological traits could do the things he did on a violin, or would conceive of doing them in the first place. The publication of Doctor Bennati's 'medical report' in the *Revue de Paris* (1831) was influential in spreading this belief. According to it, Paganini's technical abilities and artistic temperament had a somatic basis:

> In order that Paganini should become what he is today, it was necessary that his genius should be associated with organs of most delicate sensibility. His brain might have enabled him to become a great composer; but without his astonishing rhythmic sense, and the build of his body, the shoulders, arms and hands, he could never have grown into this incomparable virtuoso.[79]

Bennati's theory impressed Goethe, particularly the idea that 'the conformation of [Paganini's] body through the proportions of his members predetermined him, favourably compelled him, in fact, to bring forth the incredible, the impossible'.[80]

As we saw in Chapter 1, traces of Paganini's body can be found inscribed in his music (Example 1.1). That Paganini's virtuosity could have resulted from no other person, no other body, helped shape the idea of performance as a projection of individuality for his contemporaries. An 1829 review of a concert in Prague stated that 'his compositions *expressed the man*, and no one would have played as he did. He places thickly together the most dangerous rocks, shoals, and sandbanks, and yet there are in the prospect no lack of smiling meadows'.[81] By the 1840s Paganini's 'subjective individuality' as a performer was held up by the music critic of the *Allgemeine Wiener Musikzeitung* as the desirable standard for any aspiring soloist.[82]

Paganini did not consciously intend to make performance a site of

---

Richard Sennett, *The Fall of Public Man* (New York: Knopf, 1977), especially Chapter 8, and Gooley 'The Battle', 91.

[79] 'Notice physiologique sur Paganini', *Revue de Paris* (1831) quoted in Istel, 'The Secret of Paganini's Technique', 109–10.

[80] Letter to Zelter (9 June 1831) quoted in Berri, *Il Calvario di Paganini*, 382.

[81] *The Quarterly Musical Magazine and Review* Vol. X (1829), 203–6, quoted in Grisley, *Niccolò Paganini, epistolario*, 415 n.1, my italics.

[82] Becher used this term in his criticism of the cellist Servais, whom he judged as falling short of Paganini's 'subjective individuality'. Quoted in Weber, *The Great Transformation*, 104.

self-expression—it was in his reception that this idea emerged, whether he liked it or not. Indeed, he himself experienced performance as a loss of self—he told Schottky, 'when I step out on the stage, I'm an entirely different person: an uncontrollable seriousness comes over me till the music carries me away and I follow whither it leads me, having no will of my own'.[83] He did not see himself as 'demonic'; the widespread rumours that he was in league with the devil troubled him.[84] His public's eagerness to read personality traits into his performing style was a cultural phenomenon beyond his control. Thus strictly speaking it was the cult of Paganini (i.e. his followers) who created this legacy—not Paganini himself.

The question of self-expression in the performance of Western art music has remained substantially under-theorised, while it has been thoroughly explored for popular music. In traditional musicology, we have lacked models accounting for the relation between musical expression and the performer's self (rather than the composer's self). Although the underlying importance of self-expression for the Romantics has been amply documented, rarely has the figure of the performer displaced that of the composer as the object of enquiry. The lopsided master narrative of music history privileging composers at the expense of performers has led us to neglect the achievements and influence of the latter. Correcting this bias, we can begin to recognise that Paganini's performances and reception shaped the Romantic idea of self-expression in performance in ways that were arguably as important and influential as Beethoven's in the realm of composition. While this may not have been as profound, philosophical, or articulated in as lofty language as Beethoven's personal heroism, which was built on German Idealism, it nonetheless shared with it an emphasis on individualism and the ideal of 'being yourself' typical of nineteenth-century Romanticism. In it lies the origin of personal authenticity in popular music today—the idea that rock and heavy metal musicians simply express themselves—which is not only familiar, but also valued as a 'natural' facet of the music itself (in direct opposition to the 'inauthenticity' of pop music).[85] As Robert Walser has argued, it is this idea, and not only the prestidigitation of Paganini, that electric guitarists such as Yngwie Malmsteen and Randy Rhoads have 'appropriated'.[86]

Perhaps the most striking illustration of this idea of performance as authentic personal expression is the fictional 'death scene' in Klaus Kinski's film *Paganini*

---

[83] Quoted in De Courcy, *Paganini, the Genoese* I, 408–9.
[84] See Chapter 1, n.43.
[85] See Walser, *Running with the Devil*, 100.
[86] See *ibid.*, Chapter 3.

(1989).[87] In it, the violinist slowly plays himself to death, coughing up blood on his Guarneri, with a medley of his greatest 'hits' (Caprices Nos. 5, 6, and 24, Concerto No. 1, etc.). The music for this scene, recorded for the soundtrack by Salvatore Accardo, turns into a unique, extended 'gypsy'-style improvisation. As Paganini approaches death, the music becomes increasingly fragmented, interspersed with fleeting passages of distortion, trills, *glissandi*, flying staccato, and *sul ponticello* bowings. The musical themes unravel as Paganini falls apart, and with the final annihilation of self comes silence. The scene is imaginary, but it effectively demonstrates the intimate correlation between personhood and musical expression associated with him. The film portrays the 'demonic' Paganini in a number of ways: (soft) pornographic depictions of Paganini and women; manic performances of Caprice No. 5, Concerto No. 1, and other works; obsessions with the violin and anti-pietism; all set against Gothic backdrops.

Today, the valuation of self-authenticity remains undeniable; it is instantly recognisable to students at music conservatories from the crippling idea that, in order to succeed as performers, they must first develop an 'I' worth transmitting.[88] To counter this idea, Naomi Cumming wrote: 'It is not a matter of first having some special personal qualities and then projecting them through the instrument'.[89] Yet this is precisely the way the 'genius' argument goes: Paganini was born with a predisposition to greatness (like Beethoven)—in his case physical as well as temperamental. Cumming quite rightly insisted that the appearance of the 'I' arising from an inner source is illusory, but her transhistorical approach does not explain why the temptation to take the illusion for reality has proved irresistible, from the Romantic era to our own. Jascha Heifetz has been dubbed the *Teufelsgeiger* of the twentieth century, on the basis of reviews which noted his technical skills, lack of visible emotions, soullessness, and the hysterical reactions he elicited from the female members of the public.[90]

Although there are countless virtuoso violinists nowadays who perform Paganini's Caprices and Concertos adopting a 'demonic' image, in a sense they are not the most 'Paganinian' because it is not their own personalities that they project. The Russian violinist Alexander Markov theatricalises the left-hand pizzicato variation of the Caprice No. 24—he flails around as if possessed, bounces the bow

---

[87] Klaus Kinski, *Kinski Paganini* (SPV Recordings DVD, 2003), Chapter 7. That Kinski, who played the title role, identified himself with Paganini and cast his own wife and son adds another personal layer to this already 'self'-promoting film.

[88] This point was made by Naomi Cumming in *The Sonic Self: Musical Subjectivity and Signification* (Bloomington and Indianapolis: Indiana University Press, 2000), Introduction.

[89] *Ibid.*, 22.

[90] Fournier, *Der Teufelsvirtuose*, 238–45.

higher than is strictly necessary, and puckers his lips with fierce concentration.[91] Czech violinist Pavel Šporcl's music video of Paganini's Caprice No. 5 with digitised thunder and lightning effects, set against the backdrop of a blazing inferno, and interspliced with Paganini's silhouette, reinvents the 'demonic' virtuoso image for the MTV generation.[92] The titles, cover art, and repertory choices of recent recordings such as Rachel Barton Pine's *Instrument of the Devil* and Gil Shaham's *Devil's Dance* speak for themselves.[93] On the other side, there are certain violinists who avoid Paganini's music but who are nonetheless 'Paganinian' in that their performing styles espouse an aesthetic of personal authenticity. Gilles Apap, part French-Algerian, part 'Californian-surfer-dude', performs freewheeling jazz and gypsy-style improvisations on Mozart and Ravel that closely match his laid-back personality.[94] Tracy Silverman thinks of himself as 'a guitarist trapped inside a violinist's body' and as a rock musician with the unrepressed sexuality of a non-Classical musician.[95] They are examples of modern-day virtuoso violinists whose musical personae, for all their modern appeal, derive from a conception of self at least two hundred years old.

As the philosopher Roy Porter has written, the self-exaltation of the Romantic era represented one stage in the story of the 'self' across the sweep of Western history, a narrative of progression that began with the birth in Renaissance Italy of the idea of a 'real, undivided, inner self'. The inner self and the idea of 'life as a journey of self-discovery' have been core Western values for more than four hundred years, as Porter explains.[96] The development of Enlightenment self-determination and the self-excavation of *fin-de-siècle* psychotherapy and existentialism further charted a story of Western progress, which, as Porter also points out, is a self-congratulatory master narrative. The phenomenon of Paganini's 'self-performing' formed a chapter in this story, and it is surely in this that his larger cultural significance resides.

---

[91] Markov's performance is excerpted in *The Art of Violin*.

[92] Šporcl's performance can be seen at http://you.video.sina.com.cn/b/5693952–129870 0891.html www.youtube.com/watch?v=TnY2T4DHZ58 (accessed on 29 December 2009).

[93] Rachel Barton Pine's *Instrument of the Devil* (Cedille, 1988) and Gil Shaham's *Devil's Dance* (Deutsche Grammophon, 2000).

[94] See www.gillesapap.com.

[95] Quotes from a personal interview (November 2008). See www.tracysilverman.com.

[96] Roy Porter, *Rewriting the Self: Histories from the Renaissance to the Present* (London: Routledge, 1997), 1–6.

Coda

The above mentioned cadenza by Accardo is unusual (if not unique); it highlights the 180-degree reversal in the importance of improvisation for violinists from Paganini's time to our own.[97] Indeed, the topic of improvisation, specifically its bodily or 'somatic' basis in Paganini's characteristic physical movements and postures, needs some exploration here as it locates subjectivity in the body, thus giving more precise co-ordinates for where the 'self' resides. The word somatic, from the Greek *somat* (body), is probably more familiar to most people as part of the word psychosomatic (i.e. bodily symptoms from mental or emotional disturbances). My jumping-off point for the word 'somatic' is an understanding of the 'musical body' as theorised by the phenomenologist and violinist Elizabeth Behnke.[98] In her distinctive model of performance, she challenges the traditional mind–body duality of Western philosophers since Descartes. Following in the footsteps of Merleau-Ponty, she refuted the idea of the body as an 'object' that is controlled by a '"subject" somewhere "inside" it'. Instead, she viewed the body as 'not fundamentally a thing that I cause to move, but an original motility'. In what she called her 'body schema' the violin and bow are 'not objects to be manipulated, but modulations of a musical body, sonorous organs through which I move'.[99]

As 'an alternative to the entire paradigm of a fixed, thing-like body' with its 'holding patterns' of tension,[100] she conceived of the 'musical body' in terms of movement. Borrowing a coinage from Annie Steinhardt (a fiddler from Santa Cruz), Behnke explained that a 'swing body' is 'one that dances, flows, moves freely, fluidly, flexibly, like swing music—in contrast to the traditionally stiff and static posture of the 'classical' violinist'.[101] Whether playing from a score or improvising, it is the 'inner dance' of the music that floods the performer's body and makes it 'swing'. In Behnke's words, 'the somatic life of the player and the moving body of sound are intertwined in the essential and foundational play of a *kinaesthetic consciousness*'.[102]

Behnke's schema of the performer's body as a 'subject' locates the origin and

---

[97] The Russian TV miniseries 'Niccolo Paganini' (1982, Lenfilm production) features improvisation in Episode 3 (of 4) presumably played by Leonid Kogan, who is credited on the soundtrack.
[98] Elizabeth A. Behnke, 'At the Service of the Sonata: Music Lessons with Merleau-Ponty' in Henry Pietersma, ed., *Merleau-Ponty: Critical Essays* (Lanham, MD: University Press of America, 1990), 23–29.
[99] *Ibid.*, 24.
[100] *Ibid.*, 25.
[101] *Ibid.*, 26.
[102] *Ibid.*, 27, her italics.

impulse for music in movement. The 'subject' is not a pre-existing 'I', it is not the mind, it is not something hidden. In this sense, her view of the body as a seat of subjectivity ties into, and overlaps with, ideas developed by thinkers as diverse as Naomi Cumming, Antonio Damasio, William James, Rudolf Laban, Susan Leigh Foster, Elisabeth Le Guin, and Alexandra Pierce.[103]

Turning back to Paganini—his ability to improvise was an important contributing factor to his performance style and image as a virtuoso. De Courcy described him as 'a clever . . . musician with the gift of improvisation'.[104] Schumann considered it 'the most fascinating of virtuoso gifts'.[105] Paganini himself spoke of playing 'in the Italian manner' when he deviated from the written notes of Kreutzer's Double Concerto during the famous joint appearance with Charles Lafont in Milan (1816) that was widely interpreted as a duel. As we saw in Chapter 1, Paganini was also firmly rooted in the popular music traditions of the time, including patterns of improvisation.

Putting Behnke and Paganini together launches us onto a new line of questioning. What kind of 'musical body' was Paganini's? (This question has been sidelined by obsessive commentary on Paganini's body focusing on its unusual characteristics—especially its diseased, ravaged state.[106]) On the evidence of numerous contemporary eyewitness accounts that we have already seen in

---

[103] Susan Leigh Foster has advanced a theory of representation in dance that sees the body as more than just 'a physical instrument for an interior subjectivity', in *Reading Dancing: Bodies and Subjects in Contemporary American Dance* (Berkeley and Los Angeles: University of California Press, 1986), xvi. The focus on the body as a seat of self, rather than a reflection of self housed in the mind, has also been proposed by neurologist Antonio Damasio in *Descartes' Error: Emotion, Reason and the Human Brain* (London: Papermac, 1996). Damasio sees minds as 'embedded not only in brains but in all of the rest of the body', in the words of a reviewer for *New Scientist*. Cumming, *The Sonic Self*; William James, 'What is an Emotion?' and 'The Emotions' in C. Lange and W. James, *The Emotions* (New York: Haffner, 1967), 11–30 and 93–135; Rudolf Laban, *The Mastery of Movement*, 4th ed. (Plymouth: Macdonald and Evans, 1980); Le Guin, *Boccherini's Body*; Alexandra Pierce, *Deepening Musical Performance through Movement: The Theory and Practice of Embodied Interpretation* (Bloomington: Indiana University Press, 2007).

[104] De Courcy, *Paganini, the Genoese* I, 63.

[105] *Neue Zeitschrift für Musik* (24 January 1840), 30, quoted in Mark W. Rowe, *Heinrich Wilhelm Ernst: Virtuoso Violinist* (Aldershot: Ashgate, 2008), 75. Schumann praised Ernst for approaching Paganini in this regard.

[106] In the famous account of Doctor Bennati that we saw in Chapter 1, the aberrant body was what enabled Paganini to develop his techniques—thereby exemplifying the Romantics' readiness to link genius with disease; as theorised by Linda and Michael Hutcheon in *Opera: Desire, Disease, Death*. Texts and Contexts Series, Vol. 17. (Lincoln: University of Nebraska Press, 1999), Klaus Doerner, *Madmen and the Bourgeoisie* (Oxford: Blackwell, 1981), and others.

previous chapters, it is clear that Paganini did not hold himself still when he played. In addition to the accounts, consider the following observations: Paganini 'holds himself differently from other violinists [perfectly erect, the right foot forward]',[107] and 'when he plays, he uses the whole body'[108] (which often resulted in post-concert exhaustion). 'He is a singularly ungraceful player, he shuffles about and makes mouths, looks over his shoulder, grows peevish with the orchestra, keeps time with his head, and has as many tricks as an anxious and unskillful student.'[109] He 'beats time with it [his foot] in a most ludicrous manner. . . . When intent upon a difficult passage, his body shapes itself into a sort of triangle, the stomach forming a sharp, indent angle, whilst the head and right foot are trust outwards'.[110]

From such descriptions of Paganini's physical exertion and extravagant gestures in the midst of performance—extravagant, that is, judging by conventions of violin playing outside Italy, and by conventions that developed into tradition in subsequent generations—we can identify his body as a 'swing body'. This is significant for the following reason. The idea of music as an expression of self based on individualism and introspection, on intellect and quasi-spirituality, is a familiar cornerstone of German and French Romanticism. In contrast to this model, apt for a Beethoven or a Berlioz, I suggest that the Italian's expression of self de-privileged the mind and instead found its basis in the raw physicality of performance gestures. Put another way, the origin of musical invention in the movements of the 'somatic self' turned upside-down the trajectory of inspiration as coming from above—it originated not in the heavens, but from below.

---

[107] Matteo Niccolò de Ghetaldi's letter of 18 October 1824 quoted in De Courcy, *Paganini the Genoese* I, 235.

[108] 'Dopo il concerto chiacchierammo a lungo con Paganini, che era esausto, probabilmente perché, quando suona, usa tutto il corpo; e fisicamente è molto debole.' Matteo Niccolò de Ghetaldi, who observed Paganini at close quarters in Trieste, 2 October 1824, quoted in Grisley, *Paganini, Epistolario* 258 n.1.

[109] Anon., 'Extraordinary Performer on the Violin', *Kaleidoscope; or Literary and Scientific Mirror* Vol. 2 No. 78 (25 December 1821), 200.

[110] Anon., 'Biography', *Literary Gazette* No. 653 (25 July 1829), 491.

EPILOGUE

Paganinian Mythology

Iɴ April 1893, Czech violin virtuoso Frantisek Ondříček (1857–1922) visited Parma to give a concert and requested to see Paganini's remains. Permission was granted by either his grandson Attila Paganini or his nephew Achille Paganini (depending on the source), and accompanied by an official of the City of Genoa, some professors, and the Director of the Music Conservatory, Ondříček got his wish.[1] But what exactly was his desire, his motivation: morbid curiosity, a desire to glimpse or taste the aura of a legendary person, or a need to pay homage to a demigod? Ondříček's visit fifty-three years after Paganini's death, a period during which the coffin's multiple removals and exhumations form their own saga, stands as a metonym for a wider cultural phenomenon: the perpetuation and escalation of a Paganinian mythology in the latter half of the nineteenth century. This mythology blended together elements of 'demonic' genius, violin folklore, and what we can call anti-hagiography; it thrived and solidified on an uninterrupted trajectory throughout the twentieth century. The myth shows no signs of abating today: the 'demonic' image has eclipsed all other aspects of him and has had the effect of flattening out a multi-dimensional historical figure. Paganini saw himself as amorous, seductive, heroic, comical, business-minded, upwardly mobile, and so on, as this book has shown; some characteristics played into constructing his demonic image (unintentionally on the whole), while other aspects played no part at all. The myth arose and took hold in spite of him; it mattered to and was promoted by violinists and non-violinists alike, in performances, in writings, in historical developments in violin-playing, in the mysterious aura of his Guarneri violin Il Cannone, in cultural spin-offs, and in various representations of him in stories, plays, television, and film.

This epilogue examines the three principal ways in which the 'demonic' mythology that was engendered during Paganini's lifetime burgeoned after his death. First, I examine the illusion that an entire tradition had died with Paganini because, with a couple of notable exceptions, no other significant virtuoso violinist of international stature emerged from Italy for at least a hundred years. Second, I

---

[1] See Andreas P. Otte, Konrad Wink, and Karina Otte, *Kerners Krankheiten Grosser Musiker: die Neubearbeitung* (Stuttgart: Schattauer, 2007), 144 and Anon., 'Alleged Exhumation of Paganini', *Violin Times* Vol. 1 No. 4 (February 1894), 55, quoting from a letter of Count Luigi Francesco Valdrighi of Modena dated 23 December 1893. The former claims that Attila gave permission; the latter, Achille. See also J. D. E. Loveland, 'The Strange Obsequies of Paganini', *Monthly Review*, Vol. 25 No. 75 (December 1906), 81–9.

show that the existence of the 'Secret Red Book' can be seen to symbolise the mysterious origins of Paganini's virtuosity and what it comprised. Third, I survey the enduring popularity of 'demonic' depictions in a variety of media, which provides assurances that ultimately the potent cultural work done by them has strengthened and continues to strengthen their resistance to demythologisation.

The Fate of Virtuosity Among Nineteenth-Century Italian Violinists

What happened to Italian violin virtuosity after Paganini? He was 'the last of the great Italian violinists' according to David Boyden.[2] The widespread perception that Paganini killed off that tradition, or rather that his achievement was so great that no violinist could hope to reach it, let alone surpass it, seems to be borne out by the fact that with the exception of Sivori and Bazzini, no Italians appear in the front ranks of the famous violin virtuosi of the later nineteenth century. The fact that Paganini left no 'school' undoubtedly contributed to this situation, as noted earlier in this book. The dearth of leading Italian violin virtuosi between the death of Paganini (1840) and the birth of Salvatore Accardo (b. 1941) has been described as a hundred-year-long lull (with the possible exception of Gioconda De Vito, about whom, more below).[3] As we shall see, there were in reality quite a few aspiring virtuosi who acquired a certain degree of fame in their time, most of whom have since fallen into obscurity, giving the illusion of a lacuna in the history of Italian violinists.

Filippo Romagnoli (1822–84) of Ancona, later a resident of Macerata, was 'one of the most beloved Italian violinists', who supposedly played 'with the energy and skill of Paganini, with the fire of Sivori and the grace of Bazzini'.[4] He was 'nominated a cavalier of the order of the crown of Italy'.[5] Guido Papini (1847–1912?) of Florence was a composer and author of a violin treatise who toured to Paris, Lisbon, and London, and founded his own quartet.[6] It is unlikely either Romagnoli or Papini shared a pedagogical lineage extending from Paganini.

---

[2] Boyden, *The History of Violin Playing*, 315.

[3] Harald Eggebrecht, *Grosse Geiger: Kreisler, Heifetz, Oistrach, Mutter, Hahn & Co.* (Munich: Piper Verlag, 2000), 92.

[4] Anon., 'The Continent', *Musical Opinion and Music Trade Review* Vol. 7 No. 77 (1 February 1884), 208.

[5] Anon., 'Foreign Musical Intelligence', *Musical Standard* Vol. 25 No. 1002 (13 October 1883), 225. See also Anon., 'Waifs', *Musical World* Vol. 61 No. 41 (13 October 1883), 646 and Anon., 'Musical Notes', *Monthly Music Record* Vol. 14 No. 159 (March 1884), 68.

[6] Anon., 'The Late Guido Papini', *Musical Standard* Vol. 38 No. 983 (2 November 1912), 285.

Although Sivori taught little and one of his obituaries flatly stated that he 'leaves no pupils of eminence',[7] there are at least three pupils whom we can name. One of them was Rosario Scalero (1870–?) of Moncalieri near Turin, who also studied with Pietro Bertazzi (whose father, a celebrated violinist, was supposedly an intimate friend of Paganini's) and with Luigi Avalle (a pupil of Gianbattista Polledro).[8] Scalero played in Sivori's quartet from 1887 to 1889, and between 1891 and 1893 performed as a soloist in Leipzig, Rome, Turin, Aix-les-Bains, and Milan, in the last location with the support of Bazzini. His repertoire was extensive, including Wilhelmj's *Italian Suite*, Hubay's *Hejre Kati*, op. 32, Bach's *Adagio and Fugue* in C, the Bach *Chaconne*, the Vitali *Chaconne*, concertos by Beethoven, Dvořák, and Joachim, works by Bruch, Goldmark, Mozart, Saint-Saëns, Sgambati, and Tartini, and his own *Romance* for violin and piano (published by Edition Chanot). Judging from a number of reviews from 1895, the young Scalero's playing was virtuosic but not unfailingly so:

> His execution seems a little uneven, at times that of a great virtuoso, at others a little faulty.[9]
> *Connoisseurs* expectant of great doing were rather disappointed. Signor Scalero's *technique* is decidedly good, although not exceptional, and one or two slips were made in places where there should have been no cause for the *lacks*.[10]
> With improved physique and a few more years added to his head this artist will come to the front.[11]

Another Sivori pupil was Frenchman René Francescatti, whose son Zino Francescatti (1902–91) went on to a brilliant career as a violin virtuoso (despite his Italian name, he was also French). Zino was given an original edition of the First Concerto by his father, in turn given to him by Sivori. He débuted with this work in New York in November 1939 accompanied by the New York Philharmonic symphony orchestra. Because of this direct lineage, he can be considered a 'musical great-grandson' of Paganini's.[12]

[7] Quoted in Inzaghi, *Sivori*, 317 from *The Violin Times* (15 March 1894), 65–9.
[8] Anon., 'Crotchets', *Musical Standard* Vol. 4 No. 94 (19 October 1895), 256.
[9] Anon., 'London Concerts', *Musical News* Vol. 9 No. 244 (2 November 1895), 361.
[10] Anon., 'Other Concerts', *Musical Standard* Vol. 4 No. 96 (2 November 1895), 292. Italics in original.
[11] Anon., 'From the Editor's Note-book', *Minim* Vol. 3 No. 27 (December 1895), 47.
[12] Samuel Applebaum and Sada Applebaum, *The Way They Play* (Neptune City, NJ: Paganiniana, 1972), Vol. 1, 24, 27; Albrecht Roeseler, *Grosse Geiger unseres Jahrhunderts* (Munich: Piper, 1987), 129–34; Eggebrecht, *Grosse Geiger*; Hartnack, *Grosse Geiger unserer Zeit*, 203.

Francesco Sfilio (1876–1973), born in Catania, studied with Sivori and went on to tour Europe as a virtuoso. Saint-Saëns praised his virtuosity by calling him a 'rivale d'archetto' of the calibre of Sarasate.[13] Sfilio believed that Paganini's technique was personal rather than abstracted, with a physical and physiological basis unique to him, and that it could be acquired by others through intensive study in which quality of practice mattered more than quantity.[14] In 1916 Sfilio founded a violin school in Sanremo (where he later died). In 1932 he met Benito Mussolini, who supported the organisation of a global event dedicated to Paganini in order to glorify the Italian nation.[15] In 1937 Sfilio wrote a treatise on violin technique, *Alta cultura di tecnica violinistica*, with a section entitled 'The Secret of Paganini can be discovered'.[16] The secret, according to Sfilio, comprised the exceptional quality of Paganini's execution of techniques in the 'magics' of the instrument.[17] As he put it,

> ... already for some time, historians have dispelled every diabolical legend about the supreme violinist, agreeing and acknowledging that Paganini's art was not witchcraft, but the sovereign emanation of a supersensible spirit [*emanazione sovrana di un'anima supersensibile*] and ... nothing more! So his secret (if one can call it that) was all in his exceptional temperament and his very agile vibrating fingers.[18]

Among Sfilio's pupils was Giuseppe Gaccetta (1913–2007) of Genoa who, along with his teacher, referred often to Paganini and his supposed secret but did not place credence in the myths and legends; indeed, 'the alleged "diabolism" of Paganini's music made him smile'.[19] Thus Sfilio and Gaccetta, in the second and third generations of violinists in Paganini's lineage, for whom the possession of some kind of secret knowledge would certainly have earned them cultural prestige by association, denied the existence of such a thing. Instead, what Gaccetta drew from Paganini was a certain inner attitude towards the violin; in his own words, 'certainly, Francesco Sfilio taught me everything at an external, technical level, as

---

[13] De Martino, *Giuseppe Gaccetta e il segreto di Paganini*, 31.

[14] *Ibid.*, 69.

[15] *Ibid.*, 54–5.

[16] *Ibid.*, 33.

[17] *Ibid.*, 63–4.

[18] Isaia Billè and Francesco Sfilio, 'Botta e riposta', *Il lavoro* (20 January 1937 and 7 February 1937), quoted in *Ibid.*, 65, my translation.

[19] 'Il Maestro sorride alla presunta "diabolicità" della musica paganiniana' (*ibid.*, 40); see also 61.

well as the human. But my interior master, from whom I derived the energy to continue to live on the violin, was Paganini.'[20]

Along with teaching Scalero, Francescatti and Sfilio, Sivori was also instrumental in a project to rejuvenate music in Genoa, one product of which was the short-lived journal *Paganini* (1887–91) edited by composer-theorist-critic Lorenzo Parodi (1856–1926). Articles about Paganini and his legacy were few, topics being focussed more on musical life in general and comprising reviews, essays, portraits of contemporary composers, and so on. During the four years the journal existed, there were half as many entries on violinists as there were on pianists and few compared to those on singers. In addition to big names such as Hubay, Sauret, Ysaÿe, and of course Sivori, a number of Italian violinists were mentioned, including Leonida Bati, the Bugni brothers, Ernesto Centola, L. Chiostri, Ulpiano Chiti, Enrico Darmaro, Giulietta Dionesi, Eugenio, Angelo Ferni, Virgina Ferni, Franci, Sebastiano Gillardini, Alessandro Ravera, La Rosa, Amerlia Sarti, and Teresina Tua.

Only the last of these names is likely to be familiar to the modern reader, yet Teresina Tua (1867–1955) of Turin was not Italian-trained, having studied with Massart in Paris. Too young to be included in *Paganini*'s index was Arrigo Serato (1877–1948) of Rome, who was known for performing Paganini's First Concerto, and who was based for a time in Berlin, where he played in Joachim's quartet.[21] Another was Armida Senatra (1888–?) of Foligno (near Perugia), who studied in Rome with Romolo Jacobacci (1860–?), performing Paganini's 'Non più mesta' at age thirteen and earning praise from no less an authority than Joachim.[22]

The relative historical obscurity of these violinists contributes to the impression that Paganini's impact on the development of virtuosity among Italians was detrimental—almost like a curse. It can be asserted on the basis of this data overall that there existed no such thing as an 'Italian Violin School' in the nineteenth century. There were probably three reasons for this: 1) the types of playing taught by Sivori and by those who were close to Paganini did not coalesce into an identifiable style; 2) virtuosity was no longer an exclusive or even a central concern; and 3) violinistic pedigrees grew out of the influence of the French Violin School. Indeed, in 1867, a correspondent for the British periodical *The Orchestra* visited the 'school of music in Naples' and listened to two violin pupils of a Signor Pinto, one of whom played Bazzini's *Esmeralda Fantasia*. A report followed:

---

[20] *Ibid.*, 40, my translation.

[21] Anon., 'Arrigo Serato', *Musical Standard* Vol. 29 No. 748 (2 May 1908), 285.

[22] Anon., 'Miss Armida Senatra, Violinist', *Musical Standard* Vol. 37 No. 940 (6 January 1912), 17. Jacobacci, Roman by birth, was the first violinist of the Quartetto Romano.

Both were admirable in the French-Belgian style, which is cultivated here with especial predilection and the devotion of elective affinity; for all Italian violinists adopt this style, owing to the want of a national school. Yet in this very country lived, as recently as the last century, those great masters of the violin who marked an epoch and served as a standard for the whole world of music and of whom we still learn, even at the present day, by tradition! However incredible this fact may appear, it is true.[23]

In the twentieth century, in place of a true 'Italian Violin School' there were influences from Paris, Brussels, and Berlin as well as localised pedagogical strands in Rome and Milan that can hardly be called a national school or style. Gioconda de Vito (1907–94) of Rome studied there with Remigio (Remy) Principe (1889–1977), a native of Florence, and at the Liceo Musicale in Pesaro before settling in the United Kingdom.[24] Pina Carmirelli (b. 1914), winner of the Paganini Competition in 1940, studied with Serato and Michelangelo Abbado (1900–1980) of Milan,[25] who in turn studied with Enrico Polo (1868–1953), also of Milan. Franco Gulli (1926–) of Trieste, who revived Paganini's Concerto No. 5 in 1959 in Siena, was also taught by Serato.[26]

Salvatore Accardo, born in Turin, studied in Naples with Alfredo D'Ambrosio, a pupil of Dworzak von Walden (of Romania), who himself studied with Sarasate, a Spanish product of the French Violin School. Accardo's sensational debut at age thirteen in Trieste playing Paganini is *Caprices*, winning the Paganini Competition (1958), reviving the Concerto No. 6 and championing Paganini's works, has deservedly earned him a reputation as a Paganini specialist. Despite this, the Italian has no direct link back to Paganini; in fact his lineage can be traced to Parisian contemporaries of Paganini's. Accardo's style has been described as 'sobre', lacking the heat and demonicism of Paganini's own playing style.[27] (Ruggiero Ricci (b. 1918), another Paganini specialist, is not considered here because, although his ancestry is Italian, he is American and was born in San Francisco.)

Uto Ughi (b. 1944)[28] of Busto Arsizio performed his first Paganini *Caprices* at the age of seven at Milan's Teatro Lirico and went on to study with George

---

[23] Anon., 'Italy' [Naples, 10 July] *The Orchestra* No. 200 (27 July 1867), 277–9, quoted 278. We do not know the names of these budding Italian virtuosi.

[24] Hartnack, *Grosse Geiger*, 301; Roeseler, *Grosse Geiger*, 142–5; Eggebrecht, *Grosse Geiger*, 199–203.

[25] Hartnack, *Grosse Geiger*, 303. He was father of Claudio Abbado.

[26] Guy Graybill, *Bravo! Greatness of Italian Music* (Boston, MA: Dante University of America Press, 2008), 38.

[27] Eggebrecht, *Grosse Geiger*, 94.

[28] Roeseler, *Grosse Geiger*, 336.

Enesco. Massimo Quarta (b. 1965) studied in Lecce, Rome and elsewhere with a number of teachers including Accardo, and won the Paganini Competition (1991). His recordings of the complete concertos playing Paganini's Il Cannone on the Genoese 'Dynamic' label appear to bear an Italian stamp; however, Quarta's lineage, through Accardo, links back to the French School. In fact, with the possible exception of Gioconda De Vito, none of the abovementioned twentieth-century Italians were trained in a 'purely Italian' style—indeed it is questionable whether such a style exists any longer.

The point about Paganini's tremendous influence on virtuoso violinists who came after him is that it was 'circumpolar'—to borrow the term Carl Dahlhaus used to describe the influence of Beethoven on subsequent generations of symphonists (Schumann, Brahms, *et al.*), whose point of reference was not the generation immediately preceding them, but always led directly back to Beethoven himself.[29] The influence of Paganini was not mediated across generations, but remained an iconic absolute with a kind of ultimate gravitational pull. This is especially significant when considered in the context of the historiography of violin playing, which traces patterns of stylistic development across generations. In genealogical 'trees' mapping teacher–pupil relationships such as Margaret Campbell's chart in her book *The Great Violinists*, the pedagogical impact of Viotti on all the major violin traditions of the nineteenth century is obvious.[30] Viotti stands at the trunk of the tree, while Paganini is positioned on a branch that withers. This underscores the huge discrepancy between Paganini's minimal influence as a teacher and his tremendous influence as a 'demonic virtuoso', the latter bearing a quality that could hardly be taught or transmitted, and that could only be imitated, at best.

The 'Secret Red Book'

The cultural work accomplished by the existence of the 'Secret Red Book', never mind its contents, is immense because it carries a kind of talismanic value. The facts that Paganini kept it strictly private and that it has never been published have only added to the aura of mystery. What makes it significant is its function as a symbol for the existence of a secret key to Paganini's virtuosity, whereas in reality it contains no such thing. As Harold Spivacke, the curator of the Gertrude Clarke Whittall Foundation Collection (Library of Congress, Music Division) in which it came to be housed, quite rightly observed, 'though the book is a veritable gold mine of biographical material, it will, after all, prove a sore disappointment

---

[29] Dahlhaus, *Nineteenth Century Music*, 152–3.
[30] Campbell, *The Great Violinists*, xx–xxi.

to those who have expected to find in it either Paganini's "secret" for playing the violin or evidence of his love affairs'.[31] The book fails to compensate for the lack of the violin treatise Paganini intended to write.

As Spivacke goes on to describe, 'the book itself contains about eighty leaves and is bound in red cardboard' and was in use from around March 1828 to March 1831—in other words, the first three years of Paganini's European tour.[32] Spivacke's description of its contents can be summarised as follows:

1. Literature and poetry
   - sonnets copied by Luigi Germi and by Paganini
   - an excerpt from the story of *Lalla Rookh* copied by Germi
2. Financial records
   - travel accounts listing towns, mileage, costs for hiring horses and drivers
   - net income from individual concerts calculated by subtracting expenses from total takings
   - ticket prices, orchestral hiring costs
   - bank transactions
3. Names and addresses of professional contacts including:
   - in Berlin: Pr. Metternic [*sic*], Spontini, Mendelssohn
   - in Warsaw: 'Mr. Chopin giovine [*sic*] Pianista'
   - complimentary-ticket lists giving the names of people who attended concerts for free
4. Catalogue of his papers
5. Miscellaneous items:
   - prescriptions and various medical treatments from Dr Bennati, Spohr, and others
   - a laundry list of clothing items belonging to Niccolò and Achilles

It is worth noting several points that Spivacke did not mention concerning the 'Secret Red Book'. In category 1, the majority of the sonnets (by Lapo Gianni and Vincenzo Monti as well as Petrarch) are based on the theme of love, and the significance of *Lalla Rookh* (1817) is that it was an Orientalist poem, by Thomas Moore (the extract concerns a character called Madre Indiana).[33] These subjects give us an idea of the 'real' Paganini's personal interests. Having his friend Germi's

---

[31] Spivacke, 'Paganiniana', 51.

[32] *Ibid.*

[33] This poem served as the basis for Spontini's *Lalla Rookh* (1821), Schumann's *Das Paradies und die Peri* (1843), and Félicien David's opéra-comique *Lalla Roukh* (1862), among others.

handwriting with him as he embarked on his first trip outside of the Italian states probably had high sentimental value for him. In category 2, many of the financial records are crossed out in heavy blotted ink, indicating that this was information Paganini did not want anyone to see, even if they accidentally had access to the book that he protected so fiercely. In category 3, the names listed represented a large cross-section of society in the cities Paganini visited, including musicians (many identified specifically as violinists, pianists, singers, or theatre directors), numerous titled men and women of the nobility, journalists, editors, professors, doctors, bankers, and lawyers. The range of these people reflects the daily preoccupations of a travelling virtuoso building a professional profile from scratch. In category 5 belongs the observation that Paganini's signature appears on numerous pages throughout the book, showing that he practised his autograph constantly. Also in this category, an entry from Berlin in February 1829 reading 'Prendandone 25 Bottiglie / Se ne pagano 24' (25 bottles for the price of 24) demonstrates that he liked discounted prices as much as anybody.

The page where Paganini recorded the dates and takings of his first four concerts in Paris (19,080 francs, 15,891 francs, 21,829 francs, and 21,045 francs on 9, 13, 20, and 23 March 1831 respectively) is shown in Figure 6.1. We can see he signed his name at the bottom of this page. An excerpt from a multi-page list of contacts in Warsaw containing Chopin's name is shown in Figure 6.2. As these examples illustrate, the 'Secret Red Book' contains the quotidian details of a hustling musician very much immersed in the places and times in which he lived. They are so mundane that the book's meaning, we can confirm, lies all on the surface.

In spite of its lack of scandalous or heretical content, the 'Secret Red Book' helped to perpetuate the demonisation of Paganini by cropping up in the literature as a quasi-fetishised object of speculation (because its contents were not widely known) and by fuelling the myth that he possessed secret knowledge. The writer J. C. Lobe (1797–1881) referred to 'a little red case' in which Paganini kept his business documents written in a code resembling hieroglyphics.[34] It is not known where the coinage 'Secret Red Book' originated (Italian writers such as Codignola and Grisley have referred to the book as simply 'il libro rosso'), yet it has become a commonplace of the biographical literature. Twentieth-century biographers (e.g. De Courcy) have mentioned the book in passing, without however divulging the absence of secret knowledge, thereby contributing to the perception that the book perhaps contained a secret worth keeping. The fact that the early biographies

[34] Marian Millar, 'The Magician on the G String. A Musical Reminiscence of Weimar' (from the German of J.C. Lobe), *Quarterly Musical Review* Vol. 4 No. 13 (February 1888), 53. The full text of this article is reproduced in my Appendix.

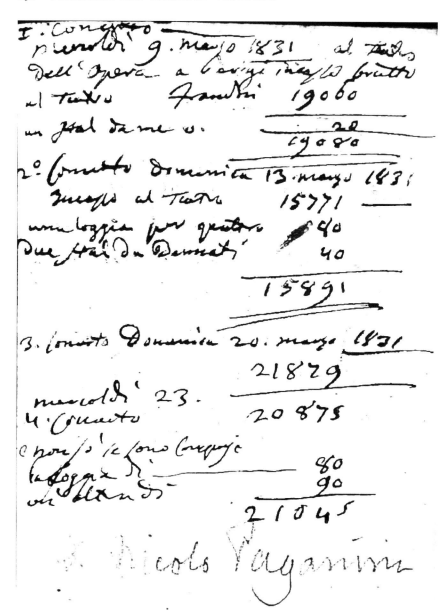

Figure 6.1 Extract from the 'Secret Red Book' (Scan 134), from the Gertrude Clarke Whittall Foundation Collection, Library of Congress, Music Division.

(Schottky, Fétis) did not mention the book at all can be read upon historical hindsight as protectiveness. Meanwhile, the unrelenting belief that there was a special secret to Paganini's technique, a topic investigated by scholars such as Kirkendale and Istel, and even acknowledged by Sfilio and Gaccetta (as we have just seen), evidences a psychological need for keys to the unknown.

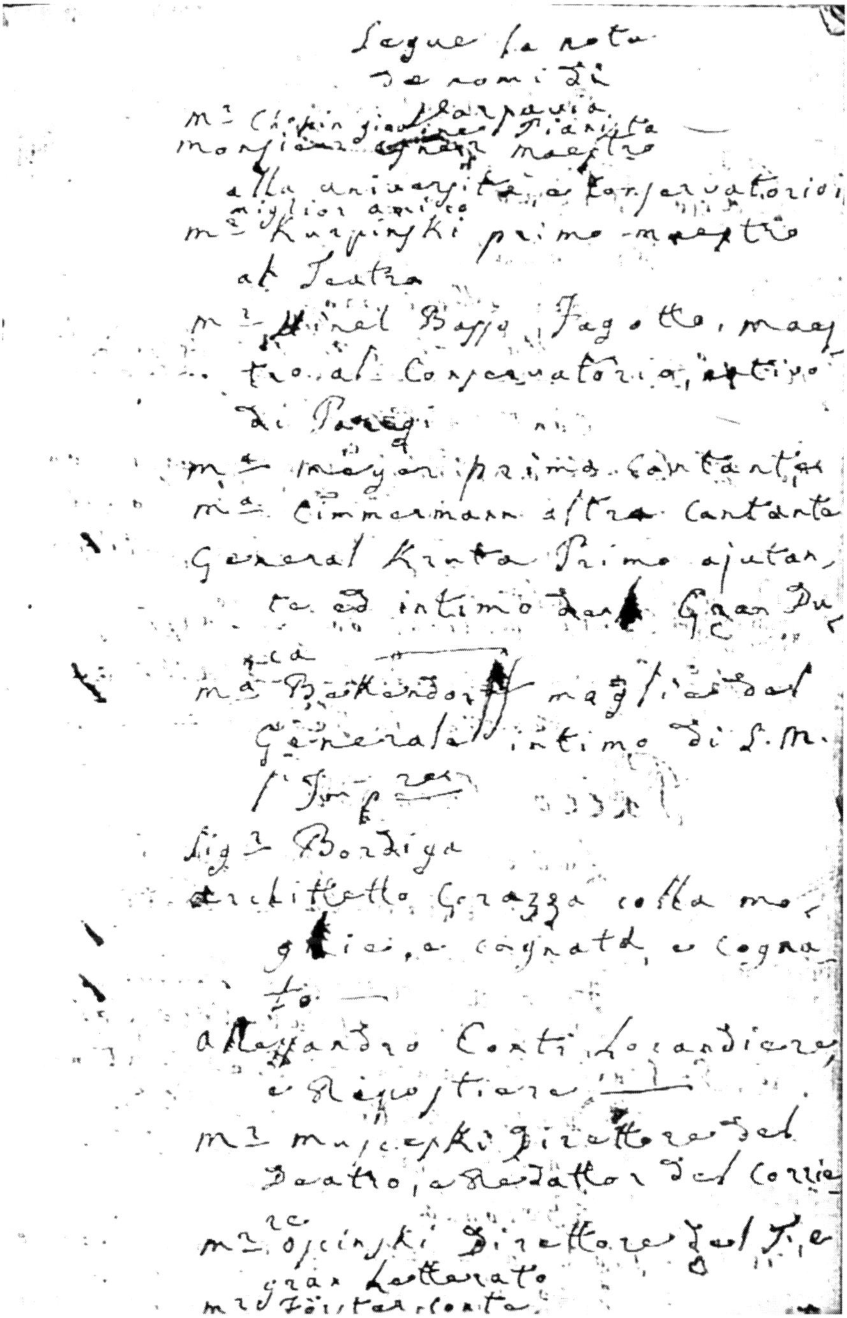

Figure 6.2 Extract from the 'Secret Red Book' (Scan 58), from the Gertrude Clarke Whittall Foundation Collection, Library of Congress, Music Division.

Paganini's 'Demonic' Mythology After 1840

As 'demonic' as Paganini was reputed to have been in his lifetime, this image was consolidated even further in the decades after his death in both direct and indirect ways. Notably, he became an icon of demonic virtuosity for those who were too young to have seen or heard him, and what became more important than his achievements as a musician observed first hand was the tantalising allure of a long-dead mysterious personage. Whenever a demonic violinist appeared in a work of fiction or theatre, Paganini hovered close by. The character Albert in George Sand's *Consuelo* (1842–43) bears Paganini's imprint when he plays his violin to the title character and seems to 'speak with the voice of Satan'.[35] So too does the character of Docteur Miracle, the violinist-hypnotist who mesmerises Antonia in Barbier and Carré's *Les Contes d'Hoffmann* (1851), an invented character inserted into the story by E. T. A. Hoffmann on which the operetta is based. The recurring motif associated with Docteur Miracle, combining violin tremolo with *obbligato cor à piston*, is even marked 'Allegro diavolo' in the score.[36]

Approaching the turn of the twentieth century, the figure of the 'demonic' violinist became increasingly established as a compositional feature: Saint-Saëns's *Danse macabre*, op. 40 (1875), Mahler's Symphony No. 4 (1892, 1899–1900, rev. 1901–10) and Stravinsky's *L'Histoire du soldat* (1918) all contain musical references to demonic violin playing (tritones, *grotesquerie*) that point indirectly to Paganini and point further back in history to the medieval *Totentanz*.

Historical factors that reinforced Paganini's 'demonicism' via counterpoint also need to be considered. The emergence of 'angelic' virtuose such as violinist Teresa Milanollo (1827–1904) and singer Jenny Lind (1820–87) set the 'demonic' male violinist into relief and helped to define him negatively.[37] (In particular, the portrayal of prima donnas as virtuous humanitarians performing acts of altruism—as demonstrated by Hilary Poriss—can be seen as directly countering Paganini.[38]) So too did the musical phenomenon of sacralisation, whereby music became a secular religion and the works of certain composers such as Bach and Beethoven came to be regarded as sacrosanct (as we glimpsed in Chapter 1). The holier Bach masterpieces became, the more demonic Paganini's virtuoso vehicles became, in comparable measure. The suggestion here is that the power

---

[35] George Sand, *Consuelo* (Amsterdam: Fredonia Books, 2004), 234.

[36] Gabriele Brandstetter, 'Die Schauspielmusik von J.-J.-A. Ancessy zu Barbier/Carrés *Les Contes d'Hoffmann* (1851)', in *Jacques Offenbachs Hoffmanns Erzählungen: Konzeption, Rezeption, Dokumentation* (Laaber: Laaber-Verlag, 1988), 472.

[37] For reviews contrasting the violin's 'demonic spirits' and Paganini's magic with the virginal Milanollo, see Hoffmann, *Instrument und Körper*, 192–3.

[38] Poriss, 'Prima Donnas and the Performance of Altruism'.

of myth-making operated by a dialectical process, offsetting the 'demonic' trope against the 'angelic' or 'holy'.

Meanwhile, the power of the written word helped to ensure that Paganini's 'demonic' image became fixed in reader's minds. The use of Gothic language to describe Paganini's performing style in 1843 was typical of the era:

> [A] tall gaunt figure, his long fleshless fingers, his wild eager and wan visage . . . convulsive . . . wild eye glancing by fits round the house, he looked not unlike some criminal escaped from the dungeon where he had been worn down by long confinement, or a lunatic who had just been released from his chains . . . waves his bow high above the strings, dashes it on them with a wild crash.[39]

An 1865 reminiscence of Paganini's performance in London still used words such as 'supernatural' and 'spectral'.[40] As late as 1891, the use of such language showed no signs of abating: the description that he cut a 'tall, weakly, skeleton-like figure', borrowed adjectives from a by-then bygone era.[41]

In the myriad music periodicals and current affairs journals in the British press, one particularly taken with Paganini, a steady stream of stories, anecdotes, poems, and semi- or fully fictionalised episodes from his life appeared in the period 1840–1900, always recycling 'demonic' tropes.[42] Because even the most cursory inspection of these texts can reveal to the reader the extent to which the legend of the 'demonic' virtuoso flourished in literature, a selection of some of them are offered in a separate Appendix ('Paganiniana in the British press (1840–1900)').

From these we can see that the demonic valences of violins and violinists in Paganini's mould only multiplied in the six decades following his death, and that Polko was by no means the only journal author in the business of fictionalising Paganini's life (as we saw in Chapter 1). In the 1870s, 1880s, and 1890s, excerpted stories about Paganini were also reprinted from books, ensuring that they reached a wider readership, in periodicals such as *Tonic Sol-fa Reporter, Magazine of Music,* and *Musical Standard.*[43]

---

[39]   Anon., 'The Violin', *British Minstrel* Vol. 1 No. 1 (January 1843), 32.

[40]   John Ross Dix, 'Paganini', *Bow Bells* Vol. 2 No. 41 (10 May 1865), 350.

[41]   Anon., 'Paganiniana', *Cornhill Magazine* Vol. 17 No. 97 (July 1891), 76.

[42]   The texts cited here can be found in full in the Appendix.

[43]   See, for instance, Anon., 'Stories of Paganini' (from Dr Phipson's "Celebrated Violinists"), *Tonic Sol-fa Reporter* (1 June 1877), 122–4, which reprinted excerpts from Thomas Lamb Phipson, *Biographical Sketches and Anecdotes of Celebrated Violinists* (London: Bentley, 1877) and Heinrich Heine, 'Paganini', *Magazine of Music* Vol. 3 No. 36 (March 1887), 256–7; 'Heine on Paganini', *Musical Standard* Vol. 43 No. 1483

The numerous publications or republications of biographical sketches in a wide variety of periodicals of the same period (not all of them music journals) showed a marked increase in number during the 1880s:

'Biographical Notice of Nicolo Paganini [from Fétis]', *Literary Gazette* 1850 (3 July 1852), 526–8.

H. R. Haweis, 'Paganini', *Good Words* 14 (December 1873), 137–43.

Anon., 'Nicolo Paganini', *Musical Opinion and Music Trade Review* Vol. 4 No. 37 (October 1880), 25–6.

Anon., 'Fiddles and Fiddlers', *Musical World* Vol. 61 No. 30 (28 July 1883), 462.

Anon., 'Paganiniana', *Musical Opinion and Music Trade Review* Vol. 6 No. 71 (August 1883), 468–9.

Anon., 'Notes about Paganini', *Musical Standard* Vol. 25 No. 1001 (6 October 1883), 207.

Anon., 'Nicolo Paganini', *Quaver* 100 (April 1884), 235–7 and 101 (May 1884), 241–2.

Ed Heron-Allen, 'Nicolo Paganini and his Guarnerius', *Musical Times and Singing Class Circular* Vol. 27 No. 519 (May 1886), 266–71.

L. E., 'Paganini', *Temple Bar* 77 (May 1886), 35–55.

Felix Weiss, 'Recollections of Nicolo Paganini', *Musical World* Vol. 64 No. 27 (3 July 1886), 420–2.

Anon., 'Paganini', *Chambers's Journal of Popular Literature, Science and Arts* Vol. 5 No. 215 (11 February 1888), 90–3.

Anon., 'A New Portrait of Paganini', *Magazine of Music* Vol. 8 No. 5 (May 1890); 93–4.

Anon., 'Paganiniana', *Cornhill Magazine* Vol. 17 No. 97 (July 1891), 76–83.

Anon., 'Recollections of Paganini' [adapted from the French of Hector Berlioz by Robin H. Legge], *Musical Opinion and Music Trade Review* Vol. 15 No. 178 (July 1892), 469–70.

Leigh Hunt, 'Paganini', [republished] *Violin Times* Vol. 5 No. 59 (September 1898), 209; Vol. 5 No. 60 (October 1898), 230; Vol. 6 No. 61 (November 1898), 4; Vol. 6 No. 62 (December 1898), 21; and Vol. 6 No. 63 (January 1899), 36.

The Paganini legend also grew in realms beyond the musical and the literary: in the 1840s a Monsieur Mareppe invented a violin-playing wind-up automaton on the model of Vaucanson's flute-player which apparently played *Nel cor più non mi*

(31 December 1892), 527, which reprinted excerpts from Heine's *Florentine Nights* in English translation.

sento 'à la Paganini'.[44] In the 1850s, 'Paganini' appeared as Figure 99 at Madame Tussaud's.[45] Curiously, at the same time, his hometown distinctly lacked material monuments—visiting Genoa in 1849, French painter Horace Vernet was 'shocked to find that the birth-place of Paganini knew little, and cared less, about him'.[46] In 1912, devotees located the house where Paganini had grown up only after great difficulty.[47] The site of the house, which was destroyed during World War II, is nowadays marked by a small placard on a wall covered in graffiti—a stone's throw from Christopher Columbus's house, which remains a popular tourist attraction by contrast. Genoa's Paganiniana, including Il Cannone, is almost entirely confined to the Comune di Genoa's collection housed at the Palazzo Tursi, which is connected to the international violin competition that bears his name. (Monuments to Paganini were erected in Parma at the cemetery where he was eventually buried, and more recently by Renzo Piano—the latter in the form of a large auditorium.)

In the twentieth century, Paganini's life and career as a virtuoso were the subject of no fewer than six novels and an operetta, listed in chronological order below.

Kuhnert, Adolfo Artur. *Paganini*. (Leipzig: Reclam, 1929).

Knepler, Paul and Bela Jenbach. *Paganini*, an operetta in three acts (1937).

Richter, Hermann. *Dämonischer Reigen: Ein Paganini-Roman* (Leipzig: Otto Janke, 1938).

Komroff, Manuel. *The Magic Bow: A Romance of Paganini* (New York: Harper & Brothers, 1940).

Reis, Kurt. *Paganini und die Frauen* (Berlin: Deutsche Buchvertriebs- und Verlags-Gesellschaft, 1952).

Waldemar, Charles. *Paganini: Liebe, Ruhm und Leidenschaft. Der Lebensroman Niccolo Paganinis* (Munich: Bong, 1959).

Maynor, Eleanor. *The Golden Key* (New York: Criterion, 1966).

The operetta *Paganini*, starring Richard Tauber as Paganini and Eveyln Laye as Princess Anna Elisa [*sic*] of Lucca, was produced on the London stage in July 1937.[48] The novels follow in the vein of that by Vinogradov mentioned in Chapter

[44] Anon., 'Automaton Violin Player', *British Minstrel* Vol. 1 No. 1 (January 1843), 39.
[45] Anon., 'Sketches of Madame Tussaud's Exhibition', *Theatrical Journal* Vol. 16 No. 820 (August 1855), 274.
[46] Morgan Rattler, 'Of Music in Italy, and Other Matters', *Fraser's Magazine for Town and Country* Vol. 40 No. 236 (August 1849), 159–71, quote from 162.
[47] Anon., 'Paganini's House', *Musical Herald* 770 (1 May 1912), 134.
[48] See Paul Knepler, 'Paganini', *Play Pictorial* Vol. 70 No. 420 (July 1937), 3, 5–18.

1 in that they romanticise Paganini's life, adding imagined dialogue and in some cases even fictional plots and scenes. Hermann Richter's *Demonic Dances: A Paganini Novel* is the most extreme example, featuring a picture of a violinist playing an instrument with only one string on the cover (Figure 6.3). The novelist poses the question, 'who was Paganini? God, demon, or both, juggler, artist, gallery slave, woman-hunter, Satan in [the same] person?'[49] He then proceeds to narrate the violinist's life in twenty-two chapters covering all the expected themes: magic, demonism, Casanova, Don Juan, Faust, Napoleon, and even a blow-by-blow account of a performance in which the violin strings snap one at a time.[50] The exception to the rule is Komroff's novel, which diverges from the prevailing Paganini imagery in that it departs from the demonic; not only is this unusual, it inverts the mythology entirely by going to the opposite extreme, depicting Paganini in the hallowed walls of the Vatican playing Beethoven's Violin Concerto—in a kind of 'double-sacralisation' (i.e. the holy venue and the canonical music of Beethoven).

Finally, in a category of its own we find *The Secret of Paganini* (1964), a film treatment by the above-mentioned violinist Juan Manén, published within a collection of stories in Manén's native Spanish.[51] In eleven scenes summarised briefly below, his proposed cinematisation of Paganini's life unfolds as a series of snapshots revealing the highpoints, turning points, and definitive moments in his career and in the making of his legend.

1. Nicolo as a boy with his mother
2. 1793 scene with Rolla, playing the *Carnival of Venice* variations
3. 1801 scene of tumult with the (fictional) Countess Camerata
4. An amorous scene on the veranda of the Countess Camerata's castle, where Paganini serenades her with his guitar
5. In a prison dungeon with his violin
6. At the palace in Lucca of Elisa Baciocchi, where he plays the *Sonata amorosa*, and meets Antonia Bianchi and kisses her passionately
7. A performance at the theatre in Ferrara of animal imitations and the *Carnival of Venice* variations
8. The 1816 'duel' with Lafont and friendship with Rossini

[49] 'Wer war Paganini? Gott, Dämon oder beides, Gaukler, Artist, Galeerensträfling, Frauenjäger, Satan in eigenster Person?' (on the front jacket).
[50] Hermann Richter also wrote fictionalised lives of Haydn, Mozart, Chopin, Schumann and Brahms, and Wilhelmine Schröder-Devrient, with a tendency to focus on romantic plots.
[51] Juan Manén, 'El secreto de Paganini (argumento para un guion de film)', *Relatos de un violinista* (Madrid: Editora Nacional, 1964), 47–76.

Figure 6.3 Cover of Hermann Richter's *Dämonischer Reigen: Ein Paganini-Roman*
(Leipzig: Otto Janke, 1938).

9. 1831 début at the Paris Opéra
10. At a villa in Nice close to the sea with seventeen-year-old Achilles, 1839
11. Death scene, 1840

Manén touches on aspects of the 'demonic' at three points in his narrative. The most obvious is in the last scene, where he states that Paganini was denied burial by the ecclesiastical authorities, who believed him to be in league with the devil. Also in Scene 11, as Paganini lies in bed dying, he plays the Prayer from *Moses*— and at the end of the first strophe does what aroused diabolical curiosity in the multitudes of his time: 'a monstrous finger, which has been brooding like a bird of prey on the artist and his medium, rapidly breaks the last string of the violin, that last link to the dominator of his life'.[52] The close connection between the diabolical and the monstrous, and between the player and his instrument, develops a theme from Scene 5, in which Paganini, imprisoned with his violin and bow in his hands, murmurs to it:

> What is your origin? Why are you the only instrument that is diabolical and divine at the same time? . . . You have a soul and a bisexual body: two people together in one, with creative energy in your top half which the other, the fertile lower half, receives and expels, transformed into a voice that sings, laughs, or cries.[53]

It is noteworthy that Manén, himself recognised as a 'Paganinian' violinist, wrote about the player's relation to his instrument in such textured terms—juxtaposing the diabolical/divine with active/passive sexual attributes.

Paganini in Film

In addition to Klaus Kinski (discussed in Chapter 5), many other actors have portrayed Paganini on screen; of them, perhaps the four most memorable are Conrad Veidt in *Paganini* (1923), Roxy Roth in *A Song to Remember* (1945), Stewart Granger in *The Magic Bow* (1946), and Vladimir Msryan in *Niccolo*

---

[52] '. . . aquel dedo monstruoso, que se ha ido cerniendo como ave de rapiña sobre el artista y su medio de expresión, baja rápido y rompe la última cuerda del violín: último ligamiento de su dominador con la vida'. 'El secreto de Paganini', Manén, 74, my translation.

[53] 'Cuál es tu origen? Por qué eres tú el único instrumento a la vez diabólico y divino? Tienes un alma y un cuerpo bisexual: dos seres reunidos en uno solo, ya que de tu mitad superior se desprende la energía creadora, que la otra, la inferior, la fecundada, acoge y expele transformada en voz que canta, ríe o llora; voz que expresa todas las emociones del corazón.' Manén, 'El secreto de Paganini', 59, my translation.

Paganini (1982). The earliest film, directed by Heinz Goldberg, appears to be lost; judging by a still shot used to publicise the film, the violinist was depicted quasi-Dracula-like in full Gothic splendour.[54] Roth's Paganini makes only a brief cameo appearance playing an excerpt from Caprice No. 24 in a scene at a Warsaw salon where Chopin (on whose life the movie is based) also plays. In Bernard Knowles's *The Magic Bow*, a swashbuckling hero in knee-length breeches—an Errol Flynn lookalike with a violin—charges around Europe giving concerts and making women swoon. Like Manuel Komroff's novel from which this film was adapted, no hint of demonism is left unneutralised; played by a matinée idol, this Paganini was squeaky clean, with countesses waving their lace handkerchiefs and coyly calling out his name.

The four-part Russian television miniseries *Niccolo Paganini* (1982, Lenfilm production) does for the small screen what Hermann Richter's *Dämonischer Reigen* did for literature. With no holds barred, every aspect of the Paganini mythology is explored, with romanticisations thrown in for good measure: here we see him practising the violin in prison while shackled at the wrists, there we see him as a boy listening to the church bells ringing out the melody that would become the theme for 'La Campanella'. The spectacle of snapping strings is enacted in a performance of the Caprice No. 24; a manic improvisation imitating animal cries follows. Unlike Kinski's film, there are no depictions of sex (probably due to censorship restrictions on Russian television in 1982). For the purposes of drama, an arch-rival is included in the form of a Jesuit priest (played by Armen Dzhigarkhanyan). On the soundtrack Leonid Kogan plays Paganini's First Concerto, seen in interspliced excerpts between scenes.

Finally, *The Red Violin* (François Girard, 1998) features a character based on Paganini called Frederick Pope (played by Jason Flemyng) who renders a demonic caprice while fornicating with his lover (played by Greta Scacchi). The figuration of inspiration as erotic arousal channelling sexual drive into musical creativity and frenzied bowings suggests a Paganinian influence, particularly the 'sense of a vigorous, irresistible vitality' of the Caprices Nos. 5 and 16.[55] Representations of Paganini on film give a false picture of him as a performer in that he did not perform the *Caprices* in public (nor the Beethoven Violin Concerto for that matter). Demonic virtuosity on celluloid is the latest in a large-scale historical process of myth-making and myth-perpetuation.

---

[54] www.conrad-veidt-society.de/bibl.ton.html

[55] 'Il senso di una vigorosa, infrenabile vitalità' is Vincenzo Terenzio's description of the caprices in *La Musica italiana nell'ottocento* (Milan: Bramante Editrice, 1976), Vol. 2, 512–13, my translation.

Paganini Today

Nowadays, Paganini's difficult techniques are mastered by child prodigies; Sarah Chang débuted aged eight playing the First Concerto with the New York Philharmonic. Precedents were set by, for example, a Nonnette Evans, a young violinist who 'performed brilliantly the Paganini Concerto in D' in London (1920).[56] The ease with which small children can play Paganini today puts a dent in the perception that his works are impenetrably difficult yet, curiously, this has not undone the power or popularity of the demonic legend. Undoubtedly, unsuccessful attempts to perform Paganini's works the world over are far more numerous than are reported; poor Jan van Oordt did not escape notice in 1896: 'his training is so far from being complete that he must surely have wished to sink through the floor after the mess he made of a passage in harmonics in a Paganini concerto.'[57] The tightrope-act of performing Paganini with 'flawless technique' (as Váša Příhoda did in 1927, in Paganini's Concerto No. 1), to bring off dazzling fireworks with apparent effortlessness, still remains a violinistic *ne plus ultra*, a gold standard of virtuosity.[58]

It is difficult to determine when the Paganini cult peaked—perhaps it is yet to happen. Since his lifetime, instead of discernable waves of interest, there has been an unflagging fascination with his myth, constantly evolving with the invention of new media. There have been opportunities to demythologise Paganini, yet to take them would be at the expense of his most salient feature as a historical figure: even more than his virtuosity, the mythology surrounding his virtuosity. An anonymous writer observed in 1886:

> The halcyon days of the virtuoso are altogether a thing of the past. Our admiration of his skill no longer takes the form of hero-worship; the mysterious atmosphere, pervaded by the vague suspicion of some terrible crime or misfortune, which clung round Paganini would soon be dispelled by the fierce light of our rational latter days.[59]

Stripped of the 'mysterious atmosphere', Paganini ceases to be 'demonic'—but what this writer did not realise was that Paganini without the 'demonic' is no Paganini at all. Fifteen years later, in the full light of rationality, another anony-

---

[56]   Anon., 'News of the Month', *Musical Herald* 867 (1 June 1920), 267.

[57]   J. F. R., 'New Music and a New Violinist', *Saturday Review of Politics, Literature, Science and Art* Vol. 81 No. 2118 (30 May 1896), 548.

[58]   F.B., 'Vasa Prihoda', *The Musical Times* Vol. 68 No. 1012 (June 1927), 546.

[59]   Anon., 'The Modern Virtuoso', *Musical World* Vol. 64 No. 2 (9 January 1886), 22.

mous writer recognised that the importance of the legend was paramount: 'today, as in the early half of the nineteenth century, the widest credence is given [to] the innumerable, fantastic stories circulated about Paganini'.[60] In other words, as yet another anonymous writer put it in 1924, 'Paganini to most of us moderns is a myth'.[61] The legend of Paganini remains a myth in this post-modern age and, like all myths, hovers in the balance between our need to believe in it and to debunk it.

[60] Anon., 'Paganini's Prison Life', *Musical Standard* Vol. 16 No. 412 (23 November 1901), 325.
[61] B. V., 'A History of Violin-Playing', *Musical Times* Vol. 65 No. 974 (April 1924), 345.

Paganiniana in the British Press (1840–1900)

T HE primary purpose of this appendix is to collect together and make accessible some of the unknown English press and literature on Paganini in the
period 1840–1900; because Paganini scholarship has tended to be dominated by
Italian, German and French scholars, the field has tended to ignore these documents in favour of texts in those languages. All of them recycle 'demonic' tropes
in a variety of ways, thereby contributing to or escalating the myth of Paganini in
the decades after his death. They reveal how the violinist's 'demonic' reputation
ensured that he remained a figure of fascination and mystery for Anglophone
readers too young to have seen or heard him in person.

These texts have been transcribed from a number of sources including micro-
films of the original publications and in some cases the digital archive of British
periodicals (Britishperiodicals.chadwyck.co.uk). I accessed them primarily at the
British Library, the New York Public Library, New York University Bobst Library,
and the Staatsbibliothek zu Berlin; I want to thank the staff of all libraries for their
help. My transcriptions retain all idiosyncrasies of spelling and format (in the case
of the poetry) with a view to giving readers a flavour of the texts in their original form; where there are obvious grammatical or typographical inconsistencies,
they are indicated ('*sic*') and, where necessary, editorial corrections are offered in
square brackets.

Leigh Hunt, 'Paganini', *British Minstrel, and Musical and Literary Miscellany* Vol. 1 No. 1 (January 1843), 244–5

*The prolific essayist [James Henry] Leigh Hunt (1774–1859) was well known in
his time for his writings on various aspects of contemporary London culture. His
poetry encompassed a wide range of themes including the political (mostly attacking Tories) and 'oriental' (narrative poems based on Islamic stories) as well as the
musical (he wrote a long poem in praise of the castrato singer Velluti, for example).
'Paganini. A Fragment' was originally intended as the first part of a four-part
poem begun in 1834. As Hunt himself noted in his* Autobiography, *the violinist
sparked his own artistic aspirations: 'I wished to write in the same manner, because
Paganini, with his violin, could move both the tears and the laughter of his audience
. . . melt you into grief and pity, or mystify you with witchcraft, or put you into a*

state of lofty triumph like a conqueror.'[1] *This poem and the one that follows below appeared a decade after Paganini's visits to London, where Hunt would most likely have seen and heard the violinist. They referred to him as the 'pale magician of the bow' and as 'a fallen angel', thus ranging in imagery from popular witchcraft to Milton. The* British Minstrel, and Musical and Literary Miscellany *was a journal published in Glasgow (a city that Paganini had visited in October 1831).*

PAGANINI has no rival—unless, indeed, you could get a whole woodfull of nightingales, and hear them in company with the person you loved best in the world. *That* would beat even him.—*Leigh Hunt*

> So play'd of late to every passing thought
> With finest change (might I but half as well
> So write!) the pale magician of the bow,
> Who brought from Italy the tales made true,
> Of Grecian lyres, and on his sphery hand,
> Loading the air with dumb expectancy,
> Suspended, ere it fell, a nation's breath.
>
> He smote—and clinging to the serious chords
> With godlike ravishment, drew forth a breath,
> So deep, so strong, so fervid thick with love,
> Blissful, yet laden as with twenty prayers,
> That Juno yearn'd with no diviner soul
> To the first burthen of the lips of Jove.
>
> The exceeding mystery of the loveliness
> Sadden'd delight; and with his mournful look,
> Dreary and gaunt, hanging his pallid face
> 'Twixt his dark and flowing locks, he almost seem'd,
> To feeble or to melancholy eyes,
> One that had parted with his soul for pride,
> And in the sable secret liv'd forlorn.
>
> But true and earnest, all too happily
> That skill dwelt in him, serious with its joy;

---

[1] Quoted in *The Selected Writings of Leigh Hunt*, ed. by John Strachan (London: Pickering and Chatto, 2003), vol. 6, 99–100 from Leigh Hunt, *The Autobiography of Leigh Hunt* (London: Smith, Elder, and Co., 1850), vol. III, 238–9.

For noble now he smote the exulting strings,
And bade them march before his stately will;
And now he was all mirth, or all for sense
And reason, carving out his thoughts like prose
After his poetry; or else he laid
His own soul prostrate at the feet of love,
And with a full and trembling fervour deep,
In kneeling and close-creeping urgency,
Implored some mistress with hot tears; which past,
And after patience had brought right of peace,
He drew as if from thoughts finer than hope
Comfort around him in ear-soothing strains
And elegant composure; or he turn'd
To heaven instead of earth, and rais'd a prayer
So earnest-vehement, yet so lowly sad,
Might with want and all poor human tears,
That never saint, wrestling with earthly love,
And in mid-age unable to get free,
Tore down from heaven such pity.

    Or behold
In his despair (for such, from what he spoke
Of grief before it, or of love, 'twould seem),
Jump would he into some strange wail, uncouth,
Of witches' dance, ghastly with whinings thin,
And palsied nods—mirth wicked, sad, and weak.
And then with show of skill mechanical,
Marvellous as witchcraft, he would overthrow
That vision with a shower of notes like hail,
Or sudden mixtures of all difficult things
Never yet heard; flashing the sharp tones now,
In downward leaps like swords; now rising fine
Into an almost tip of minute sound,
From which he stepp'd into a higher and a higher
On viewless points, till laugh took leave of him;
Or he would fly as if from all the world
To be alone and happy, and you should hear
His instrument become a tree far off,
A nest of birds and sunbeams, sparkling both,
A cottage bower; or he would condescend,

In playful wisdom which knows no contempt,
To bring to laughing memory, plains as sight,
A farmyard with its inmates, ox and lamb,
The whistle and the whip, with feeding hens
In household fidget muttering evermore,
And rising as in scorn, crown'd Chanticleer,
Ordaining silence with his sovereign crow.

    Then from one chord of his amazing shell
Would he fetch out the voice of quires, and weight
Of the built organ; or some two-fold strain
Moving before him in sweet-going yoke,
Ride like an Eastern conqueror, round whose state
Some light Morisco leaps with his guitar;
And ever and anon o'er these he'd throw
Jets of small notes like pearl, or like the pelt
Of lover's sweetmeats on Italian lutes
From windows on a fest-day, or the leaps
Of pebbled water, sparkling in the sun—
One chord effecting all; and when the ear
Felt there was nothing present but himself
And silence, and the wonder drew deep sighs,
Then would his bow lie down again in tears,
And speak to some one in a prayer of love,
Endless, and never from his heart to go;
Or he would talk as of some secret bliss;
And at the close of all the wonderment
(Which himself had shar'd) near and more near would come
Into the inmost ear and whisper there
Breathings so soft, so low, so full of life,
Touch'd beyond sense, and only to be borne
By pauses which made each less bearable,
That out of pure necessity for relief
From that heap'd joy, and bliss that laugh'd for pain,
The thunder of th' uprolling house came down,
And bow'd the breathing sorcerer into smiles.

                                           —Leigh Hunt.

Leigh Hunt, 'The Fancy Concert', *Ainsworth's Magazine 7* (January 1845), 94

Ainsworth's Magazine was the enterprise of English historical novelist William Harrison Ainsworth, who had close ties to Edinburgh (where Paganini also visited in October and November 1831). Thus, although Hunt's poems were reprinted elsewhere, such publications indicate the continuing relevance of the demonic image of Paganini for his Scottish audiences a dozen or more years after his visit there.

They talk'd of their concerts, and singers, and scores,
And pitied the fever that kept me in doors;
And I smiled in my thought, and said, 'O ye sweet fancies,
And animal spirits, that still in your dances
Come bringing me visions to comfort my care,
Now fetch me a concert—imparadise air.'*

Then a wind, like a storm out of Eden, came pouring
Fierce into my room and made tremble the flooring;
And fill'd, with a sudden impetuous trample
Of heaven, its corners; and well'd it to ample
Dimensions to breathe in, and space for all power;
Which falling as suddenly, lo! the sweet flow'r
Of an exquisite fairy-voice open'd its blessing;
And ever and aye, to its constant addressing,
There came, falling in with it, each in the last,
Flageolets one by one, and flutes blowing more fast,
And hautboys and clarinets, acrid of reed,
And the violin, smoothlier sustaining the speed
As the rich tempest gather'd, and buz-ringing moons
Of tambours, and huge basses, and giant bassoons;
And the golden trombone, that darteth its tongue
Like a bee of the gods; nor was absent the gong,
Like a sudden, fate-bringing, oracular sound,
Or earth's iron genius, burst up from the ground,
A terrible slave, come to wait on his masters
The gods, with exultings that clang'd like disasters;
And then spoke the organs, the very gods they,
Like thunders that roll on a wind-blowing day;
And, taking the rule of the roar in their hands,
Lo, the Genii of Music came out of all lands;

And one of them said, 'Will my lord tell his slave,
What concert 'twould please his Firesideship to have?'

Then I said, in a tone of immense will and pleasure,
'Let orchestras rise to some exquisite measure;
And let there be lights and be odours; and let
The lovers of music serenely be set;
And then, with their singers in lily-white stoles,
And themselves clad in rose colour, fetch me the souls
Of all the composers accounted divinest,
And, with their own hands, let them play me their finest.'

Then, lo! was perform'd my immense will and pleasure,
And orchestras rose to an exquisite measure;
And lights were about me, and odours; and set
Were the lovers of music, all wond'rously met;
And then, with their singers in lily-white stoles,
And themselves clad in rose colour, in came the souls
Of all the composers accounted divinest,
And, with their own hands, did they play me their finest.

Oh, truly was Italy heard then, and Germany,
Melody's heart, and the rich rain of harmony;
Pure Paisiello, whose airs are as new
Though we know them by heart, as may-blossoms and dew;
And nature's twin son, Pergolesi; and Bach,
Old father of fugues, with his endless fine talk;

And Gluck,[†] who saw gods; and the learned sweet feeling
Of Haydn; and Winter, whose sorrows are healing;
And gentlest Corelli, whose bowing seems made
For a hand with a Jewel; and Handel array'd
In Olympian thunders, vast lord of the spheres,
Yet pious himself, with his blindness in tears,
A lover withal, and a conqu'ror, whose marches
Bring demi-gods under victorious arches;
Then Arne,[‡] sweet and tricksome; and masterly Purcell,
Lay-clerical soul; and Mozart universal,
But chiefly with exquisite gallantries found,
With a grove in the distance of holier sound;

Nor forgot was they dulcitude, loving Saccini;
Nor love, young and dying, in shape of Bellini;
Nor Weber, nor Himmel, nor mirth's sweetest name,
Cimarosa; much less the great organ-voiced fame
Of Marcello, that hush'd the Venetian sea;
And strange was the shout, when it wept, hearing thee,
Thou soul full of grace as of grief, my heart-cloven,
My poor, my most rich, my all-feeling Beethoven.

O'er all, like a passion, great Pasta§ was heard,
As high as her heart, that truth-uttering bird;
And Banti was there; and Grassini, that goddess!
Dark, deep-toned, large, lovely, with glorious bodice;
And Mara; and Malibran, stung to the tips
Of her fingers with pleasure; and rich Fodor's lips;
And manly in face as in tone, Angrisani;
And Naldi, thy whim; and thy grace, Tramezzani;
And was it a voice? or what was it? say—
That like a fallen angel beginning to pray,
Was the soul of all tears, and celestial despair?
Paganini it was, 'twixt his dark flowing hair.

So now we had instrument, now we had song—
Now chorus, a thousand-voiced, one-hearted throng;
Now panses that pamper'd resumption, and now—
But who shall describe what was play'd us, or how?
'Twas wonder, 'twas transport, humility, pride;
'Twas the heart of the mistress that sat by one's side;
'Twas the graces invisible, moulding the air
Into all that is shapely, and lovely, and fair,
And running our fancies their tenderest rounds
Of endearments and luxuries, turn'd into sounds;
'Twas argument even, the logic of tones;
'Twas memory, 'twas wishes, 'twas laughters, 'twas moans;
'Twas pity and love, in pure impulse obey'd;
'Twas the breath of the stuff of which passion is made.

And these are the concerts I have at my will;
Then dismiss them, and patiently think of your 'bill'.—
(*Aside*) Yet Lablache, after all, makes me long to go, still.

* 'Imparadised in one another's arms'-MILTON. The word is of Italian origin.

† . . . 'I see gods ascending out of the earth'.—*Vide* the passage of 'Saul and the Witch of Endor', in the Bible. A sense of the godlike and supernatural always appears to me to attend the noble and affecting music of Gluck.

± It seems a fashion of late in musical quarters to undervalue Arne. His defects are obvious when contrasted with the natural recitative and unsought melodies of the great Italians, and with the rich instrumentation of Mozart and the modern opera; but may it be permitted an unprofessional lover of music to think that there are few melodies more touchingly fluent than 'Water Parted' and very few songs indeed more original, charming, and to the purpose, than his 'Cuckoo Song', and 'Where the Bee Sucks?'

§ Pasta, who is not dead, is here killed for the occasion, being the singer of the greatest genius it has ever been my good fortune to hear. Her tones latterly failed her, and she may have always had superiors in some other respects; but for power to move the heart and the imagination I never witnessed her equal. The reason was, that, possessing both of the most genuine sort, she cared for nothing but truth.

Anon., 'The Violin (Abridged from Blackwood's Magazine)', *British Minstrel* Vol. 1 No. 1 (January 1843), 6–7, 10–11, and 31–3

This account of notable violinists throughout history appeared in the same issue of British Minstrel *in which Hunt's poem appeared (see page 142). It was excerpted from* Blackwood's Magazine, *which was founded in 1817 and owned by William Blackwood, a friend of Ainsworth's. After an introductory section dealing with the violin as an instrument, the author turns to detailed discussion of Corelli, Geminiani, Tartini, Veracini, Giardini, Giornovichi, Viotti, De Bériot, and, at length, Paganini. In stark contrast to the preceding sections on the performing styles of his predecessors, the description of Paganini performing employs many 'Gothic' themes and imagery—for instance comparing him to an escaped criminal or a lunatic whose immense nervous energy can only be released and tamed through the violin. The excerpt concludes with commentary on Ole Bull, who is judged as being second to Paganini.*

No one will deny that music is a lovely art. It is unquestionable that its use singularly increases the innocent enjoyments of life; that it remarkably humanises the popular mind; that its general cultivation about the lower orders on the Continent has always been found to supply a gentle, yet powerful solace to the hardships inevitable in a life of labour; that to the man of literature it affords one of the simplest, yet most complete refreshments of the overworked mind; while to the higher ranks its cultivation, frequently the only cultivation which they pursue with interest, often administers the only harmless passion of their nature.

All things which have become national have more to do with nature than perhaps strikes the general eye. Music and musical instruments certainly seem to have a remarkable connexion with the climate and conceptions of a people. Among the nations of antiquity, the people of Judea were perhaps the greatest cultivators of music. Their temple worship was on the largest scale of musical magnificence, and for that worship they had especially the two most magnificent instruments known to antiquity—the trumpet and harp. In later times, the horn is the instrument of the Swiss and Tyrolean mountaineer. Its long and wild modulations, its powerful tones, and its sweet and melancholy simplicity, make it the congenial instrument of loftiness, solitude, and the life of sheepherders. The guitar is the natural instrument of a people like those of the Peninsula. Its lightness, yet tenderness—its depth of harmony—its delicacy of tone, yet power of expression—adapt it to a race of men who love pleasure, yet hate to toil in its pursuit, whose profoundest emotions are singularly mingled with frivolity, and whose spirits constantly hover between romance and caricature. The rich genius of Ireland has transmitted to us some of the noblest strains in the world, but they are essentially strains of the harp, the modulations of a hand straying at will among a rich profusion of sounds, and inspiring them with taste, feeling, and beauty. The violin is Italian in its birth, its powers, and its style—subtle, sweet, and brilliant, more immediately dependent on the mind than any other instrument—inferior only to the voice in vividness, and superior to all else in tone, flexibility, and grace. The violin, in the hands of a great performer, is the finest of human inventions, for it is the most expressive. The violin has a soul, and that soul is Italian.

Nothing is more extraordinary in this fine instrument than the diversity of styles which may be displayed on its simple construction; yet all perfect. Thus, from the sweet *cantabile* of the early masters, the world of *cognoscenti* was astonished by a transition to the fullness and majesty of the school of Tartini. Again, after the lapse of half a century, another school came, and the school of Pugnani developed its grandeur, and from this descended the brilliancy, rapidity, and fire of Viotti; and from the school of Viotti, after the lapse of another long period, the eccentric power, dazzling ingenuity, and matchless mastery of Paganini, who might seem to have exhausted all its spells, if human talent were not always new, and the secrets of harmony inexhaustible.

Thus the violin belongs to more than physical dexterity. Its excellence depends on the sensitive powers. It is more than a means of conveying pleasure to the ear; it is scarcely less than an emanation from the mind. Of course this is said of it only in its higher grades of performance. In its lower it is notoriously, of all instruments, the most intractable and unbearable. We shall now give a slight *coup d'oeil* of its chief schools and professors.

The invention of the violin is lost in the dark ages. It was probably the work of those obscure artist who furnished the travelling minstrels with th[e] *rebec* and *viola,* both common in the 12th century[.] The *violar,* or performer on the viol, was a companion of the troubadour. The name fiddle is Gothic, and probably derived from viola. Videl and fedel, are the German and Danish. About the close of the 16th century, the violin, which once had six strings, with guitar frets, was fortunately relieved from those superfluities, and was brought nearly in to its present form. But the bow remained, as of old, short—scarcely beyond the length of the violin itself. Its present length was due to Tartini.

Italy was the first seat of excellence in music, as in all the other arts; and France, in the 16th century, was, as she has always been, the patron of all that could add to the splendour of court, and the elegance of public amusement. In 1577, Catherine de Medici, the wife and mother of kings, invited her countryman, Baltazarini, to France. His performance excited universal delight; and the violin, which, in the hands of the wandering minstrels, had fallen into contempt, became a European instrument.

The first school was that of the celebrated Corelli. This famous master was born at Fusignano, in the Bolognese, in February, 1653. In 1672 he visited Paris, then the chief seat of patronage. From Paris he made a tour through Germany, and returning, fixed it at Rome; and commenced that series of composition, his twelve Sonatas, and his 'Ballate de Camera,' which formed his first fame as a composer; crowning it by his solos, which have a fortune unrivalled by any other composition of his age, or of the age following—that of being still regarded as one of the most important studies of the performers for their science, and still popular for their beauty.

It is remarkable, that in those centuries which seemed to have scarcely recovered from the barbarism of the dark ages, and which were still involved in the confusion of civil wars, *enthusiasm* distinguished the progress of the public mind. It was not pleasure, nor the graceful study of some fine intellectual acquisition, nor the desire of accomplishment; it was a wild, passionate, and universal ardour for all that awakes the mind. The great schools of classic literature, of painting, of architecture, and of music—all first opened in Italy—were a conflux of students from all nations. The leading names of these schools were followed with a homage scarcely less than prostration.

Even the masters of that driest of all studies, the Roman law, gave their prelections, not to hundreds, but to thousands. The great painter had his seguaci, who paid him almost the allegiance of a sovereign. The announcement that, in Rome, the most expressive, skilful, and brilliant of all masters of the violin presided at the Opera, drew students from every part of Italy, and even of Europe, all hastening to catch the inspiration of Archangelo Corelli. About the year 1700, he produced his celebrated solos. In 1713 he died, and was interred in the Pantheon, close to Raffaele.

Corelli's performance was eminent for grace, tenderness, and touching simplicity. It wanted the dazzling execution of later times, but its tone was exquisite. Geminiani, his pupil, said, long after, that it always reminded him of a sweet *trumpet*. For many subsequent years, his scholars performed an anniversary selection from his works over his tomb. At length the scholars themselves followed their master, and the honour sank with them into the grave.

The next celebrated violinist was Francesco Geminiani, born at Lucco [*sic*] in 1680. After acquiring the rudiments of music from Scarlatti, he completed his studies under Corelli. He now began the usual life of the profession. His fame in Rome, as the first scholar of Corelli, spread through Italy, and he commenced his career at Naples as the head of the orchestra. There his brilliancy, taste, and tone were unrivalled; yet, like many a concerto player, he was found but ill suited for the conduct of the orchestra. His impetuosity and animation ran away with him; he rose into ecstasies, and left the band wandering behind. He has been charged with deficiency as a *timeist*; but this, though the most frequent failure of the amateur, seems so incompatible with the professor, and is so easily avoided by the practical musician, that we can scarcely believe it to have been among the errors of so perfect a performer. He was still scarcely above boyhood—he was ambitious of display—he was full of fancy, feeling, and power; and in this fullness he rioted, until the orchestra, unable to follow, were thrown into confusion.

England is, after all, the great encourager of talent. It may be imitated in Italy, or praised in France, but it is in England alone that it is rewarded. In 1714 Geminiani arrived in this country. George I. was then on the throne. He has not been famed for a too liberal patronage of the fine arts, but he was a German, which is equivalent to his being a lover of music. The Baron of Kilmansegge, a Hanoverian, and one of the royal chamberlains, was the protector of the young Italian violinist. Geminiani was introduced to the royal chamber; where he played before the monarch, with Handel accompanying him on the harpsichord. The King was delighted; acknowledged the violin, in such hands, to be the master of all instruments; and Geminiani was instantly in fashion. His reign was unusually long for a sitter on the capricious throne of taste,—he reigned fifteen years. During that time no one was allowed to stand in competition with him in the qualities of finished execution, elegance of conception, and vividness of performance. After this period, he began to write books of instruction, and treatises on harmony. He seems to have been the original inventor of those pieces of imitative music, which attained their height in that most popular and most tiresome of all battles, the 'Battle of Prague'. Geminiani conceived the extravagant idea of representing the chief part of the 13th Book of Tasso's Jerusalem by music. The ingenuity of the composer must be tasked in vain, where he has to represent things wholly unconnected with musical sound. He may represent the march of armies or the roar of tempests, the heaving of the forest or the swell of ocean; but in what tones can he give the deliberations of council or the whiles of conspiracy?

After a residence of thirty-six years in England, where he ought to have died, Geminiani went to Paris, where he was forgotten, and where he found it difficult to live. He returned only to pass through England on his way to Ireland, where, in a land singularly attached to music, the great master's old age was honoured. Some faint recollection of him survives there still. His scholar Dubourg was leader of the King's band, and he delighted to do honour to the powers which had formed his own. Geminiani was frequently heard at the houses of his friends, and preserved, though in extreme old age, his early elegance. But his career was now near its close. A treatise on harmony, to which he confided his fame with posterity, was stolen or destroyed by a domestic. The loss to the world was probably slight; but to the old man was irreparable. It certainly hastened his death; he sank perceptibly, and, after a year's residence in Ireland, died in 1762, in his eighty-third year.

A phenomenon was now to appear, the famous Guiseppe [sic] Tartini. Tartini developed new powers in the violin, an instrument which seems to contain within its four simple strings all the mysteries of music, and which may be still far from exhausted.

Tartini was, what in Italy would be called a barbarian, for he was a native of Istria. His birth-place Pisano (April, 1692.) His family had been lately ennobled; and as commerce was felt to be too humble for his descent, he was destined for the law. He was fantastic from the beginning. He first exhibited a forbidden passion for music. The passion lulled, or was superseded by a passion for fencing; he became the most expert of swordsmen, at a time when all the gladiators of Europe were furnished from Italy. It may be presumed, that law made but tardy progress in the rivalry of those active competitors. Perhaps to obviate this state of things, he was sent, in 1710, to Padua, once the great school of the civilians. There he committed the natural, but still more irreparable, fault of falling desperately in love. The object of his passion was inferior to the hopes of his *parvenu* family, and he was soon cast off without mercy. The world was now before him; but it was a desert, and the future delight and pride of Italy was near dying of hunger. At length, like many another son of misfortune, he fled to the cloister, where a relative, a monk, gave him protection. There he adopted the violin, as a solace to an uneasy mind; and rapidly acquired skill sufficient to take a place in the cathedral band. During this period his existence was unknown to his family. But on a grand festival, a gust of wind blowing aside the curtain which hid the orchestra, Tartini was seen by an acquaintance. The discovery was communicated to his family, a partial reconciliation followed, and as the triumphs of the law were now fairly given up, the wayward son of genius was suffered to follow his own will, and be a violinist to the end of his days.

But there was to be another stage in his ardent career. Veracini, a most powerful performer, happened to come to Venice. Tartini was struck with a new sense of the capacity of the violin. He determined to imitate, if not to excel, this brilliant virtuoso. He instantly left Venice, then a scene of tumultuous and showy life, retired to Ancona to devote himself to labour, and give night and day to his instrument. There he made the curious discovery of the '*Third Sound*', the resonance of a third note when the two upper notes of a chord are sounded.

He now rose into fame, and was appointed to one of the highest distinctions of the art, the place of first violin to St. Anthony of Padua himself. The artist was duly grateful; for, with a superstition that can now only make us smile, but which was a proof of the lofty enthusiasm of his heart, as it was then accepted for the most striking evidence of his piety, he dedicated himself and his violin to the service of the saint for ever. His pupils had already spread his fame through the European capitals, and he received the most tempting offers from the chief courts. But his virtue was proof against all temptation. St. Anthony was his sovereign still. His violin would stoop to no more earthly supremacy, and the great master lived and died in Padua.

It is remarkable that all the chief virtuosi of the violin, if they live beyond youth, palpably change their conception of excellence. Whether it is that their taste improves, or their fire diminishes, their latter style is almost always marked by a study of elegance, a fondness for cantabile, and a pathetic tenderness. Difficulty, force, and surprise, are their ambition no more. Tartini's performance scarcely assumed superiority till mature manhood. He said 'that till he was thirty he had done little or nothing'.

Yet the well known story of his dream shows with what ardour he studied. Lalande relates it from his own lips. The story has all the vividness of a man of imagination, that man an Italian, and that Italian a devotee—for though Tartini was an Istrian, he had the true *verve* of the Ausonian; and though he was not a monk, he was the sworn slave of St. Anthony. 'He dreamed one night, in the year 1713, that he had made a compact with Satan, who promised to be at his service on all occasions. And during his vision the compact was strictly kept—every wish was anticipated, and his desires were even surpassed. At length he presented the fiend with his violin, in order to discover what kind of a musician he was. To his infinite astonishment, he heard him play a solo so singularly beautiful, that it eclipsed all the music he had ever heard or conceived during his life. So great was his surprise, and so exquisite his delight, that it almost deprived him of the power of breathing. With the wildness of his emotion he awoke; and instantly seized his instrument, in the hope of executing what he had just heard. But in vain. He was in despair. However, he wrote down such portions of the solo as he could recover in his memory; still it was so inferior to what his sleep had produced, that he declared he would have broken his instrument, and abandoned music for ever, if he could have subsisted by an other means'. The solo still exists, under the name of the 'Devil's Sonata'; a performance of great intricacy, but to which the imagination of the composer must have lent the beauty; the charm is now undiscoverable.

The late Dr. Burney thus sketches the character of Tartini's style:— 'Tartini, though he made Corelli his model in the purity of his harmony and the simplicity of his modulation, greatly surpassed him in the fertility and originality of his invention—not only in the subjects of his melodies, but in the truly cantabile manner of treating them. Many of his adagios want nothing but words to be excellent pathetic opera songs. His allegros are some times difficult; but the passages fairly belong to the instrument for which they were composed, and were suggested by his consummate knowl-edge of the finger board and the powers of the bow. Yet I must, in justice to others, own, that though the adagio and solo playing in general of his scholars are exquisitely polished and expressive, yet it seems to us as if that energy, fire, and freedom of bow, which modern symphonies and orchestra playing require, were wanting'.

Veracini's name has been already mentioned, as awaking Tartini into rivalry and excellence. He was the most daring, brilliant, and wild of violinists. His natural temperament had some share in this; for he was singularly ambitious, ostentatious, and vain. At the 'Festa della Croce' at Lucca, an occasion on which the chief Italian instrumentalists were in the habit of assembling, Veracini, who, from long absence was unknown to the Lucchese, put down his name for a solo. On entering the choir he found that his offer was treated with neglect, and that the Padre Laurenti, a friar from Bologna—for ecclesiastics were often employed as musicians in the cathedrals—was at the desk of the solo-player. Veracini walked up at once to the spot. 'Where are you going?' was the friar's question. 'To take the place of first violin', was the impetuous answer. But Laurenti was tenacious of his right, and Veracini, indignantly turning on his heel, went down to the lowest bench of the orchestra. When the time for his solo was come, he was called on by Laurenti, who appears to have acted as the director, to ascend into a more conspicuous place. 'No', said Veracini, 'I shall play where I am, or no where'. He began—the tones of his violin, for which he was long celebrated, astonished every one—their clearness, purity, and passion, were unrivalled; all was rapture in the audience, even the decorum of the church could not restrain their cheers. And at the end of each passage, while the *vivas* were echoing round him, he turned to the hoary director in triumph, saying, 'That is the way to play the first violin'.

Veracini's prompt and powerful style must have made his fortune, if he had taken pupils. But he refused to give lessons to any one except a nephew; he himself had but one master, an uncle. His style was wholly his own. Strange, wild, and redundant. Violin in hand, he continually travelled over Europe. About 1745 he was in England. He had two Steiner violins, which he pronounced to be the finest in existence, and with the mixture of super-stition and frivolity so common to his countrymen, he named one of them St. Peter and the other St. Paul! Violinists will feel an interest in knowing that his peculiar excellencies consisted in his shake, his rich and profound arpeggios, and a vividness of tone that made itself heard through the loudest orchestra.

The school of Tartini was still the classic '*academe*' of Italy. Nardini brings it nearer our own era. He was the most exquisite pupil of the great master. Of all instruments the violin has the closest connexion with the mind. Its matchless power of expression naturally takes the mould of the feelings; and where the performer has attained that complete mastery which gives the instrument a language, it is grave, gay, touching, or romantic, according to the temper of the man, and almost of the hour. Nardini's tenderness of mind gave pathos to his performance. He left the dazzling and the bold to others; he reigned unequalled in the soft, sweet, and elegant. 'His violin,' says the President Dupaty, who heard him in Italy in 1783, 'is a voice, or has one. It has made the fibres of my ear vibrate as they never did before. To what a degree of tenuity does Nardini divide the air! How exquisitely he touches the strings of his instrument! With what art he modulates and purifies their tones!'

England was never visited by this fine virtuoso; but her musical tastes were more than compensated by the arrival of Felice Giardini, who produced effects here unrivalled till the appearance of Paganini. Giardini was born at Turin in 1716, and received his chief musical education under Somis, a scholar of Corelli. At the age of seventeen he went, as was the custom of the time, to seek his fortune in the great capitals. From Rome he went to Naples, and after a short residence in the chief musical cities of his own country, passing through Germany with still increasing reputation, came to England in 1750. His first display was a concert for the benefit of Cuzzoni, who, once the great favourite of the Italian opera, was now old and enfeebled in all her powers. In her decaying voice the violinist had all the unwilling advantage of a foil. The audience were even on the point of forgetting their gallantry, and throwing the theatre into an uproar, when the young Italian came forward. His first tones were so exquisite, and so unlike anything that the living generation had heard, that they instantly put all ill-humour to flight. As he proceeded, the rapture grew. At length all was a tumult, but a tumult of applause, and applause so loud, long, and overwhelming, as to be exceeded by none ever given to Garrick himself. His fortune was now made, if he would but condescend to take it up as it lay before him. But this condescension has seldom formed a part of the wisdom of genius, and Giardini was to follow the fate of so many of his showy predecessors.

His first error was that avarice which so curiously and so often combines with the profusion of the foreign artist. In 1754 he was placed at the head of the Opera orchestra. In 1756 he adopted the disastrous idea, in connexion with the celebrated Signora Mingotti, of making rapid opulence by taking the theatre. Like every man who has ever involved himself in that speculation, he was ruined. He then fell back upon his profession, and obtained a handsome livelihood by pupils, and his still unrivalled performance. Still he was wayward, capricious, and querulous, and old age was coming on him without a provision. He had now been nearly thirty years in England, and his musical rank and the recollection of his powers would doubtless have secured for him the public liberality in his decline. But he then committed the second capital error of the foreign artists, that of restlessness, and breaking off their connexion with the country in which they have been long settled. Giardini went to recommence life in Italy with Sir William Hamilton. But Italy now knew nothing of him, and was engrossed by younger men. After lingering there just long enough to discover his folly in one shape, he returned to England to discover it in another. Five years' absence from London had broken off all his old connexions, dissolved all his old patronage, and left him a stranger in all but name. His health, too, was sinking. He was enfeebled by dropsy; his sight was failing; and he was glad to find employment as a supernumerary or tenor in the orchestra, where his talent had once reigned supreme. He attempted a burletta opera at the little Haymarket theatre, failed; took his company to St. Petersburg, failed at that extremity of Europe; took them to Moscow, failed there; and then could fail no more. In Moscow, at the age of eighty, he died.

In music, as in poetry, there have always been two schools. The classic and the romantic. The former regular, graceful, elegant; the latter wild, often rude, often ungraceful, but often powerful and postponing all things to power. A performer was now to appear whose consummate elegance gave the palm to the classic school for the time. The name of Giornovichi is still remembered by some of our living amateurs. He was a Palermitan, born in the year 1745. His life was spent in roving through the capitals of Europe. Acquiring his exquisite and touching style under the celebrated Lolli, he went to Paris. After extinguishing all competitorship for two years, he went to Prussia as first violin in the royal chapel at Potsdam. He then went, preceded by his fame, to St. Petersburg. From 1792 he remained four years in England, visiting the provinces and Ireland, to the great delight of the public taste. Then, with that love of rambling which characterises musicians and foreign artists of every description, he returned to Germany, from Germany went to Russia, and in St. Petersburg died in 1804.

Giornovichi's style was neither powerful nor brilliant. It was what is better than either—delightful. Possessing great mastery of execution, it was always subservient to a native beauty of conception, which made his performance perhaps the most charming that was ever known. Delicacy, refinement, polish of the highest order, were there; but no violinist within memory had so fine a faculty of concealing his art, and subduing the audience as with a spell. His concertos have now gone out of fashion. Intricacy, eccentricity, and novelty are the choice of instrumentalists in our day. The startling, strange, and difficult are the modern triumph of the artist. But in these feats of the finger he abandons the nobler triumph of the soul. The concertos of Giornovichi remain before us as evidence of the elegance, tenderness, and sensibility of his genius. They are, of course, neglected by the modern solo player, who must astonish or be nothing; but they form the limit of all that is delicious in the violin; and the first artist who will have the courage to try how far they may be felt by an audience, even in our day, will find that they possess at least rudiments of success, which are not to be found in the abruptness and extravagancies of the later mountebanks of the fingerboard.

By a strange contrast with the playful grace of his style, Giornovichi's temper was more than irritable. His life seems to have been a long quarrel with men and countries. He was almost a professed duellist. His caprices alienated the public; and his patrons generally found his petulance more than equivalent to their pleasure in his ability. He left England in anger, and appears to have transported this luckless spirit wherever he went. But he was a matchless musician, and his concertos must be long the study of every artist who desires to discover the true secret of captivation.

The classic school was now to give way to the romantic. Viotti, a name still familiar, appeared in London in 1790, at Salomon's concerts. He was instantly recognised as the creator of a new era of the violin. Bold, majestic, and magnificent, his style of composition was admirably seconded by the brilliancy and vividness of his execution. Unlike the majority of great violinists, he had also the talent of a great composer. No man of modern times approached so near to the sublime. His master had been the well-known Pugnani, whose breadth of performance and force of tone were long unequalled. But to these his pupil added the fire of genius.

Viotti was born in 1755, at Fontaneto in Piedmont. His musical education was early and rapid. At twenty he was first violinist in the Royal Chapel of Turin. After a few years of study there, he commenced the usual tour of artists, and passing through Germany, came to Paris. There he was the universal wonder; but his petulance at a concert in the palace at Versailles drove him from public representation.

It happened unfortunately for his peaceable career that he was a good deal infected with the revolutionary absurdities of the time, and the angry musician notoriously avenged himself by becoming the peevish republican.

Viotti, with all his republican sympathies, and we do not charge his memory with any direct attempt to put them in practice here, knew Paris too well to return there while the fever of Directories and Democracies raged. He quietly withdrew to Germany, and there, in a villa near Hamburgh, he devoted himself to a much more suitable occupation than the rise or fall of dynasties, the production of some of those works, including his duets, which will make him remembered long after his political follies are forgotten.

His career was still capable of prosperity, but his rashness unfortunately rendered him unlucky. After a few years, in which his fame as a violin composer continually rose, he returned to England; but instead of relying on his own astonishing powers as a performer, he plunged into trade, became a wine-merchant, and shortly suffered the natural consequences of exchanging a pursuit which he understood better than any other man alive, for a pursuit of which he knew nothing. He lost all that he was worth in the world. He then returned to Paris as Director of the Conservatoire; but there he found himself all but forgotten. With the usual fate of musicians and actors, long absent, and returning into the midst of a new generation, he found national jealousy combining with the love of something new; and between both, he felt himself in what is termed a false position. He now gave up his employment, and on a pension returned to England, a country, of which, notwithstanding his republican "exaltation," he was fond. Here, mingling occasionally with society, still admired for his private perform-ance on the violin—for he had entirely abandoned public exhibition—Viotti sunk into calm decay, and died March 3, 1824, aged 69. Viotti's appearance was striking—he was tall, of an imposing figure, and with a countenance of strong expression—his forehead lofty and his eye animated. As a composer for the violin he is unquestionably at the head of all his school, and his school at the head. Its excellencies are so solid, that his violin concertos may be transferred to any other instrument, without a change of their charac-ter, and scarcely a diminution of their effect. Some of the most powerful concertos for the piano are Viotti's, originally composed for the violin. The character of his style is nobleness. Pure melodies and rich harmonies had been attained by others; but it was reserved for him to unite both with grandeur. This was, in some degree, the result of his having been the scholar of Pugnani, the first man who taught the Italians the effect of combined breadth and brilliancy. But it was for the celebrated Piedmontoise to be at once supremely elegant and forcible, and to unite the most touching taste with the most dazzling command of all the powers of the instrument.

De Bériot appears to hold the highest estimation among those French violinists who have visited England within these few years. He is probably also the best of the native performers. All the violinists of France who have figured since Rode, are growing old, and we have heard of no showy and novel successor. The school of Rode, is still the taste of the Conservatoire, and it is of the nature of every school to degenerate.

De Bériot is essentially of the school of Rode, though he is understood to be ambitious of referring his skill to Viotti. But his style, dexterous rather than dazzling, intricate rather than profound, and sparkling rather than splendid, is altogether inferior to the majestic beauty of the master violin-ist of the last age. It must be acknowledged that De Bériot's conduct on the death of the unhappy Malibran must raise more than doubts of his sensibility. And the musician, like the poet, who is destitute of feeling, is deprived of the first source of excellence. He may be ingenious, but he never can be great. He is ignorant of the secret which supremely sways the mind. In Germany, Spohr is still the celebrated name. Louis Spohr was born in the Brunswick territory, in 1784. His distinctions were rapid; for at twenty-one, after making a tour of the German cities, and visiting Russia with increasing fame, he was appointed first violin and composer to the Duke of Saxe-Gotha. In 1817, he made a tour of the Italian cities, and in 1820 came to England, where he performed at the philharmonic concerts. He had already been known to violinists by the science of his compositions, and his knowledge of the capacities of the violin. His performance in this country exhibited all the command which was to be expected from German vigour. But it must be confessed that the want of conception was apparent. His style was heavy. With remarkable purity of tone, and perfect skills in the management of the bow, he was never brilliant. Sweet melodies, graceful modulations, and polished cadenzas, were all; and in these are not contained the spells of music. Even his large and heavy figure had some effect in prejudicing the ear against his style. All seems ponderous alike. The weather, too, during his visit, happened to be unusually close for the season, and the rather corpulent German too palpably suffered under a perpetual thaw. His performance in this state was the reverse of elegant; and the intricacy of his composition, the perpetual toil of science, and the general absence of expression—qualities so visible in all his written works, without the exception of his best opera, Faust—oppressed his violin.

The most popular violin composer now in Germany, or in Europe, is Mayseder. His style is singularly, yet sometimes showily toilsome. As Spohr's is the labour of science, Mayseder's is the labour of brilliancy. His works are strictly for the fashion of the time—popular airs with showy variations, some feeble and affected, but some unquestionably of remarkable richness, variety, and subtlety. His air, with variations, dedicated to Paganini, the 'pons asinorum' of our amateurs, is a well-known specimen of all those qualities, and is even a happier specimen of Paganini's style than any published composition of the great violinist himself.

In our remarks on the musical genius of Italy, we had said, that south of the Alps lay the fount from which flowed periodically the whole refreshment of the musical mind of Europe. One of these periodic gushes has burst out in our own day, and with a power which has never been rivalled by Italy herself. Paganini commenced a new era of the king of all instruments, uniting the most boundless mastery of the violin with the most vigorous conception. Audacious in his experiments on the capacity of his instrument, yet refined to the extreme of subtlety; scientific, yet wild to the verge of extravagance, he brought to music the enthusiasm of heart and habit, which would have made him eminent in perhaps any other pursuit of the human faculties. Of a performer who has been so lately before the public, and whose merits have been so amply discussed, it would be super-fluous to speak in detail. But, by universal consent, Paganini exhibited in his performance all the qualities combined, which separately once gave fame. By a singular adaptation, his exterior perfectly coincided with his performance; his tall gaunt figure, his long fleshless fingers, his wild eager and wan visage, his thin grey locks falling over his shoulders, and his singular smile sometimes bitter and convulsive, always strange, made up an aspect which approached nearly to the spectral. When he came on the stage half crouching, slowly creeping onward as if he found his withered limbs too weak to bear him, and with his wild eye glancing by fits round the house, he looked not unlike some criminal escaped from the dungeon where he had been worn down by long confinement, or a lunatic who had just been released from his chains. Of all earthly forms his was the least earthly. But it was when the first uproar of reception was stilled, when the orchestra had played its part, and the solo was to begin, that Paganini exhibited his singularity and his power in full view. He has hitherto held the violin hanging by his side; he now raises it up slowly, fixes his eye upon it as a parent might look upon a favourite child; gives one of his ghastly smiles; lets it down again, and glances round the audience, who sit in the profoundest silence looking at this mystic pantomime, as if it were an essential part of the performance. He then seizes it firmly, thrusts it close to his neck, gives a glance of triumph on all sides, waves his bow high above the strings, dashes it on them with a wild crash, and with that single impulse lets out the whole torrent of harmony.

Peculiar as this picture may seem, it is only so to those who have not heard the great master. To those who have, it will appear tame. He was extravagant beyond all bounds; yet his extravagance was not affectation, it was scarcely more than the natural result of a powerful passion acting on a nervous temperament, and naturalised by habits of lonely labour, by an all-engrossing imagination, and by a musical sensibility which seemed to vibrate through every fibre of his frame. The whole man was an instrument. It must, however, be acknowledged that his eccentricity in his latter per-formances, sometimes injured his excellence. His mastery of the violin was so complete, that he often dared too much; and by attempting in his frolic moods, and his frolics were frenzies, to imitate things altogether below the dignity of music, he offended his audience. One of his favourite freaks was the imitation of old women's voices! He imitated birds, cats, and wolves. We have heard him give variations to the pretty air of the 'Carnival de Venise', the variations consisting of imitations of all the cracked trumpets, the drums, the fifes, the squeaking of the old women, the screaming of the children, and the squabbles of Punch. These were follies. But when his better genius resumed its influence he was unequalled, and probably will remain unequalled for another generation. He enjoyed one result which genius has too seldom enjoyed, extraordinary emolument. He is said to have made, during the first year of his residence in England, upwards of £20,000. His half share of the receipts of a single concert at the King's Theatre was said to amount to seven hundred guineas. Thus, in his hands, he established the superiority of the violin as a means of production over all others, and even over the human voice. Catalani, in her days of renown, never made so much by single performances.

The novelties which Paganini introduced into his performance have been highly panegyrised. Those are, his playing occasionally on a violin with but the fourth string—his pizzicato with his fingers of the left hand, giving the instrument something of the effect of the guitar—his use of the harmonic tones, and his staccato. That these are all novelties, that they add to the general compass of the violin, and that they exhibit surprising skill in the performer we entirely allow. But excepting the staccato, which was finished and elegant, we have not been able to feel their peculiar value. That they may be the opening of future and wide triumphs to this beautiful and mysterious instrument, we believe perfectly possible. But in their present state they appear rather tricks than triumphs, rather specimens of individual dexterity than of instrumental excellence. The artist's true fame must depend on his appeal to the soul. Paganini was born in Scura, about 1784, and died at Nice, 27th May, 1840.

A new candidate for praise has lately appeared among us in the person of Ole (Olous) Bull. Half his name would entitle him to our hospitality. He is a Norwegian, and unpropitious as the remote north may be conceived to the softer arts, Ole Bull is the only artist of Europe who can remind the world of Paganini. But unlike the great Maestro, he is nearly self-taught. His musical impulse came on him when he was about eight years old. His family successively proposed the Church and the Law; he espoused the violin, and at twenty resolved to trust to it and fortune. Some strange tales are told of his destitution. But all the histories of the great musicians have a tinge of romance. Ole Bull's was ultra-romantic. He reached Paris in the period of the cholera. All was terror and silence. His purse was soon exhausted. One day after a walk of misery, he found his trunk stolen from his miserable lodging. His violin was gone with it! In a fit of despair he ran out into the streets, wandered about for three days, and finished his wanderings by throwing himself into the Seine. Frenchmen always throw themselves into the Seine, as we understand, for one or all of the three reasons:—that the

Seine has seldom water enough in it to drown any body; that it is the most public point of the capital, and the suicide enjoys the greatest number of spectators; and that, let the worst befall, there is a net stretched across the river, if river it must be called, which may save the suicide, if he can keep his head above water for a while, or at least secure his body for a spectacle in the Morgue next morning. But we believe that the poor Norwegian was not awake to those advantages, and that he took the Seine for a *bona fide* place where the wretched might get rid of their wretchedness. He plunged in, but, fortunately, he was seen and rescued. Few men in their senses ever attempt to commit suicide; not even madmen attempt it twice; and Ole Bull, probably brought back to a wiser and more pious feeling of his duties by his preservation, bethought him of trying his professional powers. He sold his last shirt to hear Paganini—a sale which probably affects a foreigner but little. He heard, and resolved to rival him.

The concert season returned. He gave a concert, gained 1200 francs, and felt himself on the road to fortune [. . .] he now made a tour of Italy, was heard with pleasure; and at the San Carlos at Naples with rapture; on one night he is said to have been encored *nine times*. From Italy, where performers learn their art, he returned to Paris, like all his predecessors, for renown, and, like them, at length brought his matured talent to England for money. He is now twenty-five years old, if at that age his talent can be spoken of as matured. Determined in all things to rival the Gran Maestro, he would condescend to nothing less than a series of concerts in the vast *enceinte* of the Italian Opera House. The audiences were numerous, but the crowd belonged to Paganini. He has since performed with great popularity at the musical festivals; and if he shall overcome the absurd and childish restlessness which has so often destroyed the hopes of the most popular artists—can avoid hiring the Opera House—and can bring himself to avoid alternate flights to Italy and the North Pole, he will make his fortune within the next ten years. If he resolve otherwise, and must wander, he will make nothing, and will die a beggar.

His performance is of a very high order, his tone good, and his execution remarkably pure, powerful, and finished. He delights in double stopping, in playing rich chords, in which he contrives to employ the whole four strings at once, and in a singularly delicate, rapid, and sparkling arpeggio. Altogether, he treads more closely on Paganini's heel than any violinist whom we have ever heard. Still he is not Paganini. The imitator must always be content to walk in the second rank; and his imitation, though the imita-tion of a man of talent, is so close, that if the eyes were shut it would be scarcely possible to detect the difference. Paganini is the parentage, and we must still pay superior honour to the head of the line. But Ole Bull will be no unfit inheritor of the title and estate.

Anon., 'The Devil's Frills: A Dutch Illustration of the Water Cure', *Blackwoods Edinburgh Magazine* Vol. 54 No. 334 (August 1843), 225–33

This strange story about 'a Dutch Orpheus' who has 'an almost miraculous mastery of the fiddle' appeared in the same magazine from which the previous article was reprinted, known variously as Blackwood's Magazine, Blackwood's Edinburgh Magazine, *or (originally)* Edinburgh Monthly Magazine. *The plot, in six parts, hinges on a soul-bartering pact between a talented violinist and the devil, known here as Satan. In exchange for glory as a violinist Frederick promises the soul of his first born—but, realizing his mistake upon the birth of his son, manages to ward off Satan's attempts to collect by placing lace frills dipped in holy water across his threshold. In defeating Satan and saving his son, Frederick in his story achieves a harmonious conclusion that was lacking from biographies of Paganini.*

CHAPTER I

A stranger who visits Haarlem is not a little astonished to see, hung out from various houses, little frames coquettishly ornamented with squares of the finest lace. His curiosity will lead him to ask the reason of so strange a proceeding. But, however he may push his questions—however persevering he may be in getting at the bottom of the mystery—if he examine and cross-examine fifty different persons, he will get no other answer than—

"These are the devil's frills."

The frills of the devil! Horrible! What possible connexion can there be between those beautiful Valenciennes, those splendid Mechlins, those exquisite Brussels points, and his cloven-footed majesty? Is Haarlem a city of idolaters? Are all these gossamer oblations an offering to Beelzebub?

And are we to believe, in spite of well-authenticated tale and history, that instead of horns and claws, the gentleman in black sports frills and ruffles, as if he were a young dandy in Bond Street?

"These are the devil's frills."

It is my own private opinion that these mystic words contain some pro-digiously recondite meaning; or, perhaps, arise from one of those awful incidents, of which Hoffman encountered so many among the ghost-seeing, all-believing Germans. But don't take it on my simple assertion, but judge for yourself. I shall tell you, word for word, the story as it was told to me, and as it is believed by multitudes of people, who believe nothing else, in the good town of Haarlem.

CHAPTER II

YES,—one other thing every body in Haarlem believes—and that is, that Guttenberg, and Werner, and Faust, in pretending that they were the discovers of the art of printing, were egregious specimens of the art of lying; for that noble discovery was made by no human being save and except an illustrious citizen of Haarlem, and an undeniable proof of it exists in the fact, that his statue is still to be seen in front of the great church. He rejoiced, while living, in the name of Laurentius Castero; and, however much you may be surprised at the claims advanced in his favour, you are hereby strictly cautioned to offer no contradiction to the boastings of his overjoyed compatriots—they are prouder of his glory than of their beer. But his merits did not stop short at casting types. In addition to his enormous learning and profound information, he possessed an almost miraculous mastery of the fiddle. He was a Dutch Paganini, and drew such notes from his instrument, that the burgomaster, in smoking his pipe and listening to the sounds, thought it had a close resemblance to the music of the spheres. There was only one man in all Haarlem, in all Holland, who did not yield the palm at fiddle-playing to Castero. That one man was no other than Frederick Katwingen, the son of a rich brewer, whom his admirers—more numerous than those of his rival—had called the Dutch Orpheus.

If the laurels of Miltiades disturbed the sleep of Themistocles; if the exploits of Macedonia's madman interfered with the comfort of Julius Caesar, the glory of Katwingen would not let Castero get a wink of sleep.

What! a man of genius—a philosopher like the *doctus* Laurentius, not be contented with his fame as discover of the art of printing; but to leave his manuscripts, and pica, and pie, to strive for a contemptible triumph, to look with an eye of envy on a competitor for the applauses of a music room! Alas! too true. Who is the man that does not feel as if the praises of his neighbour were an injury to himself? And if I must speak the whole truth, I am bound to confess that these jealous sentiments were equally entertained by both the musician. Yes,—if Castero would acknowledge no master, Frederick could not bear that any one should consider himself his rival, and insisted at any rate in treating with him on equal terms. Laurentius, therefore, and the son of the brewer were declared enemies; and the inhabitants of Haarlem were divided into two parties, each ruled over with unlimited power by the fiddlestick of its chief.

It was announced one morning that the Stadtholder would pass through the town in the course of the day. The burgomaster determined to receive the illustrious personage in proper style, and ordered the two rivals to hold themselves in readiness. Here, then, was a contest worthy of them; an opportunity of bringing the great question to issue of which of them played the first fiddle in Holland—perhaps in Europe. It fell to Frederick's chance to perform first—in itself a sort of triumph over Laurentius. The Stadtholder entered by the Amsterdam road, attended by his suite—they passed along the street, and stopped under a triumphal arch which had been hastily prepared. The burgomaster made a speech very much like the speeches of burgomasters before and since on similar tremendous occasions; and Frederick finally advanced and made his salaam to the chief magistrate of the United Provinces. The performer knew that the Stadtholder was a judge of music, and this gave him courage to do his best. He began without more ado, and every thing went on at first as he could wish; fountains of harmony gushed out from under his bow. There seemed a soul at the end of each of his fingers, and the countenance of the chief magistrate showed how enchanted he was with his powers. His triumph was on the point of being complete; a few more bars of a movement composed for the occasion—a few magnificent flourishes to show his mastery of the instrument, and Castero will be driven to despair by the superiority of his rival;—but crash! crash!—at the very moment when his melody is steeping the senses of the Stadtholder in Elysium, a string breaks with hideous sound, and the whole effect of his composition is destroyed. A smile jumped instantaneously to the protruding lip of the learned Laurentius, and mocked his mishap: the son of the brewer observed the impertinent smile, and anger gave him courage— the broken string is instantly replaced. The artist rushes full speed into the allegretto—and under the pressure of his hands, burning with rage and genius, the chord breaks again! The fiddle must be bewitched—Frederick became deadly pale—he trembled from head to foot—he was nearly wild.

But the piece he had composed was admirable; he knew it—for in a moment of inspiration he had breathed it into existence from the recesses of his soul. And was he doomed never to play this cherished work to the governor of his country?—An approving motion from that august individual encouraged him to proceed, and he fitted a string for the third time.

Alas, alas! the result is the same—the chord is too much tightened, and breaks in the middle of a note! Humbled and ashamed, Frederick gives up his allegretto. He retires, abashed and heartbroken, and Castero takes his place. Mixed up in the crowd, his eyes swam in tears of rage and disappointment when the frantic applauses of the assemblage—to whom the Stadtholder had set the example—announced to him the triumph of his rival. He is vanquished—vanquished without having had the power to fight—oh, grief! oh, shame! oh, despair!

His friends tried in vain to console him in promising him a brilliant revenge. The son of the brewer believed himself eternally disgraced. He rushed into his room, double locked the door, and would see nobody. He required solitude—but the woe of the *artiste* had not yet reached its height. He must drink the cup of humiliation to the dregs. Suddenly innumerable voices penetrated the thick walls of the brewer, and reached the chamber of the defeated candidate. Those voices—Frederick recognized them too well—were those of the faction which acknowledged Castero for their chief. A triumphal march, performed by twenty instruments, in honour of his rival, succeeded in overturning the reason of the unhappy youth. His fiddle was before him on the table—that fiddle which had disappointed his hopes. Exasperated, out of his senses, the brewer's son seized the instrument—a moment he held it aloft at the corner of the chimney, and yielding to the rage that gnawed his soul, he dashed it into a thousand pieces. Faults, like misfortunes, never come single. "Blood calls for blood," says Machiavel— "ruin for ruin."—By that fatal tendency of the human mind never to stop when once we have gone wrong, but to go on from bad to worse, instead of blushing at our folly—Frederick, after that act of vandalism, dashed like a madman out of the brewery. The sight of his instrument in a thousand fragments had completed the business—life was a torment to him. He hurried towards the lake of Haarlem, determined to seek in its gloomy depths a refuge from disgrace.—Poor Frederick!

CHAPTER III

After a quarter of an hour's run across the fields, he arrived at last at the side of the lake, with the sounds of his rival's triumphal march for ever sounding in his ears. The evening breeze, the air from the sea, 'the wandering harmonies of earth and sky', were all unable to bring rest to the perturbed spirit of the musician. He was no longer conscious of the sinful act he was about to commit. He shut his eyes—he was just going to throw himself into the water when he felt a hand laid upon his left shoulder. Frederick turned quickly round. He saw at his side a tall man wrapped up in a large cloak—in spite of the hot weather—which hid every part of him but his face. His expression was hard, almost repulsive. His eyes shot sinister glances on the youth from beneath the thick eyebrows that overshadowed them. The brewer's son, who had been on the point of facing death without a tremour, grew pale and trembled. He wished to fly, but an irresistible power nailed him to the spot. He was fascinated by the look of the Unknown.

'Madman!' said the stranger in a hollow voice—'madman who cannot resist the first impulse of anger and false shame!'

'Leave me' answered Frederick in his turn; 'I am disgraced, and have no resource but to die'.

'The triumph of Castero, then—the triumph he owes to luck—has cowed you so that you are afraid to challenge him to another trial?'—rejoined the stranger in an angry tone.

'Every thing is lost", said Frederick, 'don't you hear those sounds?' he added, holding his hands out towards the city— 'my courage cannot bear up against such mockery—*vae victis!*—my doom is sealed'.

'But you do not yet know the full extent of your rival's victory. There is a young girl who was to have been your wife—a girl who loves you—'

'Maïna!'—cried Frederick, to whom these words restored his recollection.

'Yes, Maïna, the daughter of Jansen Pyl, the burgomaster of Haarlem. Well, encouraged by his success, Castero went to the house, and demanded the hand of her you love'.

'What?—what do I hear?'—said Frederick, and looked once more towards the lake.

'The burgomaster never liked you very well, as you are aware. In consenting to receive you as his son-in-law, he yielded more to the wishes of his daughter, to her prayers and tears, than to his preference of you over the other adorers of the Beauty of Haarlem. Castero's fame had long predisposed him in his favour; and the triumph he obtained to-day has entirely won the old man's heart'.

'He has promised her?' enquired Frederick in a voice almost inaudible from anxiety.

'To-morrow he will decide between you. You are ignorant of the arrangement entered into; and, yielding to a cowardly impulse, you give up the happiness of your life at the moment it is in your grasp. Listen. The Stadtholder, who did not intend to remain at Haarlem, has accepted the invitation of the burgomaster, and will not leave the city till to-morrow afternoon. That illustrious personage has expressed a wish to hear again the two performers who pleased him so much, and his patronage is promised to the successful candidate in the next trial.

He is a judge of music—he perceived the fineness of your touch, and saw that it was a mere accident which was the cause of your failure. Do you understand me now? Maïna will be the wife of the protégé of the Stadtholder—and you give up your affianced bride if you refuse to measure your strength once more against Castero'.

The explanation brought tears into Frederick's eyes. In his agony as a musician he had forgotten the object of his love—the fair young girl whose heart was all his own. Absorbed in the one bitter thought of his defeat—of the disgrace he had endured—he had never cast a recollection on the being who, next to his art, was dearer to him than all the world. The fair maid of Haarlem occupied but the second place in the musician's heart; but not less true is it, that to kiss off a tear from the white eyelid of the beautiful Maïna, he would have sacrificed his life. And now to hear that she was about to be carried off by his rival—by Castero—that Castero whom he hated so much—that Maïna was to be the prize of the conqueror! His courage revived. Hope played once more round his heart—he felt conscious of his superiority; but—oh misery!—his fiddle—his Straduarius, which could alone insure his victory—it was lying in a million pieces on his floor!

The Unknown divined what was passing in his mind; a smile of strange meaning stole to his lip. He went close up to Frederick, whose agitated features betrayed the struggle that was going on within. 'Maïna will be the reward of the protégé of the Stadtholder, and Castero will be the happy man if you do not contest the prize', he whispered in poor Frederick's ear.

'Alas! my fate is settled—I have no arms to fight with', he answered in a broken voice.

'Does your soul pant for glory?' enquired the stranger.

'More than for life—more than for love—more than for—'

'Go on.'

'More than for my eternal salvation!' exclaimed the youth in his despair.

A slight tremour went through the stranger as he heard these words.

'Glory!' he cried, fixing his sparkling eyes on the young man's face, 'glory, the passion of noble souls—of exalted natures—of superior being!—Go home to your room, you will find your fiddle restored', he added in a softer tone.

'My fiddle?' repeated Frederick.

'The fiddle of which the wreck bestrewed your chamber when you left it', replied the stranger.

'But who are you?' said Frederick amazed. 'You who know what passes in my heart—you whose glances chill me with horror—you, who promise me a miracle which only omnipotence can accomplish. Who are you?'

'Your master', answered the man in the mantle, in an altered voice. 'Recollect the words you used a minute or two ago, "Glory is dearer to me than life—than love—than eternal salvation!" That is quite enough for me; and we must understand each other. Adieu. Your favourite instrument is again whole and entire, and sweeter toned than ever. You will find it on the table in your room. Castero, your rival, will be vanquished in this second trial, and Maïna will be yours—for you are the protégé of a greater than the Stadtholder. Adieu—we shall meet again'. On finishing this speech the Unknown advanced to the lake. Immediately the waves bubbled up, and rose in vast billows; and opening with dreadful noise, exposed an unfathomable abyss. At the same moment thunder growled in the sky, the moon hid herself behind a veil of clouds, and the brewer's son, half choked with the smell of brimstone, fell insensible on the ground.

CHAPTER IV

When Frederick came to his senses he found himself in his chamber, seated on the same sofa of Utrecht brocade which he had watered with his tears two hours before. On the table before him lay the fiddle which he had dashed to atoms against the corner of the chimney. On seeing the object of his affection, the enraptured musician, the rival of Castero, rushed towards it with a cry of joyful surprise. He took the instrument in his hands—he devoured it with his eyes, and then, at the summit of his felicity, he clasped it to his bosom. The instrument was perfectly uninjured, without even a mark of the absurd injustice of its owner. Not a crack, not a fissure, only the two gracefully shaped §§ to give vent to the double stream of sound. But is he not the victim of some trick—has no other fiddle been substituted for the broken Straduarius? No!—'tis his own well-known fiddle, outside and in— the same delicate proportion, the same elegant neck, and the same swelling rotundity of contour that might have made it a model for the Praxiteles of violins. He placed the instrument against his shoulder and seized the bow. But all of a sudden he paused—a cold perspiration bedewed his face—his limbs could scarcely support him. What if the proof deceives him? What if—; but incertitude was intolerable, and he passed the bow over the strings. Oh blessedness! Frederick recognized the unequalled tones of his instrument—he recognized its voice, so clear, so melting, and yet so thrilling and profound,

> 'The charm is done,
> Life to the dead returns at last,
> And to the corpse a soul has past'.

Now, then, with his fiddle once more restored to him, with love in his heart, and hatred also lending its invigorating energies, he felt that the future was still before him, and that Castero should pay dearly for his triumph of the former day.

When these transports had a little subsided, Frederick could reflect on the causes which gave this new turn to his thoughts. The defeat he had sustained—his insane anger against his Straduarius—his attempt at suicide—his meeting with the stranger, and his extraordinary disappearance amidst the waves of the lake.

But, with the exception of the first of these incidents, had any of them really happened? He could not believe it. Was it not rather the sport of a deceitful dream? His fiddle—he held it in his hands—he never *could* have broken it. In fact, the beginning of it all was his despair at being beaten, and he was indebted to his excited imagination for the rest—the suicide, the lake, and the mysterious Unknown.

'That must be it', he cried at last, delighted at finding a solution to the mystery, and walking joyously up and down his chamber. 'I have had a horrible dream—a dream with my eyes open; that is all'.

Two gentle taps at the door made him start; but the visitor was only one of the brewery boys, who gave him a letter from the burgomaster.

'Yoran, did you see me go out about two hours ago?' asked Frederick anxiously.

'No, meinheer', said the boy.

'And you did not see me come in?'

'No, meinheer'.

'That's all right', said the youth, signing for Yoran to retire. 'Now, then', he said, 'there can be no doubt whatever that it was all a dream'. Opening the burgomaster's letter, he ran through it in haste. The first magistrate of Haarlem informed Frederick Katwingen that he had an important communication to make to him, and requested him to come to his house.

The musician again placed his lips on his instrument, and again pressed it gratefully to his heart; and then placed it with the utmost care within its beautiful case, which he covered with a rich cloth. Locking the case, and looking at it as a mother might look at the cradle of her new-born baby, he betook himself to the mansion of Jansen Pyl.

That stately gentleman was luxuriously reposing in an immense armchair, covered with Hungary leather. His two elbows rested on the arms, and enabled him to support in his hands the largest, the reddest, the fattest face that had ever ornamented the configuration of a Dutch functionary before. Mr Jansen Pyl wore at that moment the radiant look of satisfaction which only a magistrate can assume who feels conscious that he is in the full sunshine of the approbation of his sovereign. His whole manner betrayed it—the smile upon his lip, the fidgety motion of his feet, and the look which he darted from time to time round the room, as if to satisfy himself that his happiness was 'not a sham but a reality'. But his happiness seemed far from contagious. On his right hand there was a lovely creature, seated on a foot-stool, who did not partake his enjoyment. There was something so sweet and so harmonious in her expression, that you felt sure at once she was as good as she was beautiful. There was poetry also in her dejected attitude, and in the long lashes that shadowed her blue eyes; nor was the charm diminished by the marble neck bent lowly down, and covered with long flowing locks of the richest brown. And the poetry was, perhaps, increased by the contrast offered by the sorrowing countenance of the girl to the radiant visage of the plethoric individual in the chair. Whilst the ambitious thoughts of the burgomaster rose to the regions inhabited by the Stadtholder, the poor girl's miserable reflections returned upon herself. Her eyes were dimmed with tears. It was easy to see that that had long been their occupation, and that some secret sorrow preyed upon the repose of the fair maid of Haarlem.

It was Maïna, the betrothed of Frederick. On the left of the burgomaster, negligently leaning on the back of the magistrate's chair, was a man still young in years, but so wrinkled and careworn, from study or bad health, that he might have passed for old. The man's expression was cold and severe; his look proud and fiery; his language rough and harsh. On analys-ing his features you could easily make out that he had prodigious power of mind, a character imperious and jealous, and such indomitable pride that he might do a mischief to any rival who might be bold enough to cross his path.

Now, we are aware of one at least who ran the risk; for the man was Laurentius Castero. Frederick Katwingen started back on entering the bur-gomaster's room. His eye encountered the glance of Castero, and in the look then interchanged, they felt that they were enemies between whom no reconciliation could take place. From Laurentius, Frederick turned his eye to Maïna. The sorrowful attitude of the maiden would have revealed to him all that had happened, if the self-satisfied look of his rival had left any thing to be learned. The conqueror browbeat the vanquished.

'Mr Katwingen', said the burgomaster, deliberately weighing every word, 'you are aware of the high compliment paid by the Stadtholder to our city'.

'My dream comes true', thought Frederick as he bowed affirmatively to the magistrate's enquiry.

'And you are also aware', pursued the burgomaster, 'of the Stadtholder's wishes as far as you are personally concerned?'

Frederick bowed again.

'Thanks to my humble supplications', continued Jansen Pyl, raising his

enormous head with an air of dignity, 'our gracious governor has conde-
scended to honour our good town with his august presence for twenty-four
hours longer. But what ought to fill you with eternal gratitude is this: that he
has determined to hear you a second time when he returns to-morrow from
inspecting the works at Shravnag. I hope you will redouble your efforts, and
do all you can to please your illustrious auditor; and, if any thing is required
to stimulate your ambition, and add to your endeavours to excel, I will add
this—the hand of Maïna will be bestowed on the conqueror at this second
trial'.

'But, father!—' said the maiden.

'It is all settled', interrupted the burgomaster, looking astonished at the
girl's audacity; 'you are the reward I offer to the protégé of the Stadtholder.
You hear what I say, gentlemen?' he added, turning to the rivals.

'I shall certainly not miss the appointment', said Castero, throwing back
his head proudly. 'If to-morrow is not as glorious to me as to-day has been,
I will break my violin, and never touch a bow again as long as I live'.

'As for me', said Frederick, 'if I do not make up for the check I unluckily
met to-day by a glorious victory, I swear I will renounce the flattering name
my countrymen have given me, and will hide my shame in some foreign
land. The Orpheus of his country must have no rival of his fame'.

'To-morrow, then', said the burgomaster.

'To-morrow!' repeated the rivals, casting on each other looks of proud
defiance.

'To-morrow!' whispered Maïna, and buried her face in her hands.

CHAPTER V

I shall not attempt to describe the strange sensations of Frederick on
returning from the burgomaster's house. It will have been seen from the
glimpses we have had of him already, that he was of a quick and sensitive disposition, and that the chance of defeat in the approaching struggle
would sting him into madness. He pictured to himself the ferocious joy of
Castero on being declared the victor—the agony of Maïna—the misery of
his own degradation; and there is no doubt if the mysterious Unknown,
whose appearance he now felt certain was nothing but a dream, had visited
him *in propriâ persona*, that he would have accepted his terms—his soul for
triumph over his enemy, for the possession of the girl he loved.

The morrow rose clear and cloudless. At the appointed hour Frederick
took his violin, and prepared to set out. But just when he was opening the
door, the man in the mantle—the same he had seen the day before—stood
before him.

'You did not expect to see me', said the Unknown, following Frederick to the end of the room, where he had retreated. 'I told you, nevertheless, that we should meet again', he added, placing himself face to face with the son of the brewer.

'Then it was no dream', murmured the youth, who appeared to have lost all his resolution.

'Certainly not', returned the stranger, looking sarcastically at Frederick from head to foot. 'I promised you yesterday, on the banks of the lake, that you would find your fiddle unharmed, and that I would enable you to conquer your rival. But I don't feel that I am bound to do any thing of the kind for nothing; generosity was never my forte, and I have lived long enough among the burghers of Holland to insist on being well paid for every thing I do'.

'Who are you, then; and what is it you want?' enquired the Dutch Orpheus, in an agitated voice.

'Who am I!' answered the man in the mantle, with all the muscles of his face in violent convulsions— 'Who am I!—I thought I had told you yesterday when you asked me—I am your master. What do I want? I will tell you. But why do you tremble so? you were bold enough when we met. I saw the thought in your heart—if Satan should rise before me, and promise me victory over my rival at the price of my soul, I would agree to the condition!'

'Satan!—you are Satan!' shrieked Frederick, and closed his eyes in horror.

'Didn't you find me out on the side of the lake, when you told me you would exchange your salvation for years of love and glory. Yes, I am that King of Darkness—*your* master! and that of a great part of mankind. But, come; the hour is at hand—the Burgomaster and the Stadtholder await us. Do you accept the offer I make you?'

After a minute's hesitation, during which his features betrayed the force of the internal contest, the musician made his choice. He had not power to speak, but he raised his hand, and was on the point of making the cross upon his forehead, to guard him from the tempter, when Satan perceived his intention, and seized his arm.

'Think a little before you discard me entirely', he said, raising again in the soul of the musician all the clouds of pride and ambition that had given him power over it at first; 'look into the box where your violin is laid, and decide for the last time'.

Frederick obeyed his tempter, and opened the case, but uttered a cry of desperation when he saw his Straduarius in the same state of utter ruin to which he had reduced it before. The neck separated from the body; both faces shivered to fragments—the ebony rests, the gold-headed stops, the bridge, the sides—all a confused mass of wreck and destruction.

'Frederick! Frederick!' repeated a hundred voices under the window— 'Come down, come down, the Stadtholder is impatient! Castero swears you are afraid to face him'.

They were his friends who were urging him to make haste.

'Well?' enquired Satan.

'I accept the bargain. I give you my soul!' said Frederick, while his cheek grew pale, and his eye flashed.

'*Your* soul!' replied Satan, with a shrug of infinite disdain. 'Do you think I would have hindered you from jumping into the lake, if I had wished to get it? Do you think that suicides are not mine already?—mine by their own act, without the formality of a bargain?—*Your* soul!' repeated the Prince of Darkness, with a sneer; 'I don't want it, I assure you: at least not to-day—I feel sure of it whenever I require it!'

'My soul, then, belongs to you—my fate is settled beforehand?' enquired Frederick.

'You are an *artiste*', answered Satan, with a chuckling laugh, 'and there-fore are vain, jealous, proud, and full of envy, hatred, malice, and all unchar-itableness. You perceive I shall lose nothing by waiting. No, no; 'tis not your own soul I want—but that of your first-born, that you must make over to me this hour!'

'What do you want me to do!'

'Here is the deed', said Satan, pulling a parchment from under his cloak, on which strange characters were drawn, and letters in an unknown lan-guage. 'In putting your name to this, you bind and oblige yourself to let me know when Maïna is about to become a mother; and before the baptismal water shall touch the infant's brow, you shall hang from the window a piece of lace which shall have been worn by Maïna at her wedding. One of my satellites will be on the watch; he will come and tell me when the signal is made, and—the rest is my own affair! You will find this agreement in your fiddle-case'.

'Frederick! Frederick! be quick, be quick!' again shouted the father.

'Frederick! Frederick! Castero is boasting about your absence!' cried the chorus of impatient friends.

'I agree!' cried the *artiste,* and affixed his name. While he was signing, the stranger muttered some words of mysterious sound, of which he did not know the meaning; and immediately the pieces of the broken instru-ment united themselves—rests, bridge, stops, faces, and sides, all took their proper places, and the soul of the noble violin re-entered its musical prison, at the moment when that of the future baby of Maïna was sold to the enemy of mankind!

'Now, then', said Satan, as he sank beneath the floor, 'go where glory awaits thee'.

CHAPTER VI

What need is there to tell the success of Frederick Katwingen—how he triumphed over Castero, captivated the Stadtholder, and was the pride of his native town? The Stadtholder attached him to his person, settled a pension on him of fifteen thousand florins, and treated him as the most cherished of his friends. The burgomaster was delighted to gain so illustrious a son-in-law, and hurried forward the marriage with all his might. On the day of the wedding, when Frederick was leading the bride to church, at the moment when the party was crossing the market-place, a voice whispered in his ear—'A piece of the lace she will wear at the ball this evening'. Frederick recognised the voice, though no one else heard it. He turned, but saw nobody. After the ceremony, the burgomaster handed the contract to the bridegroom, to which the Stadtholder had affixed his signature. A present of a hundred thousand florins from the governor of the United Provinces, proved the sincerity of that illustrious personage's friendship, and that his favour had by no means fallen off. The burgomaster was emulous of so much generosity, and introduced a clause in the contract, settling his whole fortune on his son-in-law, in case of Maïna's death.

Behold, then, the *artiste* praised—fêted—and happy. Possessed of the wife he loved—rich—honoured—what more had he to hope than that those advantages should be continued him? Castero was true to his word—reduced his violin to powder, acknowledged Frederick's superiority, and betook himself to higher pursuits, which ended in the great discovery of printing.

The Dutch Orpheus is freed from the annoyance of a rival. He reigns, by the divine right of his violin, the undisturbed monarch of his native plains. His name is pronounced with enthusiasm from one flat end of Holland to the other. In the splendour of his triumphal condition, he has forgotten his compact with Beelzebub; but Maïna reminded him of it one day, when she told him he was about to become a father.

A father!—ha!—Frederick! That word which brings such rapture to the newly married couple—which presents such radiant visions of the future—that word freezes the heart of the *artiste*, and stops the blood in his veins.

It is only now when Maïna is so happy that he knows the enormity of his fault.

He is about to be a father—and he—beforehand—basely, cowardly—has sold the soul of his son who is yet unborn—before it can shake off the taint of original sin. Shame! shame! on the proud in heart who has yielded to the voice of the tempter—to the wretch who, for a little miserable glory, has shut the gates of mercy on his own child—shame! shame!

If Satan would consent to an exchange—if—but no—'tis impossible. The 'archangel fallen' had explained himself too clearly—no hope! no hope! From that hour there was no rest, no happiness for the protégé of the Stadtholder—sleep fled from his eyelids, he was pursued by perpetual remorse, and in the agonies of his heart deserted the nuptial bed: while light dreams settled on Maïna's spirit, and wove bright chaplets for the future, he wandered into the midnight fields—across the canals—any where, in short, where he fancied he could procure forgetfulness; but solitude made him only feel his misery the more. How often he thought of going to the gloomy lake where he had first encountered the Unknown! How often he determined to complete the resolution he had formed on the day of Castero's triumph! But Satan had said to him, 'The suicide is condemned— irrevocably condemned'; and the condemnation of which *he* would be sure, would not bring a ransom for this first-born.

The fatal time draws on—in a few minutes more Maïna will be a mother. Frederick, by some invisible impulse, has chosen from among the laces of his wife a rich Mechlin, which she wore round her neck on her wedding-day. It is now to be the diabolic standard, and he goes with it towards the door of his house, pensive and sad. When he got to the threshold he stopped—he raised his eyes to heaven, and from his heart and from his lips, there gushed out prayers, warm, deep, sincere—the first for many years. A ray of light has rushed into his soul. He uttered a cry of joy; he dashed across the street into the neighbouring church; he dipped the lace into the basin of consecrated water, and returned immediately to hang it at the door of his apartment.

At that moment Maïna gave birth to a son, and Satan rushed impatiently to claim his expected prey. But the tempter was unprepared for the trap that was laid for him. On placing his foot on the first step of the stair, he found himself pushed back by a superior power. The Mechlin, dripping with holy water, had amazing effect. It was guardian of the house, and protected the entrance against the fallen angel. Satan strove again and again; but was always repulsed. There rises now an impenetrable barrier between him and the innocent being he had destined for his victim. Forced by the pious stratagem of Frederick Katwingen to give up his purpose, he roamed all night round the house like a roaring lion, bellowing in a most awful manner.

In the morning, when he wrapt up the babe in the precious lace to carry him to be baptized, they perceived that it had been torn in several places. The holes showed the determination with which Satan had tried to force a passage. The enemy of mankind had not retreated without leaving the mark of his talons on the lace.

On coming back from church, Frederick ran to his fiddle; and found in a corner of the case the deed of compact he had signed. With what joy he tossed it into the fire, and heard it go crackling up the chimney!

All was over now; Satan was completely floored. He confessed, by giving up the contract, that he had no further right on the soul of the newly born, when once it had been purified by the waters of baptism. The father had recovered the soul which the musician had bartered away! Since that time, whenever a young woman in Haarlem is about to become a mother, the husband never fails to hang at the door the richest pieces of lace he can find in her trousseau. That standard bids defiance to the evil one, and recalls the noble victory won over the prince of darkness by Frederick Katwingen, surnamed the Dutch Orpheus. And that is the reason that, in passing through Haarlem, the visitor sees little frames suspended from certain houses, ornamented with squares of Mechlin, or Valenciennes, or Brussels point. And that is the reason that, when he asks an explanation of the singular custom, he gets only the one short, unvarying answer—'These are the Devil's Frills!'

Anon., 'Paganini', *Mirror of Literature, Amusement, and Instruction* Vol. 2 No. 13 (23 September 1843), 211

This apocryphal anecdote is a prime example of the fanciful Gothic characterisation of Paganini that proliferated in the press both during his lifetime and after his death—in this case, by attributing magical powers to his bow. The journal was also known under the alternative title of The Mirror Monthly Magazine *and was printed, in London, from 1822 to 1847.*

This great musician is reported, just before his death, to have expressed a wish that his favourite bow should be enclosed in his coffin, saying:— 'I wish to take it with me to the other world, that, by playing a tune to Satan and his crew, I may charm them from playing [on] me any of their devilish tricks'.

Abraham Elder, 'The Wandering Fiddler', *Bentley's Miscellany* 22 (July 1847), 316–27

This story traces the social ascent of an itinerant violinist, from rural vagabond to city gentleman, by virtue of his astonishing playing. It appeared in Bentley's Miscellany, *an English magazine that was founded by Richard Bentley in 1836 and which published the work of Dickens, among other novelists, in serialised form. (For a time William Harrison Ainsworth was its editor.)*

Abraham Elder was probably a pseudonym. This author also wrote 'The Wishing Well, Isle of Wight', which was published in the same journal in 1840. Like that story, 'The Wandering Fiddler' is a typical piece of Victorian fiction. In one scene, the protagonist George Postern—referred to as 'the fiddler' almost consistently throughout—breaks off from playing pleasant quadrilles at a fashionable ball to play a mournful dirge and a series of strange variations in 'unearthly Paganini notes' (325)—by which is denoted an incongruous mixture of 'despair, violent, loud, and irregular' with a 'merry tune' and 'a tone of mockery and sardonic laughter'.

Two young men were sitting, in the evening, in a small well-furnished lodging in London, wine and glasses on the table, and the atmosphere redolent of cigars. 'John', said one of them, taking up a violin that was lying by him, 'you seem dull and flat this evening, give us 'The sea! the sea!' and you shall have my best accompaniment'; and then he flourished away the air on his instrument.

'Dull and flat', said the other: 'is it not enough to make one dull and flat to see one's best friend perfectly ruined?'

'You mean me, I suppose', said the first.

'Of course I do. You had a small independence yesterday, and today you have not a farthing'.

'Not so bad as that quite. I have got twenty pounds—twenty pounds, well stretched, ought to last some time'.

'But what will you do then? You must do something. How will you pay for your lodging and your food?'

'Lodging!—why, I must certainly give up my present lodging, but I suppose I shall find something else. Who ever heard of a gentleman being obliged to sleep in the street! And as for living—why, I know many men about town that have not a shilling, that wear kid gloves, and appear to enjoy themselves amazingly. I suppose their secret is not very abstruse'.

'Oh! not at all', said the other: 'running into debt, and not paying,—cheating,—and sponging upon their friends'.

'That won't suit me, Tom. What say you to teaching a class of young gentlemen to play upon the violin?' Here he drew his bow across his instrument, and treated his friend to an air, with elaborate variations and almost impossible fingering. 'What think you of George Postern, Professor of the Violin.—I have it now, I will teach dancing; I can soon learn a few steps'. Here he went through the pantomime of a dancing lesson. 'How grand that would be, "Monsieur Postern de Paris". Push the Madeira this way, my dear fellow; this jumping about makes me thirsty. But, what's the matter now? you do not seem to be interested in my performances: you are in low spirits,—Love is it? I'll cheer you up then. I'll play you the identical quadrille that you danced with Isabella, the night before last', and his violin accordingly went to work.

'How provoking you are. To-day you are just a beggar, and you are as merry as if you had come into a large fortune'.

'A beggar! I am the real and rightful owner of the property of Broadacre'.

'Well, I believe you are the rightful owner; but another has legal possession'.

'That's very true; but there is many a man with a large property that gets nothing to spend from it'.

'But what do you intend to do?' asked the other; 'tell me without any foolery'.

'Well, I'll tell you what, Tom, I think I shall leave London, and travel; the very sight of your face makes me melancholy'.

'What, you think you will be able to travel about, without money in the same style that you have done the last five years! How do you intend to live? You appear to have as much idea of real life as a novel-reading, boarding-school miss'.

'Live! I intend to eat, drink, and sleep, and play the fiddle, and what can I wish for more.—Good night, Tom! I'm off to bed. Have you got a pocket-book with you? Just chalk down that you are engaged to dine with me at The Crown, on the 10th of September next,—private room—bottle of champagne—punch, and some of our old songs dished up again. It's some time hence, to be sure; but I am going on my travels: this constant smoke of London sticks in my throat'.

The next day, in a small town about ten miles from London, a man with a green shade over his eyes, was seen walking up the main street, playing upon the fiddle. He was followed by a few boys, and now and then he stopped his music to pick up a halfpenny. When he came to an open space, that was less crowded by passers by, he leant his back against the wall, and continued the simplest and most well-known country airs. The group around him gradually increased, for the musician had both the power and the will to please his audience; and a handful of halfpence and two sixpences soon rewarded his toil. This flourishing state of affairs, however, was here interrupted by a man in authority, of the constable, or beadle species, who acquainted our hero that he had orders to take up any trampers or beggars that were found within the parish. The musician stoutly denied that he had ever begged.

'We will soon see that', said the man in authority. 'The petty sessions is now sitting, and I will just take you before them'. The accused was immediately ushered into the justice-room, where the magistrates were sitting behind a table, at which was seated the justice clerk.

'I found this man, sir, collecting a crowed in the streets, and stopping up the way', said the constable.

'There was no thoroughfare where I was playing', observed the musician, making a bow to the bench.

'He is just a common beggar, sir', said the constable.

'I never begged in my life', replied the musician.

'Never begged in your life!' repeated the chairman in an incredulous tone.

'I never have begged', said the fiddler with rather a proud air. 'I could produce a witness here in court that I have no necessity to ask charity of any man, and if playing upon a fiddle be a crime, the Lord help the wicked'.

'There is no statute against that', said one of the magistrates, smiling. 'Come, produce your witness'.

'Oh! sir', said the fiddler, with a sigh, 'I fear that a poor man's witness will hardly be listened to here'.

'Rich and poor shall have equal justice here', said the chairman.

'What is my witness should take up ten minutes of your honours' time, would you hear him to the end without interruption?'

'We promise that', said the chairman.

The fiddler took his violin from the case.

'Fiddlestick', said the clerk.

'That's what it is', replied the fiddler, and, putting his instrument to his shoulder, he played a few bars of a simple air, then the same with wild and beautiful variations, then the same again with different variations, scattering thousands of little sparkling notes around the simple air, and giving a specimen of the most difficult fingering within the reach of art.

'I humbly submit to your worships', said the fiddler, boldly placing his hat in the centre of the magistrates' table, 'that my witness has proved that I have no necessity to be dependent upon charity'.

'What do you put your hat there for?' said the clerk crossly.

'In case any gentleman present should think that there was any value in my humble performance'.

The magistrates laughed, and there was some silver dropped into the hat.

'Will your honours permit my witness to return thanks for the kind manner in which you have heard him?'

They nodded, and he played a plaintive tune, with the best execution that he was master of. Applause followed, and another shilling was thrown into the hat.

The fiddler took it out and laid it on the table, saying, 'all paid for before'.

'This is a very unusual mode of giving evidence', said the chairman; 'however, my brother magistrates and myself are of opinion that it is satisfactory'. The fiddler bowed and retired.

'So I am now considered by the world', thought he to himself, 'a mere beggar, rogue, and vagabond, and such like. Fiddling the justices may do for once. It's a bad look out, I am afraid'.

He took a turning leading into the country, while these desponding thoughts were passing through his mind. At length he saw a comfortable farm-house, distant about field from the road, with some children at play before the door. He walked down there, and seating himself upon a fallen tree, began playing to his juvenile audience, accompanying his instrument with his voice. He sang them a song of 'Little Red Riding-hood'. The child's voice in a high treble, while the wolf spoke in the deepest bass of his instrument. And when he sang 'high diddle diddle, the cat and the fiddle', his instrument mewed like a cat, and barked like a dog, to the delight of his hearers.

'Mother! mother! mother! come and hear the funny man'.

Mother was pulled out of the house, but the mother was as sad as her children were merry. 'We have nothing to give you', said she, 'you have come to a lone house and a cold hearth stone'.

'Never mind', said the fiddler, 'I have made a good morning's work, and I will sit here for an hour and play with your pretty children; but if you will give me a bit of dry straw to-night, to keep me out of the public-house, I will be grateful to you'.

There was not a child's song that the fiddler did not sing to them, or a queer sound that the fiddle could make, that they did not hear,—a pig was killed, first he grunted, then he squeaked, and then squealed, ducks quacked, turkeys gobbled, the show-man blew his trumpet, the boy with the white mouse played his hurdy-gurdy. Such a delightful funny man was never seen before.

The mother thanked him. 'You are kind, kind to my children. We can give you nothing. Our last shilling went for rent yesterday, the last rent we shall probably ever pay; but if you will share our dinner, you are welcome, but it is the bare, bare potatoes'.

'Thank you kindly', said the fiddler. 'Now, Johnny', said he to the elder boy, 'come with me, and I will tell you a secret'.

He took the boy aside, and slipping some money into his hand, said, 'Run and buy a piece of bacon, and we'll slip it into the pot without any one seeing, and when your daddy comes home, he'll find a nice dinner. Won't that be fun?' and he gave Johnny a poke in the ribs.

Away ran Johnny. Where can he be gone to? Nobody finds it out; farmer comes home,—out tumbles the bacon with the potatoes—great surprize and rejoicing: Johnny calls it a grand potato, and then tells all about it. Farmer's wife affected, and almost makes a scene; farmer calls the fiddler a right good fellow, but adds, that there is only one thing about him that he does not like, which is his fiddle.

'My fiddle!' said the traveller with surprise. 'Why that is my better half. What harm can it possibly have done to offend you?'

'Nothing', said the farmer; 'but our landlord spends all his time in fiddling, and leaves us to the mercies of his agent; who, because we would not graze his horse for nothing, has raised our rent, and we are just ruined'.

'Spends his time in fiddling, does he?' said the traveller. 'I'll fiddle him. Where does he live?'

Farmer and fiddler spent the evening together like old friends, and in the morning the traveller started forth on his expedition to fiddle the landlord.

It was with unpleasant feelings that he found himself entering the landlord's grounds in the guise of a mere vagrant trespasser, momentarily expecting a rebuff from constable or pampered menial. However, undisturbed and unnoticed he reached the front entrance. As he stole his way up to the door, he certainly did hear the sound of a violin. A window on the side of the front door was partially open, and though there was a gauze blind behind it, this was not sufficiently close to prevent our wanderer from getting a tolerable view of the performer within. He was a short man, with a bald head, bowing and jerking his head and body in time with the music, and at times drawing his head up to the fullest height, when he thought the music favoured such a position.

At length he took the opportunity of a pause for turning over a leaf, to treat himself with a pinch of snuff. Our fiddler seized this opportunity, and taking up the air at the point where the little gentleman broke it off, he continued with scarcely audible loudness. The effect upon the little man was singular enough; the pinch of snuff was interrupted in its way from the box to his nose by gesticulations in tune with the music. At first the little man appeared to be thinking that he was humming the tune to himself, for he shewed no surprise at the music continuing without his agency, but as the music grew louder he started and looked a little about him; at length he got up and went to the door; the music all the time getting louder, and, as the door opened, the traveller's violin gave out its full volume, like a burst of sound rushing in by the opening of the door.

'Emma, who is that playing the violin in the house?'

'Nobody but you, papa'. Indeed all was silent now.

He sat down again, and as he looked at the notes the music again stole into his ears. Again he bobbed and bowed, with the pinch of snuff in his hand still unsnuffed. Again he walked to the door.

'Emma, who *is* that playing the violin in the house?'

'Nobody but you, papa', was again the reply.

Again he walked back again. The music was heard gently stealing upon him again. He flourished again his head and hands, and again put his hand upon the door, but did not open it, apparently thinking that Emma would repeat the same story. He fidgeted about the room. At length he went to the window, not with the expectation of seeing any one there, but apparently merely to look out at the landscape, while he enjoyed his pinch of snuff, which he still held between his finger and thumb. His eyes now fell upon the wandering fiddler, who had just stopped playing. The squire threw up the sash, and, stretching his bald head out of the window, cried out, 'You are a wonderful man—a very wonderful man. Play that again'.

Upon which the fiddler began, in the very worst style of street twang, 'There was an Old Woman in Rosemary Lane'.

'Stop, my good man; for Heaven's sake, stop'. The violin was silent.

'Would your honour like to hear "Cherry Ripe?" It is a wery fashionable tune in London.'

'Play this', said the little man, leaning out of the window with his violin, and playing the tune he was employed at before.

'Oh, that's a wery easy one', said the fiddler, running over the air in his very best style of execution.

'You are a wonderful man. Come in here, come in here, and we'll play a tune together. Will you have something to eat and drink first?'

'Thank your honour kindly', said the fiddler; 'it's all that a poor fellow like myself gets to live upon'.

'A poor trade that street fiddling, is not it?' asked the little man.

'Not so very bad', said the fiddler; 'I had rather be a fiddler than a farmer any day. I had rather have this little violin than twenty thousand farms'.

'That's a very odd sentiment—a *very* odd sentiment. Now, why would not you like to be a farmer?'

'I'll tell you for why', was the answer. 'It was only yesterday that I fiddled up to a comfortable farm-house. The old people were not about, so I played and sung little songs to the children for half an hour or so. At length out comes the wife, and says, "You're a wery good man to play like this to the children; but we've no money at all to give you; but if you like to share our dinner, you are welcome; but it's only the bare-bare potatoes". So I gives one of the boys some money (for I had made a good morning's work of it), and sends him to buy some bacon, and slip it into the pot without any one seeing. Now, sir, when the bacon tumbled out of the pot along with the rest of it, and they heard where it came from, the wife took my hand in both of her's. I heard a sort of choking sound in her throat, and a large hot tear dropped upon my wrist. Don't know, sir, whether it was gratitude for the trifle, or whether it was shame in receiving charity from a tramper, or it was that her heart was just a bursting,—and a wery little made it bubble over'.

'And what did the farmer say?' asked the little man.

'The farmer, sir, said wery little; but if he was rich, and I was in distress, I should just know where to go to'.

'Did you ask them what made them so poor?'

'I did, sir. They said that their father and grandfather had had the farm before them, and just because they would not graze two of the agent's young horses for nothing, he had rose the rent upon them, and they were just ruined. Their last farthing they paid in rent the day before, and next half-year's rent they had no hopes of being able to meet.'

'But where was their landlord all this time?'

'That's just what I axed, sir. They said that he was a good enough sort of man, but that they could not get to see him. He left all to his agent'.

'Do you remember the farmer's name?'

'Not wery well, sir. It was Toddle, or Poodle, or some such thing; but the name of the farm was Two Elms. I remember that well'.

'Two Elms!' exclaimed the little landlord.

'Ay, that's the name, sir, sure enough. It make my heart ache to think of it. I have a great mind to teach their little boy to play upon the fiddle; it would be a sort of rise in the world to him, to what his prospects are now'. Then putting his violin to his shoulder, he played and sung in the regular street twang—

'And then he'll be rewarded, and have his heart's delight,
With a fiddling all the morning, and a drop of gin at night'.

'That's a very vulgar tune', said the little man.

'It is, sir; most of my friends is wulgar. It's the wulgar people that shells out the coppers; twenty coppers goes farther than the gentleman's sixpence. That style of music, sir, costs a little more in rosin, but it pays best'.

'I wonder that a man of your musical talents should ever think of playing in the street'.

'Tried playing in a room once, but it did not answer'.

'How so?'

'Baker got troublesome, sir, and the furniture, though wery accommodating in their own way, would not help me out with the rent'.

'Let me hear whether you can play this piece of music', said the little man. The fiddler performed it with great execution.

'You're a wonderful man, and here is five shillings for you'.

'Don't want the money', said the fiddler; 'it's easy enough for *me* to pick up a shilling or two. I had rather that you would promise to speak to that poor farmer's landlord'.

'I'll do both', said the little man.

So the fiddler took his departure, playing a merry tune, while the little man put his bald head out of the window, and watched him till he was out of sight, repeating to himself, 'That is a wonderful man'.

After passing through several country villages, our fiddler came to another town. He was just taking his fiddle out of its case to commence operations, when a gentleman with several ladies passed him. One of the ladies offered him a sixpence.

'I thank you, madam; I never take any money that I have not earned by my fiddle'.

'Let's have a tune, then', said the gentleman. He played them a single Swiss air in his best manner.

'That was beautiful played', said the gentleman.

'It's worth more than a sixpence', said the first lady, changing it for a shilling.

'I think so, too', said the gentleman, giving another.

The fiddler picked up two or three halfpence in going down the street. At length he made a stop before a superior description of house, with a porch before the door, and a row of evergreens in front of the wall; but the owner, a large fat man, made his appearance at the window, called him an idle vagabond, and told him to be off, at the same time throwing out a half-penny, of which the fiddler took no notice.

'Why don't you pick up the half-penny, you fool?'

'If you do not want my music, I do not want your money', was the reply, a sentiment that was received with great applause by the few idle people that had collected round him. When he had gone through the town, he went to try his luck at the Manor House that was situated in a small park behind the church. He never liked going up a gentleman's grounds; he always felt that he was then a trespassing tramper, probably in the eye of the law a rogue and a vagabond,—liable to be ejected by dog, constable, or liveried menial.

His first notes, however, before the door, brought to one of the upper windows the bright black eyes of the young lady that had offered him the sixpence as he came into the village. He determined to give them a sample of his best.

The same party that met him in the road had now come down to him, some standing on the steps of the door, some at the lower window.

'Pray what's your name?' asked a fair-haired laughing girl, after his performance had been sufficiently applauded.

'I am known by no other name than the wandering fiddler'.

And he avoided further questioning by playing another air. It required no great observation on his part to observe that the dark-haired lady, that first noticed him in the road, appeared to take great interest in him and his performance. He detected her more than once stealthily attempting to look behind or under the green shade that he wore over his eyes; and when he played, her interest in the music was intense. It was clear that she suspected him to be in disguise, and something superior to what his dress showed. The squire also was probably of the same opinion, for he invited the fiddler to join his family in the drawing-room.

After he had played two airs in his best style and most careful execution, the little fair-haired girl, who had questioned him before, renewed her attack.

'You are quite a different sort of person from any wandering fiddler that I have ever seen before. You really must tell us the history of your life'.

'With great pleasure, madam. I have got it set to music, and I sing it as I do when I go through some of the villages'. Then assuming the vulgarest street twang, and paying with the worst possible taste, he gave the following account of himself:—

> 'I was born respectably all in the town of Rye;
> Mother she sold sausingers, and father sold pig's-fry.
> Then we lived in happiness and in prosperity.
> But one Mrs. Dorothy Fudge, who lived just hard by,
> She had a tabby cat, and dog, and a monkey.
> One day this tabby cat nobody could spy;
> She swore 'twas put in sausingers by mother, dad, and I.
> And nobody our sausingers any more would buy,

They were afraid of eating Dorothy's tabby.
So, straightaway of a broken heart my father he did die,
And mother upon that account very much did cry;
And I bought me a fiddle to live melodiously;
With a titum, tiddle, tiddle, little, tum te ty.'

And he concluded with a number of quaint and extraordinary flourishes upon his violin.

Great was the shouting of the children, who had joined them in the drawing-room when he brought this anomalous piece of music to an end. 'Sing us another song!—sing us another song!' they all cried together.

'I will sing you each a song', said the fiddler; and he treated them to a similar entertainment that he had given the children at the Two Elms Farm, concluding with the little song of 'The Babes in the Wood', which he played and sang so plaintively that he sent the children all crying to bed.

One of the party made some observation upon his performance in French. To warn them that he understood the language, he suddenly changed from what he had been playing to a little French *chanson*, accompanying his instrument with his voice for the first two or three verses.

'You understand French then', said the squire.

'I have wandered in France with the instrument', was the reply.

'Where else have you travelled?' asked the fair-haired girl.

An air from 'Der Freischutz', the first verse or two sung in German, was the reply.

'Oh, that's Germany! Where else have you been?'

The instrument replied with a Swiss mountain song.

'Well, and where else?'

An Italian opera air was the reply of the violin.

'Pray give us some further account of your travels?'

The violin now turned topsy-turvy became a guitar, accompanied by his voice in a foreign language.

'I suppose this must mean Spain?'

The fiddler nodded, and putting his instrument to his shoulder again, gave them 'Auld Robin Gray' in his best and most careful style of execution, and when he came to the part where the poor girl's misfortunes began, the notes assumed a tremulousness as if the intensity of grief almost denied them utterance. Great were the praises that were lavished upon him when he concluded, for his audience had lived for many years in Scotland, and the air reminded them of days long gone by.

'That is beautifully played, indeed', said the dark-haired beauty. 'Did you ever wander as far as the Highlands?'

The fiddler made no reply, but set to work with the pegs of his instrument, screwing one down and another up, then trying the notes, and then screwing away again, till he had got matters to his liking. Then getting up from his chair, his fiddle gave one prolonged bass note very disagreeable to the ear; then upon another string he played a Highland pibroch, the bass notes continuing to act the part of drone. During the whole time he was playing, he continued walking up and down the room with bent knees and toe and heel following in one straight line. The imitation of the bagpipes was so close that the deception would hardly have been discovered if the instrument had been out of sight.

'Ah! That is the Highlands, indeed,—our own bonny Highlands; these are the real pipes, and the true piper's walk'.

Extraordinary as it may seem, this mimicry of what musicians describe as the vilest musical instrument that ever was invented, gave more satisfaction to this family of taste and refinement than the most beautiful airs he had played upon the violin—the most perfect instrument that is known. While the bagpipe notes were ringing in their ears, the fresh breeze from the blooming heather was blowing on their cheeks, and scenes of long bye-gone days were present to their view. Friends and relations who had been long gathered to the dust were restored for a few transitory moments to health and enjoyment. But when the music stopped, the heathery mountains, the rapid stream, and the joyful forms of the friends of their childhood faded away again in the dark shadows of the past.

The fiddler now rose to take his departure. He had been engaged to play at a haymaking dance at Farmer Robins's who lived a mile out of the town, and he would be sorry to keep the company waiting.

'Our good wishes attend you', said the squire. 'I have no wish to pry into your secrets, whatever they may be, but we would be happy to be of assistance to you if we knew how. What say you to our getting up a concert for you in the town-hall? I think that we could procure you an audience, and I am sure that you would give them satisfaction'.

'With regard to my secrets', replied the fiddler, 'I can only say that I am just what I represent myself to be—an itinerant fiddler, and I have at present no other means of subsistence but what I earn by wandering about with my instrument; with regard to the concert, it would be too great a presumption for a street fiddler to think of it. I understand, however, that there is to be a public ball here next Friday. If I might be allowed to be present to accompany the orchestra, and play between the dances, I shall feel very grateful'.

'I will try if I can manage it for you', said the squire, at the same time dropping a sovereign into the fiddler's hat.

He now took his departure, and, on his way towards Farmer Robins's, he stopped and played occasionally as he passed through the streets. He found his rustic company assembled and waiting for his arrival, and amongst them was a poor boy of about thirteen years of age, who, he was told, was the son of a poor pedlar who had died suddenly a day or two before in a neighbouring cottage. He liked the appearance of the lad, and told the farmer that if he would get the pedlar's little stock sold and invested in the savings' bank in the boy's name, till he was of age or in want, he would take charge of him in the meantime, and make him his travelling-companion.

The dance went on merrily, the fiddler sitting on a stool under an old oak tree: and in the course of the evening he had the satisfaction of seeing his friends, the squire and ladies from the manor-house, amongst the spectators. Shortly after their departure, he looked into his hat to see how his contributions were getting on, and, finding a half-crown there, he threw it out saying, 'Somebody has given me a bad penny!'

'You great silly man', said a buxom country-girl, 'it's a half-crown!'

'I never take silver at haymaking dances', was the reply.

'It was one of the ladies form the Manor-house that put in the half-crown'.

'Oh! That's quite a different thing', said he; and he put the silver in his pocket.

Besides the half-crown, he earned that evening one shilling and ninepence in copper, for which he expressed his gratitude.

The fiddler's fame now spread far and wide, everybody talked of the wonderful talents of the mysterious wanderer. When he played in the streets, he did, indeed, obstruct the thoroughfare, but no constable or magistrate interfered. When he played before a house, instead of being turned away, he was shewn into the parlour. Numerous messages he received to come to play in this house and in that house, and a silver shower was falling pretty steadily into his hat. He was, however, perfectly aware that it was not simply his musical accomplishments that effected all this. But there was, in the first place, the mystery,—the green shade,—the general impression that he was by birth and education a gentleman,—his rejecting the silver at the haymaking,—his continual refusing to pick up half-pence that he had not first played for,—his kindness to the pedlar's boy—and, indeed, to many others; and, secondly, the variety of his performances. When he put his violin to his shoulder, no one could guess what was coming from it. He thus kept up a constant expectation of something new.

He now announced, wherever he went, that it was his intention of leaving the place on the Saturday next, and that he would enter the neighbouring town at two o'clock on that day. He took occasion to fiddle opposite the inn at the time of the coach starting, to get an opportunity of impressing this fact upon the coachman and guard. He also spent a pint of beer upon the carrier for the same purpose. He knew that his fame had gone before him, and a good entrance into the town he thought would be greatly in his favour.

The ball in the town hall took place in due time. The fiddler ensconced himself under the orchestra, in a door-way that led into a small inner room, as much out of notice as possible. The squire and his ladies, as might be expected, soon found him out, and the fair-haired lady, looking into his hat, exclaimed: 'Bless me! who in the world has put a halfpenny into your hat?'

'I put it in myself, ma'am, it is the nest-egg'.

The first quadrille was danced, and when it was concluded, the last notes of the music appeared to be prolonged in a most unaccountable manner, but so faintly that it almost appeared to be only the impression of the sound that was left on the ear. Presently the tune that had just been concluded broke forth again, but in a different key, and then the air with a number of fanciful variations. Then the air was played in a different manner altogether, with variations altogether new. The company, who from the commencement of his playing, were gradually crowding around him, were much astonished at the taste with which he played and the wonderful command he had over his instrument: and when he concluded, shillings and sixpences showered into his hat, which was placed on the ground beside him. The next dance, a waltz, was treated in somewhat the same manner, the last note was prolonged, and then the air broke out in a new form, was tossed about and played with, and then decked out in a new costume, to have other tricks played with it.

The third dance now drew to a conclusion. The company began as before to crowd round the wandering musician; but the last note was not prolonged as before. To look at the musician, one would have imagined that he was not aware that his turn had come again. He was leaning back in his chair with his instrument in one hand and his bow in the other, apparently looking intently at the tips of his hob-nailed shoes.

'I think he is going to sleep', whispered one young lady to her partner.

'I think he is fuddled', whispered a dowager to her neighbour. 'These fiddlers are very much addicted to it'.

Presently his instrument went up to his shoulder, and his bow was laid across it, suddenly a fragment of a merry laughing air rung out so clear and sharp that it startled the whist-players in an adjoining room. It ceased as suddenly as it began, and the bow dropped again upon his knee. The bow now again crossed the strings, and gave forth a fragment of a most mournful dirge. Again the bow was lowered, and there was a pause. Again the merry air was repeated, but with a gentler, milder touch, but for the concluding notes were substituted the concluding notes of the dirge. The merry tune now broke out into all manner of fanciful variations, but never whole or unbroken, for the mournful notes of the dirge were continually thrusting themselves in. Sometimes was heard the beginning of the dirge, and then the merry laughing notes would overpower it, and trip along singing its joyful carol like the blithesome heart of thoughtless youth rejoicing in its way. But then again and again the mournful notes would creep in, deaths, sickness, or misfortunes were trampling down its spring flowers. Sometimes in the high treble the merry notes were chirping, sometimes in the tenor, or again running down into the base. Sometimes the manner of his execution was altered, as if the mirthful air was seeking a new direction: but ever would the mournful sounds intrude and mix themselves up with the rejoicing, though never able to overpower it; gradually the music became less loud, till at length it faded away into silence.

After a pause, the mournful dirge was repeated, but in a softer, gentler tone, like the sad feelings of one that feels himself left alone in this dreary world, after that which made all his joy and pride had been taken away from him; but neither could the grief remain unalloyed, for the merry tune continually crept mildly in, like gleams of sunshine flitting over the dreary waste. High and low the measure wandered, sometimes slow, sometimes fast, sometimes in one manner, sometimes another; but ever the gleams of sunshine flitted over him, though they could not brighten up his landscape. The music again faded away, and fell to silence. Again a pause.

The merry tune was now resumed, but the execution was entirely changed. There is now no softness in the air. All is harsh and coarse, with strong emphasis upon particular notes; there is a boisterousness and unevenness in his execution. It is more like the shouting of the reveller, than the merry carolling of early youth. The air is played chiefly upon the tenor and bass notes, and the mournful air continually growling in like the consciousness of utter ruin breaking in upon the drunken excitement of the gambler, or the voice of guilt whispering into the ear of the reveller, '*I am ever by your side*'. In vain the shouting is loud, and the sound of forced laughter boisterous; the demon is ever there, and the skull grinning in the corner. Suddenly, in the midst of a wild tumult of notes, the musician stopped suddenly.

After a pause, the dirge was played again, but not with the softened notes of hallowed grief, but like the voice of despair, violent, loud, and irregular, the merry tune ever breaking in upon it, as it seemed, in a tone of mockery and sardonic laughter.

Then a pause.—The two airs are now mingled together in an extraordinary manner, as if striving for victory. At length the merry tune has it all to itself, chirping and carolling its joyous notes in the high treble. Gradually it comes down again; the contest is renewed, and at length the dirge groans out unrestrained its voice of mourning. Again a pause.—Now the merry air is played simply by itself, as at the beginning. A pause, and the dirge is in like manner repeated as at first. Great applause and commendation followed this performance, attended by a substantial shower of silver into the wanderer's hat.

It would be in vain to describe in words the different freaks of the musician,—his fantasias or unearthly Paganini notes, with which he wiles away the time between the dances.

At length his friends from the Manor House persuaded him, with some difficulty, to sing one of the little comic songs that he had amused the children with the night or two before, which afforded high amusement to his present more adult audience.

The ball was now drawing to a close, and the last quadrille was about to be danced, when the fiddler, having finished his flourish, thus addressed the circle that surrounded him:—'Ladies and gentlemen, I feel so grateful to you for your kindness and liberality to me this evening, that I will attempt to play you a piece of music that I never attempted before in public. It is the tune that Patrick O'Howlegan played on the pipes when he made the table dance. The story goes, that he was engaged to play at a ball, but, arriving a long time before his company, his fingers itched to begin his tunes. So he determined to play to the table. At first, the table took no notice of him or his music; then it seemed to get a little fidgety or rickety, as they call it in a table; then it kicked out its right foot like this (giving a jerk out with his own foot) repeating the kick at regular periods in tune to the music; then the left foot kicked out, and it went right, left, right, left; then the third leg kicked out, and it went one, two, three, one, two, three, then the fourth leg, one, two, three, four, one, two, three, four; and it waltzed round the room at a terrible pace, till it tripped over the coalscuttle, and smashed itself to pieces against the fire-place. The landlord brought an action against Paddy, and got damages; and it is said, that the Irish chancellor granted an injunction against Patrick Howlegan, to restrain him from every playing that tune again in a furnished apartment'. Loud cheers, and cries of 'Bravo, fiddler'.

'The gentlemen in the orchestra are tired; and with your permission, ladies and gentlemen, I will endeavour to twist the tune into a quadrille'.

'You must bring your fiddle into the middle of the room', cried several voices.

The musician declined producing his worsted stockings and hobnailed shoes to the broad lamplight.

'You must, you must!' and several of the young people of both sexes took him by the arms and by the coat, and fairly pulled him off his chair, and led him to the middle of the room, and there they seated him again.

'I am getting quite nervous', said he; 'I really cannot do it, Patrick O'Howlegan was the prince of pipers, and I am but a poor tramper'.

After a little pressing he consented, on condition that nobody should dance that was not merry, and that they would humour the music as far as they could.

The dance commenced; it was rather a funny quaint air, but nothing extraordinarily merry in it. At length there popped in a little jerking note, most of the dancers took the hint and gave a kick, the second time they kicked all well together—they kicked in the grand rond—they kicked in the pastoral—the kicks grew double and treble and fourfold, and on the last 'Grand rond' they all fairly kicked themselves out of breath, and sank down exhausted on the benches, when the notes of the fiddle were fairly drowned by the merriment and laughter of both dancers and spectators.

It was a heavy hat when he lifted it from the ground to take his departure.

The following morning, at an early hour, he was on the tramp, he had engaged to be at the next town by two o'clock. When he arrived at a lonely part of the road he observed two ill-favoured looking men sauntering on before him, they presently stopped and joined his company.

'You made rather a nice thing of it, I should think, at that last town', said one of them to the fiddler.

'I should *rather* think I did', said the fiddler; 'that ball last night was the primest go of all. I put my hat on the ground by my side, and the great nobs of the county kept shelling their silver into it, till it was nearly half full of metal—no copper there—all silver, with just a yellow-boy here and there, like plums in a pudding. If my hat had not been a right good eight-and-sixpenny one the crown would not have stood it. As it was, I do not know how ever I should have walked home if I had not got some people there to give me two or three five-pound notes in exchange. Very pleasant it was, walking home afterwards with my hands in my pockets, making the money chink as I went along'.

While the fiddler was relating this apparently innocent tale, the two men repeatedly winked to one another. When he had concluded, one of the men familiarly nudged his elbow, saying, 'We will do you the kindness to help you to carry some of that money for you—so fork out, or you are a dead man'.

The fiddler gave a long whistle of derision, saying, 'You really do not suppose that I am green enough to carry money about me. Did you never happen to hear of such a thing as a post-office order? It's the finest thing in the world; you just go into the post-office,—shell out your money—tell them the name of a person a hundred miles off that you wish to send the money to—give the post-master a sixpence or two for his trouble, and then walk out again as light as a feather. It's very convenient, isn't it?'

'Well, I don't know', said one of his companions, apparently thinking to himself.

'Do you know', continued the fiddler, 'that I rather expected to meet you somewhere about here to-day. There has hardly been a coin dropped into my hat the last two days, without your having counted it. Good morning to you'.

A party were now seen descending the opposite hill; they turned out to be people coming to meet the wanderer. The foremost of them was a stout agricultural-looking man, with a red waistcoat. 'You are the fiddler that was at Two Elms?—Thought so.—I'm the farmer's brother—all right now—got back to the old rent again—landlord kind—agent gone to the—. Says you did it all with your fiddle.—Must come to my house and bide there while you stay in the town'.

The fiddler thanked him; for which he nearly got his hand squeezed off.

The plot now thickened; the entrance to the town was absolutely crowded. Everybody was talking about the mysterious performer; and those that had been at the ball of last night described him as something almost supernatural; and, besides, everybody expected him at two o'clock. When he produced his instrument to commence operations, there was hardly room for him to move his elbow for the crowd. Here Bobby, the boy he had taken charge of, proved himself of great value in collecting the contributions in a little tin box. Invitations without end poured in upon him, to play at this person's house, and that person's house, all [of] which he accepted, but always played in the streets as he went from one house to another. The manager of the playhouse offered to make him leader of his orchestra, which was, of course, declined; but the fiddler offered to play him one tune upon the stage, in his proper character of tramping fiddler, with Bobby and his tin box by his side, for five pounds. The manager laughed at his impertinence; but, after some time, having consulted his better-half, or some such personage, he thought it would pay, and accepted the fiddler's offer, who, however, stipulated that not only he was to appear on the stage in his own proper dress, but that his fee was to be put into the tin box by some one present in the ordinary manner.

Our hero performed with great applause, and brought the manager a full house. He was introduced upon the stage, in the middle of a play, to a turgid character called the King of Mesopotamia, as the "minstrel from the far west;" and at the conclusion of his performance, his majesty dropped the five sovereigns into the tin pot, saying, "minstrel, take this guerdon." Ten minutes after he was fiddling again in the streets.

At a day and hour appointed sometime beforehand, he made his appearance at the next town. His entry was alike triumphant, and he filled his tin box in like manner, with great honour and glory to himself. The musician continued travelling round from time to time, always taking care that his fame should precede him, and that the exact time of his entry into each place should be known beforehand. At length he thought of returning, visiting again the same places that he had passed through before. The manager got him to play again, but not at ten pounds a night. The fiddler played for him each of the four nights that he remained in that town. Again he visited the manor house, nor did he forget his friends the farmer at Two Elms, where he just got in time for the harvest home, and there he fiddle to the reapers all the evening.

He arrived in London again on the 9th of September. He first called upon a private friend with whom he had previously deposited his clothes and other articles, and to whom he had consigned his earnings day by day. He then established himself in a room at the Crown, and wrote the following letter:__

'DEAR TOM,

'Don't forget that you are engaged to dine with me to-morrow at six o'clock.

'Ever yours,

'GEORGE POSTERN.'

Tom arrived at the hour appointed, and was delighted and surprised to see his friend looking so flourishing. Dinner was served, Bobby waiting behind his master. 'That's not one of the regular waiters here, is it?' said Tom, when the lad had left the room.

'Oh! that's my valet', said the fiddler; 'he is rather young, to be sure; but he is very trustworthy; he has been in the habit of being trusted with untold money'.

'But where does all the money come from?'

'Oh, it does not cost much, but really I *could* not go on any longer without a servant'.

'Now the cloth is off', said Tom; 'I will tell you some news. Sniggins, who got hold of your property of Broadacre, has no more right to that property than I have'.

'Well, I knew that two years ago,—what of it?'

'Why, it can be *proved* that he has no right to it!'

'There is something in that, however'.

"But there is one great difficulty in the way, it will cost you at least forty or fifty pounds to establish your claim. How in the world are we to manage that? You know I cannot help you'.

'I think I have got rather more than that in my pocket just now', pulling out a purse heavy with gold on one side, and stuffed full of bank notes at the other. The fact is, I have got plenty of money,—indeed, I don't know that it is worth while my bothering myself about this little property, except, you know, it is a sort of family thing,—one ought not to let a property go out of one's family."

The next morning they consulted their lawyer, who said that he thought it very probably that Sniggins would give up the property quietly, rather than subject himself to a criminal prosecution. The lawyer judged correctly, and George Postern became the undisputed owner of Broadacre; and our wandering fiddler immediately started for his new possession. He did not, however, take the shortest road to Broadacre Hall, but contrived that the manor house should come in the way.

He drove up to the door in an elegant equipage, and sent in his card,

MR. POSTERN,
Broadacre Hall

Neither the squire nor the fair-haired lady recognised him in his new character of a country gentleman; but the dark-haired lady blushed up to the eyes when he entered the room. His visit was first extended from a few hours to a few days, then to a few weeks, and at the end of the month Mr. Postern departed to take formal possession of Broadacre Hall, attended by the black-eyed lady, in the character of Mrs. Postern.

Anon., 'The Fiddler's Fate', *Ainsworth's Magazine* 23 (January 1853), 325–9

This story loosely based on Ole Bull's time in Paris appeared in Ainsworth's Magazine *eight years after Leigh Hunt's 'The Fancy Concert' (see above). The fictional violinist Pierre (characterised as a 'young magician of the bow' and as 'Paganini's young rival') is a nervous character who obsesses over his Cremona*

violin, pines for a pretty girl named Lisette, and has thoughts of drowning himself
in the Seine. This melodramatic mise en scène *thus depicts a violinist aspiring to*
Paganinian virtuosity as a self-involved, overly romanticised figure, like a character
from a late nineteenth-century French opera. If the tenets of tragic-heroic individu-
alism associated with later French Romanticism were anachronistically applied to
Paganini himself, it was partly because of literature such as this.

I

It promised to be a very brilliant season. The monarchy of the modern
Nestor—Louis Philippe—was established; the storms that had passed over
the political heavens left behind them a clear atmosphere of repose and
good humour; and all classes vied with each other as to the quantity of
amusement that should be crowded into an interval of peace, so unusual in
the volcanic world of Paris.

It may readily be imagined, therefore, that the advent of a new musician, of whom report spoke highly, was an event that drew a large and
impatient audience to the great concert room at the Opera House; and that
the person principally concerned in the success of the *début—videlicet,* the
violinist himself—was, during that cold and gusty March morning, in a
state of nervous anxiety little calculated to improve the chances of a highly
successful performance.

He strode about, then, this young magician of the bow, with his long fair
hair floating behind him, as the energy of impatience drove him from one
end of his apartment to the other; the soft blue eye, that told of northern
origin, assumed unusual fire, as the thought flashed through and through
his mind that, on the success or failure of that morning's work, depended
fame, fortune, friends, and gratified ambition. The placid expression, habitual to that good-looking face, gave way to nervous and agitated glances; and
still he strode from room to room, and found no relief from his anxious
anticipations. He lives in one of the streets branching from the Boulevards
with a brother musician, who, on the morning in question, has vainly
endeavoured to soothe the irritation of Paganini's young rival; and has left
him—hopeless of succeeding in his friendly design—to commune with his
own thoughts, which at length find expression in a soliloquy, addressed,
with all the ardour of a lover's language, to the object that was to be either
the sharer of his success or the companion of his failure—his cremona.

'To thee, faithful friend—to thee I look for hope and consolation—
solace of weary hours of labour—untiring in thy responses to my wishes—
inspiration of my genius!—hope of my future—joy of my past—to thee I
must confide my anxieties. Thou wilt not betray me'. And here he passed

his bow across the strings, and drew forth a sweet and touching melody in answer to his appeal. 'No, I feel that though wilt be faithful still—and yet—'

How very nervous our young friend is! Go, if you be wise, friend, and seek relief from this care that afflicts you in the crowd out of doors. Pah! the confined air stifles you; the furniture looks grim, and faces stare at you from the walls; go out, and see faces more anxious than your own; go and meet vagabonds with *no* hope before them—no pleasant memories bygone; go and look at the poor old invalid who is drawn by you in the carriage that he shall soon exchange for a hearse; and watch that sick child smiling faintly in its dear mother's tearful face; look at that eager wretch that rushes headlong through the crowd—he has just issued out from the gaming-table, where his last Louis has been won by sharpers—there is no hope for *him.* There is for you; cheer up, brave heart, and learn the lesson of endurance from the myriads round you. Whatever *your* griefs or trials may be, depend on't you would shrink, shaming, back into your ungrateful heart, could you but know how much your neighbour bears without complaint.

He follows my advice: already the cold air revives and strengthens him. Pierre, his servant, will carry the beloved cremona to the concert-room, where he will meet him, anxious, but ready to abide the critical judgment of the fashionable assembly that is to decide his doom. He has traversed the cheerful Boulevards, he passes the classical Madelaine, he strides through the Place de la Concorde, and reaches the Quays; a crowd is round the landing-place hard by, in which he has obtained a place in time to witness the raising of a woman's body on the shutter that shall bear her to the Morgue—there to lie for some days for the chance of a friendly claim to the possession of that livid mass of what once was warm life and perilous beauty—failing that, to be removed to an unmarked, unhonoured grave, and this world's oblivion for the worm that perished in sin.

Shocked and startled through he was, our young friend took to speculating on the subject of suicide; and, as many do who indulge fancy to the exclusion of stern morality, concluded, finally, that if the candle gives not light enough, it is well to extinguish it altogether. Musing thus, and calling to mind the noble simplicity with which so many of the ancients passed out of the world when they were wearing of it—until at length *felo-de-se* assumed the lustre of a virtue to his eyes—the *débutant* marches to the theatre, consoled to think that he may comfortably evade the pangs of disappointment should he meet with it, and very indulgent to the morose and gloomy view of things that his morning's adventure had excited.

Behold him at the gates; with a palpitating heart and trembling hand he pushes open the portal, and with faltering voice inquires for his servant.

He has not yet come; but it wants some minutes yet of the time fixed for the commencement of the concert, and the fashionable crowd is content to anticipate the feast of reason prepared for its entertainment by a preparatory survey of its individual members. Pleased with himself, every man appears gratified with his neighbour; he is there for amusement, and finds it (not, as we do, in an uncharitable spirit of ridicule, or, still worse, in morose resentment of the idea of being pleased under any circumstances whatever), in receiving and rendering those little civilities of act and word that distinguished the Frenchman of those long-past days. *O tempora! O mores!* how changed all these things now.

Time flies, and yet no Pierre, no cremona. A messenger is despatched to the musician's home, and returns, bearing the information that servant and idol have left the house some time, and may be momentarily expected. Patience—patience. Offers are made of the use of other instruments, and despairingly rejected; no hope but in *the* one, and that is lost or strayed. Finally, the impatient expectation is wrought to the pitch of intolerance both in audience and performer, and the latter determines on a personal effort to recover his fiddle and opportunity, and rushes madly through the streets homeward. It is in vain; no Pierre—no kit—no case even.

The man is new to Paris—he has lost his way; or, it may be, has met a friend who tempts him to the wine shop, to drink success to the master whom his delay is ruining. There is no trace—no hope! Ah! yes, there is hope of relief—the Seine, the Seine! Pierre will find him at the Morgue, and perhaps follow him there in his turn! Fate will be cheated of his destined disappointment, and Paris will be entertained no less by the death than it would have been by the *début* of the romantic and broken-hearted Russian.

If the thought was rapid, its execution was not tardily accomplished. Again he finds his way to the scene of the morning's visit; a hasty glance around, through the gathering mists of evening, a silent plunge, and all is over—perhaps.

There is in the Seine at Paris nearly as much mud as water, and he who desires to drown must manage well to avoid suffocation by solid in place of liquid agency. This fact will explain, perhaps, how it was that our young friend, finding himself in some danger of taking up permanent quarters in the bed of the river, evaded that unpleasant risk by striking out with considerable energy, and floating, aided by the current, adown the course of the river; but coats and other articles of usual dress are not calculated to assist efforts of natation; consequently, despite of a strong disposition to prolong the pleasures of a voluntary death, by resisting the embraces of the god of rivers as long as might be, the poor suicide found his legs too heavy for him, and his lungs not sufficiently buoyant, and, in short, after a few moments of severe mental agony and repentance, found himself dreaming of pleasant green fields, taking a rapid survey of his past life, thought of his mother and home, of the days when he said his prayers, and slept without dreams.

II

CERTAINLY pretty! not, perhaps, so refined as you, madame; her hands are not so delicate, nor her figure so *élancée*; she is not *bien gautée*, nor *bien chaussée*, nor *bien* anything but *bien* good-looking, and as good as she looks. Youthful, healthful bloom is on her cheek, and that is a pleasant thing to see; there is no double meaning in those glances that sparkle so merrily, or melt so sweetly into expressive sympathy; those rosy little lips are certainly not used to say what they do not mean; and, to judge by their expression, they should be accustomed to say the best-natured things in the world. Look at her as she sits by the invalid's bedside: how watchful yet silent—how eager in her attention, yet collected in her demeanour. Were it our privilege to read her thoughts, how much we might edify our readers with a homily on the duties of nurses, with compassionate details of the sufferings she has had to assuage; when, my dear young lady, you have watched that dear old lady through a month of rheumatic gout, and silently endured all the ill-humours so inseparable from such a curdling of the milk of human kindness as is caused by that, or any other ailing, you will form some idea of the patience requisite for the performance of such a dutiful attention;—you, my dear fellow, who expect that old gentleman to make his will before he dies (a legal ceremony he is much indisposed to perform, owing to a vague notion that when that is done he shall have forfeited instanter the privilege of continuing to bear his loving relatives of the melancholy satisfaction of paying his earthly remains the last testimonies of respect)—you, I say, my dear fellow, will symphathise, perchance, with the trials, and admire the endurance, of my darling little Lisette, when your daily devotion and watchfulness turn at last to the despairing hope that a merciful Providence cannot much longer continue to afflict humanity with the 'hope deferred'—of release from anxiety and pain.

'Pierre, you villain! destroyer of my peace! you did it to ruin me! My idol! my ideal! my delight! lost to me for ever!'

Poor Lisette looks very eager now, and, truth to tell, not too well pleased. 'How', thinks she, half aloud—'how could his delight have the heart to be lost to him for ever? If I were his delight, I would not let any one be the destroyer of his happiness. No, dear fellow—so young, to be so unhappy. I wish I could console him'.

Here the invalid turned round, and fixing those speculative eyes upon the musing maid, faintly begged for drink; and when those kind hands gave him the refreshing draught, they were retained for a few moments in that fevered grasp, and pressed with grateful tenderness. It is very odd that an incident so simple should cause much sensation in anybody's mind; but, when my pretty Lisette met the glance of those big blue eyes, and felt the gentle pressure of the hand, her impulse was to bend over it; and when, after a few moments' interval the blushing face was raised avertedly, some drops of a refreshing dew had fallen on the emaciated palm, and on the clothes that had buried that good face awhile.

'Lisette! Lisette!' cried a loud and startling voice from another room.

And Lisette, with a kind word of caution to the half-sleeping invalid, darted in the direction of the summons, drying her eyes as she went.

III

'MY sweet angel! my guardian and preserver! What shall I do to show you gratitude and love? Yes, love! for my heart is full of you and your goodness. You are my idol! my ideal! my delight!'

Poor Lisette cannot answer him. The very words! A week ago, and somebody else was his idol, ideal, and delight! and was lost to him for ever—and now! the cant phrase that had brought misery to that unhappy one, was applied to her, to be—who knows how soon abandoned or 'lost' in her turn. The very heart of our dear Lisette turned cold at such wholesale devotion, and there is no saying to what extreme her indignation might not have reached, had she not been restrained by generosity towards the invalid, and something or other that she read in those very good-looking blue eyes.

IV

PIERRE is in a state of distraction, and Paris rings with the mysterious disparition of our young friend. Fortunately for my story (for else I should have had none to tell) the police of Paris is, and was, little disposed to concern itself with the private affairs of people, and a few murders, robberies, abductions, and suicide, are matters foreign to the functions of those guardians of the civil liberties. Had any one observed within earshot of a gendarme that the King of the French had a head like a pear, he might have found himself speedily located in close durance—but, as for suicide, if monsieur does not like Paris, and takes to the Seine as a means of quitting it—'c'est son affaire'—politeness prohibits interference.

Pierre is, therefore, almost unassisted in his exertions to trace the lost fiddler. Many and ardent are the *sacrés* with which he anathematises the easy disposition that led him to accept the solicitations of Jacques Bonhomme to drink his master's health on his road to the Opera House. Why did he get so excited—so indiscreet?—why did that *gobemouche* Orleanist say so much in favour of the citizen-king, when Pierre's tendencies were so strongly Jacobinical?—why on earth did they not permit him to leave the cremona for his master on his road to the prefecture? Why, madame, because a *process verbal* must be drawn up; and it is impossible to know whether the fiddle-case may not turn out an important witness in the evidence for the prosecution.

Thus it was that master and man were playing at cross-purposes; thus it was that the Seine found an odd fish the more in it; thus that Lisette found little time to spare from the sick room for the diurnal occupation of beating shape and substance out of the various linens confided to the charge of 'Madame Duchesne Blanchisseuse', her respected mother; thus it was that some short space after the events herein set forth occurred, Pierre was rewarded for the fidelity with which he sought and mourned his lost master, by obtaining, through his means, the prettiest and kindest mistress in all Paris; and the hero of my little history found himself blessed in the possession of *two* idols—*two* ideals—*two* delights; the one had saved his life, the other made his living.

In its main points, this little tale is true. The record must close with some touch of sadness in the writer's mind.

The hand that drew those thrilling tones from the stringed toy is nerveless now; the high heart has ceased to beat—the simple nature, to rejoice. The generous giver has no more to give; the ambitious soul has soared its highest now; and the machine that enshrined some of the finest feelings and gentlest thought of our kind, was known among us by the name of Ole Bull.

'Zeta', 'Paganini', *Musical World* Vol. 35 No. 25 (20 June 1857), 397

A letter to the editor of a reputable London music periodical, written under the pen-name Zeta, asking about the circumstances surrounding Paganini's exile to Siberia (Paganini was never exiled to Siberia) stands as an instance of the growth of the Paganini myth through the mischievous spreading of false rumours. The tongue-in-cheek tone of the letter and of the editor's brief response suggests a certain playfulness in deliberately perpetuating the Paganini legend through outrageous insinuation. Similarly, the only other letter this 'Zeta' wrote to the journal, ten years

earlier, was jocular, not serious, in tone, asking 'has Correlli [sic] in any known
passage violated or departed from the laws of harmony'.[2] The Musical World,
founded by the music publisher Novello, was published weekly in London from 1836
to 1891 and dealt with musical topics and events of the time.

To the Editor of the Musical World.

SIR—Could you kindly (if in your power) answer me the following questions, the first one particularly, in your next number:—

1st.—At what age was Paganini exiled to Siberia?

2nd.—Had he, previous to his exile, shewn any of that wonderful power over the fiddle for which he afterwards became so celebrated?

3rd.—How many years was he in exile?

Your obedient servant,

ZETA

[We are unable to answer any one of the three questions. We did not know that Paganini was ever in Russia—much less exiled to Siberia.—ED.]

W. J. Prowse, 'The Mazed Fiddler', *Once a Week* Vol. 4 No. 85 (2 February 1861), 154–9

The titular 'mazed fiddler' ('mazed' meaning 'mad' in the dialect of Coombetown,
the English seaside village where the story takes place) refers to the story's protago-
nist, Willy Basset. While Paganini 'played . . . like a man who had sold himself to
the devil', this man 'plays as a devil might to whom Paganini had sold himself'.
Basset escapes life as a poor fisherman by achieving great success as a violinist in
Italy. But when he returns home to marry his sweetheart, he finds her in the arms
of his old rival. The two men fight, the girl suddenly dies, and Basset loses his mind.
He plays a crazed requiem for her and then, while playing a last air on the violin
that causes it to crack, himself dies. The simultaneous 'deaths' of the violin and
its player recall the ending of E. T. A. Hoffmann's 'Councillor Krespel' (in which
Antonia expires as the violin shatters to pieces). Both stories underscore the theme of
a psychic bond between a human being and an instrument. William Jeffrey Prowse
(1839–70) was an English writer and journalist from the coastal town of Torquay,
Devon. Once A Week *(printed from 1859 to 1880) was a literary journal primarily*
featuring fiction in serialised form that was originally launched to rival Dickens's
All The Year Round.

---

[2] 'Zeta', 'Original Correspondence', *Musical World* Vol. 22 No. 17 (24 April 1847), 269.

I. THE VIOLIN

'STUNNING weeds', said the Tourist, who was a Londoner, and flippant in his speech.

'The cigars', rejoined the Village Schoolmaster, 'are indeed of an excellent savour and fragrance; and methinks that if King James—a ripe scholar, Mr. Smith—'

Mr. Smith nodded; his notions of scholarship were hazy.

'—a ripe scholar, as became one who was the pupil of George Buchanan, and the friend of Isaac Casaubon,—could have sat with us here, in this little parlour,—could have looked out over yonder garden, and watched, as he did so, the long luxurious curls of smoke, he would, perchance, have somewhat mitigated the fury of his famous "Counterblast."'

Mr. Smith thought it likely, and then, with every demonstration of placid bliss, returned to the consumption of his cigar. He had come down for a stroll in North Devon, and the kindly, if somewhat formal old schoolmaster of Coombetown, happy enough to see a strange face, had quickly fraternised with him. Thus it befell that they sat together one July evening in the schoolmaster's parlour, and there, cigar in mouth, talked lazily as men who have much leisure on their hands. The day was very hot; but through the open window came the breath of many flowers; the little air that stole in was thick and sweet with summer, and from the street without came the voice of a young girl, crooning over some plaintive old west-country ballad. The conversation flagged, for the cigars were undeniably good. At last:

"What's that?" cried Smith, starting up.

"Wait and listen," answered his friend.

It was only the sound of a violin in the next house; and Smith, who was a practised musician, trembled lest he should hear some eccentric jig, such as country fiddlers alone can perpetrate or even imagine. He was wrong. In five minutes a look of wonder was in his face; in ten, he cried, "the fellow has genius!" There was an immense pathos in the music; the divine instrument (the instruments own the organ for their king, but they claim the violin for their poet) seemed to be telling some strange tale, of love ineffable and of infinite sorrow; now, it would seem to sink into a wail of utter desolate weariness, and anon there was a wild exultation,—rapid, passionate, vibrant, in every tone. Of mere technical skill, the player had evidently abundance; but then, besides this, there was a soul in his playing—there was passion, poetry. Silently the two men sat, listening with reverence to the wonder-worker; at last the music grew confused, even harsh, as if the player had sought to go beyond the limits of possible expression, and had found some strange harmony in what, to ears less finely attuned or to hearts less hotly excited, seemed utter discord. Then he ceased, and our friends looked gravely at each other.

'You are astonished to hear such music in a little fishing hamlet?'

Said the Londoner: 'If that man comes to town he will make a fortune in a year. I have heard Paganini; he played, they said, like a man who had sold himself to the devil. Why, this man plays as a devil might to whom Paganini had sold himself! Who taught him?'

'Two masters', said the schoolmaster, with a half-frown at the Londoner's rather irreverent words, 'two masters—Love and Vanity—and the latter, I fear me, was the stronger of the two. The man is mad—'mazed' as we call it here. His is a painful story. Will you hear it?'

The Londoner, really interested, gave a rapid *yes*, and his friend began.

II. THE SCHOOLMASTER'S STORY

'I CAME to this place a man of thirty, and I am sixty now. It suits me well enough. I was never fitted to struggle in the great cities; and here I know every one. My work is simple; its reward is sufficient for my few wants, and I know that the children love me. There is much comfort in that, sir, for one who has never been a father. Well, when I came here, the prettiest girl for many a mile round was Mary Lee. You have seen our North Devon girls— dark eyes, dark hair, and ready speech? Mary had all this, and she had more; she had the bearing of a born lady, so that, though our folks are plain and rough, no one ever dreamt of uttering a coarse jest before Mary Lee. Her father, a small farmer, had left her tolerably well to do; and the old maiden aunt, with whom she lived, had been to her a very mother. You will suppose that she had many lovers. In a manner, she had; every lad in Coombetown felt a kind of pride in her; but she was "grandlike,"—there was something about her with rather awed than invited them, and only John Hamlyn had any reason to hope for her hand. He lives next door still—a plain old sailor now, but in years gone by, as fine and daring a fellow as breathed along the coast. Like Mary, he was sufficiently rich; that is, his father had owned two or three small coasters (people *did* talk of his smuggling, but that is no affair of mine) and, dying, left them to his only son. Mary and he had grown up side by side, and always there was a quiet kind of affection between them. There was more than that, one wild winter morning when John was brought speechless and bleeding into the village, and Mary heard how, in the tempest of the night before, he had manned a boat, pushed off to a large brig that had struck upon the Tangle Rock in the offing, and saved the lives of some of her crew at the imminent peril of his own. A spar had struck him during his work, and there was a great ghastly wound in his head.

Dr. Woodbury—the old gentleman whom you saw to-day upon his little chestnut mare—met the men, as they silently brought John Hamlyn up the steep path from the pier, and saw him carried to his house; and Mary, going home, knelt down beside her bed, burst into wild tears, then into prayers as wild, and felt, for the first time, as if she really loved the great strong sailor. He recovered slowly;—some traces of the wound indeed remained, but he could have had, I think, no scars more glorious, and ere long he hoped to bring Mary home as his wife'.

'And this brave fellow is the one who was playing?'

'Pray let me go on. No, he is not. Genius he never had; only the courage of a lion and the affectionate gentleness of a child. Poor Mary! It had been well had these sufficed her, and so for a time they did; but, unfortunately for her, unfortunately for John, there was a lad in the village *who had* genius, and, alas! who knew it. Willy Basset was but a poor young fisherman—not a strong one, not even a brave one; but one of singular parts. If I was too partial to him, and if my praises helped to turn his head and fill him with the demon of vanity, may God forgive me. I did all for the best. Suffice it, sir, that whatever time he could steal from the drudgery of his daily life, was given partly to the books I lent him, and partly to practising upon an old violin which had belonged to his father, the village fiddler.

'John Hamlyn passed the cottage where he lived one day, and heard him playing. "Willy Basset, lad", cried the big curly-haired John, "it seems to me you might spend your time better than in fiddling, with your poor old mother bed-ridden at home. There's the herring-hawks off the bay, man, and the shoal will be round the head before you finish Bobbing Joan. Out to the boats, Willy". Willy looked up, and was about to answer angrily; but John looked alarmingly big. Said Willy: "It is very generous of you, John Hamlyn, to talk of my mother's poverty. You are richer than we, I know; but you need not remind us of it!" These were mean, false, cowardly words of his; but John—placable John—felt as if he had spoken too roughly, and held out his hand. Willy refused it, and turned away. From that hour, as I fear, he often thought how he could best injure the strong prosperous fellow who had reminded him of his duty.

'You have noticed that we are a musical race down here. Mary Lee had this passion almost to excess, and sang with singular sweetness. One evening, at my house, she had been singing some of her quaint old songs, when Willy Basset came up to return some of my books. He sat down, and I asked him to play a tune or two, as he often would when he came to see me. As yet he was but a poor player, though already he gave some faint promise of that wondrous skill to which he afterwards attained. This night, whatever was his inspiration—and Mary Lee's dark eyes had surely much to do with it—he played as he never had before, with quite new passion and energy. This was indeed the first time on which I ever heard him improvise. Hitherto he had simply played the ordinary country tunes; to-night, he struck boldly away from them, trusted to his own heart, and succeeded. Have I said that he was not handsome? At ordinary times he was not; but *now*, as his eyes lighted up with the excitement of his music, there was a wild beauty about them which, to a romantic girl, would have far more charm than ordinary comeliness. When he ended, I asked Mary to sing—and behold, Mary was crying.

'It is the old story. What was John Hamlyn, plain and bluff, to this Willy Basset, so gifted and so passionate? Mary asked herself this question too often for her first love to last. It died out. John saw the change, but would not believe it. A year passed by. Willy Basset's bed-ridden mother died— proud of her son, and loving him wildly to the last. The poor soul cried out, as she lay dying, in her wretched cottage, on a rough December day, "He will be the pride of the county yet, my Willy—a wonderful boy, sirs! a wonderful boy!" But the neighbours said that little good would ever come of one who had been fiddling to please himself when he should have been fishing to help his mother; and I could not but feel that what they said was true.

'And now, sir, came a time which, to Mary, I think, was one of the purest happiness; but which brought pleasure less pure to Willy Basset, and absolute torture to the brave John. Willy—let me not be unjust to him—was thoroughly sincere in all his professions of love; but there mingled with them always, I fear, a base sense of triumph over his richer, stronger, handsomer, manlier rival. And as for John, though the poor fellow blundered about in his big, uncouth, righteous way, still sang at his work, and never left a duty undone, yet was he as assuredly smitten with a deep and terrible grief as if he had testified thereto by jumping over the cliffs—which often he was very much inclined to do—for, struggle against the conviction as he might, he could not but see that Mary Lee, though she had ever a kindly word and a bright smile for him, no more intended to *marry* him than she intended, say, to marry *me*! Thus went down all the poor fellow's card-castles, shattered by a fiddle-stick. He was not imaginative, this big John; but, smoking his honest pipe of evenings in the sanded kitchen of his old homestead, he had had his little visions of happiness and ease, the central figure in every such vision being that of Mary Lee. Well, *that* was over now. I don't pity him the less because he could not write a sonnet about his "blighted hopes".

In the April after his mother's death, Willy Basset, with his violin and with ten pounds in his pocket—my savings were very small, and I could give him no more—sailed away in a ship that was bound to Naples. He went as a common sailor; but I knew that what he chiefly wanted was to reach some land where he might obtain really good musical teaching; and, for my own part, I encouraged him in this scheme, wild as it might appear. An old friend of my own lived at Naples, and I recommended Willy to him as a youth of rare and brilliant promise. For, whether it was through his love for Mary Lee, or whether it was through a mere ambitious desire to show his kinsfolk and his townsfolk that, if he *was* a humble fisherman, he was yet something superior to *that*, certain it is that his genius had taken a rapid and sudden start, and that he would oftentimes play with really wonderful expression and power. Ere he went, Mary Lee, with little urging, had promised that if in a few years he came back in a position to maintain a wife she would be his.

'I remember well the morning on which his vessel sailed—a drizzly uncertain April day, with now and then some faint and fitful gleams of sunshine over the sea. His friends, Mary amongst them, stood upon the pierhead as the ship went slowly away to the west. Soon they could no longer see the waiving of his red fisherman's cap; the vessel went on, growing fainter and fainter to the sight; a cold cheerless rain began to fall; at last the ship could be seen no more, and Mary Lee, as the Good Endeavour went fairly out of sight, sank back fainting in John Hamlyn's arms. He was not far from fainting himself, I think, the big brave man, as he led her home; and if I found some tears in my own eyes that day, I do not think I was worse for them.

'Letters came from Willy in due time—hopeful, eloquent letters. My friend at Naples was very kind to him; procured him a master; and, at last, plain Willy Basset, ex-fisher-boy, had a seat in the orchestra of an Italian opera. Mary was proud enough of this, be sure; but when three years passed by, and he still said nothing of returning, she became uneasy. His letters grew less frequent. "He has found new friends", thought she, "and forgets old Coombetown folk". Indeed, indeed, sir, if *she* was sorely tried, yet was he as sorely tempted! I learnt afterwards that he had progressed in his art with startling rapidity; at last he became a celebrity; and you know, doubtless far better than I, to what seductions an artist is exposed in the south.

'Six years after his departure there came a letter from him which made Mary's face flush and glow again. He was coming home—successful, famous, rich. Home to his little Mary, "whom he loved better than any signora of them all". Home to his "dear old friend", naming me with words far more flattering than I liked. Home to old Coombetown, "where, perhaps, he would be valued rather more than formerly". And so on: a vain, egotistical letter, as I see now, but which made Mary's heart as light as a bird's. She had waited long, waited faithfully, but she had not waited in vain, it seemed. Was she not right in her choice?

'John Hamlyn? John Hamlyn was doing very well in the coasting-trade between Coombetown and Bristol.

'Willy Basset? He was a famous artist—and she would be an artist's wife.

'The artist reached home. He landed at Bristol, where he lodged almost all his money with a well-known banker, and thence posted on to the little Devonshire village with what speed he might. You will pardon me if I do not attempt to describe his meeting with Mary Lee. I could tell you of its gladness, of its vehement passion, but even as I speak the sad memory is with me of all those trials, all those afflictions, which so speedily followed this hour of intense delight. I found him changed—not altogether for the better. His face, though he came from the south, was very pale; his eyes, brilliant as ever, had now a light in them which was not that of cheerfulness and health; and in his whole bearing there was somewhat of ostentation, somewhat of affectation, which it pained me bitterly to see. Despite all this, he could be very fascinating when he chose, and the faults which I, a grave bookman, saw, were doubtless invisible to the girl who loved. John Hamlyn indeed conceived an utter loathing for him; but John had very strong provocation; for Willy now took it into his head to be *jealous* of John—jealous of the man whose life-happiness he had ruined! and gradually John's relations with Mary Lee grew to be formal and constrained. It was hard for John to keep quiet under this: but Love, if it had worked wonderfully upon the artist, if it had fired and kindled him into genius, had tried John Hamlyn also in its magic crucible, and found him utterly pure; so that, rather than cause one tear, one shadow of anxiety to Mary Lee, he would even—keep away from her! He was very seldom at her house now, and Willy made his visits exceedingly trying to him. The time fixed for the marriage was now close at hand.

'John Hamlyn, returning from a coasting-voyage to Bristol, went home, smoked a huge pipe in the kitchen, and then, contrary to his wont, walked up to visit Mary Lee. He saw Willy, from a distance, leave the house, so he knew that Mary would be alone. The same evening Willy called to see me. He seemed overflowing with happiness; all the better part of him—and, believe me, sir, he had much that was very loveable!—shone out. And, oh, how he played! You have heard him to-night, and you know his genius; but *then*, this heart was so full of joy, the future stretched before him so bright and so gay in its every aspect, that his music was as the warbling of an angel rejoicing over the beauty of the earth. He left me at last; but, excited by the conversation and the music, he could not go home to sleep. He walked on towards Mary's house, to wander round it, to dream about it, as lovers will. As he approached, he saw a light in her window, though it was strangely late—and there was the shadow of a man upon the curtain! It stung him, this shadow, like a snake. With a cold biting jealousy at his heart, he crept into the darkness of the hedge and waited.

'Presently he heard the door open, and then a voice which he knew to be John Hamlyn's, said: "but she had been crying, he could tell that". John's big form came out into the light. He walked slowly, silently, up the hill. Silently, slowly, the artist followed him. God forgive the poor man if he meant to use a knife—I know he carried one; but, on the brow of the hill, John, turning, saw that he was followed, and marched back upon his follower. Evening in the faint starlight, he recognised Willy by his wide foreign cloak, and said, with a strange grave earnestness in his voice:—

'"I have bad news for you, Basset: I would rather you learnt them from some one who is less hateful to you than I am—*why*, I cannot tell—I never wronged you in any way."

'"Never tampered, I suppose, with my intended wife? Never tried to lure her away from me? Never came to her like a thief in the night? Never 'pitied the poor fiddler', as one would pity a maimed cur?'

'"You are very hot about it, Basset—but you shall know all to-morrow morning".

'"I insist, sir, upon knowing all to-night—to-morrow you may be busy, discharging your bales at the pier-head!"

'John felt the insult: but still, very stubbornly, very nobly, held down the passion that was rising in him. Willy—for rage had blinded him—mistook this silence for timidity, and went on, rapidly, tauntingly, till at length John answered:—

'"I went up to Mary Lee to-night, if you *will* have it, to tell her that Johnson, the Bristol banker, has absconded, and that you are a beggar!"

'With a hoarse shriek, Basset leapt upon him, and struck him in the face. And then, the suppressed rage of years concentrated into one single blow, John lifted his huge arm and beat him down. It was a terrible blow: the passionate artist lay stretched like a dead log upon the ground—senseless. Suddenly the moon shone out large and full. The light fell through the thick hedgerow trees, right upon Basset's face. John knelt down, and saw that it was bloody—bloody. He groaned with shame, the big John, that he should have struck one so frail; but, at last, Basset's eyes slowly opened, and John still knelt by his side, weeping like a babe.

'What made him leap up, and then stagger back, as if a knife had struck him to the heart? This: as he knelt by the artist, and watched him return to consciousness, he expected to hear a curse from his lips: he heard, instead, a low, feeble, chuckling *laugh*. It was the laugh of an idiot. Willy Basset was insane.

'Three months afterwards, I followed Mary Lee to her grave; and when the clamour and the noise of the affair had died away, John Hamlyn took the mad artist to his home, and has supported him ever since.

'Willy Basset had lost all recollection of that terrible night. He wanders about, harmlessly, quietly: the villager, who call him "the Mazed Fiddler", never molest him; and at times he will take his violin and play so sweetly and so well, that the few strangers who visit Coombetown will hardly believe me when I tell them he is mad'.

III. WHAT FOLLOWED

HOWEVER feebly the old schoolmaster had told his tale, there had been something in it which had riveted the attention of his listener. The two men sat for a while silently, smoking and thinking. At last, as the evening closed in, the schoolmaster was rising to light his lamp, when he heard a tap at his door. In another minute John Hamlyn entered.

The Londoner gazed at him with interest. There was nothing romantic or picturesque in his appearance. He was simply a big sea-captain, with prematurely grey hair, and mild eyes: for the rest, he wore a rough pilot's jacket, and smelt strongly of Cavendish tobacco. He said quietly:

'I have been down to the pier, sir; the Sarah Jane has just come in: and now I find that poor Basset has left the house. I am going to look for him. Would you like to come with me, sir? There's a wildish look about the sky to-night, and I should be loath to have him caught in the storm that is rolling up.'

'I suppose we shall find him in the churchyard?' said the schoolmaster.

'Most like, most like, sir. I always notice that on nights like this, he steals away there. Poor fellow! it can't be helped *now*. But I would rather lose my right hand than use it as I did one night!'

The schoolmaster sighed; and, after a few words with the Londoner, all three set out together for the churchyard.

John Hamlyn had been right enough when he said that a storm was coming. The day, as I have hinted, had been one of intense heat, and now there was not a breath of air stirring. As they walked on, they felt oppressed by the close, sultry deadness of the night. Their road lay uphill, through a thick deep lane, such as every Devonshire tourist knows; and ere long the utter silence of the place grew almost terrible. Not a leaf moved above them; and when, after half an hour's walk, they reached an open space from which the sea was visible, they were still more struck with the gloomy look it wore. A dull, heavy, leaden look—now and then there was a little white flash below them, when a larger wave than usual rolled slowly in and broke upon the rocks—but there was no *life* in the sea, so to speak.

As they paused at the little churchyard gate, they heard the sound of the violin. Willy Basset, standing by the grave of Mary Lee, was playing such a requiem as never yet musician has expressed in notes—a requiem of such depth of lamentation, such bitterness of regret, such vehemence of self-accusation, yet such overwhelming love and tenderness withal, that the three men almost wept as they listened, and not another sound was heard save the magical tones with which the Mazed Fiddler mourned over his dead love. They did not dare to interrupt him; but at length the music ceased; he walked towards them, staggering like a drunken man; and then, as he reached the gate, sank heavily, fainting, on the ground. At that instant there was a peal of thunder in the east, which rolled on, crashing and reverberating as it rolled, till it seemed to break right above their heads; then for a minute utter silence; and then a blinding sheet of rain fell suddenly upon them. They lifted the Mazed Fiddler from the earth; John Hamlyn, flinging off his rough jacket, wrapped Willy in it as a shelter from the rain; and they turned homewards. The rain still fell, but far away towards the horizon vivid flashes of lightning leapt over the sea like swords.

'Make haste, for the love of God!' cried John, striding along with his burden as one who carried nought: 'make haste! He is wet to the skin already—it will be the death of him!'

They brought him home, and laid him gently in his bed. The Londoner ran off for Dr. Woodbury, but the good doctor was ten miles off, tending a sick woman; and when Smith returned, the artist was raving in his delirium. He said not a word now of Mary, not a word of John Hamlyn, his thoughts were away in the south.

'A poor fisher-boy, Signora!—Money, money, always money! can I coin it?—On the Red, then—I back the Red! For the eighth, ninth, tenth time, *Red*! Red it is!' he screamed, half starting out of his bed. 'Do you believe in my fortune, now?—In notes, in notes! I have no lackey to carry my gold for me—an artist, nothing more!'

Through the whole weary night, while the rain fell in torrents without, the three men watched beside him; but as it drew on towards morning, and the storm slowly and sullenly abated, he became much calmer. He slept for an hour or two, and at daybreak turned to the old schoolmaster, with a peculiar smile upon his face:

'You will give me my violin?' There were several in the room, his friend handed him the nearest. 'Not *that*, not *that!*' I played that at the San Carlo, when la Catarina sang so grandly: give me the old one—the one I had when a boy.' He took it from the schoolmaster's hand, and looked at it lovingly. Just then the morning light came full into the room, flooding it with its lustre. 'I played it often enough, sir, down among the rocks, when there were none to hear me but the merry sea-gulls. Ah! the beautiful light! The birds will be singing after the storm, and the lambs will be running in the meadows over the fresh wet grass. I loved to see them once, but I fear me, I fear me, that I'll never move from this bed till they carry me away to the grey old churchyard yonder, close by the dear old sea. And, well, I have had troubles enough, God knows! and I'm weary, weary, and I shall rest by her side at last!'

Was he mad now? He spoke softly, but there was a *raised* look in his eyes, and at times a cold, nervous trembling went right over him.

'Let him have his way, sir', whispered John Hamlyn: 'it is nearly over'.

The artist played a few feeble notes upon his old violin, and smiled sadly as he preluded with a bar or two of a simple country air. *Crack!*

It was but the snapping of a fiddle-string; but as it snapped his heart broke too. Another hour had passed away. The artist, with his lean, long hand still upon the instrument, had fallen back upon his pillow: and big John Hamlyn, kneeling by the bed, and shaking terribly with the great strong sobs that seemed to be choking him, suddenly cried out, 'Lead us not into temptation, lead us not into temptation! but, oh Lord, deliver us from evil!'

Anon., 'Paganini's False Teeth', *The Orchestra Musical Review* Vol. 1 No. 11 (12 December 1863), 168

This 'true story' (probably apocryphal) concerns Paganini and an incident involving a set of false teeth he purchased in Paris—specifically, his great distress upon learning its exorbitant cost and the spectacle that ensued. This is a good example of the fetish of celebrity: an anecdote told with absurdly disproportionate gravitas about a famous man and an utterly trivial matter. The story, presented as true, and related by someone whose 'friend' it was who introduced Paganini to the dentist, thus blatantly implicates the narrator in the perpetuation of the Paganini myth. The journal was published in London.

The Paris correspondent of the *Daily Telegraph* writes thus under date of Sunday last:—I must tell you a true story of Paganini. The great violinist had no teeth. A friend sent him to a dentist, telling him that he would find 'his affair' there in a minute. Paganini bought a set, ate with it, liked it, and bought another, never asking the price. A few weeks after, he was just out of his bath, clothed only in a large towel, when the man came with his little 'account'; it was 1,000 francs. Paganini, always very passionate, was frantic, and played an air with variations, of which 'robber' was the theme, and the coarsest epithets the fioritura. The man remonstrated. 'It was reasonable, very cheap; it was even artist's price'. Paganini, forgetful of his airy costume, rushed at his creditor, and shook him. Suddenly he paused, was silent, motionless, and the blood streamed from his mouth. Two friends, who were there, thought he had broken a blood vessel. It was a tragic scene—the dentist, a small man, with upright hair, shivering in the hands of the two spectators, who had rescued him from the claws of the enraged fiddler,—the violinist himself just as much dressed as when he entered this troublesome world, at his feet a cloth like a shroud, his mouth open, gasping! The friends approach, and find that Paganini, in his passion, had displaced his set of teeth, the spring of which had broken, and stuck in his throat and gagged him.

Anon., 'Paganini', *Argosy: a Magazine of Tales, Travels, Essays, and Poems* 21 (January 1876), 74–80

The frame story, of a 'Lord M------' who regales a certain nobleman and his daughter ('Lady Arabella') with anecdotes about Paganini, is a barely disguised device for introducing the most popular strands of the Paganini myth: the Ferrara 'donkey' incident and the abduction of a young girl (in this case a Florentine merchant's daughter), the murder of her relatives, and his subsequent imprisonment in a dungeon with nothing but his violin. Above all, Paganini's 'demonic' reputation is underscored in a section discussing 'various theories' about him; some claimed that he was 'in reality an angel sent down to this world' while others believed that he 'had a league with Satan' and had, after dying, 'only come back to life by magical agency'. According to further rumours he burst into 'fits of demoniacal laughter' and performed with dark shadows 'directing his hand' or 'hovering about the strings'.

What is interesting about this particular retelling of endlessly recycled mythology is the late date and the vehicle, a London magazine (1865–1901) which typically printed articles related to literature or social issues, thus possibly suggesting that awareness of the Paganini myth had by this time and among a certain literary London set become a staple of cultural knowledge. (Note: the article erroneously names Paganini's teacher 'Allessandro Stella'.)

Towards the afternoon of a hot July day in the early part of this century there rattled through the streets of Ferrara a post-carriage, drawn by four horses. It drew up before the principal hotel in the place. The postilion sprang to the ground, and threw coverings over his smoking cattle. A waiter hurried out and opened the carriage door. An excited Englishman came forth from under a mountain of rugs, and, seizing hold of the man by the arm, exclaimed: 'Is he here still? Is it too late? Are we in time?'

The startled waiter stammered 'Who here? Whom do you seek, Milord?' A young lady, who stepped out of the carriage after the gentleman, came to his aid, crying, in enthusiastic tones, 'Ah! My father means the great Paganini, who was to have given a concert here to-day. Is he still in the town? And does he really play to-day?'

'At your service, Signora', answered the relieved waiter. 'All Ferrara is in an uproar, for he has promised a concert for this evening'.

The Englishman drew a handful of money out of his pocket; threw the postilion a splendid reward for his hot and hasty journey, and giving the waiter some gold pieces, and orders to buy tickets for himself and his daughter for the evening's entertainment, he ascended the hotel steps, followed by the young lady; piles of luggage being borne up after them.

The name of Paganini was at that time a household word in Italy. The fame of this man as a wonderful musician had spread with amazing rapidity. He was born at Genoa, on the nineteenth of February, in the year 1784. It is said that his mother foresaw his future renown in a vision. In his sixth year, the boy played violin solos in the church, and, when nine years old, he stepped on the boards of a theatre for the first time. His principal teacher was Allessandro Stella, of Parma, but he was also taught by Ghiretti, and others. When but thirteen years old he made an artistic tour through Lombardy; and, at fourteen, he gave concerts on his own account. At twenty, he stood on the pinnacle of fame as a violin player; but, from that time forward, except when he made his triumphal journeys through Europe, his life was very much veiled in mystery, as regards the outer world. He continually disappeared for months together, leaving no trace or clue by which his whereabouts could be discovered, and then, again, as suddenly as he had vanished, he would reappear; now here, now there, but always where he was least expected: and, before again hiding himself, would give a few concerts—three, or, at the most, four.

There were, of course, various theories afloat as to his private history. Many of his admirers warmly upheld it as their opinion that he was in reality an angel sent down to this world, in pity, for the purpose of lightening the miseries of earthly life by giving man a foretaste of what the heavenly harmonies will be hereafter. They said, with truth, that it was as if a choir of sweet-voiced spirits lay hid within the instrument, and that, at times, it seemed as though this choir turned into a grand orchestra. In further support of this opinion, they said that Paganini lived on air, or, at most, a little herb-tea. On the other hand, his detractors hinted that his private life was a most ill-regulated one, and that, far from living upon air, he ate in a ravenous and almost brutal manner, although he at times chastised himself with long fastings, by which he had ruined his health.

Paganini's detractors further stated that he despised all forms of religion, and never put his foot upon consecrated ground. Some declared that he had a league with Satan, and held interviews with him in an old Florentine castle, much frequented by the artist, from which, they said, fearful sounds were heard proceeding on stormy nights, and where the great master was known to have lain as one dead, for hours together, on different occasions. These persons believed that at such times Paganini had only come back to life by magical agency. In all probability what gave rise to this latter story is the fact that Paganini destroyed his health and nervous system by continual use of Leroy's so-called life elixir. He was, at any rate, credited liberally by some with dealings in the black art. His glance was said to be irresistible, and to partake of some of the qualities ascribed to the evil eye. A flower girl told how she had met him one day in a lonely neighbourhood, and had remained standing still as one fascinated—as a bird is petrified by the gaze of a serpent—while he paced up and down before her, declaiming loudly; and bursting into fits of demoniacal laughter. Another swore to having seen a tall dark shadow bending over him at one of his concerts, and directing his hand; while a third testified that he had seen nine or ten shadowy hands hovering about the strings of the great master's violin.

But all these rumours only increased the fame and attractions of this wonderful man. When it became known that he was about to give a concert at Ferrara, visitors streamed thither from all directions, consumed with feverish impatience to accomplish their various journeys; half dreading lest, on their arrival, they should learn that the man they sought had again disappeared. Amongst the rest came the pair of English travelers, with the scene of whose arrival this sketch opened. They rested but for a few hours, and then hastened early to the theatre, in order to secure their places. The house was, of course, thronged; but the expectant audience was at first bitterly disappointed. A favourite singer had promised Paganini her aid in the evening's performance; but, at the last moment, had left him shamefully in the lurch. To fill the gap caused by her absence, the violinist had engaged a young dancer, who had a tolerable voice, and undertook to sing a few light pieces at the beginning of the entertainment. The more she endeavoured to give satisfaction, however, the more the disappointed public hissed and hooted her down, until at least, in despair, the girl ran away, and took refuge behind the curtain.

As soon as she disappeared a breathless silence fell upon the whole house. The audience waited, with strained nerves, for the master's appearance, prepared to give him an enthusiastic reception. But some evil fortune seemed to pursue the spoiled favourite on this particular evening. Like some shadow out of the demon world, a lean, gaunt, haggard figure slipped from behind the curtain. All held their breath. His strange appearance was familiar to his admirers; the wan thin face, with pale cheeks, framed in long black hair hanging wildly about; the features, continually twisted into some grimace; the sharp hooked nose; the dull, lurking, half-quenched glow in the eyes, buried under dark brows; the unsteady gait, as though the man were weak and powerless, and might, at any moment, bend or break in two like some tender reed; the strange scornful smile, hovering constantly about the ill-tutored lips;—for all this they were prepared; his picture hung in every shop and public place. They in a manner reverenced his peculiarities; viewing them with a sort of shudder of half pity, half horror; but, to-day, an additional and unexpected peculiarity distinguished him. He had wounded his foot with a nail in Livorno, from whence he had come; and, in place of gliding to his place like a ghost, as usual, he hobbled awkwardly across to his desk. The ludicrous appearance he made proved irresistible. In place of the storm of applause that usually greeted him, he was met by smothered, and then immoderate, bursts of laughter. The most enthusiastic of those present endeavoured to drown the ridicule by loud cheering, and finding this impossible fell into extravagant anger—our two English visitors being amongst the most angry—until the uproar became tremendous, and promised to be endless.

On a sudden, however, all again grew hushed into silence, as though influenced by the moving of a magic wand: as, indeed, they were.

By a violent effort Paganini composed himself, and grasped his violin. The frail, wavering figure straightened itself and became imposing. Every muscle was strained to its utmost tension. His eyes shone like stars of glowing fire. As though made of brass, his nervous fingers clenched his instrument, while the bow in his other hand moved like a powerful sword over the strings, drawing from them a tone so soft, so ethereal, so ravishing, and withal so sharp and clear, that it is hard to describe the listeners' sensations otherwise than by the term, an agony of pleasure; for all their diverse feelings were comprised in this.

This keen, heart-stirring tone hovered in the air like a clear, trembling star for a little space of time, and then the powerful fingers moved, the bow flashed up and down like lightning over the strings. It was as if that first keen tone had distilled itself into a rain of soft, refreshing notes; as though the start had burst, and fallen to the ground in beauteous fragments. Paganini kept his audience on entranced from that moment. Melting passages, in which harp-like tones blended, were exchanged for full sounds as of a mighty host of instruments, in which the waves of melody roared and jostled against each other in their exuberance. All eyes were drawn, as by a magnet, to the wonderful player. No sound came through the whole house to disturb the attention of the audience; except, now and then, that of a hysterical, smothered sob, which gave evidence of some overstrained and excited nerves.

When the music had ceased those present still sat on, as if under an enchanted tree, silent and scarcely breathing; but when Paganini bowed, with a malicious smile curling up his lips, the enthusiasm of delight manifested knew no limits. It was as if an earthquake shook the house. The musician had nobly revenged himself upon the public, and had forced them to admire in place of ridiculing him. But his soul hankered after a revenge of a different sort. He hobbled to the very front of the platform, with his violin still in his hand. He lifted his bow and stooped to begin afresh.

Breathless stillness, as before. From the magical instrument there suddenly burst out a perfect simulation of a donkey's bray: 'E-ah! E-ah!' No ass in the country could have done it better. Everyone looked at everyone else in horrified surprise. The musician bowed again, and, with his cynical smile still on his lips, said, 'This for those who hissed before, and laughed!'

The result was electrical. The enthusiasts applauded, clapped, and laughed, but the greater number of those present burst into a storm of wrath, filling the air with abusive epithets. The Ferrarese in the house took the joke as specially personal to them, as it was very much the custom of the surrounding aristocracy to nickname the city-folk asses, and to greet them with 'E-ahs,' when it was their pleasure to insult them.

Long after Paganini had taken refuge in his hotel, and had locked himself up from all the world, as was his custom, the storm he had raised still raged within the theatre. The police had at last to interfere between the two parties. With wounded bodies, and torn clothes, the greater number of those present left the building; watches, chains, and all other ornaments having, in most cases, disappeared totally. Lord M------ and his daughter of course amongst those whose admiration and reverence for the great master had only been increased by the night's occurrences. Amongst all his enthusiastic followers, they were, perhaps, the very warmest and most devoted.

At the table d'hôte next day, the conversation naturally turned entirely on the previous evening's entertainment. The greater number of voices were united in condemning the musician for his joke, and in criticizing his whole character and behaviour severely. Lord M------ observed that a middle-aged gentlemen sitting opposite to him seemed continually about to take part in the conversation, but as often checked himself with a visible effort. At last, when some very censorious remarks were made on Paganini, he burst out into vehement defence, as though he were well acquainted with everything concerning the musician's private life. His whole air and manner was that of one who says to himself inwardly, 'If you all knew what I know, you would not talk so foolishly'.

When dinner was over, Lord M------ succeeded in establishing an acquaintance with this gentleman; and, during subsequent intercourse, he was induced to confide many interesting particulars concerning Paganini to the nobleman and Lady Arabella.

He told how he had first made acquaintance with the genius. He was at a wedding one day in Florence, and, in the evening, he and the other guests were amusing themselves with jests and laughter on the banks of the Arno. Music and song also beguiled the time, and he was sitting down, playing on a guitar to a circle of admiring listeners, when on a sudden, with a cry of affright, the little company started aside, surprised at the appearance of a tall, pale man, with black disheveled hair flying about him, and with wild, gleaming eyes. This strange figure strode up to the player, took the instrument from his astonished hand, and began to play in his turn, gesticulating excitedly the while. The music he brought forth seemed to those who listened perfectly divine; but with a harsh chord he suddenly broke off, and, as if in an access of rage, dashed the guitar to pieces against a tree, and then disappeared as quickly as he had appeared, and as unexpectedly.

The following day the wedding guests learned that their strange entertainer was Paganini, whom the Grand Duchess had bidden to the Court to give a concert. It may be imagined how carefully the teller of the tale treasured up the broken fragments of the guitar. He was as much surprised as pleased a few days later, when the great master came to him with an apology for the odd jest he had played, and offering a liberal recompense for the harm done. This latter was naturally refused; but a friendship between the two, thus strangely brought together, was the result of the interview. They travelled about continually in company, and the musician had received trusty service from Lord M------'s new acquaintance, and had given him his fullest confidence. This latter entreated the nobleman and his daughter not to give credence to the many tales circulated to the disadvantage and discredit of his friend. Knowing that he spoke to trustworthy ears and sympathizing hearts, he confided to them the true secret of the great master's strongly developed peculiarities and misanthropy.

While at the Florentine Court, a certain noble lady had conceived for him a violent passion, which caused him much discomfort. It was entirely and exclusively on her side, his heart being given to a lovely young girl, the daughter of a rich merchant in the city. She was also much attached to him. Unfortunately, she betrayed her feelings one evening at one of Paganini's concerts. During an effective pause made by him in playing, she heaved a deep sigh. Tears streamed from her eyes, and she was near fainting. Her lover betrayed uneasiness concerning her; and went to the front of the boards, looking towards where she sat. Everyone saw the two exchange glances.

Suddenly a strange gentleman made his way to the young girl's side, took her hand, and whispered some words into her ear. She grew deadly pale, but allowed him to lead her away. A few curious persons crept out after the pair, and saw them driving quickly away in a black carriage. Whither they went is unknown, but the girl was seen no more in Florence. Nearly everyone laid the blame of her disappearance on Paganini. Two of the girl's relations challenged him on her account. He stabbed them both, one after the other. Later, he also disappeared mysteriously for a very lengthened period. His friend vowed never to rest until he had found him out; and at last, after three years' searching, he discovered him imprisoned in a castle in Tuscany belonging to some relatives of the lost girl. He was confined in a gloomy dungeon; his only furniture a broken table, an old chair, a miserable bed, and a water jug; his only solace some writing materials, which he had made use of in putting on paper many musical compositions, and his beloved violin, of which, however, every string but one had, by degrees, become useless. Nevertheless, he contrived still to play on this one string, so as to delight his own heart, and the hearts of all who listened to him. His jailors were so much attached to him that it was with their connivance that his friend succeeded in releasing him from his sad captivity.

Lord M------ and Lady Arabella so entreated of their new acquaintance to get them a personal interview with Paganini, that at last he did what he could to please them by introducing them secretly into a garden where he knew his friend was, and whence he could not easily escape. It was late in the evening, and was growing dusk, but they could see the musician listlessly stretched at full length upon the grass, with his back turned to them.

At some slight noise, however, which betrayed their presence, he started hastily up, drew the loose cloak he wore over his face, and with one bound disappeared from their sight into a sheltering grove of trees.

Paganini died at the age of fifty-six, in the year 1840, after a year of painful wasting sickness. It was in the night of the 27th of May that he breathed his last. He awoke suddenly out of a peaceful sleep, feeling refreshed, and, as he thought, re-invigorated. He drew aside the curtain of his bed and looked out into the night. His windows were open, and the soft balmy Italian air was filling all the room with sweet freshness. The moon had risen, and was pouring a flood of light across his bed, but his eyes were dim, and to him everything seemed overshadowed. He stretched out his hand, we are told, and grasped his beloved violin, which always lay beside him. He took up his bow, and endeavoured to bring some sound out of the instrument. But the magic power and strength had left his fingers; and, when he found that his efforts were in vain, he fell back on his pillow broken-hearted, and sighed his soul away.

Norman Oliphant, 'A Vision of Paganini', *Magazine of Music* Vol. 2 No. 21 (December 1885), 203–4

This piece of fiction, set in a French casino, portrays Paganini gambling at the roulette table and, upon hitting a losing streak, playing his violin to stake a bet. The entire scene is imagined, of course, yet the prose is notable for faithfully reprising themes that originally arose in his reception. A 'tall thin figure' with a 'half-ironic flash in the heavy eyes' arrives with a violin case at the casino entrusting 'the great goddess Luck' or else the devil. When he plays, the 'curious medley' ranges from 'melodic sweetness' to 'a half ironic but curiously realistic imitation of a person sobbing and crying'—which is compared to the 'grim sneer' of Heine's poetry. A description of virtuoso effects, a reference to the Totentanz, *and an emphasis on Gothic attributes follow in quick succession, thereby gathering together aspects of the 'demonic' Paganini in a bundle—from the perspective of a writer looking back to events that occurred half a century before.*

It was far on in the evening, and the orchestra was hard at work with that revived energy which is proverbial in the case of a horse with its nose turned homeward. The violins, more nearly in tune than they gener-ally were, for it was a performance of more than common interest, were complaining in a wild, rambling fashion about nothing in particular, it being the habit of violins, in their more serious moments, to lapse into transcendental pessimism. Presently the glittering cynical laughter of the piccolo changed complaint into remonstrance, and the indignant violins worked themselves up into the conventional fury which heralds the close of the piece. Then came the final crash, and the basses arpeggioing heavily down to the lower D, punctuated the whole in irreproachable, if not altogether novel, fashion.

Before the note of dismissal, however, had released the enthusiastic audience from their places, a little door at the side of the building had opened and closed behind a tall thin figure, which stood for a moment or two irresolutely on the steps. Then it turned and walked rapidly with a curious kangaroo-like gait down the narrow alley which led into a main street, scarcely wider than itself. The place was almost deserted, for the loungers had taken up their station at the front of the concert room, to watch the outgoing tide of faces. An occasional clamour of laughter and music streamed out, with a glare of light, into the pervading darkness from some popular wine-shop; but the most noteworthy thing was certainly this lank, looping skeleton, which hurried past them, as if desirous of escaping notice. At length, in the dark corner of a square, into which the street suddenly broadened, the figure halted abruptly, descended two or three steps, rapped thrice, and waited, rapped twice in quick succession, and then, as the bolt was withdrawn, threw open the door, and entered. Speech was apparently at a discount, for he said nothing as he went down the passage to a long and well-lighted room at the end of it, threw a violin case on a chair, leaned his elbows upon the back of it, and dropped his chin upon his slack inverted wrists. Even the half-reluctant applausive murmur, which ran round the room at his appearance, called forth no further sign of recognition than a momentary and half-ironic flash in the heavy eyes, where were instantly turned towards the table. No one knew better than he that the brief recognition of his fame as a virtuoso would, in a few seconds more, be forgotten by everyone in the enthrallment of the game.

The whole room, indeed, with its misty brilliance and thick, heated atmosphere, seemed to throb with suppressed excitement. There was no noise or bustle, the feet fell silently on the carpeted floor, the figures shifted a little now and then, as some pale or flushed face fell back from the group and a new one took its place, but the only sound was a low, deep hum of voices, broken by the rustle of paper, the clink of gold, and the whirring of the modern wheel of fortune. It was not long before the last comer, who had remained motionless, like a vulture craning its neck in the direction in which its scents carrion, raised himself erect, and took a stride towards the table.

'Messieurs, faites votre jeu', sang the croupier in a soft chant, not less potent than that of the sirens.

A long arm and attenuated hand was stretched out to him with a rouleau of gold, and a voice, the lowness of which failed to hide its discordance, muttered the words, 'Numero treize'.

'Numero treize', echoed the croupier, as the louis were deposited, the wheel revolved, and the song rose, 'Le jeu est fait. Rien ne va plus'.

The luck, however, was against the player, whose face took a keener expression as the words, 'Trente-deux; rouge. Pair et passe', announced his discomfiture. But when the initial formula, 'Faite votre jeu', was repeated, the same long, thin arm and skeleton hand was thrust forth again with its gold almost automatically, and the same low harsh voice said—'Numero treize'. The players looked at him and then stealthily at each other, but said nothing, though one or two of them followed his strange leadership in placing their stakes. Failure again resulted, and the gold was raked away, but it appeared to have no influence upon the player's steadfastness of purpose. Again and again in quick succession came his single utterance, 'Numero treize'; indeed, renewed failure seemed to kindle more vigorous life within him. The vulture stoop went out of the neck, the dull eye took an unnatural lustre, the pale hollow cheeks were flushed and moist, even the weak voice seemed to acquire new force and vibrancy. The players were stirred. This man had faith. Whether he had discovered a system or had had a dream: whether he trusted in the God of the Christians or the goddess of the gambler—the great goddess Luck; or whether (which seems more likely) he had faith in and friendship with the devil—it was all one to them. His faith inspired them; his curious presence bound them with a strange mesmeric influence. One after another they began to back his play in the chase of the elusive fortune which danced attendance upon 'Numero treize'.

How much he lost himself he appeared neither to know nor to care any more than he knew or cared who followed, lost, and cursed him as they slunk back penniless from the table. But when at length he drew forth his last rouleau of gold, it was obvious that his excitement became intense. Almost before the croupier's cry the hand was thrust nervously forward. 'Numero treize?' asked the croupier with a shade more expression than usual in his monotone. There was a pause, and then the voice answered— 'Trente-deux—en plein'. A bombshell dropped in the room could not have created more sensation than this sudden change without apparent reason, and something very like a groan of astonishment rose form the group. Then the wheel ran round, an hour seemed to pass, and the ball rattled into a compartment. 'Le jeu est fait. Rien ne va plus', sang the croupier, and then, as the players turned instinctively to the tall gamester, came the statement of the winning number—Numero treize.

To their surprise, however, so far from showing any mortification, the victim of this freak of fortune simply laughed—first a low demoniac chuckle, and then with all the heartiness of which he seemed capable. It was an expensive joke, but it was a joke which he evidently appreciated—that he should have thrown up his hands just as he was about to touch the shore; and his laughter found a sympathetic echo from more than one who had waited to see Numero treize out and had profited by their patience.

The loser had fallen back from the group and was resuming his violin case, when one of the watching crowd went up to him and drew him aside.

'Do you care to stake more?'

'Why?'

'Here is money; you are welcome to the loan of it, or you can stake it for me, or', and he hesitated, 'I would gladly give you it in return for one favour'.

'And that?'

'That you should play me something on your violin'.

'You expect me to sell my art like that?' was the rejoinder, 'It is well that you—'

'Messieurs', came the croupier's monotone, 'faites votre jeu'.

The violinist paused in his sentence, and then flung to the floor the purse which the other had proffered him.

'As you will', said its owner. 'I did not mean to offend you. Take it or not; play on the violin or at the table, or leave them, just as you please; but the purse will lie there till it rots so far as I am concerned'. And he turned away to the crowd again.

The violinist looked at the purse with his head quaintly askew, as the jackdaw of Rheims might at the Bishop's ring. Then he looked after its departing donor and laughed. Finally, as the clink of the gold under the rakes struck his ear, he stooped, took up the purse, and following the owner of it, pulled his coat, and whispered, 'I will earn your money, you fool'.

He lifted the violin case, went to the end of the room, took out his instrument, plucked the strings to ascertain their condition, but made no attempt to tune it, and then, leaning his left shoulder against the side of the window, began to play. Whether or not his bad luck, or the environment, or some innate whimsicality of disposition affected his playing, it was certainly a curious medley. It opened with a phrase of unequalled melodic sweetness, as it commenced in pure round tones and sang upwards with the clearness of a flageolet. Then, before the responsive phrase was completed, he shifted his bow to the fourth string in a half ironic but curiously realistic imitation of a person sobbing and crying. It was not unlike the grim sneer with which Heine at times rounds off some sentimental lyric. The playing, however, did not end there, for the bow suddenly darted off in a series of astonishing sequences as he slid his fingers with the rapidity of lightning along the strings till the violin almost raved in enharmonics. As an exhibition of technique it was unequalled, though little method was discernible in the madness, until the gamesters, who had been momentarily attracted by it from their game, turned to the tables, and the inevitable croupier's song—'Messieurs, faites votre jeu' arose again. Then the violin, pausing in a headlong downward flight, suddenly commenced to echo the chaunt [*sic*] in almost human tones, dropped it and took it up again, ran with it over all the strings and up and down the scale, interspersing it with quaint turns and inversions—'Messieurs, faites votre jeu, faites votre jeu; Messieurs, Messieurs, votre jeu; le jeu est fait—est fait; rien ne va plus: Trente-deux, rouge; pair et passe, pair et passe!'

Gradually this shaped itself into a sort of dance; till, as the tall gaunt figure swayed to and fro, and the black hair shook about the dead waxen face, it seemed as thought the figure of Holbein's picture, in the grimmer mockery of modern masquerade, was standing there playing on its crossed bones, a more tremendous and terrible Dance of Death. The gamblers forsook their table under its spell. They might not realize its full potence and meaning, might not see the vision which was ready to shape itself before them—the vision of the weird circle of the dead, hollow-eyed, with grinning teeth and shredded finery clinging to their limbs, who flung themselves in tumultuous dance about the player, and sang in horrible chorus—'le jeu est fait—rien ne va plus'. But some suggestion of it could not fail to touch them as the bow leapt and swung, and the long bony fingers wound grotesquely over the strings, singing out the measured phrases, shrieking back unearthly comments with more than mortal anguish, other than human mirth.

Suddenly he stopped, bowed abruptly and awkwardly to his listeners, with a smile that was almost a grin, and the words, 'Rien ne va plus'. Then turning to the owner of the purse, he added the question, 'Have I earned it?'

'Have you!' muttered the other under his breath, with a sigh between gratitude and relief.

'Very well, then', said the violinist, 'Monsieur, faites votre jeu'; and as the croupier took his seat he flung the unopened purse down with the cry—'Numero Treize'.

The wheel revolved and the crowd bent forward as if to witness a miracle.

'Le jeu est fait', said the croupier . . . . 'Zero!' With a laugh the gambler seized his violin and chuckled his way down the passage and into the street.

'Who is that?' said a new comer.

'That?' answered a second. 'That is Paganini or the Devil'.

Elise Polko, 'Paganini's First Love', *Merry England* Vol. 7 No. 40 (August 1886), 271–5

*This story about Paganini at the age of twelve imagines an innocent romance with a girl his own age, how hard his childhood must have been under his father's unreasonable demands that he practise constantly, and his emotional attachment to a spider who keeps him company during those lonely hours with his violin. Elise Polko (1822–99) was a German novelist whose biography (*Nicolo Paganini und die Geigenbauer*) had appeared twelve years prior to the publication of this story in the London magazine* Merry England. *In it she had taken considerable liberties filling in the unknown blanks of his life, as she does here. The story is unusual in that it portrays an uncorrupted Paganini, in the days before his virtuosity and his legend obliterated any glimmer of possibility that such a 'normal' child—with 'normal' emotional needs—would grow up to be a 'normal' adult. It thus suggests that at least in part, the father's brutality was responsible for the way Paganini turned out—and thereby implies that the legend of the dehumanised virtuoso began with a strong negative paternal influence.*

A MAY day under Italy's brilliant, cloudless sky has a magic the natives of northern climes can but faintly picture to themselves even in their dreams. The earth laughs, radiantly decked as she is with her brightest gems, while, like an ardent bridegroom, the sun enfolds her in his warm embrace, and the air is full of a nameless enchantment. Under such conditions, the human heart expands early, and human eyes wear a look as joyous and impassioned as the gaze of the sun. Seldom does one see a melancholy expression in the faces of the children of this land; but on this bright May day of 1793 there was sadness in the eyes of a boy sitting on the shore where beautiful Genoa rests on the Mediterranean Sea. He was not more than twelve, with a slender figure, clear cut, pale features, dark hair, and thick eye-lashes shading the most expressive dark eyes, which were one moment full of a proud light, and the next were sad as death.

As he was musing, looking weary and unhappy, a clear, childish voice called his name, and a pretty girl about his own age threw her arms round his neck with the words: 'Oh, you bad Nicolo! where have you been hiding all the afternoon? Everywhere have I been seeking you!' and she kissed him again and again before emptying into his lap her white apron full of roses, myrtle, and orange blossom.

Nicolo put his arm round the young prattler, and stroking her thick black locks, answered: 'I have slipped away from father, Gianetta, to dream a little in peace and quiet by the beautiful water; but you know well I love to be here'.

'Your father is cruel!' she answered, vehemently; 'he will work you into the grave. My mother says Nicolo is not strong and hearty like other boys, his weary fiddle-playing and his hard-hearted father will kill him outright, and I know she is right'.

'Do not believe it!' cried Nicolo; 'I shall not die, I cannot die; I must first become a great man; and see! I am not weak'; and he sprang to his feet, and seizing the girl suddenly in his arms, he held her suspended for some moments over the water. Gianetta did not wince, only sighing softly as he put her on her feet again. She looked at him shyly, and sat silently leaning against him.

But, child-like, she soon recovered her spirits, and laughed and chatted about her flowers and her doves; and if she saw the shades of sadness gathering over Nicolo's face, her innocent kisses and the soft little hand stroking his hair soon chased away all clouds. So they sat happily together on the shores of the beautiful blue sea; and, with the sunlight falling on the two dark heads, they looked the perfect embodiment of the poet's ideal of Love and Spring.

When darkness fell, they wandered home, with arms twined round each other through the stately streets of Genoa, till they reached two little neighbour-houses overgrown with vines. Gianetta's mother was anxiously looking out for her child, who rushed into the loving arms, and Nicolo, sighing, entered his father's door, and climbed up to his lonely attic under the roof. Then he opened the little casement set in the vines, and taking up an old violin, he kissed it passionately before beginning to play. Wonderful was the voice and strange the song that little hand drew from the strings. It was an improvisation—tender, triumphant, a musician's inspiration. As he played, the boy looked out of the open window, and smiled when a large spider (known as the Cross spider, being marked with a white cross on the back) appeared upon the sill. 'Welcome, Silver Cross', whispered Nicolo, as he took up the creature and placed it on the bridge of his violin, where it remained motionless, as if overpowered by the rush of sound around it. The boy played till his arm sank exhausted, and his eyelids were heavy with sleep, and the dewy day broke upon him. Then he laid down his beloved fiddle and took the spider to the window, where it disappeared amongst the vines. It was a whimsical companionship that of the spider and the lonely boy. Night after night, at the first stroke of his bow it appeared, drawn by the music, and only those who have experienced the same heart-loneliness can imagine the attraction this had for Nicolo, deprived as an infant of his gentle mother's love, and entirely dependent upon his strict and morose father. Boys of his own age either teased or avoided him; only Gianetta kissed and consoled him during the day, and the spider was the sole companion of his vigils, and no one knew the depths of love the boy felt for these two, so different beings, who alone seemed to care for him. It was a drawback that Gianetta neither liked nor could understand his feeling for Silver Cross. 'It is a witch', she would say, shuddering, and Nicolo never placed the spider on his violin when Gianetta was there, but if, on these occasions, he looked out of the window, he would see it sitting motionless on one of the leaves. When he was tired of playing, Gianetta would coax him to tell her wonderful stories, and all the plans of what he would do when he had achieved greatness were confided to the faithful little maiden, who would clasp his feverish hand in her own, and gaze at him with clear, wondering eyes, which lighted up under his enthusiasm.

He would tell her of the great German tone master, Mozart, who had composed a Concerto in his sixth year, and had been as a planet in the heaven of Music, and tears would burst from his eyes as he cried: "Ah! I am but a miserable bungler compared to such as he," and all Gianetta's endearments would fail to console him.

One hot day Nicolo had been playing dreary exercises for hours under his father's supervision, till his arms ached, his head burned, and all strength and life seemed exhausted, when Gianetta's mother entered in haste with the news that the child was attacked by fever, and kept crying out for her play-fellow and his music.

Nicolo seized his violin and hastened to the girl's bedside; she looked at him long and earnestly, and then signed to him to play. 'Yes', he cried, 'I will play you a slumber song, then you will sleep and get well'. She smiled faintly as the boy drew forth from the strings the most marvelous lullaby that had ever rocked mortal to sleep, and when he had ended Gianetta raised herself up and held out her arms to him. With a cry he hid his face on her breast and began to sob convulsively—'Thank you, my dearest', she whispered, 'now I shall sleep sweetly, Nicolo—but you must not rest yet, you must shine upon earth. Go away from here to distant lands, but do not forget me' and laying her cheek upon his bowed head, she breathed out her soul with a soft sigh.

All night long Nicolo watched by the side of his little sweetheart, and the next day he wandered about aimlessly, as if seeking her in their old meeting places. Late in the evening he returned to his dark silent attic, from the open window of which he could plainly see into Gianetta's death chamber.

Tapers were burning there, and the child lay on her bier, clothed in white, and almost buried in flowers, only her calm pale face was visible; beside her knelt a monk praying for the little soul which had so early left its beautiful earthly dwelling.

'Farewell, farewell, sweetheart', whispered the heart-broken boy, as the tears stream from his eyes, 'yes, I will go away—as far away as I can; no one cares for me here, lonely and unloved as I am', and he fell sobbing upon his knees. At that moment something touched his hand, he started and lifted his head, it was Silver Cross. 'Ah! is it you, my old companion?' he cried as he gazed for a moment at the little animals; then he seized his violin. 'One farewell to Gianetta'. The strings began to sing in notes of pain and longing, which were borne across on the soft night air to the girl in her last long sleep; the dead lips seemed to smile, the odorous flowers trembled, and the praying monk unclasped his hands, while he dreamed wonderful dreams. When the morning arose in all its splendour it saw a fainting boy lying on the narrow attic floor, his violin upon his breast, and to its strings clung a dead spider.

Was Gianetta's prophecy fulfilled?

That boy was Nicolo Paganini.

Marian Millar, 'The Magician on the G String. A Musical Reminiscence of Weimar' (From the German of J.C. Lobe), *Quarterly Musical Review* Vol. 4 No. 13 (February 1888), 45–58

Johann Christian Lobe (1797–1881) was a German violinist and composer born in Weimar, where he saw Paganini perform in 1829. At the age of seventy-five, Lobe wrote an account of 'the magician' (his word). Lobe recalled that Paganini had baboon-like arms, and that he reminded him of Hoffmann's 'Kapellmeister Kreisler' or Ahasuerus the Wandering Jew. Of particular interest in this account are Lobe's observations from the perspective of a German musician and as a violinist himself. He described Paganini's performance style in vivid detail, noting that he held the bow much closer to his body than other players; that he created 'electric sparks of tone'; that his technical display defied belief ('absolutely incomprehensible'); that the tone of delivery varied widely in mood; and that he made the violin a direct means of communicating emotion. Just as interesting are Lobe's observations of the personal characteristics of the mysterious Italian: that he wrote in secret hieroglyphics in 'a little red case' and that he had a singular obsession in the violin. Alongside these traits of abnormality that contributed to the 'demonic' legend, it is unusual that Lobe also underscored Paganini's benevolence ('his ever-ready kindness') towards Berlioz and to other young aspiring musicians—thus humanising the violinist. For Lobe, Paganini was weird but no monster. This characterisation was translated into English for readers of the short-lived Manchester journal Quarterly Musical Review *(1885–88), which was expressly aimed at the general public rather than the music specialist.*

On the 25th of March, 1828, [there] appeared in the Viennese theatrical paper the following notice: 'A very interesting item of intelligence for the musical world is the announcement of the arrival of the celebrated violin, Nicolo Paganini, of Genoese birth, who has determined at last on undertaking an artistic tour outside Italy, and will first make art-loving Vienna acquainted with his performance', &c.

Celebrated? Possibly in Italy! But we in Germany looked down from a very considerable height upon the Italian masters. Their operas might be given throughout the whole musical world, but they were regarded by the German critics but as ear-catching trifle, musical jingle. They were quite incapable of producing instrumental music—a symphony, for example— and as for their executive talent, it was long since there had been any mention of such a thing. There Germany and France held the honours. As violinists there towered above all the rest amongst us Spohr, a giant physically and artistically, Lipinsky, Kiesewetter, Mayseder, &c., and in France there were Rhode [sic], Baillot, and others. But few had so much as heard of the Genoese violinist: the general public knew nothing whatever of him. Add to this that he gave the impression of a decrepit old man; and, as a matter of fact, had already attained the age of forty-four. At best then a ruin, but still good enough for the German barbarians! And thus it was not to be wondered at that at his first concert, given on the 29th March, there was but an indifferent attendance.

But—on the day afterwards! Then the whole of Vienna seemed verily to have gone music-mad. To obtain tickets for the concerts which followed, the house was besieged from the early morning hours by immense crowds of people; and though the prices were first doubled, then trebled, many a one in lieu of a ticket carried away but bruises, scratches, and torn garments.

To judge by the articles which now appeared in the Viennese newspapers, either all the musical critics had gone mad or else the Genoese fiddler was in truth the most extraordinary and phenomenal executant which the world had ever seen or heard of. For example, one critique ran thus: 'Whoever has not heard Paganini can form no notion of him. To give a detailed account of his playing is utterly impossible; and, further, an oft-repeated hearing will be of no avail'. The calm and reasonable critic Castelli wrote, 'Never has an artist within our walls created such a sensation as this God of the Violin. His performance is the most perfect, the most marvelous, and the most admirable which can possibly be heard in executive musical art. He begins exactly where others come to an end; he produces the incredible, nay—since we are absolutely in the dark as to the means whereby he gets his effects—he produces *for us the impossible!*'

And from all the town which he now visited, Breslau, Berlin, Frankfort-on-the-Maine, there resounded the same rapturous plaudits.

As though we could help being curious! 'Will he come to Weimar?' This was now the question, for me, at that time as momentous as poor Hamlet's, 'To be or not to be?'

Our little capital with its meagre purse, I said to myself, can hardly offer sufficient inducement to entice him, when one reads of the enormous sums which the larger cities must expend upon him. Yet the little capital has, nevertheless, a great name, so I consoled myself. There still live Goethe, Hummel, and Marie Pawlowna, herself a pianoforte player of the first rank. If Paganini is a true artist he will not pass by Weimar. Thus I talked to myself: for I am an old man, and old age is garrulous. And for this reason I stroke my pen through many a page of my manuscript, upon which I have described my waiting sensations, and at once pass to that evening of the 29th October, 1829, when our orchestral factotum, Buchholz, came to me with the announcement 'To-morrow morning, at nine o'clock, rehearsal on the stage for Signor Paganini's concert'.

And for the reasons referred to above I pass by even the rehearsal, and at once give my account of the concert in the evening. All those in the town or surrounding neighbourhood who could afford the double prices of admission had flocked thither. The house presented a splendid appearance. Those present were so closely packed, nay, so wedged into each other, that (I wish to be taken literally), an apple falling could not have reached the ground. A solemn stillness lay over the assembly. All eyes were directed toward the stage, every ear vibrated in anticipation to the tones of the famous magician. The overture was ended; the poor thing had struggled its best in vain, since no one paid the slightest attention to it. At length, after a tolerably long pause, Paganini (like some other great lords we know, he loved to be waited for) stepped forward. In his left hand the violin, in his right the bow, he glided with soft, hasty tread through our ranks till he reached the footlights. No desk was placed there, for he played everything from memory. He made some slight and rather clumsy bows, lowering his bow like a general on parade salutes his sovereign with his sword.

Never in my life have I seen a man whose appearance pained me so much, or who touched with such emotion and pity. There he stood—a meagre figure in an old-fashioned dress coat, and in black trousers, which touched the ground and hung loosely about his lean limbs, as though about a veritable skeleton. From out his long locks and singularly curly whiskers there looked forth a long visage, fleshless and bloodless, with a long aquiline nose. From his shoulders there hung down arms like those of a baboon, to which were attached very long and thin hands of snowy whiteness. I could not but, involuntarily, think of Callot Hofmann's [*sic*] 'Kapellmeister Kreisler'. Or again, as he looked down upon the assembly, so far away, so isolated, one might say so unsympathetic, did he appear, that it seemed to me as though I saw before me Ahasuerus, the poor cobbler of Jerusalem, who for an insult to our Lord, must still, in the nineteenth century, wander on and on over the earth vainly seeking death.

He opened with his E major concerto. The *ritornello* began. He had naturally high shoulders; and, whilst playing he had a trick of approaching them so closely together, that his head assumed the appearance of being impaled *à la Turque*. He held the bow, contrary to the practice of all other violin players, close to his body. Thus he led the orchestra; and, during the *tutti*, flashed through and above it with electric sparks of tone.

But what am I to say of his playing? All those were indeed perfectly right who said that you had to hear him, since no one could possibly describe him. Meyerbeer once said to Cafil [*sic*] Blaze: 'Imagine to yourself the most wonderful effects which it is possible to produce upon a violin, dream of all the marvels of the bow and of melody, and Paganini will still surpass your expectations'.

Once in a certain assembly of Frenchmen, where there happened to be a noted curmudgeon, a collection was made for a charitable purpose. The collector accidentally came a second time to the skinflint. He replied, 'I have already contributed, sir'. The collector answered, 'I beg your pardon, I did not see it, but I believe it'. Very promptly a witty neighbour of the harpagon broke in, 'As for me, I saw it; and still I do not believe it'. So it was with Paganini. Those who had just listened to his performance came out saying, 'They who have not heard him will not believe', and one of his critics wrote, 'I have heard him, yet still I cannot believe'.

And just as little were the more minute descriptions of his absolutely unheard-of tricks able to give anything more than a distant conception of the essence and reality of the effects he produced.

For to what purport are all such descriptions as these. 'You hear beside the tones peculiar to the violin, sounds not as of an instrument, but, as it were, voices of primitive nature—now resembling the simple twitter of a bird, now again the trill of a nightingale or the silvery tinkling of a bell, now flute-like and softly dying away like the western wind, now rushing on stormily in double-stoppings and seeming to rule the entire orchestra'. He executed certain runs, leaps, and double-stops which had never yet been heard from any violin-player; he played the most difficult two, three, and four-part passages; he gave, in the highest octave close to the bridge, the chromatic scale pure and distinct. In the first solo of his E major concerto he climbed by a chain of four-part *arpeggio* chords, with the swiftness of lightning, to such a height as caused us fiddlers absolutely to lose our violin understanding, since even for the initiated the riddle was unsolvable. The greatest violinists thought much of it if they were able to bring out easy little passages in harmonics. Paganini made use of them in the most various and utterly unexpected, the boldest and most unusual forms. In the 'Sonate Militaire' upon one string, by means of harmonics, he brought before the listener almost the whole range of sounds capable of being produced upon all four strings; so that any one not looking entirely forgot that all this in reality was evolved from the one string only. Absolutely incomprehensible, even upon the full-stringed violin, were the passages in thirds, sixths, octaves, tenths, and double shakes of arrowy swiftness; and the semiquaver runs, in which one part was brought out *pizzicato* and the other produced by the bow. He evolved the sweetest sounds so close to the bridge of the instrument that the bow could scarcely find room betwixt it and the finger. The most wonderful feat of all was when with the left hand he plucked a marvelous *pizzicato*, whilst he continued the theme with all its incidental difficulties absolutely undisturbed: nay, he even produced in one long swift run, from the very topmost height to the deepest depth of sound, a constant interchange of notes in pizzicato and notes produced by long bow strokes.

If, after the delivery of the Concerto and the Sonata on the G string, any one believed that his feats had come to an end, and that he could not possibly bring forth anything new, this belief was presently dispelled; for, in the variations on 'Nel cor piu non mi sento', which he gave at the finish, unaccompanied by the orchestra, he displayed new and inconceivable wonders. Without the aid of an orchestra he provided his own accompani-ment. He maintained a theme upon the E string, whilst at the same time he accompanied it on the A, D, and G strings. Again, he sustained the tone upon one string during one, two, and three bars, whilst at the same time he was playing runs and *pizzicato* on the other strings. All this, and more besides, he carried on throughout with the greatest ease and the purest intonation, without missing a single note.

All this belongs to his *technique*, the highest and most perfect which human ear had ever heard. But, after all, this magic *technique* was but the interpreter of his incandescent soul. In his playing, seriousness and playfulness, profundity and lightness, tragic melancholy and rollicking humour were varied and interchanged in the most perfect fashion. André has on this point given us the happiest dictum, and from his paper in 'Hesperus' we take the following:—

'Are we to consider Paganini a musician in the higher sense, and a musician of a pronounced and distinct individuality? Without having regard to his incredible mechanical facility, this is a question which I feel constrained to answer in the affirmative, for he breathes into his execution a soul such as no one else is able. It is this *anima* which produces such an indescribable effect upon all finely-strung and susceptible minds—which gives to his tone that peculiar characteristic colouring—and for this reason he will ever remain inimitable, since it is his own soul which pours forth in his playing, and his own proper individuality which he causes to speak. For he has succeeded in making his violin into the organ of speech: the voice of his own feelings and of his own peculiar state of mind and culture. The emotions which pass through his own mind are expressed upon the instrument with rare truth, fidelity, and subtlety. If we may be permitted from his playing to draw an inference of the state of his innermost mind, we find contending therein (if only perhaps in the form of reminiscences) the stormiest passions with the tenderest feelings, intense suffering with the most unutterable joy, brooding melancholy with child-like playfulness. And were I to sum up all together I should say that we have here, finding an outlet, a mind torn by volcanic passions'.

It can well be imagined what a commotion the magician raised amongst us. The applause of the Weimar public, always hitherto remaining strictly within the limits of moderation, burst all bounds, and roared through the house like an advancing tide. Even the calmest-minded caught the infection and were carried away by delight. Paganini knew well that an artist must himself feel before he can awaken feeling in others. He had chosen as his motto, 'To call out strong emotion you must yourself feel strongly'; and with reference to the impression of his playing left upon the heart, Holtei wrote, after his drastic fashion, 'Paganini has played at Weimar; and there also, wriggling upon his four miserable strings, he has caused men's souls to cut capers within them'.

He approached the footlights as a poor, decrepit-looking man of weakly build; but as soon as he took his violin, raised the bow, and began to play, a giant-like strength, which had been but asleep, seemed to awake—nerves, muscles, and limbs were all strength, rigidity, and high tension. Spirit, force, and life were within and about him.

How is it that he has become so great—so absolutely incomparable? On that subject we shall have to question the history of his life.

Paganini was born at Genoa, on the 18th February, 1784. His father was a not particularly well-to-do tradesman, who was passionately fond of music, and cultivated it 'with little talent, but much pleasure'. He soon discovered his son's natural bent, and taught him the rudiments of the violin. He was a hard and severe man, who forced the boy to stick to his instrument the whole day, and who, if the lad did not seem to him sufficiently industrious, drove him to redouble his efforts through force of hunger.

In his ninth year the young violinist was first heard publicly, at a concert in his native town, Genoa, amidst the unprecedented plaudits of an enthusiastic audience. After receiving instruction at Parma, from the famous Rolla, and in composition from Chivetti [sic], he gave himself up to solitude, carrying on his studies most assiduously. From the age of fifteen, he, for two and twenty years, travelled and gave concerts throughout Italy, perfecting more and more his marvelous attainments. For some years he held a post at Court in Lucca. But passion had awoke to life in the fiery young Italian. He led a dissipated life and became a terrible gambler, which resulted in shattered health and pecuniary distress. When he made his appearance in Germany, he had sobered down and become even frugal in his habits; and it is from Vienna that his world-fame may be said to have taken rise. He now visited Germany, France, England, Spain, Poland, &c., and, at last, after an absence of ten years, he returned in the summer of 1834 to Italy, loaded with fame and riches; from that time living either in Genoa, Milan, or Parma. After a short stay in Paris—where, on account of his shattered health, he was no longer able to give concerts—he hastened to return by sea to Genoa, fancying that there he might recover. It was a vain hope. Nice was to be his last abiding-place. His malady—consumption—there made rapid strides. His voice completely failed him, his strength fast ebbed away. On his last evening he seemed quieter than usual, and slept a little. When he awoke he had the bed curtains put aside, that he might look upon the moon, just rising in full glory in a cloudless heaven. At that sight, his senses once again sprang to life; he seized his violin, the faithful companion of all his travels, and in its tones was wafted to heaven his last sigh.

The great master died on the 27th May, 1840, in the 56th year of his age.

But, with the death of this extraordinary man, all was not yet over. He was an Italian and a Catholic. He believed in God, but not in the priests. He liked to visit churches and cathedrals to admire the heaven-inspired masterpieces of the architect, the sculptor, and the painter; or to enjoy the sacred music of the old Italian and other composers. But the multiplicity of ceremonies and the clouds of incense, which mystify and obscure the minds of the people, he hated. This, no doubt, had come to the ears of the Catholic priesthood. The Very Christian Archbishop of Nice forbade him burial in consecrated ground; and it was only after long entreaties from his son and his friends that Christian burial was at length accorded to him.

Paganini bequeathed to his son Achilles a fortune of two millions, and to his two sisters legacies of from fifty to sixty thousand, francs: but to the mother of his son—the vocalist, Antonia Bianchi, of Como—only an annuity during her lifetime of twelve hundred francs. He also left behind a collection of the most valuable stringed instruments of Guarneri, Amati, Straduarius [sic], &c.; the last-named, being the instrument which he ever used at his concerts, he bequeathed, it is said, to his native town of Genoa, not wishing that another artist should possess it after him. According to another account, he left it to Ernst.

Not only, during his lifetime, was he tormented by continued acute bodily suffering, but he was also pursued by the basest calumnies from the many who envied his success and his fame. They went so far as to accuse him of actual crime. 'In his youth he had been an associate of thieves'—'in a fit of jealousy he had murdered his wife'—or, seeing that he could show that he never was married, 'his mistress'. Some asseverated that, in expiation of this crime, he had spent many years at the galleys, 'as might be seen from his uncertain, swaying gait'. Others asserted that he had 'suffered long imprisonment, during which, one by one, the strings of his violin had cracked, until only the fourth was left; and this was what had caused him to bring his playing upon the G string to such an astonishingly skilful pass'.

Paris, who plumed herself that she led the march of civilization, eminently distinguished herself in the invention of such-like tales. Fétis wrote: "There are, in this city, a by no means inconsiderable portion of the population who live upon the evil which they do, and upon the good which they prevent." Nay, even in his own native country, where grows the orange, and where priest and bandit flourish, many a one maintained, in all seriousness, that he had made a pact with the devil, and had given over to him his hopes for the world to come, in return for being taught in this life all manner of magic arts.

No doubt after Paganini's death all these fables were satisfactorily demonstrated to be but shameful inventions and stupid credulity; but during his lifetime they were held by many as true; for mankind believes in the evil much more easily and much more readily than in the good; particularly when it concerns great and famous men, or those whom fortune has specially favoured.

Beyond these fables next to nothing was known of Paganini's character and private life until he came to Germany. But, afterwards, he was in the habit of selecting from time to time companions to accompany him on his tours, and to look after his business arrangements; in fact, to act as his *impresarii*. One of these—the Hanoverian writer George Harrys—for some time kept a circumstantial diary, from which we obtain many an interesting glimpse into the habits and peculiarities of Paganini.

As a rule, artists are great lovers of nature, but Paganini formed a striking exception. If, on his journeys, he passed through the most beautiful landscape, by lovely villas and stately castles, or through the most romantic scenery, he took no notice; for him there was no charm. If he did not talk, he was thinking of his art, of his composition, or was lost in melancholy reverie. Another reason, and that a very good one, why he could not look about him was because he was constantly shivering, and would always keep the curtains of the carriage drawn close. He would sit in a temperature of 82 degrees wrapped in his fur coat, and every curtain drawn tight, crouching in his corner, and scarcely allowing his companion, at the side where he sat, occasionally to let in a little air. He continually grumbled at the German climate; and ascribed to it a great portion of the bodily ailments which he had brought with him from Italy. Often he used to say to Harrys, whilst wrapping himself in his fur coat, 'This is an excellent article for Germany: one can never travel without it, even in the middle of summer'. Odd to say, *per contra*, he liked best to sit in his room betwixt open doors and windows, which he called 'taking an air bath'. The frequent colds which he caught in consequence had much to do with his bodily weakness

Like all weakly persons, Paganini loved sleep. He would often sleep two hours at a stretch in his travelling carriage, and this three times a day. After these naps he was more lively and talkative, and was inclined, sometimes, to joke.

When he arrived at the post stage he would remain in the carriage, or else promenade, whilst the horses were being changed or fed; but he never entered an inn nor posting house before he had reached the place fixed as the termination of his day's journey.

His luggage gave him but little trouble. His most valuable possession, his instrument—a Guarneri—lay in a shabby and worn-out case, in which he was accustomed to keep at the same time his money, some little jewellery, and his fine linen. A travelling mechanic might easily have carried the whole of Paganini's wardrobe in his knapsack. His papers, more important than those of many a man of business, were all contained in a little red case. And although they numbered but some twenty loose scraps, yet they held a succinct account of his business transactions since had left Italy for Germany. But it was all in hieroglyphics, which no one but himself could decipher. There the papers lay huddled together—Vienna and Carlsruhe, Frankfort and Leipzig, income and outgoing expenses, post horses and concert tickets; and yet he could find his way in a marvelous manner though this labyrinth; and rarely reckoned to his own disadvantage, though he was no arithmetician.

Paganini was satisfied with whatever was given him in the hotels upon his tours. It was all the same to him whether he had a garret or the best room, a good bed or an indifferent one: all he bargained for was that it must be in the back part of the building, for the noise of the streets was absolutely unbearable to him. "I have to stand noise enough in the large towns," he would say: "on my journeys I must have quiet."

Once arrived at his destination, no sternly-guarded state prisoner could lead a more monotonous and tedious life than did the great master in his apartment. Nevertheless, he left it seldom, and then unwillingly; for he seemed to find himself most comfortable when left in absolute solitude.

Vocalists and instrumentalists have painfully to attain facility in their art by dint of persevering industry; and by several hours' daily practice of scales, solfeggi, and difficult passages, seek to maintain flexibility of throat and finger. But even in this respect this wonderful man was an almost incredible exception. It is a proved fact that during all his tours no human ear even heard the voice of his fiddle proceeding from his room, with the very occasional exception of the tuning of his violin, and that only on concert days, a few minutes before the rehearsal, or before the concert itself. Paganini, moreover, made no secret of it that he never cared to touch his violin unless he were obliged. 'I have practiced enough in my lifetime', he would say; 'and am thankful when I need not take my fiddle from out its case'.

Since Paganini was absolutely unoccupied when at home, one would have thought that he would give his time to composition. But it was not so.

The works (concertos, variations, &c.) with which he made his appearance on his tours had all been written in Italy; and not a single new production fell from his pen during all his travels.

There could be no question that he was not a well-read man; for, except a smattering of French, he understood no language but his own; and he showed no inclination for reading, and made no secret of it (at any rate to his companion) that he possessed no scientific culture whatever. His excuse was: 'One can only know *one* science thoroughly. I have devoted my whole life to my fiddle and to the theory of music; and have had no time left for other scientific pursuits'. And he had just as little taste for other mundane matters. In political events he took no part: the most stupendous phenomena and changes in the world's history, the down fall of the most exalted personages, the fate of Napoleon, the insurrection of the Greeks, or the thought of his own politically torn and distracted country made less impression on him than did the snapping of a fiddle-string in the orchestra during one of his public performances.

But, after all, this extreme one-sidedness of mind, this concentration upon one thing alone—his violin playing—made him the greatest phenomenal *virtuoso* which the world has ever seen.

Taking him all in all Paganini was a misanthrope, as is the case with most people to whom days of health are but rare occurrences. The sickly body is a murky window through which the mind can perceive no more cheerful prospect without. Yet even the melancholy man has moments of brightness, and perhaps of merriment. And so it was with Paganini. When with acquaintances he could be the most talkative and amusing of companions. At such times he liked best to relate anecdotes of his life; and he knew how to recount them with great piquancy and humour. He was a sworn foe to all great gatherings and feasts; and it always required great persuasion to get him to accept an invitation. On such occasions he would talk little at table, but enjoy the feast the more. At a great banquet he would seldom leave a dish untasted. His appetite was of the best. He could go on eating for several hours without suffering the slightest inconvenience, and he was not disinclined to sacrifice to Bacchus. Withal he was generally so *distrait* that he seldom knew of what he had partaken, or whether it was good or bad. He took but little share in the conversation; and after the feast was over he would soon withdraw, in order to enjoy his siesta. In the evening social gatherings, where there was less constraint, he was more accessible; but if anyone wanted to talk with him about music, or to arrange with him a musical *soirée,* then his good humour was irrecoverably gone. In cards or social games he took no interest. For persons he had an extraordinarily faithful memory, but none whatever for places—even the names of towns where he gave his concerts vanished from his memory before he was well out of them.

It was remarkable how nature seemed to have specially adapted him for violin-playing. His fingers were of extraordinary length and flexibility; he could bend the thumbs so far back that he was able to touch with the nails the back of his hand. Just as extraordinary was the suppleness of his arm: without the least effort he could bend the two elbows close together.

Paganini's behaviour on the way to the concerts, in the concert rehearsals, and behind the scenes, was most remarkable. On rehearsal mornings he was altogether more serious than usual. Although perfectly sure as regarded his execution, he could not rid himself of a certain nervousness. On such occasions he could do nothing but sit still. A few minutes before going to rehearsal he would open his violin-case to see that no strings were broken, tune his fiddle, play a couple of chords, close his case again, and set in readiness the music required for the day. All the time he would, almost uninterruptedly, be taking snuff—a sure sign with him of inner restlessness. If he found that listeners had dropped in, as happened not seldom, he would merely outline his solos, sometimes only indicating them by a soft *pizzicato*.

Nothing finer than his ear can possibly be imagined: the slightest faint never escaped him. In the loudest orchestral *tutti* he would call out, 'The second clarinet [*sic*] is not playing'; or, 'I don't hear the viola', &c. if the orchestra did not play to his satisfaction he could be very angry; but if he were accompanied with precision he would shout in the middle a loud 'Bravissimo!' We had heard that, during an orchestral pause, he would display his greatest skill; and we pricked up our ears when his first solo came. So it happened that we were greatly taken by surprise, and not agreeably so, when he put down his violin with the words, 'And so on, gentlemen: let us go on'. From fear lest anyone should purloin or copy any of his pieces, he would always take his music carefully away with him, although the principal part was not there, for he played everything by heart. After rehearsal he would enjoy a solitary meal and then rest. It was remarkable that he who during the whole of a concert day was silent and melancholy, should from the moment when he entered the anteroom until his appearance before the public shake off all the seriousness which had clung to him during the day. Whilst waiting, he usually carried on nothing but jests and jokes, and would keep this up until the kapellmesiter apprised him that it was now his turn, when suddenly he would return to his habitual seriousness, and go forward to meet his audience.

A pleasing trait in his character was his ever-ready kindness. Young musicians who ofttimes brought to him their ponderous scores, young ladies who wished to learn from him whether their voices were powerful enough for the stage, fiddlers who were brought to him for his artistic judgment as to their merits, artists whose talent he had recognized and who came to him for recommendations—to all of these he was affable, and advised them according to his convictions. He himself was fond of praise, and would, with eagerness and satisfaction, read the papers in which it was lavished on him. He carried on his correspondence in Italian; his French letters he was obliged to have corrected; his handwriting was not the most legible.

Outer splendour and luxury were not to his taste; even his Orders were seldom used, except when he was appearing in public, and then he wore ribbons only. Often he would say, 'What is the use of it all? I am not proud'. To part with money was for him (the former spendthrift), after his change to frugality, the most difficult of tasks. He would get into the most violent passion over what he considered an imposition in the way of *pour boire*. He was always bargaining, and, consequently, soon got the reputation of being a miser—particularly since his means had accumulated rapidly in consequence of the extraordinary takes at his concerts, where the prices of admission were always doubled or trebled. But that he could be generous, when he deemed it expedient, he has given such a proof as is rarely to be met with. It is well known that Berlioz, during the greater part of his life, was in poor circumstances, from no fault of his own, except that he remained consistently true to his ideal; and ideal at that time not congenial to the French. The works of Berlioz made a wonderful impression upon Paganini; and when he had heard the 'Romeo and Juliet', and become cognizant of Berlioz's poverty-stricken condition, he wrote to him on the very next day:—

'My Dear Friend,—Since Beethoven has departed, it could only fall to Berlioz to recall him to life; and, after enjoying your heaven-inspired compositions, which are worthy of a genius like yours, I must beg of you to accept, as a token of my reverence, twenty thousand francs, which will be paid to you by Baron Rothschild on presentation of the enclosure'.

Paganini appeared to me at that time (in the heyday of my youth) the most consummate and incomparable artist in the highest sense of the words; and such he still seems to me, now, when the blood flows with slow cadence in the veins of the old man of seventy-five. Whether there ever will be found anyone to equal him on the violin, I cannot say: such a one has yet to appear. For, whatever commotion he created amongst us fiddlers, with whatever mad zeal they have struggled since his time, in their attics and whenever they handled a fiddle, to learn and imitate his tricks, even to the very pauses in the rehearsal (in the Berlin orchestra the practicing of Paganini's artistic feats had to be actually prohibited), yet no one has succeeded in rivaling him.

There have been all manner of *virtuosi* after him, who have learned many of his arts and imitated them with more or less success; but all his best followers (be their names whatsoe'er they may) are, at most, but fragments of him. This much I know, and all those who have heard him likewise know, that it is not given to mortals to excel him. Robert Schumann said, and rightly, 'Paganini has attained to the highest pinnacle; he is the very apex of the virtuoso's skill'.

Walter Spinney, 'The Dead Violin. An Account of a Strange Occurrence. Related by Walter Spinney', *Musical Standard* Vol. 36 No. 1294 (18 May 1889), 410–11

Walter Spinney (1852–94) was an English organist and composer based in Leamington, Warwickshire. This short story, a piece of Victorian literature, is written in the first person, as if the events in question came from the author's own recollection. He relates a nocturnal encounter with Paganini's ghost at a concert hall in an English town where the violinist had once played. The author describes Paganini's appearance in familiar Gothic terms ('skeleton-like', 'wax-coloured face', 'bead-like eyes', 'half-mocking sneer of sardonic pity', 'unearthly eyes' etc.). As if by compulsion he then visits the house where Paganini had stayed and discovers his violin, kept there by the housekeeper for many years. Despite being told he must not touch it, he cannot resist temptation—and the violin falls apart (hence 'the dead violin'). This story is thus not about Paganini per se, but rather about the strange desire of a later generation to somehow taste a piece of his legend. The Musical Standard *was published in London and covered secular and sacred music, professional and amateur; most contributors wrote anonymously.*

I found myself a few years ago in a fine concert hall in one of the large towns of this country, listening to the delightful strains of the violin and piano as discoursed by Mdme. Norman-Néruda and Charles Hallé.

It is not too much to say that it is not only the mind that is affected by such music, but the bodily frame as well. It can bring to the hearer a feeling of perfect rest, almost impossible to describe, and to such a feeling, I, being at that time tired in body and worried in mind, was especially inclined.

I entered the room alone, and selected the quietest corner I could find, so that I could sit and close my eyes, and thus enjoy the music to the fullest extent.

The evening wore on, and I leaned on the seat before me. Scarcely anyone was within some yards of me, for the hall was only about one-third full.

How the soirée ended I cannot say, for I was asleep—fast asleep. I suppose the fact of my being bent down caused the caretaker to overlook me, and when I awoke I was startled by finding myself in the darkened room with no light save that of the rays of the moon, which streamed through the heavy windows.

I tried all the doors I could find, knocked, banged a chair on the ground, shouted, and made every noise imaginable, but all to no purpose. No attendants dwelt within the dwelling, or if they did, they were quite out of hearing.

I must confess that the dying echoes of the din I caused made me somewhat nervous. They seemed to be such a long time in ceasing, and I, more than once, half expected to see some ghostly figures flitting about as if disturbed by such unwonted clamour.

I soon found that unless something unexpected occurred, I was doomed to pass the night in this novel prison; and, consequently, I began with an ill grace to make up as good a bed as I could upon the seats.

I had a thick overcoat with me, so I did not suffer at all with cold, and almost as soon as I had laid down, I fell fast asleep for the second time in this vast bed chamber.

But not, it would seems, for long.

Presently I could hear strains of music in the distance. The hall gradually grew lighter and lighter, and to my utmost astonishment I saw that the seats were filled. The audience was a crowd of silent and awe-stricken individuals.

Strange and quaint dresses were there—costumes of the kind made familiar to us in the drawings of Leech, 'Phiz' and Cruikshank, limned when the century was still young. But my attention was not by any means drawn towards these details. No; the gaze of every one present was immovably fixed, in almost terrified amazement, upon a performer who stood before us.

Was he human?

He was a tall skeleton-like man, with pale, narrow wax-coloured face, and with most brilliant, bead-like eyes. A violin was firmly grasped in his left hand. A half-mocking sneer of sardonic pity quivered upon his thin lips, and those unearthly eyes roved and roamed about until they had brought all under their magic spell. It was mesmerism. No one spoke. Deep sighs were frequent, as if the tension upon the nerves was more than could be borne. Slowly the figure raised the bow and placed it upon the strings, and then one soft sound—how soft passes the power of words to tell—began to fill the room, until we were conscious of nothing else, save that we were breathing music.

On he moved from the slow, soft satin-like notes, on and on in an ecstasy of inspiration, carrying us with him as the waters of a river are carried to the sea. We were no longer individuals with separate wills and understandings. He swayed us hither and thither as his fancy moved him. Now it was a light and dancing strain, relieving the breast as if from a long pent-up woe. Now it was a sad tale which told of misery more eloquently than words could ever speak. During one of these changes, I, overcome, leant my head once more on the seat before me to let my tears flow unobserved, and when I raised my head again I was startled to find that he and I were alone in the moon-lit room. The glare of the candles had vanished with the mysterious audience. There was no mistaking the evident intention of the imperious player. Still wielding his bow, he made gestures towards me which plainly said 'Come'. And in spite of my fearful disinclination to do so, I found myself following him, dreading all the time some unseen danger, yet powerless to prevent myself fulfilling his will. Noiselessly his feet moved over the ground, whilst he seemed breathing with his instrument, as if he lived through its medium. We passed through doors which opened as he approached; into the black night air; through the busy streets, as if we were not of the world. We disturbed no one. Yet all the while he was filling the very sky with pathetic outpourings of the wildest melody. Presently he touched me by the hand and led me to a cottage by the roadside. There he stopped, and pointed to the door with a commanding yet almost wistful look. Another second, and he was gone.

I rubbed my eyes, sat up and discovered that it was broad daylight, and further, that I was still on my impromptu bed, instead of being on the road where my supernatural guide had left me. It was evidently a dream, but what a dream! Do what I would it haunted me, and I could think of nothing else when I felt fully awakened.

The care-taker arrived soon after eight in the morning and I had considerable difficulty in persuading him that I was not a burglar. At last, against his will, he let me go unmolested.

On my way to the hotel, I dropped in at the ticket-seller's office, to ask if any inquiry had been made after me during the night, and in the course of a few minutes' conversation, up came the subject of my dream. Nothing, indeed, could keep me away from it.

'Do you mind giving me a few particulars about your dream?' the ticket seller said in an evidently interested voice.

Seeing I had something more than an idle, curious mind to satisfy, I did so, not forgetting to describe the weird and unearthly aspect of the player of my vision.

'Do you know' the ticket seller said, 'that an old friend of mine was nearly put into a lunatic asylum about ten years ago, for declaring *he* had heard Paganini perform under almost exactly similar circumstances in that same room'?

'Indeed', I replied, growing deeply interested. 'I should much like to converse with your friend'.

'He died soon after, but on his death bed he held to the veracity of his tale. And now we are upon that subject, it may interest you to know that Paganini did play in this town and in that very room in 1831, and it is said, by some, upon what authority I do not know, that there are still persons living who remember him, and who have even conversed with him'.

'I should much like to find them out, and tell them of my dream', I said.

My informant went on. 'Paganini, whilst here stayed at the house of an old gentleman on the Heath. This old man was a fit companion for the wild musician, for he was eccentric to a degree. I believe he died at nearly the age of 100 some years ago, but his housekeeper still lives in the old house'.

'Thank you very much', was my reply, 'if I can any way make the time during my short stay here I shall certainly look up the old lady'.

Upon this I left, and found my way to my hotel, where not a little anxiety had been felt on my account.

I tried to attend to my business the rest of the day, but it was of no avail, and before the clock struck four in the afternoon I found myself on the Heath searching for the house where Paganini had stayed.

All buildings of anything like an ancient appearance I scrutinized with the zeal of an antiquary.

'Ah; here it is', I said aloud, as I paused in front of the identical door before which the ghostly musician stood last night.

There was no mistaking the old carved lintels and the quaint iron knocker. The whole was photographed on my mind. Without hesitation I raised the hammer, and gave a stirring rat-a-tat.

'Pardon me, Madame', I said, as a very old and wizened-faced woman appeared. 'Pardon me, I am a musician, and am seeking the house in which the great violinist lived when in this town'.

These words seemed to flow without any effort from my mouth, without thought on my part.

'This is the house, sir, but all are dead and gone, save myself, who ever remembered him'.

'May I come in and sit down? I should like to get a few particulars about him'.

'Certainly, but you will find it dull work listening to the tales of an old woman like myself'.

I learned from this poor old lady that Paganini had been very friendly with her master, and when the great violinist quitted his dwelling, he left with the old gentleman a violin in a case, with the strictest injunctions that no one was ever to be allowed to touch it. Paganini promised to come himself, or send a messenger for it whose credentials should be beyond all doubt. About ten years ago her old master died, and she and others that same night heard unmistakable sounds of a violin outside, though no one was visible at the time within at least half a mile. 'Last night', she went on, with increasing solemnity, 'I heard the player again, and I feel sure something will come of it'. 'He is not of this world', she added. 'Such beautiful sounds are beyond the reach of any living man'.

I said, 'Have you the violin yet?'

'Yes'.

'May I look at it?'

'Yes, but no finger must touch it'.

She reached, with my help, from the top of an old carved oak cupboard a violin-case—opened it—and I—*in spite of my promise, was literally compelled as if by an unseen hand to grasp the instrument.*

As my fingers touched the wood the whole crumbled into dust.

With a face crimson with shame I turned to the old woman, who said slowly, 'It was not to be. The great master said in my hearing, "*This is a part of my life, when I die this will die also.*"[']

Anon., 'New Story of Paganini', *Violin Times* Vol. 5 No. 51 (January 1898), 57

This fictional story about Paganini buying a 1711 Stradivarius at a London auction is presented as fact. Despite being apocryphal, there are two elements of interest here in terms of escalating the Paganini legend. The first is the account of Paganini mesmerising listeners playing this violin—causing them spontaneously to dance or to cry, overcome—which he handles 'fondly as if it were his little child'. The second is the overlapping mythologies of Paganini and of Stradivari violins, which carried their own mysterious aura. The Violin Times *magazine was printed from 1893 to 1907.*

When in Genoa, Italy, I was told a thrilling incident which has not been published until now, says a contributor to an exchange. In the year 1831, at an auction in London, England, which drew a small crowd of fashionable people, was a black, greasy violin, said to be an ancient Cremona 120 years old, and to have been made by Antonius Stradivarius. When the violin was lifted from its case and given to the auctioneer he held it very gently as if it were sacred. Having described its supposed history, he handed it to a well-known professional artist to show its sweetness and power; but though the musician no doubt did his best, the tone was not specially fine, nor did its power excel that of a high class modern fiddle. The people looked disappointed, and with a long face, but trying to speak cheerfully, the auctioneer called for bids.

After some coaxing he began with an offer of a guinea, and gradually worked the people up to six guineas, beyond which it seemed impossible to move. At a rapid rate, in one breath, he cried, 'A real grand, original, genuine Cremona Antonius Stradivarius!' Someone said, 'It does not bear his name!' but the auctioneer explained that some of the violins which had the name were modern and shams, the name having been added to increase the value; and as no one denied it he triumphantly held up the case bearing the fiddle like a baby in the cradle, crying, 'See the sweet little beauty, gentlemen!' He then levered up the bids to ten guineas, where he stuck; but he made frantic efforts to advance, beads of sweat bursting from his brow, running along his nose, from which they were flirted off with the bank of his hand. 'Really, gentlemen, only ten guineas for an instrument worth its weight in gold! Ten guineas; going! Going! Any advance? Why gentlemen, this is an angel violin! Such a chance has never been before the British public!—a real genuine Antonius-----'.

At this point a middle aged Italian in a velvet coat entered the auction room, and, as if drawn by a magnet, gently pushed his way to the front. Lifting the violin from its case, he keenly examined it, putting it to his ear and listening as if he thought, perhaps, something inside might whisper to him, and he handled it fondly as if it were his little child he had found in a shop. He seemed to forget that the auctioneer and the fashionables were watching him. He now stretched out his hand for the bow, and when, in the almost breathless silence of the crowd, he turned his face, some of them recognized him, and softly uttered the magic name, Paganini!

The first three of four notes thrilled everyone: in another moment many were in tears; soon their feet moved as if they wished to dance, one of them exclaiming 'It is superhuman!' Another. 'It is divine!' Now they smile and nudge one another for gladness; again tears start to their eyes; they are nerved as if for battle, and when Nicolo Paganini reverently kisses the violin and places it in its case, half-a-dozen person cry, 50 guineas! Another 60; others 70, 80, 90, and then, followed by a great cheering, the fiddle is knocked down to the famous musician for 100 guineas.

At Drury Lane that night, Paganini stood before a packed throng with the ancient fiddle he had bought a few hours previously, and the people were spellbound. He so roused their enthusiasm that they waved their hats, crying 'Hurrah!' But when he breathed himself into the G string he so much loved, and with unequalled pathos, made it, as the crowd imagined, pronounce the words, 'Home, sweet home', a mighty sob burst form the people, and it was some time before they sufficiently overcame their emotion to listen to the next piece.

R. E. Andrews, 'The Violin of Human Strings', *Idler: an Illustrated Monthly Magazine* (June 1898), 709–14

*Originally in Italian, this story about a fictional German Paganini imitator was published in two slightly different translations twelve years apart. The author, Antonio Ghislanzoni (1824–93) was an Italian writer and librettist for Verdi (*Aida, La Forza del Destino*). The earlier version, by an anonymous translator ('The Violin of Human Strings' [trans. anon. from the Italian of Antonio Ghislanzoni], Magazine of Music Vol. 4 No. 45 (December 1887), 199–200) substitutes the word 'demon' for 'incomparable' in the second line (which thus reads 'Paganini, the demon Paganini'), yet the bulk of the story is identical. It concerns Franz Sthoeny of Stuttgart who sets out to win glory as the world's foremost violinist—by challenging the 'incubus' Paganini. Sthoeny and his teacher Samuel Klauss believe that Tartini's 'satanic' playing was due to his instrument carrying the soul of a virgin who died out of love for him and that Paganini had strung his violin with the entrails of his beloved in order to make it sound like the human voice. Klauss sacrifices his own life so that his protégé can make strings out of his entrails (never mind that the precedents were presumably young beautiful women). Franz puts the 'fatal strings' on the violin (the gruesome details of how he extracts his teacher's intestines are mercifully skipped over). He travels to Ghent to challenge Paganini ('the demoniac artist' in the 1887 version, 'the great man' in the 1898 version) to a duel, playing* Le Streghe. *When Paganini plays, 'his satanic eyes were fixed upon his instrument as though to invoke the infernal sounds'. Next comes Franz's turn but his violin does not work and so, humiliated, he rips the strings off the violin and prostrates himself at Paganini's feet. The story ends with Paganini telling Franz that his strings do not work because they need to be from an Italian (a nationalist sentiment from the*

Mazzini devotee Ghislanzoni). The Idler *printed fiction, poetry, and short articles and reviews for light entertainment from 1892 to 1911.*

It was in the year 1831. Paganini, the incomparable Paganini, had been performing at the Opera, where he had given six concerts, exciting an enthusiasm even greater than that which had accompanied him during his triumphal tours in Italy and Germany. His reception in Paris baffles description: at each performance the crowded house had been moved to a pitch of excitement rarely witnessed even among Parisians—nor was this emotional demonstration confined merely to the audience, for, some orchestra professors of the great theatre, carried away by this master genius—who seemed to exercise a magic spell wherever he went—actually threw down their instruments before the great artist. Now there was in Paris just at this time another violinist, named Franz Sthoeny, a man who was gifted with unusual ability, but was, nevertheless, quite ignorant of the great world of art.

Born at Stuttgart—where he had been quietly brought up—Franz had passed his time in that city alternating the severe meditations of philosophy with exercises on the four-stringed instrument. At thirty-five years of age he had lost both parents, and was alone in the world. On the death of his mother, who had adored him, and exhausted all the savings of a rather slender patrimony for her only son, Franz realised the fact that he was poor, and the prospect of the future presented itself in very gloomy colours.

What was he to do?

His old music-master, Samuel Klauss, undertook to solve this serious enquiry, and his mute response to it was far more eloquent than any words could have been.

Klauss took his beloved pupil by the hand, and led him to the little room in which they had so often improvised together delightful musical 'Fantasias', and silently indicated the little case in which was enclosed the violin like a living thing in a neglected tomb.

That look opened out a new career before Franz Sthoeny. After selling the furniture and chattels of his home, the artist left for Paris in company with his master and friend.

Before Paganini had given his marvellous concerts at the Opera, Franz had become imbued with a secret confidence in his own abilities as a musician—having made mental comparisons in his competitions with other players—and believed that his skill could even surpass that of the most renowned violinists who had been heard in the capital of France.

This belief gradually became a settled conviction, and Franz inwardly resolved that he would break his instrument and terminate his own existence with it rather than fail to rank above the players of the period, and he duly confided this resolution to his master.

Old Klauss was delighted with such noble pride, and honestly believed that he was fulfilling a grand design by flattering it.

But before bringing himself into public notice, Franz waited with feverish impatience for the much lauded Italian to make his appearance in Paris.

The name of Paganini had been for some months a cruel 'thorn in the flesh' to Franz—an incubus, a threatening phantom to the heart of old Samuel. Both had inwardly shivered at that artist's name; both alike had unpleasant misgivings of his coming to Paris.

Words utterly fail to describe the pangs, the heart burnings, the unbounded enthusiasm of that unlucky evening. Franz and Samuel shuddered as Paganini drew the first few notes on his violin—both master and pupil were dumbfounded by the tumultuous applause, which was unspeakable anguish of spirit to them; they dared not look at one another; neither exchanged a syllable with the other.

At midnight, after the concert, they returned silently and sadly to their lodgings.

'Samuel!' said Franz with a dispirited air, throwing himself into a chair, 'here's a pretty thing. We are good for nothing. Do you understand? Nothing whatever. I say, we are out of it altogether'.

The features of the old man became livid. After a brief silence, Samuel answered in a hollow tone:

'Still, you are wrong, Franz; I have taught you all that a master can teach, and you have learnt everything that one man can learn from another. What fault is it of mine, if these d—d Italians have recourse to satanic inspirations, and the infamies of magic, in order to excel in the realm of art?'

Franz glared at his old master with a sinister expression—the look on his face seemed to say: 'What do I care about scruples? Just exalt me to that position in art, and I would only too willingly give myself over to the devil, body and soul'.

Samuel guessed what was passing in his pupil's mind, but resumed with simulated calmness: 'You know the wretched history of the celebrated Tartini. He died one Saturday night, strangled by his familiar spirit who had taught him how to put soul into his violin, incorporating in it the spirit of a virgin. Paganini has done even more. Paganini, in order to breathe into his instrument the groans, the cries of desolation, the most telling notes of the human voice, has become the murderer of the most devoted friend he ever possessed; and he has made the four strings of his matchless violin with the entrails of his victim. There, you have the secret of that subtle fascination, of that irresistible power of sound, which you, my poor Franz, could never equal, except—'And the old man paused abruptly.

His voice seemed to be paralysed with a sort of mysterious dread.

After a brief silence Franz, lowering his eyes, resumed in this strain:

'And you think, Samuel, that I should really obtain those unheard of effects, and create the unbounded outbursts that everywhere greet Paganini, if my instrument were composed of this human cat-gut?'

'Only too much so!' exclaimed the master with unwonted emotion; 'but in order to obtain that consummation it is not merely necessary that the strings should be composed of human fibre; it is also required that the said fibre shall have been part of a sympathetic body. Tartini communicated life to his violin by introducing into it the soul of a virgin—but that girl died out of love for him; whilst the satanic artist—who was present with her during her last agonies—caused the spirit of the dying to pass into his instrument through the medium of a small cane. As for Paganini, I have already told you . . .

'Oh! the human voice; the miracle of the human voice', pursued Samuel, after a brief silence. 'Do you suppose, my poor Franz, that I should not have instructed you in its production, if it could have been obtained by means of art, of that noble and blessed art which I long to see embodied in you yourself, that art which shines by the light of its own genius alone, which despises meanness and holds crime in abhorrence'.

Franz could not trust himself to say a word. He stood up, and, with an assumed calmness, which revealed the deepest agitation, took the violin in his hand, gave a threatening and scornful look at the strings, then grabbing them with savage frenzy, tore them from the instrument.

Old Samuel uttered a cry, the strings, reduced to shreds, had been flung on to the burning cinders in the grate, and there they were curling and hissing through the heat of the fire like tortured serpents.

Samuel took a candlestick from the table, and, without wishing his pupil good night, made his way upstairs to bed.

. . . . . . '

Weeks passed, months passed. A deep melancholy had taken possession of Franz. The violin, bereft of strings, dusty and neglected, hung in a corner.

Every day Samuel and Franz dined together, and in the evening they used to sit facing each other in the same little salon, but neither dared to enter into conversation with the other; they maintained a strict silence, like two mutes.

Ever since the violin had been ruthlessly destroyed, these two animated beings appeared to have lost the use of speech.

'This has lasted long enough', exclaimed old Samuel at length. And that same evening, before retiring to rest, he came up to his friend to kiss his forehead. Franz, diverted from his sad reflections, mechanically repeated the words of his master.

'This has lasted long enough'.

They separated and both went to bed.

On the following morning when Franz opened his eyes to the light of day, he was surprised at not finding this old master in the room at his bedside as usual—the latter generally rose before him.

'My good Samuel! My dearest Samuel!' shouted Franz, jumping out of bed and hurrying into the master's room.

Franz was startled by the sound of his own voice, but still more so by the silence to his cries.

'There is no silence like the silence of Death'. At the bed of Death, and in the stillness of the tomb, silence acquires that mysterious intensity which strikes the heart with awe.

The rigid head of Samuel was lying motionless on the bolster; the salient features of that head were an open forehead brilliant with light and a grey sharp beard that seemed to be raised upwards.

At the sight of the corpse Franz experienced a dreadful quaking, but the nature of the man and the nature of the artist awakened strongly in him at the same time, and in that conflict of passions grief almost dazed him, but the affections of the artist prevailed and subdued the weaker instincts of the man.

A letter addressed to Franz was lying on the dressing-table. The violinist opened it trembling.

It read as follows:—

'MY DEAR FRANZ,—

'When you have read this letter I shall have fulfilled the greatest and last sacrifice that I, your master, and only friend, can accomplish for your renown. He who loves you above everything else in this world is now a dead man; there is now nothing remaining of your old master but impassive organic matter. I will not suggest to you what remains to be done.

'Do not allow yourself to be carried away by vain scruples or foolish superstitions. I have given up my body that you may use it for your everlasting glory.

'You could not sully your fair name by a more heartless ingratitude than by rendering my sacrifice of no effect. When you will have restored the strings to your violin—when those strings composed of my fibre give forth the voice, the groan, the weeping of my ardent love—then—Oh, my dear,

Franz, you need fear nothing, take your instrument, track the footsteps of the man who has done us so much harm, present yourself on the field where he has proudly held sway until now, throw down the gauntlet to him. Oh! what an inspiration will stir within you as the thrilling note of passion will sound from your violin, and you will remember, when fondling the strings, that they were a part of your old master, who now kisses you for the last time, and blesses you.

'SAMUEL'.

Two tears dimmed the eyes of Franz, soon however to be dispelled by the fire that lurked within. He stood, stunned and motionless, by the bedside of his dead master.

Let us pass what followed by remarking that the dying wish of the heroic Samuel was carried into effect, as Franz did not in the least hesitate to arrange with the doctors to obtain the fatal strings, with which he hoped to impart soul to his violin.

A fortnight afterwards those strings were stretched upon his instrument. Franz could not bear to look at them. One evening he was desirous of trying the tone of them, but the bow trembled in his nerveless grasp like a knife in the hand of an assassin.

'Never mind', he muttered to himself, replacing the violin into the case, 'these foolish fears will vanish when I appear before my powerful rival. The wish of my poor Samuel shall be fulfilled. It will be a great triumph for me and for him if it results in my equalling, or surpassing, Paganini'.

But the celebrated violinist was no longer in Paris. At that time Paganini was giving a series of concerts at Ghent Theatre.

One evening, as the great man was seated at a round table, surrounded by a selected company of musicians, Franz entered the hall of the hotel, and, stepping lightly towards Paganini, handed him a visiting-card, but without saying a word.

Paganini read it, darted a keen glance at his unknown visitor, which would have disconcerted anyone less rash, but, seeing that the other was quite unmoved by it he answered dryly, 'Signor, your wishes shall be complied with'. And Franz, bowing courteously to the assembled guests, took his departure.

Two days afterwards, in the city of Ghent, a notice was posted up announcing the final concert of Paganini. In the last lines thereof, printed in very large letters, there appeared a singular announcement, which provoked never ceasing comments and excited the public curiosity in no small degree.

'On the said evening', ran the notice, 'the famous German violinist, Herr Franz Sthoeny, will be present for the first time. He has come to

Ghent expressly to challenge the illustrious Paganini, declaring himself prepared to compete with him in the most difficult pieces. The illustrious Paganini having accepted the challenge, Herr Franz Sthoeny will execute the Fantasia-Capriccio entitled *Le Streghe* (the witches) in comparison with the insuperable violinist'.

The effect of this poster was simply electrifying. Paganini, who never lost sight of the main chance even in the midst of his greatest successes, did well on this occasion by doubling the prices of tickets. Needless to say, his calculations proved correct. By common consent the whole city of Ghent seemed to have assembled at the theatre that evening. As the great eventful hour arrived, Franz was found in the actor's room, whither Paganini had just preceded him.

'Bravo, my son', said Paganini, 'you have done well by coming early. It would be as well if we inverted the order of the programme. It bothers me having to rush through this business, as you will not be disturbed by my playing my other pieces afterwards. Are you ready?'

'I am quite at your service' replied Franz calmly.

Paganini then gave the word for the curtain to be lifted, and at once presented himself to his audience amid a tempest of applause and frantic shouts.

Never before had the Italian artist exhibited so masterly a power in the execution of that difficult composition *Le Streghe.* The strings of the violin, under the pressure of the long, bony fingers, twisted like throbbing heart-strings. The sounds seemed to take human form, and dance deliriously with fantastic shapes around that magician of art. In the vacant space of the stage an inexplicable phantasmagoria, formed by the sonorous vibrations, represented the wanton orgies of the witches' meeting.

When Paganini was at last able to withdraw from the scene to which the tumultuous acclamations of his audience were ever recalling him, he met Franz in the rear. The latter had just finished testing his violin, and was about to step forward on to the stage. Paganini was stupefied on beholding the complete self-possession of his competitor and the air of confidence which shone in his face. Franz advanced towards the footlights, being welcomed with frigid silence by the audience. Satiated by the fascination of Paganini, the spectators looked upon the new arrival as upon some poor weakling who dares an absurd contest with a rival who is immeasurably his superior.

Nevertheless, after Franz had drawn the first few notes the interest of the audience was visibly awakened.

Franz was a very able executant—one of those executants to whom the word difficulty conveys no meaning. Old Samuel was not mistaken when he said, 'I have taught you all that one can teach, and you have learnt all that one can learn'.

But that which Franz had dreamed of obtaining by means of those sympathetic strings—the groan of passion, the piercing cry of anguish, the roar of the forest, and the shrieks of the damned—that which old Samuel wanted to communicate to his pupil and friend—all this fabric of illusions and hopes that had been received in simple faith by the German artist fled in a moment.

Under the shock of this dreadful disillusion, Franz lost courage and power. He invoked, in a low voice, the name of the defunct master, entreated him, cursed him in his secret soul, then called him aloud, 'Traitor! Scoundrel!' At last, tired of the contest, desperate, and despairing of the issue, he wrenched the fatal strings from the violin and started trampling on them in an access of madness and fury.

'He is mad! He is mad! Stop him! Help him!' shouted a hundred voices from the pit.

Franz hurried from the scene and rushed away from the stage out of sight, to throw himself prostrate at the feet of Paganini.

'Pardon! a thousand times pardons!' groaned Franz, in deep despair. 'I believed—I hoped—'

Paganini extended his arms to that poor discomfited man, raised him from the ground, and, embracing him like a brother, said:

'You played divinely . . . . You are a great artist . . . . What you lack is—'

'Oh, I know but too well what I lack', broke in Franz, sobbing; 'but old Samuel has deceived me'.

And Franz narrated to Paganini the story of the human strings, ingenuously explaining the illusions upon which he had relied.

'Poor Franz!' exclaimed the Italian violinist, with a touch of sarcastic pity. 'You have forgotten one circumstance through which the strings of your violin could not compete with mine—in vivacity, in the ardour and impetuosity of passion. Did you not tell me that your old master was a German?'

'Yes', replied Franz, 'and so am I'.

'Well, then that accounts for it', continued Paganini, slapping poor Franz on the shoulder. 'Another time when you wish to infuse into your violin the soul, fire, passion, the life, which I possess, be sure that your strings are composed of Italian fibre'.

Bibliography

Archival Sources

Biblioteca Casanatense, Rome
Bibliothèque de l'Opéra, Paris: 'Dossier d'artiste: Nicolo Paganini'
Gertrude Clarke Whittall Foundation Collection, Music Division, Library of
    Congress, Washington, DC

Newspapers and Periodicals

Ainsworth's Magazine
Allgemeine Musikalische Zeitung
Allgemeine Wiener Musikzeitung
Allgemeine Wiener Zeitung
Argosy: A Magazine of Tales, Travels, Essays, and Poems
Athenaeum
Bentley's Miscellany
Blackwoods Edinburgh Magazine
Bow Bells
British Minstrel
Caecilia
Il caffè di Petronio
Chambers's Journal of Popular Literature, Science and Arts
Cornhill Magazine
Dziennik Powszechy (Universal Country Journal)
L'Entracte
Figaro in London
The Foreign Quarterly Review
La France Musicale
Frankfurt Journal
Fraser's Magazine for Town and Country
Der Freischütz
Gazzetta di Genova
Gazzetta musicale di Milano
Gazzetta Piemontese
Good Words
Harmonicon
Idler: An Illustrated Monthly Magazine
L'Illustration
L'Indépendent

Journal of the American Musicological Society
Journal des débats
Journal général de France, politique, littéraire et militaire
Kaleidoscope; or Literary & Scientific Mirror
Il lavoro
Leipziger Allgemeine Musikalische Zeitung
Leipziger Kometen
Literary Gazette
Lokal-Anzeiger
Lute
Magazine of Music
Ménestrel
Merry England
Le Miroir
Minim
Mirror Monthly Magazine
Mirror of Literature, Amusement, and Instruction
Monthly Magazine
Monthly Music Record
Monthly Review
Morgenblatt
The Morning Chronicle
Music & Letters
Musical Herald
Musical News
Musical Opinion and Music Trade Review
Musical Quarterly
Musical Standard
The Musical Times
The Musical World
Musik & Ästhetik
Nuova rivista musicale italiana
The Observer
Once a Week
Orchestra
Paganini
Le Plaisir à Paris
Play Pictorial
Quarterly Musical Review
Quarterly Music Magazine and Review
Quaver
Review
Revue de musicologie
Revue de Paris
Revue et gazette musicale de Paris
Revue musicale

Romantisme: Revue de la Société des Études Romantique
Saturday Review of Politics, Literature, Science and Art
School Music Review
The Strad
Temple Bar
Theaterzeitung
Theatrical Observer
Tonic Sol-fa Reporter
Violin Times
Vossiche Zeitung
Zeitung für die Elegante Welt

Primary Sources and Secondary Literature

Abrams, M. H. *The Mirror and the Lamp: Romantic Theory and the Critical Tradition* (London: Oxford University Press, 1953).

Adorno, Theodor W. *Introduction to the Sociology of Music*, trans. E. B. Ashton (New York: Continuum, 1989).

_____. *Essays on Music*, trans. Susan H. Gillespie, ed. Richard Leppert (Berkeley: University of California Press, 2002).

Anon. *Il libro del perché* ([Publication place unknown]: [Publisher unknown], n.d. [18c]).

_____. *Zur Erinnerung an Louis Eller* (Dresden: Rudolf Kuntze, 1864).

Applebaum, Samuel, and Sada Applebaum. *The Way They Play*, 4 vols (Neptune City, NJ: Paganiniana, 1972).

Aretino, Pietro. *Ragionamento*, ed. Giorgio Barberi Squarotti and Carla Forno (Milan: Biblioteca Universale Rizzoli, 1988).

Athanassoglou-Kallmyer, Nina. 'Blemished Physiologies: Delacroix, Paganini, and the Cholera Epidemic of 1832', *The Art Bulletin* Vol. 83 No. 4 (2001), 686–710.

Bachmann, Albert. *Les Grands Violinistes du passé*, trans. Theodore Baker (Paris: Fischbacher, 1913).

Baillot, Pierre Marie François de Sales. *The Art of the Violin* [Paris, 1835] trans. Louise Goldberg (Evanston, IL: Northwestern University Press, 1991).

Baker, Theodore. *Baker's Biographical Dictionary of Musicians*, rev. Nicolas Slonimsky, 7th ed. (New York: Schirmer Books, 1984).

Balma, Mario. 'La tradizione popolare fonte di ispirazione per Paganini', in Maria Rosa Moretti, Anna Sorrento, Stefano Termanini, and Enrico Volpato, eds, *Paganini divo e comunicatore, atti del convengointernationale* (Genoa, 3–5 December 2004) (Genoa: Serel International, 2007), 227–54.

Barizza, Andrea and Fulvia Morabito, eds. *Nicolò Paganini Diabolus in Musica*. Studies on Italian Music History, vol. 6 (Lucca: Brepols Publishers, 2010).

Bartsch, Cornelia. 'Virtuosität und Travestie: Frauen als Virtuosinnen', in Heinz von Loesch, Ulrich Mahlert, and Peter Rummenhöller, eds, *Musikalische*

Virtuosität. Perspektiven musikalischer Theorie und Praxis (Gebundene Ausgabe) (Mainz: Schott, 2004), 77–90.

Barzun, Jacques. *From Dawn to Decadence: 500 Years of Western Cultural Life* (New York: Perennial, 2001).

Battaglia, Marco. 'Mosaico Ottocentesco. Mazzini e Paganini tra musica, filosofia, lettere, memorie e due storiche chitarre', in Maria Rosa Moretti, Anna Sorrento, Stefano Termanini, and Enrico Volpato, eds, *Paganini divo e comunicatore, atti del convengointernationale* (Genoa, 3–5 December 2004) (Genoa: Serel International, 2007), 205–16.

Beales, Derek. *The Risorgimento and the Unification of Italy* (London: George Allen & Unwin, 1971).

Behnke, Elizabeth A. 'At the Service of the Sonata: Music Lessons with Merleau-Ponty', in Henry Pietersma, ed., *Merleau-Ponty: Critical Essays* (Lanham, MD: University Press of America, 1990), 23–9.

Bennett, Betty T., ed. *The Letters of Mary Wollstonecraft Shelley*, 3 vols (Baltimore, MD, and London: The Johns Hopkins University Press, 1983).

Berkley, Harold, ed. *Niccolo Paganini Op. 1 Twenty-Four Caprices for the violin* (New York: Schirmer, 1944).

Bernstein, Susan. *Virtuosity of the Nineteenth Century: Performing Music and Language in Heine, Liszt, and Baudelaire* (Stanford, CA: Stanford University Press, 1998).

Berri, Pietro. *Il Calvario di Paganini* (Savona: Liguria, 1941).

_____. *Paganini: Documenti e testimonianze* (Genoa: Sigla Effe, 1962).

_____. *Paganini: La vita e le opere* (Milan: Monti, 1982).

Beyle, Henri. *Life of Rossini*, trans. Richard Coe (London: Calder & Boyars, 1970 [Originally published 1824]).

Bianchi, Luigi Alberto. 'Il virtuosismo violistico nell'opera di Rolla e Paganini', *Nuova rivista musicale italiana* 1 (1975), 10–34.

Blanchard, Henri. 'Physiologie du violon', *Revue et gazzette musicale de Paris* Vol. 6 No. 38 (25 August 1839), 331–32.

_____. 'Antonio Bazzini', *Revue et Gazette Musicale de Paris* Vol. 20 No. 17 (24 April 1853), 152.

Bloom, Peter, ed. *Music in Paris in the Eighteen-Thirties* (Stuyvesant, NY: Pendragon Press, 1987).

_____. 'Virtuosités de Berlioz', *Romantisme: Revue de la Société des Études Romantiques* 128 (2005), 71–94.

Bone, Philip J. *The Guitar and Mandolin: Biographies of Celebrated Players and Composers*, 2nd ed. (London: Schott, 1972).

Bongiovanni, Carmela. 'Osservazioni sulla musica a Genova nell'età di Paganini', in Maria Rosa Moretti, Anna Sorrento, Stefano Termanini, and Enrico Volpato, eds, *Paganini divo e comunicatore, atti del convengointernationale* (Genoa, 3–5 December 2004) (Genoa: Serel International, 2007), 101–60.

Borchard, Beatrix. 'Der Virtuose—ein "weiblicher" Künstlertypus?', in Heinz von Loesch, Ulrich Mahlert, and Peter Rummenhöller, eds, *Musikalische Virtuosität. Perspektiven musikalischer Theorie und Praxis (Gebundene Ausgabe)* (Mainz: Schott, 2004), 63–76.

Bordas, Éric. 'Ut musica poesis? Littérature et virtuosité', *Romantisme: Revue de la Société des Études Romantiques* 128 (2005), 109–28.

Bork, Camilla. 'Theatricality in the Concert Hall: Paganini's Virtuosity', Paper read at the 3rd German-American Frontiers of Humanities Symposium, Humboldt University, Berlin (2006).

Bouissac, Paul. *Circus and Culture: A Semiotic Approach* (Bloomington: Indiana University Press, 1976).

Bourdieu, Pierre. *The Field of Cultural Production* (New York: Columbia University Press, 1993).

Boyd, Malcolm, ed. *Music and the French Revolution* (Cambridge: Cambridge University Press, 1992).

Boyden, David D. *The History of Violin Playing from its Origins to 1761* (New York: Oxford University Press, 1965).

_____ . 'Der Geigenbogen von Corelli bis Tourte', in Vera Schwarz, ed., *Violinspiel und Violinmusik in Geschichte und Gegenwart: Bericht über den Internationalen Kongress am Institut für Aufführungspraxis der Hochschule für Musik und Darstellende Kunst in Graz, vom 25. Juni bis 2. Juli 1972* (Vienna: Universal Edition, 1975), 295–310.

Boyden, David D. *et al. New Grove Violin Family* (New York: Norton, 1989).

Brandstetter, Gabriele. 'Die Schauspielmusik von J.-J.-A. Ancessy zu Barbier/Carrés *Les Contes d'Hoffmann* (1851)', in *Jacques Offenbachs Hoffmanns Erzählungen: Konzeption, Rezeption, Dokumentation* (Laaber: Laaber-Verlag, 1988), 465–75.

Brittnacher, Hans Richard. *Ästhetik des Horrors. Gespenster, Vampire, Monster, Teufel und künstliche Menschen in der phantastischen Literatur* (Frankfurt am Main: Suhrkamp, 1994).

Brossard, Sebastien de. *Dictionnaire de musique* (Paris: Ballard, 1703).

Brown, Clive. *Louis Spohr: A Critical Biography* (Cambridge: Cambridge University Press, 1984).

_____ . 'Bowing Styles, Vibrato and Portamento in Nineteenth-Century Violin Playing', *Journal of the Royal Musical Association* 113 (1988), 97–128.

Brumana, Biancamaria. *Teatro musicale e accademie a Perugia. Tra dominazione francese e Restaurazione* (Florence: Olschki, 1996).

Burk, J. N. 'The Fetish of Virtuosity', *Musical Quarterly* 4 (1918), 282–92.

Burnham, Scott. *Beethoven Hero* (Princeton, NJ: Princeton University Press, 1995).

Butler, Judith. 'Performative Acts and Gender Constitution: An Essay in Phenomenology and Feminist Theory', in Sue-Ellen Case, ed., *Performing Feminisms: Feminist Critical Theory and Theatre* (Baltimore, MD, and London: The Johns Hopkins University Press, 1990), 270–82.

C., M.-D. 'Les Violinistes compositeurs et virtuoses', *Musical Times* Vol. 64 No. 965 (July 1923), 471.

Caduff, Corina. 'Heinrich Heine: Die Musikperson als Medium der Musikkritik' [Heinrich Heine: The Musician as a Medium of Music Criticism], *Musik & Ästhetik* Vol. 6 No. 22 (April 2002), 96–105.

Campbell, Margaret. *The Great Violinists* (Garden City, NY: Doubleday, 1981).

Canetti, Elias. *Crowds and Power*, trans. Carol Stewart (London: Phoenix Press, [1962] 2000).

Cantú, Alberto. *Invito all'ascolto di Nicolò Paganini* (Milan: Mursia, 1988).

Carse, Adam. *The Orchestra* (New York: Chanticleer, 1949).

_____. *The Orchestra in the XVIIIth Century*, 2nd ed. (Cambridge: Heffer, 1950).

Cartier, Jean-Baptiste. *L'Art du violon* (Decombe: À l'Accord Parfait, ca. 1796).

Carver, Terrell. *The Postmodern Marx* (University Park: Pennsylvania State University Press, 1999).

Case, Sue-Ellen, ed. *Performing Feminisms: Feminist Critical Theory and Theatre* (Baltimore, MD, and London: The Johns Hopkins University Press, 1990).

Castil-Blaze, François-Henri-Joseph. *L'Académie impériale de musique de 1645 à 1855*, 2 vols (Paris: Castil-Blaze, 1855).

Charlton, David, ed. *E.T.A. Hoffmann's Musical Writings:* Kreisleriana, The Poet and the Composer, *Music Criticism*, trans. Martyn Clarke (Cambridge: Cambridge University Press, 1989).

Codignola, Arturo. *Paganini intimo* (Genoa: Edito a cura del municipio, 1935).

Cohn, Norman. *Europe's Inner Demons: The Demonization of Christians in Medieval Chistendom*, rev. ed. (Chicago, IL, and London: University of Chicago Press, 2000).

Cone, Edward. *The Composer's Voice* (Berkeley and Los Angeles: University of California Press, 1974).

Conestabile, G. C. *Vita di Niccolò Paganini* 2nd ed. rev. by F. Mompellio (Perugia: Bartelli, 1851 [reprinted 1936].

Cook, Peter, Alastair Dick *et al.* 'Extra-European and Folk Usage', in *The New Grove Violin Family*, ed. Stanley Sadie [The Grove Musical Instruments Series] (New York: W. W. Norton, 1989).

Cooke, John. *History and Method of Cure of the Various Species of Epilepsy* (London: Longman, 1823).

Cowgill, Rachel and Hilary Poriss, eds. *The Arts of the Prima Donna in the Long Nineteenth Century* (Oxford: Oxford University Press, 2012).

Cumming, Naomi. *The Sonic Self: Musical Subjectivity and Signification* (Bloomington and Indianapolis: Indiana University Press, 2000).

Dahlhaus Carl. *Nineteenth-Century Music*, trans. J. Bradford Robinson (Berkeley, Los Angeles, and London: University of California Press, 1989).

Damasio, Antonio. *Descartes' Error: Emotion, Reason and the Human Brain* (London: Papermac, 1996).

Dancla, Charles. *Notes et souvenirs* (Paris: Delamotte, 1893).

Darnton, Robert. *Mesmerism and the End of the Enlightenment in France* (Cambridge, MA: Harvard University Press, 1968).

Davies, J. Q. '"Velluti in speculum": The Twilight of the Castrato', *Cambridge Opera Journal* Vol. 17 No. 3 (2005), 271–301.

Day, Lilian. *Paganini of Genoa* (London: Victor Gollancz, 1966 [originally published New York: The Macaulay Company, 1929]).

Deaville, James. 'The Making of a Myth: Liszt, the Press, and Virtuosity', in James Deaville and Michael Saffle, eds, *Analecta Lisztiana II: New Light on Liszt and His Music* (Stuyvesant, NY: Pendragon Press, 1997), 181–95.

_____ . 'La figura del virtuoso da Tartini e Bach a Paganini e Liszt', in Jean-Jacques Nattiez, ed., with the collaboration of Margaret Bent, Rossana Dalmonte and Mario Baroni, *Enciclopedia della musica*, Vol. IV (Turin: Giulio Einaudi, 2004), 803–25.

_____ . 'A Star is Born? Czerny, Liszt and the Pedagogy of Virtuosity', in *Beyond the Art of Finger Dexterity: Reassessing Carl Czerny*, ed. David Gramit (Rochester, NY: University of Rochester Press, 2008), 52–66.

Deaville, James and Michael Saffle, eds. *Analecta Lisztiana II: New Light on Liszt and His Music (Essays in Honour of Alan Walker's 65th Birthday)* (Stuyvesant, NY: Pendragon Press, 1997).

De Courcy, Geraldine I. C. *Paganini, the Genoese*, 2 vols. (Norman: University of Oklahoma Press, 1957).

_____ . *Chronology of Nicolo Paganini's Life* (Wiesbaden: Erdmann Muskverlag, 1961).

Delfino, Vanda. 'Niccolo Paganini e la critica musicale inglese', *Nuova rivista musicale italiana* Vol. 14 No. 4 (October–December 1980), 555–60.

De Martino, Giorgio. *Giuseppe Gaccetta e il segreto di Paganini: La biografia del violinista anche scelse di non essere il più grande* (Genoa: De Ferrari, 2001).

DeNora, Tia. *Beethoven and the Construction of Genius: Musical Politics in Vienna, 1792–1803* (Berkeley: University of California Press, 1997).

Denys, Odet. *Qui était Le Chevalier de Saint-George (1739–1799)?* (Paris: Pavillon, 1972).

Devrient, Therese. *Jugenderinnerungen* (Stuttgart: Carl Krabbe Verlag, 1905).

De Wailly, P. 'Rapports de Boucher de Perthes avec Paganini', *Revue de musicologie* Vol. 9 (August, 1928), 167–9.

Diderot, Denis. *Rameau's Nephew and D'Alembert's Dream*, trans. Leonard Tencock (Harmondsworth: Penguin, 1966).

Doerner, Klaus. *Madmen and the Bourgeoisie* (Oxford: Blackwell, 1981).

Doni, G. B. *Annotazioni sopra il Compendio de' Generi, e de' Modi della Musica* (Rome: [Publisher unknown], 1640).

Döpfner, M. O. C. and Thomas Garms, *Erotik in der Musik* (Frankfurt: Populäre Kultur, 1986).

D'Ortigue, Joseph. *Le Balcon de l'Opéra* (Paris: Renduel, 1833).

Downes, Stephen. *Muse as Eros: Music, Erotic Fantasy and Male Creativity in the Romantic and Modern Imagination* (Aldershot: Ashgate, 2006).

Dunning, Albert. *Pietro Antonio Locatelli, der Virtuose und seine Welt*, 2 vols (Buren: F. Knuf, 1981).

Durant, John, and Alice Durant. *Pictorial History of the American Circus* (New York: A. S. Barnes, and Toronto: Copp Clark, 1957).

Durant, Will and Ariel Durant. *The Age of Napoleon: A History of European Civilization from 1789 to 1815* (New York: Simon and Schuster, 1975).

Eckermann, Johan Peter. *Gespräche mit Goethe* (Leipzig: Brodhaus, 1925).

Eggebrecht, Harald. *Grosse Geiger: Kreisler, Heifetz, Oistrach, Mutter, Hahn & Co.* (Munich: Piper Verlag, 2000).

Einstein, Alfred. 'The Military Element in Beethoven', *The Monthly Musical Record* Vol. 49 (November 1939), 270–4.

Elfenbein, Andrew. *Byron and the Victorians* (Cambridge: Cambridge University Press, 1995).

Ellis, Havelock, ed. *The Prose Writings of Heinrich Heine* (London: Walter Scott, 1887).

Elster, Alexander. *Musik und Erotik* (Bonn: Marcus & Weber, 1925).

Erickson, Raymond, ed. *Schubert's Vienna* (New Haven, CT, and London: Yale University Press, 1997).

Farga, Franz. *Geigen und Geiger. English Violins & Violinists*, trans. Egon Larsen [with a chapter on English violin-makers by E. W. Lavender] (London: Rockliff, 1950).

_____ . *Paganini: Der Roman seines Lebens* (Zurich: Albert Müller, 1950).

Farmer, H. G. 'Military Music and its Story', *Musical Standard* Vol. 36 No. 934 (25 November 1911), 342–43.

Fauquet, Joël-Marie. *Les Sociétés de musique de chambre à Paris de la Restauration à 1870* (Paris: Aux Amateurs de Livres, 1986).

_____ . 'Quand le diable s'en mêle', *Romantisme: Revue de la Société des Études Romantiques* 128 (2005), 35–50.

Fayolle, François. *Paganini et Bériot: Avis aux jeunes artistes sur l'enseignement du violon* (Paris: Legouest, 1831).

Feldman, Allen and Eamonn O'Doherty, *The Northern Fiddler* (London: Oak Publications, 1979).

Fétis, François-Joseph. *Notice biographique sur Ch-Aug de Bériot* (Brussels: [Publisher unknown], 1871).

_____ . *Biographical Notice of Nicolo Paganini with an Analysis of his Compositions* (New York: AMS, 1976 [1876]).

_____ . *Notice Biographique sur Nicolo Paganini suivie de l'analyse de ses ouvrages* (Paris: Flute de Pan, 1981 [originally published 1851]).

Fiske, Roger. *Beethoven Concertos and Overtures* (Seattle: University of Washington Press, 1970).

Flotzinger, Rudolf, ed. *Oesterreichisches Musiklexicon* (Vienna: Österreichischen Akademie der Wissenschaften, 2002).

Flower, Newman. *Franz Schubert: The Man and His Circle* (London: Cassell, 1928).

Foster, Susan Leigh. *Reading Dancing: Bodies and Subjects in Contemporary American Dance* (Berkeley and Los Angeles: University of California Press, 1986).

Foucault, Michel. *Power/Knowledge*, ed. Colin Gordon (New York: Pantheon, 1980).

Fournier, Pascal. *Der Teufelsvirtuose: Eine kulturhistorische Spurensuche* (Freiburg im Breisgau: Rombach, ca.2001).

François-Sappey, Brigitte. 'Pierre Marie François de Sales Baillot (1771–1842) par lui-même', *Recherches sur la musique française classique* 18 (1978), 126–211.

Fraser, Elisabeth A. *Delacroix, Art, and Patrimony in Post-Revolutionary France* (Cambridge and New York: Cambridge University Press, 2004).

Frith, Simon and Andrew Goodwin, eds. *On Record: Rock, Pop, and the Written Word* (New York: Pantheon Books, 1990).

Frith, Simon and Angela McRobbie. 'Rock and Sexuality (1978)', in Simon Frith and Andrew Goodwin, eds, *On Record: Rock, Pop, and the Written Word* (New York: Pantheon Books, 1990), 369–424.

Fuchs, Eduard. *Geschichte der erotischen Kunst*, 3 vols (Munich: A. Langen, 1922–26).

Fuller-Maitland, J. A. *Joseph Joachim* [Living Masters of Music VI], ed. Rosa Newmarch (London: John Lane, 1905).

Gay, Peter. *The Cultivation of Hatred.* The Bourgeois Experience, Victoria to Freud, No. 3 (New York: Norton, 1993).

_____. *The Naked Heart.* The Bourgeois Experience, Victoria to Freud, No. 4 (New York and London: Norton, 1995).

Gelrud, Paul G. 'Foundations and Development of the Modern French Violin School' (MA thesis, Cornell, 1940).

Gibbs, Christopher H. and Dana Gooley, eds. *Franz Liszt & His World* (Princeton, NJ: Princeton University Press, 2006).

Gill, Dominic, ed. *The Book of the Violin*, 2nd ed. (New York: Rizzoli, 1987).

Gjerdingen, Robert O. *Music in the Galant Style* (Oxford: Oxford University Press, 2007).

Goehr, Lydia. *The Imaginary Museum of Musical Works: An Essay in the Philosophy of Music* (Oxford: Clarendon Press, 1992).

_____. *The Quest for Voice: Music, Politics, and the Limits of Philosophy* (Berkeley and Los Angeles: University of California Press, 1998).

Goethe, Johann Wolfgang. *Sulla musica*, ed. Giovanni Insom (Pordenone: Studio Tesi, 1992).

Gold, Joseph. 'Paganini: Virtuoso, Collector, and Dealer', *Journal of the Violin Society of America* Vol. 14 No. 1 (1994), 67–88.

Goldstein, Michael. 'Charles de Bériot', trans. Simone Luciani, *Cahiers Ivan Tourgéniev, Pauline Viardot et Marie Malibran* Vol. 10 (1986), 64–72.

Gooley, Dana. *The Virtuoso Liszt.* New Perspectives in Music History and Criticism (Cambridge and New York: Cambridge University Press, 2004).

_____. 'Franz Liszt: The Virtuoso as Strategist', in William Weber, ed., *The Musician as Entrepreneur, 1700–1914: Managers, Charlatans, and Idealists* (Bloomington: Indiana University Press, 2004), 145–61.

_____. 'La Commedia del Violino: Paganini's Comic Strains', *Musical Quarterly* Vol. 88 No. 3 (2005), 370–427.

_____. 'The Battle Against Instrumental Virtuosity in the Early Nineteenth Century', in Christopher H. Gibbs and Dana Gooley, eds, *Franz Liszt & His World* (Princeton, NJ: Princeton University Press, 2006), 75–112.

Gramit, David, ed. *Beyond the Art of Finger Dexterity: Reassessing Carl Czerny* (Rochester, NY: University of Rochester Press, 2008).

Graybill, Guy. *Bravo! Greatness of Italian Music* (Boston, MA: Dante University of America Press, 2008).

Grisley, Roberto. *Niccolò Paganini, epistolario 1810–1831* (Rome: Accademia Nazionale di Santa Cecilia and Milan: Skira editore, 2006).

Gross, Jonathan David. *Byron: The Erotic Liberal* (Lanham, MD: Rowman & Littlefield, 2000).

Guest, Ivor. *Fanny Cerrito: The Life of a Romantic Ballerina*, 2nd ed. (London: Chameleon, 1974).

Guhr, Carl. *Ueber Paganinis Kunst die Violin zu spielen* (Mainz: Schott, 1829).

Haas, Robert. 'The Viennese Violinist, Franz Clement', *Musical Quarterly* Vol. 34 No. 1 (1948), 15–27.

Hadlock, Heather. *Mad Loves: Women and Music in Offenbach's* Les Contes d'Hoffmann. Princeton Studies in Opera (Princeton, NJ: Princeton University Press, 2000).

Halski, Czeslaw Raymond. 'Paganini and Lipinski', *Music and Letters* Vol. 40 No. 3 (1959), 274–8.

Hansell, Sven. 'Marchesi, Luigi', in *Grove Music Online*, accessed 15 April 2009.

Hanslick, Eduard. *Geschichte des Concertwesens in Wien* (Hildesheim and New York: Georg Olms Verlag, 1979).

Hanson, Alice. *Musical Life in Biedermeier Vienna* (London: Cambridge, 1985).

Harrys, George. *Paganini in seinem Reisewagen und Zimmer, in seinem redseligen Stunden, in gesellschaftlichen Zirkeln und seinen Konzerten* (Tutzing: Schneider, 1982 [originally published 1830]).

Hart, George. *The Violin and its Music.* (London: Dulau, 1881).

Hartnack, Joachim W. *Grosse Geiger unserer Zeit* (Zurich: Atlantis, 1993).

Heine, Heinrich. *Florentine Nights*, trans. Frederick Carter (London: Gerald Howe, 1933).

Hemmings, F. W. J. *Culture and Society in France, 1789–1848* (Leicester: Leicester University Press, 1987).

Heron-Allen, E. and Lynda Macgregor, 'Wilhelmj, August', in Stanley Sadie, ed., *The New Grove Dictionary of Music and Musicians*, 2nd ed. (London: Macmillan, 2001), Vol. 27, 386.

Hibberd, Sarah. 'Cette diablerie philosophique': Faust Criticism in Paris c. 1830', in Roger Parker and Mary-Ann Smart, eds, *Reading Critics Reading* (New York: Oxford University Press, 2001), 111–36.

Hobsbawm, Eric. *The Age of Capital: 1848–1875* (London: Vintage, 1996).

Hoffmann, E. T. A. *Tales of Hoffmann*, trans. R. J. Hollingdale (London: Penguin Books, 1982).

Hoffmann, Freia. *Instrument und Körper* (Frankfurt and Leipzig: Insel, 1991).

Hogarth, George. *Musical History, Biography, and Criticism* 2nd ed. (London: John W. Parker, 1838).

Howard, Vernon. 'Virtuosity as a Performance Concept: A Philosophical Analysis', *Philosophy of Music Education Review* Vol. 5 No. 1 (Spring 1997), 42–54.

Hunt, Leigh. *The Autobiography of Leigh Hunt*, 3 vols (London: Smith, Elder, and Co., 1850).

Hunt, Lynn. *Politics, Culture, and Class in the French Revolution* (Berkeley: University of California Press, 1986).

Hunter, Mary. 'The Idea of the Performer in Early Romantic Aesthetics', *Journal of the American Musicological Society* Vol. 58 No. 2 (Summer 2005), 357–98.

Hutcheon, Linda and Michael H. *Opera: Desire, Disease, Death.* Texts and Contexts Series, Vol. 17. (Lincoln: University of Nebraska Press, 1999).

Huyghe, René. *Delacroix*, trans. Jonathan Griffin (London: Thames & Hudson, 1963).

Ince, R.B. *Franz Anton Mesmer: His Life and Teaching* (London: William Rider and Sons, Ltd, 1920).

Inzaghi, Luigi. *Alessandro Rolla: vita e opera del grande musicista, maestro di Niccolo Paganini* (Milan: La Spiga, ca. 1984).

_____ . *Camillo Sivori: Carteggi del grande violinista e compositore allievo di Paganini* (Varese: Zecchini, 2004).

Iovino, Roberto. *Niccolò Paganini: Un genovese nel mondo* (Genoa: Fratelli Frilli Editori, 2004).

Istel, Edgar. 'The Secret of Paganini's Technique', *The Musical Quarterly* Vol. 16 No. 1 (1930), 101–16.

Jacq-Mioche, Sylvie. 'La Virtuosité dans le ballet français romantique: Des faits à une morale sociale du corps', *Romantisme: Revue de la Société des Études Romantiques* 128 (2005), 95–108.

James, E. *Camillo Sivori: A Sketch of his Life, Talent, Travels and Successes* (London: Pietro Rolandi, 1845).

James, William. 'What is an Emotion?', in C. Lange and W. James, *The Emotions* (New York: Haffner, 1967), 11–30.

_____ . ' 'The Emotions', in C. Lange and W. James, *The Emotions* (New York: Haffner, 1967), 93–135.

Jankélévitch, Vladimir. *Music and the Ineffable*, trans. Carolyn Abbate (Princeton, NJ: Princeton University Press, 2003).

Joachim, Joseph. *Letters from and to Joseph Joachim.* Selected and translated by Nora Bickley (London: Macmillan, 1914).

Johnson, James. *Listening in Paris: A Cultural History* (Berkeley, Los Angeles, and London: University of California Press, 1995).

Kallberg, Jeffrey. *Chopin at the Boundaries: Sex, History, and Musical Genre* (Convergences: Inventories of the Present) (Cambridge, MA: Harvard University Press, 1996).

Kapp, Julius. *Paganini: Eine Biographie mit 60 Bildern* (Berlin: Schuster & Loeffler, 1922 [1914]).

Kawabata, Maiko. 'Drama and Heroism in the Romantic Violin Concerto' (PhD dissertation, UCLA, 2001).

_____ . 'Virtuoso Codes of Violin Performance: Power, Military Heroism, and Gender (1789–1830)', *19th-Century Music*, Vol. 28, No. 2 (November 2004), 89–107.

_____ . 'Violinists "Singing": Paganini, Operatic Voices, and Virtuosity', *Ad Parnassum* Vol. 5 No. 9 (April 2007), 7–39.

_____ . 'Paganini's Legacy', in Andrea Barizza and Fulvia Morabito, eds, *Nicolò Paganini: Diabolus in Musica.* Studies on Italian Music History, Vol. 6 (Lucca: Brepols Publishers, 2010), 353–8.

Kearney, Patrick J. *A History of Erotic Literature* (London: Macmillan, 1982).

Kendall, Alan. *Paganini: A Biography* (London: Chappell, 1982).

Kennedy, Emmet. *A Cultural History of the French Revolution* (New Haven, CT, and London: Yale University Press, 1989).

Kerman, Joseph. *Concerto Conversations* (Cambridge, MA: Harvard University Press, 1999).

Kierkegaard, Søren. *Either/Or*, trans. D. and L. Swenson (Princeton, NJ: Princeton University Press, 1944 [1843]).

Kirkendale, Warren. 'Segreto comunicato da Paganini', *Journal of the American Musicological Society* No. 18 No. 3 (Autumn, 1965), 394–407.

Klein, Hans-Günter. Liner notes to *Accardo plays Paganini*, trans. Clive Brown (Deutsche Grammophon, 1988).

Kolneder, Walter. *The Amadeus Book of the Violin: Construction, History, and Music*, trans. and ed. Reinhard G. Pauly (Portland, OR: Amadeus Press, 1998).

Kross, Emil. *The Study of Paganini's Twenty-four Caprices*, trans. Gustav Saenger (New York: Carl Fischer, 1908).

Laban, Rudolf. *The Mastery of Movement*, 4th ed. (Plymouth: Macdonald and Evans, 1980).

Lange, C. and W. James, *The Emotions* (New York: Haffner, 1967).

Laphelèque, G. Imbert de. *Nicolo Paganini: Notice sur ce célèbre violiniste* (Paris: Guyot, 1830).

Layton, Robert, ed. *A Guide to the Concerto* (Oxford and New York: Oxford University Press, 1996).

Le Guin, Elisabeth. *Boccherini's Body: An Essay in Carnal Musicology* (Berkeley and Los Angeles: University of California Press, 2006).

Leppert, Richard and Susan McClary, eds. *Music and Society: The Politics of Composition, Performance and Reception* (Cambridge: Cambridge University Press, 1987).

Lister, Warwick. *Amico: The Life of Giovanni Battista Viotti* (Oxford: Oxford University Press, 2009).

Löbl, Franz and Edith Hänfling, eds. *Paganini in Berichten, Zitaten und seltenen Bildern: Eine Dokumentation* (Wien: F. Löbl u. E. Hänfling, 1988).

Loesch, Heinz von, 'Virtuosität als Gegenstand der Musikwissenschaft', in Heinz von Loesch, Ulrich Mahlert, and Peter Rummenhöller, eds, *Musikalische Virtuosität. Perspektiven musikalischer Theorie und Praxis (Gebundene Ausgabe)* (Mainz: Schott, 2004), 11–16.

Loesch, Heinz von, Ulrich Mahlert, and Peter Rummenhöller, eds. *Musikalische Virtuosität. Perspektiven musikalischer Theorie und Praxis (Gebundene Ausgabe)* (Mainz: Schott, 2004).

Loesser, Arthur. *Men, Women and Pianos: A Social History* (New York: Simon and Schuster, 1954).

MacArdle, Donald. 'Beethoven and Schuppanzigh', *Music Review* Vol. 26 (1965), 3–14.

Macdonald, Hugh. 'Paganini in Scotland', in Raffaello Monterosso, ed., *Paganini e il suo tempo* (Genoa: Comune di Genova, 1984), 201–18.

Malvinni, David. *The Gypsy Caravan: From Real Roma to Imaginary Gypsies in Western Music and Film* (New York: Routledge, 2004).

Manén, Juan. *Relatos de un violinista* (Madrid: Editora Nacional, 1964).

Mann, Michael, ed. *Zeitungsberichte über Musik und Malerei* (Frankfurt am Main: Insel-Verlag, 1964).

McClary, Susan. 'A Musical Dialectic from the Enlightenment: Mozart's *Piano Concerto in G Major, K.453*, Movement 2', *Cultural Critique* (1986), 129–69.

———. 'The Blasphemy of Talking Politics During Bach Year', in Richard Leppert and Susan McClary, eds, *Music and Society: The Politics of Composition, Performance and Reception* (Cambridge: Cambridge University Press, 1987), 13–62.

———. *Feminine Endings: Music, Gender, and Sexuality* (Minneapolis: University of Minnesota Press, 1991).

———. *Conventional Wisdom: The Content of Musical Form* (Berkeley and Los Angeles: University of California Press, 2000).

McVeigh, Simon. 'Brahms's Favourite Concerto', *The Strad* (April 1994), 343–7.

———. '"An Audience for High-Class Music": Concert Promoters and Entrepreneurs in Late–19th Century London', in William Weber, ed., *The Musician as Entrepreneur, 1700–1914: Managers, Charlatans, and Idealists* (Bloomington: Indiana University Press, 2004), 162–82.

Medkova-Strakova, Ljuba. Unpublished leaflet from the Dvořák Museum, Prague (n.d.).

Mehl, Margaret. 'Japan's Early Twentieth-Century Violin Boom', *Nineteenth-Century Music Review* Vol. 7 No. 1 (2010), 23–43.

Mell, Albert. 'Paganiniana in the Muller Collection of the New York Public Library', *Musical Quarterly* Vol. 39 (1953), 1–25.

———. 'Antonio Lolli's Letters to Padre Martini', *Musical Quarterly* Vol. 56 No. 3 (July 1970), 463–77.

Mellor, Anne K. *Romanticism and Feminism* (Bloomington and Indianapolis: Indiana University Press, 1988).

———. *Romanticism and Gender* (New York: Routledge, 1993).

Merleau-Ponty, Maurice. *The Phenomenology of Perception*, trans. Colin Smith (Boston, MA: Routledge and Kegan Paul, 1962).

———. *Sense and Non-Sense*, trans. Hubert L. Dreyfus and Patricia Allen Dreyfus (Evanston, IL: Northwestern University Press, 1964).

Metzner, Paul. *Crescendo of the Virtuoso: Spectacle, Skill and Self-Promotion in Paris during the Age of Revolution* (Berkeley and Los Angeles: University of California Press, 1998).

Milligan, Thomas B. *The Concerto and London's Musical Culture in the Late 18th Century* (Ann Arbor, MI: UMI Research Press, 1983).

Minazzoli, Gilbert, ed. *Dictionnaire des oeuvres érotiques: Domaine français* (Paris: Mercure de France, 1971).

Mocinova, Bozhanka. 'Compositori bulgari ispirati a Paganini', in Maria Rosa Moretti, Anna Sorrento, Stefano Termanini, and Enrico Volpato, eds, *Paganini divo e comunicatore, atti del convegnointernationale* (Genoa, 3–5 December 2004) (Genoa: Serel International, 2007), 517–26.

Mongrédien, Jean. *French Music from the Enlightenment to Romanticism 1789–1830*, trans. Sylvain Frémaux (Portland, OR: Amadeus Press, 1996).

Monterosso, Raffaello, ed. *Nicolò Paganini e il suo tempo* [*Nicolò Paganini and His Times*] (Genoa: Comune di Genova, 1984).

Moretti, Maria Rosa and Anna Sorrento. *Catalogo tematico delle musiche di Nicolò Paganini* (Genoa: Comune di Genova, 1982).

Moretti, Maria Rosa, Anna Sorrento, Stefano Termanini, and Enrico Volpato, eds, *Paganini divo e comunicatore, atti del convengo internationale* (Genoa, 3–5 December 2004) (Genoa: Serel International, 2007).

Morgan-Browne, H. 'An Approximation to the Truth about August Wilhelmj', *Music & Letters* Vol. 3 (1922), 219–28.

Moser, Andreas. *Geschichte des Violinspiels*, ed. Hans-Joachim Nössel, 2nd ed. (Tutzing: Hans Schneider, 1967).

_____. *Joseph Joachim: A Biography (1831–99)* trans. Lilla Durham (London: Philip Wellby, 1901).

Mourão, Manuela. 'The Representation of Female Desire in Early Modern Pornographic Texts, 1660–1745', *Signs* Vol. 24 No. 3 (1999), 573–602.

Moysan, Bruno. 'Virtuosité pianistique: Les Écritures de la subjectivité', *Romantisme: Revue de la Société des Études Romantiques* 128 (2005), 51–69.

Mozart, Leopold. *A Treatise on the Fundamental Principles of Violin Playing* (1756), trans. Editha Knocker (New York: Oxford University Press, 1948).

Müller-Funk, Wolfgang. 'E. T. A. Hoffmanns Erzählung Der Magnetiseur, ein poetisches Lehrstück zwischen Dämonisierung und neuzeitlicher Wissenschaft', in Heinz Schott, ed., *Franz Anton Mesmer und die Geschichte des Mesmerismus* (Stuttgart: Franz Steiner, 1985), 200–15.

Murray, Marian. *From Rome to Ringling: Circus!* (New York: Appleton-Century-Crofts, 1956).

Musgrave, Michael. *A Brahms Reader* (New Haven, CT, and London: Yale University Press, 2000).

Myerly, Scott Hughes. *British Military Spectacle: From the Napoleonic Wars through the Crimea* (Cambridge, MA: Harvard University Press, 1996).

Nattiez, Jean-Jacques, ed., with the collaboration of Margaret Bent, Rossana Dalmonte and Mario Baroni, *Enciclopedia della musica*, Vol. IV (Turin: Giulio Einaudi, 2004).

Neill, Edward. *Nicolò Paganini: La vita attraverso le opere, i documenti e le immagini* (Genoa: Cassa di risparmio di Genova e Imperia, 1978).

_____. Liner notes to Paganini's 'La Carmagnola' played by Franco Mezzena, violin and Adriano Sebastiani, guitar (Dynamic, 1994).

_____. *Paganini: Con la riproduzione integrale dei disegni del Lyser*. Graphos-Musica no. 5 (Genoa: Graphos, 1994).

Nelson, Sheila M. *The Violin and Viola: History, Structure, Techniques* (Mineola, NY: Dover, reprinted 2003).

Neocleous, Mark. 'The Political Economy of the Dead Marx's Vampires', *History of Political Thought* Vol. 24 No. 4 (2003), 668–84.

Newman, Ernest. *More Essays from the World of Music* (London: John Calder, 1958).

Nicholls, Angus. *Goethe's Concept of the Daemonic: After the Ancients* (Rochester, NY: Camden House, 2006).

Nisbet, John Ferguson. *The Insanity of Genius and the General Inequality of Human Faculty Physiologically Considered*, 3rd ed. (London: Ward & Downey, 1893).

Otte, Andreas P., Konrad Wink, and Karina Otte, *Kerners Krankheiten grosser Musiker: Die Neubearbeitung* (Stuttgart: Schattauer, 2007).

Palmer, David L. 'Virtuosity as Rhetoric: Agency and Transformation in Paganini's Mastery of the Violin', *Quarterly Journal of Speech* Vol. 84 No. 3 (August 1998), 341–57.

Parker, Roger and Mary-Ann Smart, eds, *Reading Critics Reading: Opera and Ballet Criticism from the Revolution to 1848* (Oxford and New York: Oxford University Press, 2001).

Penesco, Anne. 'Paganini et l'école de violon Franco-Belge', *Revue Internationale de Musique française* Vol. 9 (1982), 17–60.

_____. 'Le Violon en France au temps de Baillot et de Paganini', *La musique en France à l'époque romantique: 1830–1870* Vol. 25 (1991), 199–229.

_____. 'L'estro paganiniano et son empreinte jusqu'à nos jours', in Anne Penesco, ed., *Défense et illustration de la virtuosité*. Cahiers du Centre de Recherches Musicologiques (Lyons: Presses Universitaires de Lyon, 1997).

_____. 'Portrait de l'artiste violiniste en virtuose', *Romantisme: Revue de la Société des Études Romantiques* Vol. 128 (2005), 19–34.

Petrey, Sandy. 'Robert le diable and Louis-Philippe the King', in Roger Parker and Mary-Ann Smart, eds, *Reading Critics Reading* (New York: Oxford University Press, 2001), 137–54.

Phipson, Thomas Lamb. *Biographical Sketches and Anecdotes of Celebrated Violinists* (London: Bentley, 1877).

Pierce, Alexandra. *Deepening Musical Performance through Movement: The Theory and Practice of Embodied Interpretation* (Indianapolis: Indiana University Press, 2007).

Pietersma, Henry, ed., *Merleau-Ponty: Critical Essays* (Lanham, MD: University Press of America, 1990).

Pincherle, Marc. 'Virtuosity', trans. Willis Wager, *Musical Quarterly* Vol. 35 No. 2 (April 1949), 226–43.

_____. *The World of the Virtuoso* (New York: Norton, 1963).

Place, Adélaïde de. *La vie musicale en France au temps de la révolution* (Paris: Fayard, 1989).

Pleasants, Henry, ed. *The Musical Journeys of Louis Spohr* (Norman: University of Oklahoma Press, 1961).

Poriss, Hilary. 'Prima Donnas and the Performance of Altruism', in Rachel Cowgill and Hilary Poriss, eds, *The Arts of the Prima Donna in the Long Nineteenth Century* (Oxford: Oxford University Press, 2012).

Porter, Roy, ed. *Rewriting the Self: Histories from the Renaissance to the Present* (London: Routledge, 1997).

Pougin, Arthur. *Viotti et l'école moderne de violon* (Paris: Schott, 1888).

_____. *Le Violon, les violonistes et la musique de violon du XVIe au XVIIIe siècle* (Paris: Fischbacher, 1924).

Praz, Mario. *The Romantic Agony*, trans. Angus Davidson, 2nd ed. (London: Oxford University Press, 1951).

Prefumo, Danilo and Alberto Cantù. *Le opere di Paganini* (Genoa: Sanep, 1982).

Prendergast, Christopher. *Napoleon and History Painting* (Oxford: Clarendon Press, 1997).

Prod'homme, J. G. *Nicolo Paganini: A Biography*, trans. Alice Mattullath (New York: Fischer, 1911).

Proust, Marcel. *A Search for Lost Time: Swann's Way*, trans. James Grieve (Canberra: Australian National University, 1982).

Pulver, Jeffrey. *Paganini: The Romantic Virtuoso* (London: Herbert Joseph, 1936).

Punter, David. *The Literature of Terror: A History of Gothic Fictions from 1765 to the Present Day* (New York: Longman, 1980).

Puppo, Mario. 'Divinità e demonismo della musical nella cultura romantica', in Raffaello Monterosso, ed. *Nicolò Paganini e il suo tempo* [*Nicolò Paganini and His Times*] (Genoa: Comune di Genova, 1984), 79–99.

Putnam, Allen. *Mesmerism, Spiritualism, Witchcraft, and Miracle: A Brief Treatise, showing that mesmerism is a key which will unlock many chambers of mystery* (Boston, MA: Bela Marsh, 1858).

Rangoni, Giovanni Battista. *Saggio sul gusto della musica, col carattere de'tre celebri suonatori di violino Nardini, Lolli e Pugnani* (Livorno: Tommaso Masi, 1790).

Ratner, Leonard. *Classic Music: Expression, Form, and Style* (New York: Schirmer, 1980).

Rey, Xavier. *Niccolo Paganini* (Paris: L'Harmattan, 1999).

Reynaud, Cécile. 'Présentation: Misère et accomplissement de l'art dans la virtuosite romantique', *Romantisme: Revue de la Société des Études Romantique* Vol. 128 (2005), 3–17.

Ringer, Alexander L., ed. *The Early Romantic Era* (Englewood Cliffs, NJ: Prentice Hall, 1991).

Robertson, Ritchie. *Heine* (London: Halban, 2005).

Roeseler, Albrecht. *Grosse Geiger unseres Jahrhunderts* (Munich: Piper, 1987).

Rosenthal, Albi. 'An Intriguing copy of Paganini's "Capricci" and Its Implications', in Raffaello Monterosso, ed. *Nicolò Paganini e il suo tempo* [*Nicolò Paganini and His Times*] (Genoa: Comune di Genova, 1984), 235–46.

Rosselli, John. 'Castrato', *Grove Music Online* accessed 1 February 2010 www.oxfordmusiconline.com/subscriber/article/grove/music/05146.

Roth, Henry. 'Violin Sound from a Century Past', *The Strad* (July 1994), 687–8.

Rowe, Mark W. *Heinrich Wilhelm Ernst: Virtuoso Violinist* (Aldershot: Ashgate, 2008).

S., P. Théâtre de la Nation (Opéra), *Le Violon du Diable*', *Revue et gazette musicale de Paris* Vol. 16 No. 3 (21 January 1849), 18–19.

Sachs, Curt. *The History of Musical Instruments* (New York: Norton, 1940).

Sadie, Stanley, ed. *The New Grove Dictionary of Music and Musicians* (London: Macmillan, 1980).

_____. ed. *The New Grove Violin Family* [The Grove Musical Instruments Series] (New York: W.W. Norton, 1989).

Salone, Anna Maria. 'The Paganini–Cavanna event', 'La vicenda Paganini–Cavanna', in Maria Rosa Moretti, Anna Sorrento, Stefano Termanini, and Enrico Volpato, eds, *Paganini divo e comunicatore, atti del convengointernationale* (Genoa, 3–5 December 2004) (Genoa: Serel International, 2007), 371–424.

Salzedo, S.L. *Paganini's Secret at Last* (London: Nicholson & Watson, 1946).

Samson, Jim. *Virtuosity and the Musical Work: The Transcendental Studies of Liszt* (Cambridge: Cambridge University Press, 2003).

Sartori, Claudio. *L'avventura del violino: l'Italia musicale dell'Ottocento nella biografica e nei carteggi di Antonio Bazzini* (Turin: Edizioni Rai Radiotelevisione Italiana, 1978).

Saussine, Renée de. *Paganini*, trans. Marjorie Laurie (London: Hutchinson, 1970 [1953, 1954]).

Schering, Arnold. *Geschichte des Instrumentalkonzerts* (Leipzig: Breitkopf und Härtel, 1905).

Schoenfeld, M. R. 'Nicolo Paganini: Musical Magician and Marfan Mutant?', *Journal of the American Medical Association* Vol. 239 No. 1 (2 January 1978), 40–2.

Schott, Heinz, ed. *Franz Anton Mesmer und die Geschichte des Mesmerismus* (Stuttgart: Franz Steiner, 1985).

Schottky, Julius Max. *Paganinis Leben und Treiben als Künstler und als Mensch* (Prague: Calve, 1830).

Schwarz, Boris. 'Beethoven and the French Violin School', *The Musical Quarterly* Vol. 44 (1958), 431–47.

_____. *Great Masters of the Violin* (New York: Simon & Schuster, 1983).

_____. *French Instrumental Music Between the Revolutions (1789–1830)* (New York: Da Capo Press, 1987).

Schwarz, Vera, ed., *Violinspiel und Violinmusik in Geschichte und Gegenwart: Bericht über den Internationalen Kongress am Institut für Aufführungspraxis der Hochschule für Musik und Darstellende Kunst in Graz, vom 25. Juni bis 2. Juli 1972* (Vienna: Universal Edition, 1975).

_____. 'Zur Programmgestaltung des Violinabends in Wien 1880–1920', in Vera Schwarz, ed., *Violinspiel und Violinmusik in Geschichte und Gegenwart: Bericht über den Internationalen Kongress am Institut für Aufführungspraxis der Hochschule für Musik und Darstellende Kunst in Graz, vom 25. Juni bis 2. Juli 1972* (Vienna: Universal Edition, 1975), 52–5.

Sennett, Richard. *The Fall of Public Man* (New York: Knopf, 1977).

Sfilio, Francesco. *Alta cultura di tecnica violinistica* (Varese: Zecchini, 2002).

Sheppard, Leslie. '19th-Century Violinist-Composers', *The Strad* (August 1980), 252–4.

Sheppard, Leslie and Herbert R. Axelrod. *Paganini* (Neptune City, NJ: Paganiniana Publications, 1979).

Siber, Julius. 'Niccolò Paganini. Eine psychologische Studie von Dr. Jules Siber', *Jahrbuch für sexuelle Zwischenstufen* (1914), 39–44.

Silverman, William A. *The Violin Hunter* (Neptune City, NJ: Paganiniana Publications, 1981).

Solomon, Maynard. *Mozart: A Life* (New York: HarperCollins, 1995).

Spector, Jack. *Delacroix: The Death of Sardanapalus.* Art in Context (New York: Viking Press, 1974).

Spitzer, John. 'Metaphors of the Orchestra: The Orchestra as a Metaphor', *Musical Quarterly* Vol. 80 No. 2 (Summer 1996), 234–64.

Spivacke, Harold. 'Paganiniana', *The Library of Congress Quarterly Journal of Current Acquisitions* Vol 2, No 2 (February 1945), 49–67.

Spohr, Louis. *Louis Spohr's Autobiography*, trans. anon., 2 vols (New York: Da Capo Press 1969 [1865]).

Steblin, Rita. 'Death as Fiddler: A Study of a Convention in European Art, Literature and Music', *Basler Jahrbuch für historische Musikpraxis* Vol. 14 (1990), 271–323.

_____ . 'The Gender Stereotyping of Musical Instruments in the Western Tradition', *Canadian University Music Review* Vol. 16 No. 1 (1995), 128–44.

Storck, Karl. *Musik und Musiker in Karikatur und Satire* (Oldenburg: Stalling, 1910).

Stowell, Robin. *The Cambridge Companion to the Violin* (Cambridge: Cambridge University Press, 1992).

_____ . 'Nicolo Paganini: The Violin Virtuoso *in excelsis*?', *Basler Jahrbuch für Historische Musikpraxis* Vol. 20 (1996), 73–93.

_____ . *Beethoven: Violin Concerto* (Cambridge: Cambridge University Press, 1998).

Strachan, John, ed. *The Selected Writings of Leigh Hunt*, Vol. 6 (London: Pickering and Chatto, 2003).

Stratton, Stephen S. *Nicolo Paganini: His Life and Works* (London: Strad, 1907).

Sugden, John. *Niccolo Paganini: Supreme Violinist or Devil's Fiddler?* (Tunbridge Wells: Midas Books, 1980).

Swift, Jonathan. *Journal to Stella*, ed. J. K. Moorehead (London: J. M. Dent and Sons, 1948 [1924]).

Taruskin, Richard. *The Oxford History of Western Music* (Oxford: Oxford University Press, 2005).

Taylor, Charles. *Sources of the Self: The Making of the Modern Identity* (Cambridge, MA: Harvard University Press, 1996).

Teijirian, Edward. *Sexuality and the Devil: Symbols of Love, Power, and Fear in Male Psychology* (New York and London: Routledge, 1990).

Terenzio, Vincenzo. *La musica italiana nell'ottocento*, 2 vols (Milan: Bramante Editrice, 1976).

Tienhooven, Marie-José. 'All Roads Lead to England: *The Monk* Constructs the Nation', *Romanticism on the Net* Vol. 8: www.erudit.org/revue/ron/1997/v/ n8/005777ar.html (online article, accessed 1 March 2007).

Tinterow, Gary and Philip Conisbee, eds. *Portraits by Ingres: Image of an Epoch* (New York: Metropolitan Museum of Art and Harry N. Abrams, 1999).

Todd , R. Larry, ed. *Mendelssohn Studies* (Cambridge: Cambridge University Press, 1992).

Tonazzi, Bruno. *Paganini a Trieste* (Trieste: Edizioni LINT, 1977).

Tuite, Clara. 'Cloistered Closets: Enlightenment Pornography, the Confessional State, Homosexual Persecution, and *The Monk*', *Romanticism on the Net* Vol. 8: www.erudit.org/revue/ron/1997/v/n8/005766ar.html (online article, accessed 1 March 2007).

Tyler, Linda and Caryl L. Clark, 'Süssmayr, Franz Xaver', in Stanley Sadie, ed., *New Grove Dictionary of Music and Musicians*, 2nd ed. (London: Macmillan, 2001) Vol. 24, 734.

Vallat, George. *Études d'histoire de moeurs et d'art des musicale: Alexandre Boucher et son temps* (Paris: Quantin, 1890).

Vyborny, Zdenek. 'The Real Paganini', *Music and Letters* Vol. 42 (1961), 348–63.

Walker, Alan. *Franz Liszt*, 2 vols (Ithaca, NY: Cornell University Press, 1987).

Walmsley, Donald. *Anton Mesmer* (London: Hale, 1967).

Walser, Robert. *Running with the Devil: Power, Gender and Madness in Heavy Metal Music* (Hanover, NH: Wesleyan University Press, 1993).

Weber, William. 'Mass Culture and the Reshaping of European Music Taste, 1770–1870', *International Review of the Aesthetics and Sociology of Music* Vol. 8 No. 1 (June 1977), 5–22.

_____. *Music and the Middle Class: The Social Structure of Concert Life in London, Paris and Vienna Between 1830 and 1848* (London: Ashgate, 2003).

_____, ed. *The Musician as Entrepreneur, 1700–1914: Managers, Charlatans, and Idealists* (Bloomington: Indiana University Press, 2004).

_____. 'The Musician as Entrepreneur and Opportunist, 1700–1914', in William Weber, ed., *The Musician as Entrepreneur, 1700–1914: Managers, Charlatans, and Idealists* (Bloomington: Indiana University Press, 2004), 3–24.

_____. 'From the Self-Managing Musician to the Independent Concert Agent', in William Weber, ed., *The Musician as Entrepreneur, 1700–1914: Managers, Charlatans, and Idealists* (Bloomington: Indiana University Press, 2004), 105–29.

_____. *The Great Transformation of Musical Taste: Concert Programming from Haydn to Brahms* (Cambridge: Cambridge University Press, 2008).

Wechsberg, Joseph. *The Glory of the Violin* (New York: The Viking Press, 1972).

Weissmann, Adolf. *Berlin als Musikstadt: Geschichte der Oper und des Konzerts von 1740 bis 1911* (Berlin and Leipzig: Schuster & Leffler, 1911).

Wen, Eric. 'The Twentieth Century', in Robin Stowell, ed., *The Cambridge Companion to the Violin* (Cambridge: Cambridge University Press, 1992), 79–91.

White, Chappell, ed. *Giovanni Battista Viotti: Four Violin Concertos* (Recent Researches in the Music of the Pre-classical, Classical, and Early Romantic Eras Volume IV) (Madison, WI: A-R Editions, 1976).

_____. *From Vivaldi to Viotti: A History of the Early Classical Violin Concerto* (Phildaelphia, PA: Gordon and Breach, 1992).

Whitlark, James. 'Heresy Hunting: *The Monk* and the French Revolution', *Romanticism on the Net* Vol. 8: www.erudit.org/revue/ron/1997/v/n8/005773ar.html (online article, accessed 1 March 2007).

Wicke, Peter. 'Virtuosität als Ritual: Vom Guitar Hero zum DJ-Schamanen', in Heinz von Loesch, Ulrich Mahlert, and Peter Rummenhöller, eds,

Musikalische Virtuosität: Perspektiven musikalischer Theorie und Praxis (Gebundene Ausgabe) (Mainz: Schott, 2004), 232–43.

Williams, Anne. *Art of Darkness: A Poetics of Gothic* (Chicago, IL, and London: University of Chicago Press, 1995).

Williams, Linda. *Hardcore: Power, Pleasure, and the 'Frenzy of the Visible'* (Berkeley and Los Angeles, University of California Press, 1989).

Wilson-Smith, Timothy. *Delacroix: A Life* (London: Constable, 1992).

Wise, Sue. 'Sexing Elvis', in Simon Frith and Andrew Goodwin, eds, *On Record: Rock, Pop, and the Written Word* (New York: Pantheon Books, 1990), 390–409.

Woolf, Stuart. *A History of Italy 1700–1860: The Social Constraints of Political Change* (London: Methuen, 1979).

X., Doctor Jacobus. *L'Amour au colonies* (Paris, 1893).

Zaslaw, Neal. 'The Italian Violin School in the 17th Century', *Early Music* Vol. 18 (1990), 515–18.

Novels

Komroff, Manuel. *The Magic Bow: A Romance of Paganini* (New York: Harper & Brothers, 1940).

Kuhnert, Adolfo Artur. *Paganini* (Leipzig: Reclam, 1929).

Maynor, Eleanor. *The Golden Key* (New York: Criterion, 1966).

Polko, Elise. *Nicolo Paganini und die Geigenbauer* (Leipzig: Bernhard Schlicke, 1876).

Reis, Kurt. *Paganini und die Frauen* (Berlin: Deutsche Buchvertriebs- und Verlgas-Gesellshaft, 1952).

Richter, Hermann. *Dämonischer Reigen: Ein Paganini-Roman* (Leipzig: Otto Janke, 1938).

Sand, George. *Consuelo* (Amsterdam: Fredonia Books, 2004).

Vinogradov, Anatoli. *The Condemnation of Paganini: A Novel*, trans. Stephen Garry (London: Hutchinson, n.d.).

Waldemar, Charles. *Paganini: Liebe, Ruhm und Leidenschaft. Der Lebensroman Niccolo Paganinis* (Munich: Bong, 1959).

Scores

Eller, Louis.*Valse diabolique*, op. 10 (Leipzig: Gustav Heinze, n.d.; Dresden: Guillaume Paul, n.d.; Paris: Richault, n.d.).

Monterosso, Raffaello *et al.*, eds. *Nazionale delle opere di Niccolò Paganini*, Vols I IX (Rome: Istituto Italiano per la Storia della Musica, 1976 ongoing).

Niccolo Paganini, Op. 1: Twenty-Four Caprices For the Violin. Study version and Preface by Harold Berkley (New York: Schirmer, 1944).

Paganini, Niccolò. *Le Streghe*, op. 8. New Edition by Fritz Kreisler (London and New York: Ernst Eulenburg, 1905).

Paganini, Niccolò. *Konzert für Violine und Orchester D-dur, Op. 6*, (Wiesbaden, Leipzig, Paris: Breitkopf & Härtel, 1993).

Paganini, Niccolò. *Concerto no. 1 in D major, opus 6, for violin and piano*, ed.
    Zino Francescatti (New York: International Music Co., ca.1980).
Paganini–Wilhelmj. *Einleitung. Thema und Variationen nach Nicolo Paganini
    für Violin mit Orchester oder Clavier-Begleitung* (Mainz: Schott, n.d.).
Wilhelmj, August. *Italienische Suite nach Nicolo Paganini für Violin mit
    Orchester oder Clavier-Begleitung* (Berlin: Schlesinger, n.d.).

Select Recordings

Accardo, Salvatore. *Accardo plays Paganini* (Deutsche Grammophon, 1988).
Barton Pine, Rachel. *Instrument of the Devil* (Cedille, 1988).
*Joseph Joachim: The Complete Recordings (1903). Pablo de Sarasate: The Complete
    Recordings (1904). Eugène Ysaÿe: A Selection of His Recordings (1912).*
    (Reissued by Pearl, 2003).
Kaplan, Mark. *Paganini Concerto No. 1.* Mitch Miller, London Symphony
    Orchestra (Mitch Miller Music, 1994).
Lakatos, Sandor. *Konig der Zigeunergeiger* (Capriccio, 2004).
Mezzena, Franco and Adriano Sebastiani. *Paganini's 'La Carmagnola'* (Dynamic,
    1994).
Shaham, Gil. *Devil's Dance* (Deutsche Grammophon, 2000).

Films Inspired by Paganini

Girard, François. *The Red Violin* (1998).
Goldberg, Heinz. *Paganini* (1923).
Kinski, Klaus. *Kinski Paganini* (SPV Recordings DVD, 2003).
Knowles, Bernard. *The Magic Bow* (1946).
Monsaingeon, Bruno. *The Art of Violin* (Idéale Audience, 2000).
Niccolo Paganini (1982, Lenfilm production) [Russian TV miniseries]
Vidor, Charles. *A Song to Remember* (1945).

Useful Websites

Grove Music Online: www.oxfordmusiconline.com
http://you.video.sina.com.cn/b/5693952–1298700891.html
www.conrad-veidt-society.de/bild.ton.html
www.gillesapap.com
www.tracysilverman.com

Index

References to illustrations are shown in *italics* and those to musical examples in ***bold italics***. References to footnotes consist of the page number followed by the letter 'n' followed by the number of the footnote, e.g. 5n12 refers to footnote no. 12 on page 5. A page number followed by the letter 't' refers to a table.

genius, concept of 25, 41, 46, 50, 77, 87, 113,
114, 116, 119n106, 121
Genoa
Paganini's birth-place and Palazzo Tursi
collection 135
types of music (18th-19th centuries) 7–8
see also Paganini (journal)
German aesthetics
'demonic' concept 46–7
see also Goethe, Johann Wolfgang von;
Heine, Heinrich; Romanticism
Germi, Luigi 38, 40, 41, 44, 56, 57, 79,
128–9
Ghetaldi, Matteo Niccoló de 30n13, 88,
120n107, 120n108
Girard, François Girard, *The Red Violin*
58n24
Gitlis, Ivry 4
Goethe, Johann Wolfgang von
cult of 18
daemonic concept 46–7
Faust 27, 44, 45, 47, 62
on impact of Paganini's music on women
73
on Paganini and Napoléon 87
on Paganini's body 114
on violinists preferring playing their
own music 105n39
Goldberg, Heinz 138–9
Gollmick, Carl 113n77
Gothic image
and alterity 71n65
Gothic archetype 57, 61, 62–3
Hugo's 'Der Geiger' 69, 69
Kinski Paganini (film) 116
Paganini's Gothic aura 1, 30–1, 34, 133
Paganini's music titles 40
post-Paganinian violinists 100
see also 'demonic' mythology; vampire
metaphor
Gothic novels 1, 31, 61, 74n81
see also novels (on Paganini)
Grandville, Jean Ignace Isidore 31
Granger, Stewart 138
see also Magic Bow, The (film)
Great Britain *see* Britain
Grisi, Giulia 59
grotesque
cholera as metaphor for 37
grotesque Sensualism 45–6

Guarneri instruments 4, 81
Il Cannone 64, 81, 116, 121, 127, 135
Guhr, Carl 10, 16, 17, 65, 109
guitar playing 8, 20, 22n63, 23, 44, 51, 53, 71,
115, 117, 136
Gulli, Franco 126

Halen, Eddie van 71
harmonics 5, 10, 12, 16, 32, 43, 50, 92, 98,
100, 106, 109, 140
Harrys, George 24, 78
heavy metal music 22n63, 71, 115
Heifetz, Jascha 116
Heim, Ernst 109
Heine, Heinrich
Atta Troll 46
Faust ballet 46
'ghostly fiddler' poem 61n39
'Lisztomania' coinage 72
on Malibran's death 60
on Paganini and Satan 'disguised as a
black poodle' 44
on Paganini and violinists' virtuosity 26
on Paganini's bowing style 31
on Paganini's hunger for wealth 82–3,
84
on Paganini's physical appearance 34,
37
on Paganini's relationship with Sivori
24
perspective on art history 83
Sensualism and Spiritualism 45–6
Hendrix, Jimi 71
Herz, Henri 81
historical context 3–10
Hoffmann, E. T. A. 43, 46, 60, 132
homosexuality 24, 62n43, 63n48
Hubay, Jenö 123, 125
Hugo, Melchior von, 'Der Geiger' 69, 69
Humler, Sophie 96
Hummel, Johann Nepomuk 79
hypereroticism 51–7
see also sexuality

improvisation
and 18th-century musicians 8–9
composer–improviser vs interpreter 104,
105–6, 110
'gypsy'-style improvisation 116, 117
and the 'musical body' 118, 119